Mass Media Education in Transition

Preparing for the 21st Century

LEA'S COMMUNICATION SERIES
Jennings Bryant / Dolf Zillmann, General Editors

For a complete list of other titles in LEA's Communication Series, please contact Lawrence Erlbaum Associates, Publishers

Mass Media Education in Transition
Preparing for the 21st Century

Tom Dickson
Southwest Missouri State University

LAWRENCE ERLBAUM ASSOCIATES, PUBLISHERS
2000   Mahwah, New Jersey   London

Copyright © 2000 by Lawrence Erlbaum Associates, Inc.
All rights reserved. No part of this book may be reproduced in any form, by photostat, microfilm, retrieval system, or any other means, without prior written permission of the publisher.

Lawrence Erlbaum Associates, Inc., Publishers
10 Industrial Avenue
Mahwah, NJ 07430

Cover design by Kathryn Houghtaling Lacey

Library of Congress Cataloging-in-Publication Data

Dickson, Tom, 1946–
Mass media education in transition : preparing for the 21st century / Tom Dickson.
      p. cm. — (Communication)
Includes bibliographical references and index.
ISBN 0-8058-3097-9 (alk. paper)
1. Mass media—Study and teaching (Higher)—United States.
   I. Title. II. Series : Communication (Hillsdale, N.J.)
P1.5.U5D53 1999
302.23'071'173—dc21   99-23014
                                                              CIP

Books published by Lawrence Erlbaum Associates are printed on acid-free paper, and their bindings are chosen for strength and durability.

Printed in the United States of America
10 9 8 7 6 5 4 3 2 1

Contents

Preface

As the 21st century approaches, mass media educators are in the midst of a decades-long debate over the nature and purpose of mass media education. Some of its most pressing challenges are related to changes in curriculum because of the evolution of the media industries and new technologies. But perhaps the most vexing questions are related to its structure: Should it exist as an integrated field, merge with other communication subfields, or fragment into two or more separate fields? Media educators also must continue to respond to practitioners who ask whether mass media education is really necessary. How such issues are resolved will have a profound effect on media-related education in the new century as well as on the media industries they serve. The purpose of this book is to give the reader—not only media educators but also media practitioners and others interested in academic issues—some understanding of how media-related education has evolved as well as the nature of the debate that threatens to cause the disintegration of mass media education into separate academic fields.

The story of mass media education parallels to a large extent the story of the evolution of higher education from the classical college to the modern comprehensive university. Its precursors and founders were some of the main players in U.S. government, public life, and higher education of their day—sage, journalist, and politician Benjamin Franklin; general and educator Robert E. Lee; publisher Joseph Pulitzer; and university presidents Charles Eliot of Harvard and Andrew Dickson White of Cornell. The history of mass media education is the story of how the concepts of liberal education and professional education have evolved and intertwined. It also is a story that indicates how higher education has changed to reflect Americans' changing understanding of democracy, citizenship, and the common good.

Any discussion of mass media education necessitates the use of the term *journalism* in a variety of ways. Because journalism existed as a professional field before the beginning of academic training for journalists, the term journalism began to be used by educators to represent the new field of study. Journalism education developed in departments of English at liberal arts colleges at the same time that departments and professional schools of journalism were established at fledgling comprehensive universities. As coursework in other media-related fields was added to journalism programs, the term journalism continued to be used as an overarching term for the field. With the introduction of the term *mass communication* in the 1940s, that term also began to be used to refer to the entire field, as well as to professional training for media-related fields other than journalism and to a more-theoretical course of study, also called *media studies* or *communication studies*.

Today, media-related programs, departments, schools, and colleges go by such names as journalism, journalism and mass communication, mass media, media studies, communication, communications, communication and mass media, and a variety of other names. Authors cited in this book have used journalism and mass communication in a variety of ways. I use the term journalism education for the field until the addition of media-related sequences. I use the term mass media education for the broader field of media-related education and the term journalism education for print and broadcast journalism after other media-related subfields emerged.

Some of the concerns of the book are as follows:

- The reasons for the founding of journalism education, particularly the efforts of its founders to develop a curriculum that would result not only in trained journalists but also broadly educated and ethical journalists.
- The broadening of journalism education that led to the incorporation not only of advertising and, later, broadcast journalism but also public relations.
- The increasing emphasis on the more theoretical concerns of the mass media with the birth of mass communication and communication studies.
- The struggle over programs of interpersonal communication as to where the boundaries of mass communication and interpersonal communication should be.
- The academic versus professional debate and the debate over whether mass media education should provide the entire campus with an understanding of the mass media as well as prepare students for media-related careers.
- The role of the liberal arts in mass media education and the extent to which media education itself provides a liberal education.
- The integration movement that proposed the development of a "generic communicator" who could take his or her place in a variety of media-related occupations.
- The development of the concept of a *new professionalism* that challenged mass media programs' structure and mission.
- The debate over whether or not mass media education should separate itself from training for the media industries and become a part of a larger, more-theoretical communication discipline.
- The question of whether journalism education should revert to its roots and cast off subfields that are concerned with persuasion and propaganda rather with than the objective dissemination of information in order to promote the public good.

Chapter 1 describes publisher Benjamin Franklin's attempts to improve the "scurrilous" newspapers of the day, the efforts of Robert E. Lee to establish a journalism school to educate men who could help get the war-ravished South on its feet following the Civil War, the evolution of the comprehensive university and the movement for education for practical professions, the emergence of journalism coursework in universities in the midwest, and the contributions of publisher Joseph Pulitzer and educator Charles Eliot that led to two different visions of journalism education.

Chapter 2 discusses the transformation of journalism education from a practical, vocational program to a broad professional program. It tells of the rise of journalism educational organizations and curriculum standards, the connection between journalism education and the Progressive Movement, the growing ties between journalism education and the liberal arts and social sciences, the question of professional accreditation, the attacks on journalism education for vocationalism, the debate over vocationalism in scholastic journalism education, and the post-World War II growth of journalism education.

In chapter 3, I describe the broadening of journalism education with the advent of new media and the growth of other media-related fields. I also describe the birth and growth of advertising education, the development of broadcast education and improvement of curriculum standards, the emergence and expansion of public relations education in journalism programs and development of curriculum standards, and recent research concerning advertising, broadcast journalism, and public relations education.

Chapter 4 focuses on the development of communication education. It provides an overview of the history of speech communication and its development of programs that crossed the boundaries between interpersonal communication and media-related education. The chapter also tells of the growth of the theoretical side of mass media education with the advent of the study of mass communication as a media-related subfield. It discusses the emergence of communication studies in journalism schools and its success in finding a friendlier home in speech communication, leading to conflicts over defining the term *communication*.

In chapter 5, I delve into mass media education's so-called "split personality": the struggle between the practical media educators (the "green eyeshades") and the theoretical media educators (the "chi-squares"). The chapter also provides an overview of the attempts by media educators to achieve respect as an academic program of study and growth in the importance of media-related research.

Chapter 6 describes the academic–practitioner debate, an apparently unending "dialogue of the deaf." It tells of the lengthy history of attacks on journalism education from practitioners for being alternately too practical or too theoretical and the assumed gap between the instruction provided and the needs of media-related industries. The chapter gives an overview of research about the gap between instruction and practice and the on-going debate between educators and practitioners over whether media educators need a doctorate and/or practical experience, a discussion of mass media education's role in promoting the public service role of practitioners, and the recent debate over civic/public journalism.

In chapter 7, I discuss whether mass media education is a liberal art or is merely allied with the liberal arts. I discuss mass educators' concern that the liberal arts and social sciences are too specialized and fragmented to best serve mass media education, as well as the implementation of accreditation standards designed to provide graduates with practical skills in addition to a liberal education.

Chapter 8 looks at what the configuration of mass media education might be in the future and where it belongs within the structure of the liberal arts college, comprehensive university, and research university. It also investigates various paths mass media education might take: toward a unified communication discipline of interpersonal and mass communication, toward an integrated curriculum for media-related sequences, toward partial integration of closely allied media-related subfields called *integrated communication*, or toward fragmentation of mass media education into a variety of separate fields. It details the debate between advocates of the new professionalism, a proposal to restructure the undergraduate media curriculum by replacing the occupational thrust with a focus on a revitalized concept of the liberal arts, and the movement to separate journalism education from the other media-related sequences that were traditionally under the journalism school umbrella.

In chapter 9, I provide responses to a number of questions that still are the focus of debate among media educators; and in chapter 10, I present visions of the future of mass media education by educators, media practitioners, and friends of media education. These two chapters provide an overview of the issues facing media education at the end of the 20th century and what lies ahead at the start of the 21st century. The appendix provides an overview of the major reports and studies concerning mass media education.

Mass media education is in transition. I hope this book helps increase the understanding of the history of the field and the major issues that face it, as well as offer some insight into what the next stage in its development might be, whether it be a new professionalism, a return to an older vision of media-related education, or something quite different.

ACKNOWLEDGMENTS

The genesis of this book was a study I undertook with Ralph Sellmeyer on mass media educators' responses to calls for curricular reform. My research on the topic was spurred by my being named cochair of the Association for Education in Journalism and Mass Communication Curriculum Task Force by President Maurine Beasley. The project became a reality after Bill Christ suggested the need for such a book to the editors of Lawrence Erlbaum Associates. In addition to professors Sellmeyer, Beasley, and Christ, I thank the editors at LEA for their understanding when I found myself in the hospital in traction as the deadline loomed. I would particularly like to thank LEA's Linda Bathgate and Kathryn Scornavacca for their patience and assistance during the preparation of the manuscript. I also would like to thank the contributors to chapter 10 who shared their visions and insights about mass media education: Maurine Beasley, Bill Christ, Jerry Ceppos, Robert Dardenne, Donald Gillmor, Arnold Ismach, Lillian Lodge Kopenhaver, Ralph Lowenstein, Paul McMasters, Betty Medgser, Melvin Mencher, Doug Newsom, Charles Overby, Elise Parsigian, Betsy Plank, Lana Rakow, Stephen Reese, Bill Ross, and David Weaver. In addition, I thank Elizabeth Topping for her many hours of copyediting the manuscripts and her insightful suggestions along the way.

—Tom Dickson

1

The Beginnings of Journalism Education

The story of journalism education in America is a story of good intentions, weak support, irresolution, ambiguity, and even deception and hypocrisy.
—Dennis (1988, p. 4)

Until the late 1870s, journalism education in the United States was in the hands of professional tradesmen, usually printers. The most famous of these early printers was Benjamin Franklin, who wanted to improve the press by improving the virtue of printers. Franklin felt most printers of the time were endangering democracy by publishing defamatory essays. He wrote that "nothing is more likely to endanger the liberty of the press than the abuse of that liberty by employing it in personal accusation, detraction, and calumny" (Frasca, 1995, p. 5). About Franklin's mission, Frasca noted that "Franklin's challenge in the early republic was thus doubly formidable—not only to impart moral instruction to a mass audience, but also to overcome the deleterious effects of scurrilous journalism which eroded the edifice of public virtue that Franklin had devoted a lifetime trying to erect" (p. 8).

In the mid-1780s, Franklin decided to form partnerships with several young printers in an effort to promote moral virtue. However, his plans were frustrated and later collapsed without measurable success with the dissolution of his partnership with Francis Childs and the death in 1798 of another partner, his grandson Benjamin Franklin Bache. Frasca (1995) stated about the effort, however, that "Childs' ability to avoid partisanship captured the essence of Franklin's early code of journalistic conduct" (p. 26).

Education for future journalists in a college setting was proposed long before formal journalism education began in the United States. John Ward Fenno, editor of the *Gazette of the United States*, made one of the earliest known statements of support for college training for journalists. He called the newspapers of his day the "most base, false, servile and venal publications that ever polluted society" (O'Dell, 1935, p. 1) and called for journalists to become college-trained. He stated in the *Gazette* on March 4, 1799:

I have not the vanity to recommend any preservative, but I cannot concede the propriety of requiring some qualifications and pledges from men on whom the nation depends for all the information and much of the instruction it receives. To well-regulated colleges we naturally look for a source whence such qualifications might in proper form be derived. (Mirando, 1995, p. 4)

THE GROUNDWORK IS LAID FOR PROFESSIONAL
TRAINING AT COLLEGES

The structure of both the media and higher education in the United States made classroom-oriented journalism instruction seem unimportant to most practitioners during the 1700s and most of the 1800s. Mirando (1995) noted two reasons for that situation. First, printing was seen as a trade to be learned through apprenticeship. Such journalistic terms as *scoop, slug, sidebar, headline,* and *byline,* Mirando noted, "gave journalism strong identification as a trade rather than a profession." Second, the "primary values educators hoped to pass on to their students were not as much concerned with gaining expertise as they were with overall notions of morality, refinement, maturity and respectability" (p. 4). The four notions mentioned by Mirando were tenets of a classical liberal education, the model for college education until the late 1880s. They were based on the Romans' Seven Pillars of the Temple of Wisdom: the Trivium (grammar, rhetoric, and logic) and the Quadrivium (music, arithmetic, geometry, and astronomy). The Trivium and Quadrivium were the basis for a liberal education for 800 years. They were added to when Aristotle's three "philosophies" (natural, moral, and mental) were rediscovered in the 12th century (Hoskins, 1988).

A typical first-year course of study at an American colonial college, as in England, included Latin, Greek, logic, Hebrew, and rhetoric. Logic, Greek, and Hebrew were continued in the second year, and natural philosophy was added. In the third year, mental philosophy or metaphysics and moral philosophy (the predecessors of economics, ethics, political science, and sociology) were started. The fourth year consisted of review in Latin, Greek, logic, and natural philosophy and an introduction to mathematics. The standard course of study in the early 1800s had changed little. It included ancient languages, mathematics, natural philosophy, chemistry, and moral philosophy (Rudolph, 1962).

Students usually went to college to prepare for a profession, such as the ministry, law, or medicine. The college role in education for journalism and the other nontraditional professions had to wait until colleges moved away from providing a classical education toward providing vocational education and a variety of practical subjects. The classical studies curriculum was challenged in the 1820s and 1830s when a nonclassical "parallel course" of study was added at some colleges as they began to include modern languages, new branches of mathematics, and science. Colleges were not willing to give up the classical curriculum without a struggle, however. The Yale Report of 1828 put that institution, headed by President Jeremiah Day, squarely behind classical studies. Other prestigious eastern colleges, such as Princeton and Dartmouth, added their reputation to the cause of trying to head off a new curriculum. Rudolph (1962) stated of the Yale Report:

The report echoed everywhere. Behind it the American college curriculum remained almost immovable until after the Civil War. Behind it President Lord of Dartmouth was able to declare that a college education was not meant for people who planned to "engage in mercantile, mechanical or agricultural operations." (p. 135)

The idea of training for the vocation of journalism did have supporters, however. For example, Duff Green, the editor of the *United States Telegraph*, in 1834 proposed what would have been the earliest journalism school in order, he said, to raise the standards of journalism. The school was to be called the Washington Institute. It was to be a "manual labor school" with up to 200 boys from 11 to 14 who would work 8 hours each day at the newspaper and spend 5 hours a day in classes in language, arts, and sciences. Students would be paid for working in his print shop, but at a rate considerably lower than what journeyman printers earned. His printers, however, saw the plan as a threat to their jobs and wage scale and boycotted the newspaper, forcing Green to abandon his plan (Mirando, 1995).

Much like Franklin before them, reformers in the mid-1800s argued that journalism could be improved if journalists were better educated and, thus, more ethical. In an 1856 speech, George Lunt, an early advocate of college training for journalists, stated that educated people are "less liable to petty temptations—less easily controlled and led away" and called for journalists to be educated for public service (Steiner, 1994, p. 50). In 1857, the board of directors of Farmers' High School (now Pennsylvania State University) requested that the state legislature institute a journalism curriculum (O'Dell, 1935). In 1869, a St. Louis journalist, Norman J. Coleman, also proposed study in journalism at the University of Missouri. Neither proposal was to be acted on at that time, however.

LEE'S EXPERIMENT AT WASHINGTON COLLEGE

The two main obstacles to college training for journalists—the nature of the craft of journalism and the classical college curriculum—became less of a barrier in the post-Civil War period. The newspaper was becoming an institution and was more professional, and higher education began to move from the classical curriculum to a specialized, practical curriculum.

The movement toward a practical curriculum after the Civil War was spurred by the Morrill Federal Land Grant Act of 1862, which was designed "to promote the liberal and practical education of the industrial classes in the several pursuits and professions of life" (Rudolph, 1962, p. 249). The act provided land for every state to have at least one college "where the leading object shall be, without excluding other scientific or classical studies, to teach such branches of learning as are related to agriculture and the mechanic arts" (p. 252). Another idea that evolved from the Morrill Act was service. According to Boyer (1990), service in the 1870s and 1880s not only meant spreading knowledge to practical problems, but it had a moral meaning as well: "The goal was not only to *serve society,* but *reshape* it" (p. 6).

At the time of the Civil War, journalism education in the United States still was almost exclusively provided by the newspaper office. In 1869, a plan for merging practical training at a newspaper office with a college degree was proposed by Robert E. Lee, then president of Virginia's Washington College (now Washington and Lee University). The Washington College plan shared some of the principles of the Morrill Act in that Lee saw the need for educated professionals, including journalists, in rebuilding the South. From 1865 to 1868, Lee had added science, engineering and other practical courses to the classical curriculum and had introduced an elective system. Freeman (1935) quoted Lee as writing about the proposal in 1867: "The importance of a more practical course of instruction in our schools and colleges, which, while it may call forth the genius and energies of our people, will tend to develop the resources and promote the interests of the country" (Mirando, 1995, pp. 8–9).

Professor William Preston Johnson presented three resolutions to set up scholarships for journalism students on March 12, 1869. Johnson stated that the reason for the scholarships was "that printing is one of the arts which diffuse education and we should therefore seek to qualify printers for the task of educating as far as possible" (O'Dell, 1935, p. 16). In a letter to the board of trustees on March 30, 1869, Lee requested "fifty scholarships for young men proposing to make printing or journalism their profession" (O'Dell, 1935, p. 14). Students would pay no tuition or college fees "on condition that when required by the faculty they shall perform such disciplinary duties as may be assigned them in a printing office or in other positions in the line of their professions, for a time equal to one hour in each working day" (Mirando, 1995, p. 10). According to Freeman (1935), Lee wrote:

> The great object of the whole plan is to provide the facilities required by the large class of our young men, who, looking to an early entrance into the practical pursuits of life, need a more direct training to this end than the usual literary courses. The proposed departments would also derive great advantage from the literary schools of the college, whose influence in the cultivation and enlargement of the mind is felt beyond their immediate limits. (Mirando, 1995, pp. 9–10)

According to Mirando (1995), the college offered journalism scholarships to five students in 1869 and to seven students the following year. However, Lee died Oct. 12, 1870, and the following year only five scholarship students were registered. The scholarship program was abandoned in late 1878. Journalism wasn't revived at the college until 1926, when the Lee Memorial School of Journalism was established (O'Dell, 1935). Mirando (1995) blamed the demise of the program on the press, stating, "In general, the press was upset with the implication that college boys who had not paid their dues working for newspapers could become editors and that a college purposed to know enough about the subject to be able to teach journalism" (p. 23).

Jandoli (1957) noted that "General Lee's apparent intention in 1869 was to train the printer to be a well-educated editor rather than to qualify the prospective editor in the art of printing" (p. 63). Mirando (1995) differentiated the program from those proposed at Yale, Cornell, and Missouri in the 1870s, which consisted of only discussion or lectures and not practical experience. He wrote:

> Some attributes that set editors apart from typesetters, compositors and press operators were writing ability, public affairs knowledge, legal and ethical principles and communication skills. General college curricula could handle much of this kind of training at the time because few specialized reporting and newswriting procedures had become standardized journalistic practice.
>
> Much of this kind of thinking is very much alive in today's journalism and mass communication education. (Mirando, 1995, p. 22)

THE EMERGENCE OF JOURNALISM INSTRUCTION

Following the failure of Lee's scholarship program, journalists continued to debate the merit of college training for journalists. According to Sutton (1945), those lined up in favor of such training included Whitelaw Reid of *The New York Tribune*, George W. Curtis of *Harper's Weekly*, William Penn Nixon of *The Chicago Inter-Ocean*, David G. Croly of the *New York Graphic*, and Joseph Pulitzer of *The New York World*. Opponents included E. L. Godkin of *The New York Evening Post*, Frederic Hudson of *The New York Herald*, Horace Greeley of *The New York Tribune*, J. C. Goldsmith of *Frank Leslie's Illustrated,* and William Hyde of *The Missouri Republican*.

Despite Washington College's failed experiment, individual journalism courses began to appear at colleges, mainly in the midwest, as the college vocational movement spread. In 1872, Whitelaw Reid of *The New York Tribune* announced a plan for a college curriculum that merged the liberal arts and practical journalism. The same year, the first journalism textbook, *Hints to Young Editors* (An Editor, 1872), was written anonymously by "An Editor." The first journalism course is said to have been a course in newspaper printing established at Kansas State College in 1873 (O'Dell, 1935).

Cornell University, founded as a land-grant institution in 1864, became a leader of the movement for providing a liberal education with practical training. Its founder, Ezra Cornell, stated about the new university: "I would found an institution where any person can find instruction in any study" (Rudolph, 1962, p. 266). In 1875 in a letter to New York newspaperman Charles F. Wingate, Andrew Dickson White, Cornell's first president, proposed a journalism curriculum that was to be "the first blueprint for a professional program" (Wilcox, 1959, p. 3). The 1875–1876 catalog announced a "Certificate in Journalism." All students would work under the director of the University Press and must learn "phonography" and telegraphy at their own expense outside the university. Students in literature or philosophy needed no further coursework for the certificate. Students in the arts were also required to take one term of French and two of German. Students in science were required to take coursework in history, languages, philosophy, and letters in addition to taking a examination in Latin grammar (O'Dell, 1935).

The program was listed in the catalog for 4 years before being abandoned. Because the program was not successfully implemented, White proposed that Cornell students interested in journalism undertake a major in history and political science instead, "especially since that program also required moral and political philosophy, Latin, and English" (Steiner, 1994, p. 56). White persisted in his desire for college training for journalists, however. In 1884, a year before he resigned as president, he noted the need for "journalists whose knowledge is extended and thorough, whose opinions are based upon well-ascertained principles, whose powers both of thought and statement have been carefully cultivated" (White, 1884, p. 31). According to O'Dell (1935), White's "position on the side of journalism education gave the movement weight at a time when it needed the support of such a national figure" (p. 28).

In 1875, the same year that White wrote Wingate about his plan for journalism education, Wingate wrote a volume titled *Views and Interviews on Journalism* (Wingate, 1875), which included opinions of 20 journalists. Several of them mentioned journalism education and were critical of the idea. Henry Watterson of the *Louisville Courier-Journal* stated, "There is but one school of journalism and that is a well-conducted newspaper office" (O'Dell, 1935, p. 30). Horace White of the *Chicago Tribune* wrote, "I do not think there is room for a distinctive school of journalism, though such a school is possible, just as a swimming school is possible" (p. 32). Others suggested that no specific courses were necessary for college training for journalists. R. R. Bowker of *The New York Mail*, for example, wrote, "The college itself is the school of journalism, for the breadth of the curriculum, and that alone, corresponds to the breadth of training, principle and information a journalist requires" (O'Dell, 1935, p. 34). According to O'Dell, "By throwing this controversial subject into the cauldron of public discussion in 1875, Wingate performed a lasting service to this educational movement" (p. 34).

A course in the history of journalism in addition to tutorials was started at the University of Missouri by David R. McAnally, Jr. in 1878, though the course ended in 1885 when McAnally returned to newspaper work (O'Dell, 1935). The first journalism curriculum is thought to be one offered at a Detroit journalism school for women run by Martha Louise Rayne from 1886 to 1900 (Steiner, 1994). The school was part of the academy movement that developed after the American Revolution around Benjamin Franklin's call for vocational preparation. Rayne's 1893 book titled *What Can a Woman Do: or, Her Position in the Business and Literary World* promoted women developing practical skills in case they ever needed a job (Steiner, 1994).

On March 27, 1888, Eugene M. Camp of the *Philadelphia Times* gave a speech titled "Journalists, Born or Made?" (Camp, 1888) at the University of Pennsylvania's Wharton School of Finance in which he stated, "Journalism is a trade. It ought to be a profession." In preparing for his speech, he collected comments from journalists concerning the importance of college training. Typical of the comments against the idea, Frederic Hudson of *The New York Herald* stated, ". . . I cannot see how it could be made very serviceable. . . . The only place where one can learn to be a journalist is in a great newspaper office" (Sutton, 1945, p. 9).

J. C. Goldsmith of *Frank Leslie's Illustrated* argued for a liberal education in addition to practical experience, saying, "Give the boy a good academical education, not omitting Latin and the modern languages, put him to writing wrappers on a large daily journal, and let him work up to the city department" (Sutton, 1945, p. 9). Likewise, Charles Dana of *The New York Sun* stated, "The scheme of teaching journalism by a college professor who is to give special attention to English Composition and to be helped out by courses of lectures given by professional journalists seems to me just as much mistaken as would be an attempt to teach medicine in the same manner (O'Dell, 1935, p. 42). On the other hand, Joseph Pulitzer of *The New York World* said, "I have thought seriously upon this subject and think well of the idea, though I know it is the habit of newspaper men to ridicule it" (O'Dell, 1935, p. 42).

According to O'Dell (1935), Camp's "favorable consensus of opinion for journalism education in the college curriculum" and his proposal to establish a journalism curriculum at the Wharton School of Business was directly responsible for the establishment of "the first comprehensive journalism curriculum offered in the United States" (p. 46). Emery and McKerns (1987) called the program at the University of Pennyvania the first definitely organized journalism curriculum. It was offered from 1893 to 1901 by Joseph French Johnson.

The Pennsylvania program, titled "Courses in Journalism," had a large component of practical coursework—the news side of newspapering as well as advertising and business management, a combination soon to be proposed by President Charles Eliot of Harvard—in addition to a liberal arts component. Coursework consisted of Art and History of Newspaper Making (1 hour); Law of Libel, Business Management, Typographical Union, Cost and Revenue, Advertising, Method of Criticism (1 hour); Newspaper Practice, Exercises in Reporting, Editing of Copy, Conversation (3 hours); Current Topics, Lectures on Live Issues in the United States and Foreign Countries (3 hours); and Public Lectures by Men Engaged in the Active Work of the Profession (B. I. Ross, 1993). Sutton (1945) stated that the program "although more limited than most modern programs, compares favorably in many respects with the journalism curricula being offered in present-day schools" and "served as the pattern for many schools since then" (p. 11).

Bessie Tift College of Forsyth, Georgia, announced the creation of the School of Literature and Journalism in 1898. Its coursework included Summary Writing, Practical Journalism, Business Writing, Interviewing, Space Writing and Reporting, Short Story Writing, Personal Adventure, Newspaper Correspondence, Editorial Paragraphs, Graphic Writing, Pictorial Writing, Imaginative Writing, Novel Writing, Proofreading, and Practical Work in Newspaper Writing. However, no journalism courses were mentioned in the next year's catalog (O'Dell, 1935).

Sutton (1945) concluded that "[i]n numbers, the opposition far outweighed the proponents for the new type of instruction in the beginning, and the objections they set forth undoubtedly had great influence in forestalling a rapid spread of the movement after it once had started." He added, however:

> Likewise, schools that initiated programs of journalism despite these pressures none the less developed in a healthy atmosphere of sharp criticism—a characteristic which they of necessity were to instill in their graduates if they hoped to serve one of the primary missions of education for the profession of journalism. (p. 10)

Despite the difficulties it faced, by the end of the 19th century journalism education had grabbed a foothold in a number of colleges, mainly in the midwest. Research by O'Dell (1935) determined that 14 colleges and universities began offering journalism courses between 1873 and 1903. Such institutions as Denver, Indiana, Iowa, Kansas State, Michigan, Missouri, Nebraska, Ohio State, and Pennsylvania all offered journalism courses prior to 1900.

JOURNALISM EDUCATION IN THE EMERGING STATE UNIVERSITY

The growth of journalism education and other practical courses of study in the post-Civil War period came at a time when the state university was being established and defined in the midwest and west, "where frontier democracy and frontier materialism would help to support a practical-oriented popular institution" (Rudolph, 1962, p. 277). One of the hallmarks of the practically oriented university was the elective system, which was being built on the ruins of the classical curriculum. The elective system has been called "[o]ne of the most creative, and also one of the most destructive, education developments of the post-Civil War years" (Rudolph, 1962, p. 290). It was devised to overcome students' lack of interest in the existing curriculum. Though it did not necessarily do that, according to Rudolph, the elective system succeeded in helping to bring the university into "the mainstream of American life, where it had long been sorely needed and where it for long had sorely needed to be." It also resulted in chaos in the curriculum "by encouraging the notion that one subject was no more important than any other and by making it possible for the nonserious student to find an easy berth" (p. 306).

Though Robert E. Lee experimented with election at Washington College, the champion of the elective system was Harvard President Charles Eliot, who also was soon to be a major influence in journalism education. Implementation of election was begun at Harvard in 1872 with the abolition of required courses for seniors. By 1897, the only prescribed course was a year of freshman rhetoric. The prescribed curriculum at Yale was first relaxed in 1876, and juniors and seniors were released from all course requirements by 1902. Though the elective system became widespread, it found its home in the universities of the midwest and west. As Rudolph (1962) noted, "Unquestionably the large state universities of the Midwest and West, with their commitment to public service and to learning, were more friendly than any other group of institutions to the elective principle" (p. 303).

Journalism education also began to emerge at a time when the German university with its emphasis on graduate education and research was beginning to influence American higher education. Boyer (1990), for example, noted that by the late 1800s "colonial college values, which emphasized teaching undergraduates, began to lose ground to the new university that was emerging" (p. 9). It was also a time when the university's role in training for professions was gaining momentum. J. W. Carey (1978) stated that the professionalization of higher education "was not driven by a lust for equality but what we have come to call a lust for meritocracy" and "pivoted on the substitution for the authority of knowledge—specifically of scientific knowledge—for the authority of an absent tradition" (p. 849). He added:

> In short, the struggle which the American university led on behalf of the professions was a struggle between professional studies versus practical ones, academic studies versus the apprenticeship system, social-science knowledge versus common sense, ethical practitioners versus amoral hacks. (p. 849)

PULITZER'S AND ELIOT'S CONTRIBUTIONS TO JOURNALISM EDUCATION

Polson (1924) argued that the 1869–1908 period that led up to the founding of the first journalism school was significant for journalism education because the first steps were taken toward academic programs in journalism and because of the growth within the academic community of an appreciation of the value of journalism education. The push for journalism professionalism around the turn of the century was linked to the Progressive movement (Schudson, 1978). It also was seen as a way for journalists "to regain some of the lost prestige suffered during the era of yellow journalism" (Steiner, 1994, p. 56). Joseph Pulitzer, himself a major player in the yellow journalism era of the 1890s and early 1900s, is credited with being the driving force in attempts around the turn of the century to professionalize the field of journalism by merging the profession and academics. Pulitzer first proposed funding a school of journalism at Columbia University in 1892, 4 years after his response to Eugene Camp's question about the feasibility of college training in journalism (O'Dell, 1935). Through his proposed school of journalism, Pulitzer "sought to bring the full liberal education resources of the university into the journalism school" (Wilcox, 1959, p. 3). In 1902, Pulitzer set forth his vision of the role of the journalism school and of journalism education in general: "My idea is to recognize that journalism is, or ought to be, one of the great and intellectual professions, to encourage, elevate and educate in a practical way the present, and still more, future members of that profession, exactly as if it were the profession of law or medicine" (Dennis, 1988, p. 11). In 1903, Pulitzer asked Dr. George W. Hosmer to prepare a brochure to be titled *The Making of a Journalist: Why a Technical and Professional School Is Needed* and to present it to President Nicholas Murray Butler of Columbia University and President Charles W. Eliot of Harvard. The pamphlet stated about the need for a journalism school:

> The newspaper man must be qualified for his higher profession, first, by ample information, much of which is already included in collegiate courses in history, geography, political science, international relations, economics, and particularly the study of the English language; second, by acquiring much special information that is at present not taught outside the newspaper offices. This knowledge must be analyzed, classified and systematized, so that it may be conveyed by oral instruction, preferably by newspaper men themselves, as none other are likely to know those things, at least in the beginning. (O'Dell, 1935, pp. 102–103)

Pulitzer sent along a promise of a large endowment for a journalism school if either university would accept it. Butler was quick to accept Pulitzer's $2 million gift; however, Columbia's school wouldn't open until 1912. Pulitzer said the school would "begin a movement that will raise journalism to the rank of a learned profession, growing in the respect of the community as other professions far less important to the public interest have grown" (Steiner, 1994, p. 50–51). As J. W. Carey (1978) put it, "Journalism education begins, for all practical purposes, when Joseph Pulitzer pressed many dollars into the somewhat reluctant hands of Columbia University" (p. 848).

Pulitzer proposed an integrated curriculum focusing on style, journalism law, ethics, literature, truth and accuracy as well as referencing techniques, history for the journalist, sociology, economics, "the enemies of the republic," arbitration, statistics, modern languages (French for style and German as a key for gaining information), an overview of science, the study of newspapers (including values of the news and ethics), the power of ideas, principles of journalism, including publishing a newspaper, and the news (Pulitzer, 1904). O'Dell noted, "Following the trend of [Charles] Wingate, Joseph Pulitzer insisted that training for journalism should concern itself primarily with the editorial department. This basic implication naturally precluded instruction in general newspaper manufacture, advertising, circulation, or allied fields" (1935, 93–94).

Like Pulitzer, President Charles Eliot of Harvard proposed to improve journalism through journalism education, but he defined journalism education more broadly. Eliot was out of the state when Hosmer brought the brochure he had prepared for Pulitzer. On his return, Eliot wrote Hosmer three letters detailing his interest in which he proposed his own journalism curriculum. Like the Pennsylvania curriculum of 1893, it consisted not only of editorial work (including news and editorial writing), but also the operation of the business office and advertising office and the close connection with the mechanical department. O'Dell (1935) stated the newspaper "was, in the mind of Dr. Eliot, primarily a business." He added, "Its purpose was to sell a commodity—the commodity of news—and every factor involved in this sale was to be evaluated in the light of the possible training for the potential newspaper worker" (p. 84).

Eliot proposed courses in newspaper administration (organization, functions and services), newspaper manufacture (printing presses and other mechanical devices), the law of journalism, ethics of journalism, history of journalism, and literary forms of newspapers (approved newspaper style and usage). In contrast to Pulitzer's plan, background courses would be taken in other departments rather than inside the journalism school itself (O'Dell, 1935). Pulitzer objected to Eliot's proposal because it did not distinguish between the business and editorial sides of the profession. In an article in *North American Review*, Pulitzer (1904) wrote that "if my wishes are to be considered, business instruction of any sort should not, would not, and must not form any part of the work of the college of journalism." He added that "nothing, in fact, is more inconsistent and incompatible with my intentions or repugnant to my feelings than to include any of the business or commercial elements of a newspaper in what is to be taught in this department of Columbia College" (M. L. Lee, 1918, p. 13). O'Dell said of Eliot's contribution to journalism education:

> The development of this concept of journalism, in which all the forces which have an immediate effect on the newspaper development within the plant are to be included, constitutes Dr. Eliot's main gift to education for journalism today. And it must be remembered that the acceleration of this movement within journalism education has been due, in the main, to the presentation of the list of journalism courses recommended by Dr. Eliot. (pp. 87-88)

Eliot's curriculum is usually thought of today as being essentially practical and vocational, though "perhaps unjustly" (Dressel, 1960, p. 23). Likewise, Wilcox (1959) stated that the philosophies of Pulitzer and Eliot "were to have a lasting, if often misconstrued, impact on journalism education" (p. 3). He said that their plans "later were commonly, if somewhat inaccurately, used to distinguish between emphasis upon a broad liberal education as opposed to emphasis upon a specialized technical education" (p. 4). Dennis (1988), for example, stated: "Harvard's President Charles William Eliot was slow to respond to Pulitzer's soundings; and when he did, he somewhat perversely (in light of later history) proposed a trade school with courses in advertising, circulation, and typesetting" (p. 11).

Jandoli (1957), like Dressel (1960) and Wilcox (1959), argued that the liberal arts–vocational distinction often made between the ideas of Pulitzer and Eliot was not an accurate perception because both men agreed that journalism education should be largely oriented toward the social sciences. He wrote:

> Indeed, chroniclers of journalistic history have too often perverted the facts for the sake of dramatic contrast. Just as journalism education did not evolve from technical training, so, too, the schools established in 1908 and thereafter did not actually align themselves into opposing camps of diehards who stood either for the "practical" business officer instruction ascribed to Dr. Charles W. Eliot of Harvard or for the "background" editorial room approach attributed to Joseph Pulitzer of the New York *World*. It was not like that. (p. 64)

According to O'Dell (1935) and other journalism historians, Eliot's so-called practical, even vocational, approach to journalism education was not put into practice at Harvard but at what became the first journalism school—the School of Journalism at the University of Missouri. For example, Sutton (1945) stated that the Missouri curriculum "provided for a practical approach to the problem" of training journalists and "was fashioned closely after the one proposed some time before by Dr. Charles W. Eliot" (p. 12). Also, Dennis (1988) stated that "[a] program similar to the one proposed by Eliot was later organized at the University of Missouri" (p. 11).

The Missouri School of Journalism was founded in 1908 with pressure from the state press association while Columbia University was deciding how to spend Pulitzer's money; however, planning for it began long before Eliot became involved in journalism education and only shortly after Pulitzer first proposed his plan. A bill to establish a journalism school was defeated by the Missouri legislature in 1895. After the defeat, the Missouri Press Association took up the cause. The proposed curriculum at Missouri was based on the concept of the newsroom and emphasized drills built around journalistic techniques (Dressel, 1960). In "The Journalist's Creed" of 1908, Walter Williams, the first dean, noted that the interests of the new school would be greater than just the news side of journalism, however. The creed stated, "I believe that advertising, news, and editorial columns should alike serve the best interests of the readers; that a single standard of helpful truth and cleanness would prevail for all; that the supreme test of good journalism is the measure of its public service" (O'Dell, 1935, p. 91).

Even though the Missouri School of Journalism curriculum was similar to Eliot's, the proposed curriculum was first published in 1898—5 years before

Eliot's curriculum. It consisted of Art and History of Newspaper Making (including the history of printing and newspapers in addition to typography and presswork), Newspaper Making (including business management, advertising, reporting, and criticism), and Current Topics (including constitutional law, political science, U.S. and Missouri history, economics, journalism law, and issues in journalism) (O'Dell, 1935). The 1908 curriculum was similar. It consisted of History and Principles of Journalism, Newspaper Making, Newspaper Administration, Magazine and Class Journalism, Newspaper Publishing, Newspaper Jurisprudence, News-Gathering, Correspondence, and Office Equipment (S. L. Williams, 1929).

Walter Williams (1908) noted that the coursework was not just practical but provided for a broad education. In his remarks for the opening of the new school in 1908, he stated about the school's purpose:

> I believe it is possible for this School to give dignity to the profession of journalism, to anticipate to some extent the difficulties that journalism must meet and to prepare its graduates to overcome them; to give prospective journalists a professional spirit and high ideals of service; to discover those with real talent for work in the profession, and to give the State better newspapers and a better citizenship. (S. L. Williams, 1929, p. 25)

According to O'Dell (1935), the 1908-1912 period saw the "first establishment of journalism education in accordance with the philosophies of Pulitzer and Eliot, and a mushroom spread of courses in newspaper training throughout the country" (pp. 92–93). Sutton (1945) noted that "[t]he attention that both of these men—each an outstanding leader in his particular field—lent encouragement to the spread of instruction in journalism" and "bolstered a widespread and growing faith among educators and many newspapermen in the soundness of programs for training in journalism" (p. 13).

Most journalism programs were not to be organized into journalism schools following the example of Columbia and Missouri, however. Typically, they were begun in departments of English, but English departments at the time were more interested in the reading of literature than in writing. As J. W. Carey (1978) stated,

> the creation of these professional schools did not occur until a coalition was formed between teachers of journalism and the state press association. And this coalition did not form until journalism teachers were blocked by the English departments that housed them from further development of the curriculum. Thus, an uneasy partnership was created, decades after editors started calling for the establishment of journalism schools. (p. 848)

2

The Transformation of Journalism Education

The history of journalism education is part of the history of the transformation of the American university into a professional school, and the transformation of American society into a domain of professional power and expertise.
—J. W. Carey (1978, pp. 847-848)

Evidence suggests that journalism education in the early years of the century was not well respected, even by some journalism educators. An article in the November 1927 *Journalism Bulletin* of the American Association of Schools and Departments of Journalism noted, for example, that before 1910, "it is generally known that conditions in education for journalism were bad, that few journalism schools were equipped to provide a comprehensive education for the profession" (Farrar, 1993, p. 57).

Part of the reason why journalism education was slow in gaining a prestigious place along with the established professional schools can be traced to its practical roots. Journalism educators had a difficult time overcoming the commonly held opinion that journalism was no more than a trade. Academic critics stated that it might best be taught in a trade school rather than a college or university, and many journalists continued to state that it could be better learned on the job. Another obvious difference between journalism and older and more prestigious professions such as law, medicine, and theology was that journalism education was almost everywhere an undergraduate experience. Few programs were organized as separate professional schools, and those few schools were dependent on the rest of the university to provide background coursework.

Yet another reason journalism education was not taken as seriously as early journalism educators had hoped was its development at universities in the midwest, south and far west, far from the major media centers. Dennis (1988) termed the phenomenon the "Harvard Non-Model." He wrote concerning the phenomenon:

> The fact that journalism and mass communication studies never got a department, let alone a school, at Harvard—or at any of the other establishment institutions which set the agenda and determine the "respectability" for many fields—helped other universities either to reject the idea of journalism education or to keep their struggling departments "down on the farm." (Dennis, 1988, pp. 13–14)

The situation journalism education found itself in during the first decade of the 20th century was not particularly unique to journalism, however. Whereas the

14

classical college was preprofessional—preparing students for study for the professions of law, medicine and theology—the emerging university of the late 1800s had developed its own professional programs. Rudolph (1962) stated about the new professions that were created by the so-called University Movement:

> The new professions . . . were not as respectable as the old professions. The old professionalism was characterized by a serious regard for the liberal studies and by the degree to which the central subject of every liberal study was man himself. . . . There was, therefore, a difference, a *real* difference in kind between the old and the new professions, a difference that had once been clarified by the distinction between profession and vocation. The flowering American university took what were vocations and turned them into professions; the old distinction would be lost in the process. (p. 343)

THE RISE OF JOURNALISM EDUCATION ORGANIZATIONS AND CURRICULUM STANDARDS

The *Journalism Bulletin* noted that in 1910 three departments of journalism (the University of Wisconsin, New York University and the University of Washington) had been organized in addition to the school at the University of Missouri (Editorial, 1927, p. 25). Walter Williams, dean of the school of journalism at Missouri, sent a survey to 200 colleges and universities in 1912 and determined that 32 of them offered instruction in journalism (Sutton, 1945). Three of the 32 institutions (Columbia, Marquette, and Missouri) were professional schools, and seven (Iowa State, Kansas, Kansas State, Notre Dame, Oregon, Washington, and Wisconsin) were departments.

The American Association of Teachers of Journalism (AATJ) was founded at what was called the third annual American Conference of Teachers of Journalism in Chicago on November 30, 1912, under the instigation of Willard G. Bleyer of Wisconsin, who became its first president. The previous meetings had been informal ones in California in 1910 and at the University of Missouri in 1911, but no constitution had been adopted or officers elected. Eighteen educators and five media professionals attended the 1912 meeting. The first AATJ directory listed 31 teachers. At the time, 33 colleges and universities were thought to offer journalism instruction. The first organization for advertising teachers, the National Association of Teachers of Advertising, was founded in 1915 through the efforts of George B. Hotchkiss of New York University (Emery & McKerns, 1987).

Starting with the founding of the AATJ, journalism school organizations began to establish curriculum standards to meet the needs of a growing discipline. In

1915, *Editor & Publisher* magazine called for licensing of journalists, but it later changed its mind because journalism schools were setting sufficiently high standards for students who became professional journalists (Steiner, 1994). In 1916, Walter Williams of Missouri proposed an association of the largest programs. An organizational meeting was held April 5, 1917, before the AATF meeting in Chicago with 10 invited member universities: Missouri, Wisconsin, Columbia, Kansas, Ohio State, Oregon, Texas, Montana State, Washington, and Indiana. The members voted 5 to 4 to call it the American Association of Schools and Departments of Journalism (AASDJ). Williams was elected first president. At that first meeting, the AASDJ began the movement toward standards by requiring that students in member schools take 24 semester units of journalism, including two units of history and principles, two units of editorial writing, six units of news writing and reporting, and three units of copy reading (Emery & McKerns, 1987). By 1920, 131 institutions were offering instruction in journalism. Many of them were in English departments, and a number were at 2-year institutions. Twenty-eight of them were offering a professional curriculum. Ten of them belonged to the AASDJ (Sutton, 1945).

A tentative attempt at setting curriculum standards for the new discipline was begun when the Council on Education for Journalism (CEJ) was established jointly by the AATJ and the AASDJ in 1923, after a Committee on Classification dropped its efforts to rate existing journalism programs as A, B, or C. In 1924 the CEJ presented its Principles and Standards of Education for Journalism, outlining what should be required of a quality journalism program (Council on Education for Journalism, 1925). The Principles and Standards proposed that not less than 120 semester credits be required for a bachelor's degree; that such subjects as history, economics, government and politics, sociology, literature, natural science, and psychology should be part of a journalism student's 4-year course of study; and that a foreign language was desirable. The document proposed journalism courses in reporting, copy reading, editorial writing, writing of special articles, the history of journalism, and principles and responsibilities (or ethics) of journalism (Emery & McKerns, 1987).

By 1929, journalism was being taught at 190 institutions, 56 of them offering a professional curriculum. A study in *Journalism Quarterly* ("Journalism Education," 1929) reported that 5,108 students were training for journalism careers at the schools reported to be offering a professional curriculum. The author concluded that "[s]ixty Class A schools of journalism can easily take care of the needs of the profession. . . . There is danger that schools already started may over-expand" (pp. 2–3). The author also called for higher standards and controls on enrollment. The number of 2- and 4-year institutions with journalism programs grew to 326 in 1932 and 894 in 1936. The first count of 4-year institutions, conducted in 1940, found 542 such institutions offering journalism (Sutton, 1945).

After nearly 30 years of discussion, the first steps toward a formal accrediting program were begun by the AASDJ in collaboration with newspaper groups in 1939 with the establishment of the National Council on Professional Education for Journalism (NCPEJ). It was formed by journalism educators, the American Society of Newspaper Editors, the American Newspaper Publishers Association, the National Newspaper Association, the Inland Daily Press Association, and the Southern Newspaper Publishers Association (Sutton, 1945). NCPEJ became the American Council on Education for Journalism (ACEJ) in 1945. In 1948, the first 35 schools with accredited sequences were named. The National Association of Radio and Television Broadcasters joined the ACEJ in 1952, and the Magazine Publishers Association joined in 1957. The number of accredited journalism schools reached 47 in 1965 and 89 in 1987 (Emery & McKerns, 1987). The number of accredited programs reached 106 in 1997 (ACEJMC, 1997).

The American Society of Journalism School Administrators (ASJSA) was founded in 1944 among administrators of smaller programs. The Association for Education in Journalism (AEJ) replaced the American Association of Teachers of Journalism (AATJ) in 1950. Ten AEJ special interest divisions were approved in 1965 and began operation at the 1966 convention. In 1982, the AEJ became the Association for Education in Journalism and Mass Communication. In 1984 the AASDJ and the ASJSA merged to become the Association of Schools in Journalism and Mass Communication (Emery & McKerns, 1987).

JOURNALISM EDUCATION AND
THE PROGRESSIVE MOVEMENT

While the schools at the University of Missouri and Columbia University were being discussed, the first 4-year curriculum was put in place at the University of Illinois by Frank W. Scott in 1905. The first journalism instruction there began in 1902 in a course titled Business Writing–Business Correspondence in the Department of Rhetoric and Oratory. It provided instruction in "the making of summaries and abstracts, advertising, proof-reading, and the preparation of manuscripts for the press." A second course, Newspaper Writing, was added in the 1903–1904 school year. It proposed "to give, on the side of theory, an insight into the history of the newspaper and the aims and ideals of modern journalism, and on the side of practice to give exercise under criticism, in the more practical forms of newspaper writing" (O'Dell, 1935, p. 68). According to O'Dell, Scott "drew on the plans of both Pulitzer and Eliot and provided the needed development in the transitional period between the presentation of their plans, and the first fruition of their programs as seen in the work of [Willard G.] Bleyer and Walter Williams" (p.

69).

Willard G. Bleyer began teaching English and the first journalism course (News Writing) at the University of Wisconsin in 1905. And by the time the Columbia University School of Journalism opened in 1912, according to J. W. Carey (1978), "the center of journalism education had passed to the state universities" (p. 849). Bleyer was soon to propose a 4-year journalism curriculum based on a broad liberal arts foundation. Bleyer stated that he based his curriculum on ideas developed by both Joseph Pulitzer and Charles Eliot about journalism as liberal education. O'Dell (1935) argued, however, that Bleyer instituted Pulitzer's plan rather than Eliot's. O'Dell wrote of Bleyer's curriculum: "Emphasis is placed on preparation for the editorial department. Training is given in journalism only after the student has made preliminary preparation in literature and in the social sciences. The business interests of the newspaper are given attention, but are not as heavily emphasized as the editorial department" (p. 71). Because it became accepted myth that the distinction between Pulitzer and Eliot was a vision of a liberal education versus a vision of a practical education, Wisconsin and Missouri became models for what were seen as the two contrasting visions of journalism education, the former providing a liberal education and the latter a more practical one (Dressel, 1960; D. K. Ross, 1957).

Though Bleyer was interested in providing students a broad liberal arts education, the curriculum was also practical. The University of Wisconsin at the time was a center for Progressivism, an extension of the University Idea of the late 1800s with its emphasis on public service ideals embodied in the Morrill Act that set up vocationally oriented land-grant colleges. Progressivism flowered from the end of the Spanish-American War to World War I. Rudolph (1962) stated about that movement and the University Idea:

> The simultaneous spread of the Progressive spirit and of the university idea would of course tend to reinforce the service element of both. Both movements would in a sense argue for stability in society, for an equality of opportunity now challenged by labor unionism and socialism from below and by vast concentrations of wealth and power from above; both would serve the idea of inevitable material and moral progress and see the future as a place that would not only be bigger but also better. (p. 357)

A part of the Progressive Movement, but not unique to it, was the extension curriculum—in part a public relations effort "to extend the influence and the popularity of the university into communities beyond the immediate vicinity of the institution" (p. 363).

Wisconsin President Charles R. Van Hise strongly supported Progressivism through what became known as the Wisconsin Idea: "the concept of a partnership between the university and the state to work together to improve conditions of everyday life" (Bronstein & Vaughn, 1998, p. 5). In 1908, Harvard President Charles Eliot called Wisconsin the leading state university of the time. Rudolph (1962) credited Wisconsin for "the success with which it incorporated in its rationale two curiously conflicting currents in Progressivism: the resort to an *expertise* in the affairs of state, and the development of popular nontechnical lectures which carried the university to the people" (p. 363).

Though hired to teach freshman English at Wisconsin for the 1904–1905 school year, Bleyer was more interested in journalism. According to Bronstein and Vaughn (1998), Bleyer thought of the journalist as "an expert who served as interpreter of information and guide to the public." His ideas about journalism fit well with the goals of President Van Hise, who agreed to let Bleyer revive the university news service, which had been founded in 1896 but had fallen into disuse. Bleyer also began the weekly *Press Bulletin*, another effort to promote the university. Bronstein and Vaughn stated about Bleyer's use of the press:

> Like many progressives, Bleyer saw a potential for community uplift in a press that informed individuals about the workings of their institutions. He believed that newspapers could improve public life by disseminating information about research, and could make citizens feel connected to the university by keeping them abreast of discoveries in knowledge and their real-world applications. Certainly these ideas dovetailed nicely with the Wisconsin Idea and Bleyer urged Van Hise to foster relationships between journalists and the university. (p. 6)

BLEYER'S CURRICULUM AND ITS TIES
TO THE SOCIAL SCIENCES

Bleyer outlined his junior–senior curriculum in 1906. He realized the impossibility of developing an undergraduate journalism program on the model of a medical or law school—with all courses taught by journalism school faculty—as advocated by Pulitzer. Therefore, he provided for a liberal education through a curriculum that consisted of courses in economics, political science, history, and English as well as journalism. Sociology, psychology, and the natural sciences were added later. The structured curriculum was particularly progressive for the time. It wouldn't be until 1919 that the total permissiveness of the elective system would begin to be put in check with the advent, at Columbia University, of a general education curriculum. Rudolph (1962) called the general education curriculum "an attempt to capture some of the sense of a continuing intellectual and spiritual heritage that had fallen victim to the elective principle" (p. 456). Bleyer saw his curriculum in much the same way. In a March 1931 article in *Journalism*

Quarterly, he wrote:

> Unfortunately for too many of the students enrolled in our liberal arts colleges, lack
> of purpose and direction in their work results, under the elective system, now
> generally in vogue, in a more or less haphazard choice of studies, with little effort
> on their part to think seriously about what they are studying in application to
> present-day problems. (Bleyer, 1931b, pp. 43–44)

Bleyer's curriculum took journalism education in a different direction from other professional schools. He stated that journalists need a much broader education than members of other professions and that the curriculum "that includes government and politics, economics, sociology, psychology, history, science, and literature, would seem to be the minimum requirements as preparation for intelligent newspaper and magazine work" (Bleyer, 1931b, p. 38). Bleyer believed that trained journalists were needed to improve democracy and, according to Rogers (1994), he believed that journalism could not survive at a research university like Wisconsin as a vocational program. Thus, he "pioneered in promoting journalism as a legitimate university discipline, with an emphasis on teaching journalism as a social science rather than a vocational subject" (p. 19).

D. K. Ross (1957) noted that the 1906 curriculum "roughly approximates that adopted by most of the major journalism schools of today" (p. 468). The course was split into two levels, one for freshmen and sophomores and one for juniors and seniors. Between one third and one fourth of the courses were in journalism, with the balance in social and natural sciences and liberal arts. Graduates had a minimum of 31 hours in journalism and a maximum of 40. In 1907, Bleyer expanded on his ideas about what the best journalism curriculum should be. He wrote that it should have three kinds of courses (the first two kinds of courses being the basis of a good general education curriculum and the third specifically related to the major):

> Those designed to familiarize the student with the present and past social, political,
> and industrial conditions and with the literature of his own and other languages;
> those designed to develop the students' power of expressing ideas effectively in
> writing; and those intended to give necessary instruction in the history,
> development, organization and methods of modern journalism. (D. K. Ross, 1957,
> p. 468)

Bleyer's 4-year plan of study for journalism, both inside and outside the major, was put into the catalog in 1909, the same year that a course of journalism was established. In 1912 a department was established. By 1914 the journalism curriculum at Wisconsin was enlarged to include courses in history and ethics, and by 1920 law of the press was introduced as a journalism rather than a political science course. In 1927 a school of journalism was established (O'Dell, 1935). In the 1920s, Bleyer proposed master's and doctoral degrees in journalism built around postgraduate seminars and established such a graduate program at Wisconsin. Bleyer came to propose journalism education as an additional 1 or 2 years beyond the 4-year general college degree, but he realized that students would not feel it worth their time to study for 6 years for the low salaries newspapers provided (D. K. Ross, 1957). A proposal for providing professional journalism courses only at the graduate level in a one-year master of journalism program was revived in 1975 (Stephenson & Merrill) and revised in 1980 (Merrill).

Bleyer also was early to note the need for research in journalism education. In a 1923 paper presented to the American Association of Teachers of Journalism, he noted the importance of research in enhancing the teaching of journalism and recommended that research papers be presented at the group's annual conventions (Durham, 1992). In addition, he wanted to further journalism education by sending his disciples into leadership positions at other research universities. According to Rogers (1994), "Wisconsin in the 1930s was the seed institution for journalism training based in the social sciences, and Daddy Bleyer was the pioneering figure" (p. 19).

THE WISCONSIN CURRICULUM AND LIBERAL EDUCATION

Though the Progressive era that was the momentum behind the curriculum designed by Willard Bleyer at Wisconsin did not survive World War I, the Progressive Movement was to remain important in higher education in the United States, particularly in journalism education (Rudolph, 1962). Progressive educator John Dewey's 1916 work, *Democracy and Education*, was to have a major impact on higher education and journalism education years after it was published. In it, he defined the requirements for thought and learning: that there must first be an experience that the student finds to be of interest and a problem to be solved coming from that experience. He stated that a "curriculum which acknowledges the social responsibilities of education must present situations where problems are relevant to the problems of living together, and where observation and information are calculated to develop social insights and interest" (Dewey, 1966, p. 192).

President Arthur Twining Hadley of Yale, a supporter of Progressivism, provided a test to determine what courses were legitimate liberal arts courses. The text was: "[A] public motive rather than a private . . . [one] must constitute the dominant note in its appeal" (Rudolph, 1962, p. 365). Bleyer saw the public motive—and the liberal arts—at the center of journalism education. In a statement that seems current even today, he wrote, "Therefore, it seems to me that the function of most of the courses in journalism is to teach students how to think straight about what is going on in the world at large and how to apply what they have learned to understanding and interpreting the day's news" (Bleyer, 1931b, p. 39).

Though Bleyer's curriculum was practical, it was not a trade school curriculum. For example, he stated that a course in reporting involved "a survey of the whole community and all its important activities, as a means of showing students how to discover and evaluate the news that they may furnish." In addition, he stated that a course in copy reading is more than writing headlines and correcting copy: "Its most important function is to teach students how to evaluate the news . . . in the light of its significance to readers of a particular newspaper as citizens of the local community, of the state and the nation" (Bleyer, 1931b, p. 40). Likewise, editorial writing "is devoted to the careful, impartial, logical analysis of the latest phases of the social, political, and economic problems that they have studied in other courses. . . . It is designed to teach them how to think straight about what is going on in the world day by day, and to write interestingly and effectively concerning these things" (p. 41).

In response to attacks by Flexner (1930) on journalism education in general and Bleyer's Principles of Journalism course specifically, Bleyer (1931b) stated that the course "undertakes to lead students to consider what influence the newspaper may exert on the opinions, morals, tastes, and standards of living of readers" as well as "the manner in which attitudes, opinions, beliefs, and habits of thought and action develop in the individual" and the "nature of public opinion and its relation to individual private opinion." He concluded: "In this way, the material in courses in psychology, sociology, ethics, and the history of morality is brought to bear upon the problems of the journalistic handling of news of crime, scandal, and vice" (p. 41).

Though Bleyer's proposed journalism curriculum had from one quarter to one third of a student's courses in journalism with the rest in liberal arts studies, Bleyer (1931b) also thought that his journalism courses could be seen as liberal studies. He wrote:

> Moreover, even the courses in journalism in so far as they undertake to train students to think straight, to write clearly and effectively, and to apply what they have learned in other fields to the practice of journalism, are broadly cultural rather than narrowly technical. . . . [T]hey aim to give greater significance to liberal arts studies, because they show students how to apply these studies to the events and problems of today. (p. 43)

Bleyer thought that many students enrolled in liberal arts programs were not getting the broad education expected of such programs. He gave much of the blame for that to the elective system of the day that allowed students' studies to be too broad and unfocused. He saw journalism as a means for giving students focus and direction as well as showing them "what these other studies mean in relation to the life and the work of the world" (p. 44).

JOURNALISM EDUCATION: TRADE SCHOOL OR ACADEMIC ENTERPRISE?

The question of accreditation brought with it the question of which vision journalism education should follow, and the issue to be faced by journalism educators before 1930 continued to be the balance between vocational instruction and academics. In many cases, critics charged, vocationalism won (E. W. Allen, 1924; Cowles, 1928). Sutton (1945) stated that two conflicting philosophies emerged from early attempts to establish journalism education: "one which called for a very 'practical' type of training, and another which emphasized the need for broad cultural programs including a minimum of technical subjects" (p. 35). He also suggested that two competing viewpoints were Eliot's and Pulitzer's. He wrote that the "Eliot plan, which placed major emphasis on 'practical' training, held greatest favor for many years" (p. 14). Sutton, like O'Dell (1935), suggested that Eliot's vision was favored by journalism educators for several years both because of Eliot's stature in academe and because it was thought to be favored by practitioners. Sutton concluded, however, that "the gradual trend toward less stress on technical courses in favor of a background instruction in the social sciences points to a growing shift to the Pulitzer point of view." He attributed the assumed shift to a similar shift in higher education itself. He stated, "This tendency of certain schools to favor one plan over another perhaps was due largely to the confusion which still exists in an interpretation of the real meaning of 'vocational subjects' contrasted with 'liberal or cultural studies'—a condition that has persisted for many years" (Sutton, 1945, p. 14).

Though O'Dell's and Sutton's contention that the difference between Pulitzer and Eliot was a difference between a liberal education and a practical one can be questioned, their conclusion that the use of practical classroom experience was prevalent early in the century is supported. Wilcox (1959) constructed a timetable of journalism education during those early decades. It was roughly in three parts: 1908–1920, the early and mid-1920s, and the late 1930s onward. During the first period, he concluded, journalism programs were largely vocational. Harrington (1919) explained that journalism educators were "pioneers in an untracked wilderness" trying to determine the best teaching methods, but that it was becoming more evident to them that "the most fruitful instruction in journalism is that which realistically duplicates the conditions of the newspaper office." He noted that teaching students "in a natural setting of work pleasantly pursued, has proven best adapted to fulfilling the ends we have in view" (pp. 198–199).

Wilcox (1959) stated that in the second period of his timetable, through most of the 1920s, journalism educators "looked increasingly to the social sciences as taught in other departments of the university" (p. 4). That educators' opinions of what journalism education should be had changed from what Harrington had stated in 1919 is evident in a statement by E. W. Allen (1927) that "[i]f journalism means anything more than a mere trade, it must be based upon some depth of understanding." Allen added:

> Schools of Journalism will utterly fail of their deeper purpose if they do not attempt and succeed in producing a graduate who is thoroughly grounded not only in the separate social sciences, but also in the habit of keeping up with the authentic progress of the best current thought and actually applying the most enlightening conception of social science to his work as a reporter and as an editor. (Sutton, 1945, p. 24)

Wilcox (1959) wrote that starting during the late 1920s "journalism brought to its own curriculum an increasing measure of applied social science" (p. 4). Similarly, Jandoli (1957) wrote that by the time the American Association of Schools and Departments of Journalism stated the importance of the social sciences in 1924 "the need for integrating and correlating became more evident than before" and "journalism educators quickly devised methods of teaching social science under journalism-titled courses in the journalism school. . . . For some, journalism itself was a social science" (p. 64). Dressel (1960) noted that from 1908 to 1925, "[j]ournalism educators were torn between desire for academic respectability and the demands of the working press for technical instruction" (p. 24). He added:

> Although by 1918 the social sciences were regarded as basic to journalism, journalism educators gradually become concerned about the fragmentation of the social sciences and moved to organize social science-oriented courses within the journalism schools. By the late 1920s there was evident a trend toward thinking of journalistic education as a broad liberal education with a minimum of attention to techniques. (pp. 24–25)

Likewise, Hyde (1937) wrote that journalism education began to see the value in the social sciences around 1918 and by the late 1920s had determined that "the social sciences were not accomplishing what we had hoped." Their response was to determine that they must help students relate the social science courses "with each other and with the problems of journalism" (Sutton, 1945, p. 23).

Wilcox (1959) noted that "there was something of an explosion in the development of journalism education" in the second two decades of the 20th century. Wilcox credited part of the growth to the increase in the trend toward specialization that had begun in the late 1800s. Specialization was part of the University Movement, which was represented by the birth of the new professions. Wilcox concluded that specialization provided "a benign climate" for journalism programs to emerge from English departments and that it caused a reduction in the number of liberal arts graduates available to newspapers, both of which helped the fledgling journalism programs. He added that, gradually, "the press came to accept the existence of the journalism school, although it can hardly be said that there was wild enthusiasm—or even an adequate degree of understanding—concerning teaching methods and curricula" (p. 4). Career guidance books were beginning to note by the 1920s that the value of a college education for journalists was "an established fact." Talcott Williams, the first director of the Columbia School of Journalism, predicted in 1922 that journalism education would be provided in all "urban universities" and that states would eventually require that reporters have professional training and certification (Steiner, 1994, p. 51).

The president of the American Association of Teachers of Journalism, Edward Marion Johnson, spoke against the trade school approach to journalism education in his presidential address at the 1929 annual convention. He stated that three approaches to journalism education were possible: teaching journalism as a social institution, as a craft, or as a profession. If journalism were seen as a social institution, he said, journalism schools would offer cultural courses focused on that fact. If it were seen as a craft, journalism schools would be trade schools preparing students for journalistic jobs. If it were considered a profession, journalism schools would teach students about the "nature of the services of the press, the measuring of these services, and the ascertainment of the methods by which they may be made to contribute to social progress" (Johnson, 1930, p. 31). He concluded that teaching journalism as a craft was the main approach of his day. He added:

> I believe that cultural courses and professional courses in journalism are just as essential, if not more so, than our present vocational instruction. Trade school instruction is nothing more than presenting a blueprint of the current practices; it does not train for journalistic leadership.
>
> Failure to fix clearly the objectives of our instruction has led us to operate trade schools. We prepare our students for jobs as reporters and copyreaders. There does not exist a genuine professional school of journalism. (pp. 31–32)

THE ATTACK ON JOURNALISM EDUCATION INTENSIFIES

Wilcox (1959) stated that there were main characteristics of the period from 1930 to 1950. One was that journalism education "faced a storm of criticism, largely bearing on vocationalism." The second was that the idea of interpretive reporting—adding context to the news—emerged, causing journalism educators to "take a close look at the nonjournalism content of the curriculum, including a critical appraisal of the social sciences and the humanities." The third was the rise of new media and "the increasing cognizance of the necessity for effective communications in an ever-more complex society created pressure to expand the curriculum" (p. 6).

Attacks against journalism education for vocationalism abounded at the start of the 1930–1950 period. In 1930, Flexner stated that journalism education was "on par with university faculties of cookery and clothing" (Flexner, 1930, pp 160–161). The American Society of Newspaper Editors' Committee on Schools of Journalism called for almost a total liberal arts education for journalists and proposed that journalism schools become graduate schools instead (Armstead, 1930), something the ASNE had proposed at its first meeting in 1923 (Sutton, 1945). The ASNE report concluded: "The schools are out of place. The time of life at which they seek to give the boy the tricks of the trade is out of joint" (Wilcox, 1959, p. 6). The ASNE also passed a resolution the next year charging that journalism educators were refusing to meet newspapers' needs and editors' demands ("Report sees," 1931).

Some educators challenged such charges, however. For example, Johnson (1930) stated that journalism was "an academic subject of the highest order" and was to the social sciences what mathematics was to the physical sciences. "Without mathematics we could not have the physical sciences," he stated. "Without journalism we could not have the social sciences." He added that it is impossible to classify mathematics as a physical science or journalism as a social science. "None the less," he wrote, "both are sciences" (p. 32). Johnson charged that one of the greatest faults of journalism education was that "we have treated journalism as though it were something sufficient unto itself" (p. 38). He called for funding for research on problems of significance to journalists and for training journalism specialists "to deal with the complicated issues of the day— men who can serve as teachers for the masses through the agencies of journalism" (p. 39).

In an address to the American Association of Schools and Departments of Journalism on its 20th anniversary in 1931, Casey (1932) stated that editors and faculty had begun "to bring about the closest and most sympathetic cooperation between schools and newspapers and to arrive at a common understanding on problems relating to education in journalism" and concluded that "massed attacks were no longer in fashion" (Sutton, 1945, p. 22). As the 1930s continued, journalism education began moving further away from vocational training and doing more to integrate with the social sciences as journalism educators expanded research and teaching into other communication fields. Steiner (1994), for example, wrote that in the 1930s "the philosophy of journalism programs shifted away somewhat from the vocational approaches (again combined with courses taken in other disciplines) to a social-science focus" (p. 52). It began to be expected universally that students should obtain not only a broad liberal arts background and a solid training in journalistic skills, but also an understanding of the impact of the media on society.

During the late 1920s, journalism educators began a reevaluation of the liberal arts programs that provided background for their students. Though the problem had been noted by Pulitzer (1904) years earlier, educators in the late 1920s and the 1930s became vocal in their criticism of the fragmentation and specialization taking place in the liberal arts because it made it difficult for journalism students to get an overall view of the social sciences. Cunliffe (1926), E. W. Allen (1927), Bleyer (1931a), Casey (1932), Hyde (1937), and Nash (1938) all noted the failure of liberal arts education in the United States. Journalism educators determined that the trend toward specialization in the previous 50 years or so that had led to collegiate professional training in journalism had had similar effects on the liberal arts programs that journalism educators looked to for adding breadth to their majors' coursework. The disciplines on which they depended for a student's broadening experience had been splintering and narrowing their courses, which were designed for their majors, not the university at large.

Dressel (1960) noted of the situation in the late 1920s and 1930s, "As journalism educators recognized this trend and as they simultaneously achieved some accepted and respected philosophy of a broad liberal education, they dared to criticize the adequacy of the liberal arts offering" (p. 27). Dressel stated that journalism education began as being heavily vocational in most schools, but that period was followed by a "period of attention to the liberal arts, with perhaps some leaning toward the social sciences" (p. 36). He concluded that the increased specialization of the liberal arts led later to a widespread acceptance of journalism education as an applied social science.

In contrast to the momentum of the time toward the social sciences, the Columbia School of Journalism founded by Pulitzer went the opposite direction. In 1935, it became a professionally oriented graduate school. It required students to complete their bachelor's degree, with a liberal arts degree preferred, before undertaking their program of study. Dennis (1988) called it "a kind of educational 'bait-and-switch' scheme" (p. 12). Though it might be argued that what he described took place earlier, Dennis stated about the Columbia Graduate School of Journalism, "Columbia (and other schools that subsequently followed its model) played a less and less active role in generating new knowledge about journalism and communication. The intellectual center of journalism education shifted to the Middle West, where the land grant colleges forged their own traditions, cut off from the Northeastern centers of the media industry" (p. 12).

As U.S. newspapers began a trend to in-depth, "interpretive" reporting in the 1930s, journalism educators began to see journalism courses "as catalytic agents in giving unity, meaning, and reality to the liberal arts courses" while liberal arts brought more depth and substance to journalism (Dressel, 1960, p. 28). Some educators, such as Morrill (1938, p. 32) went further and predicted journalism education would turn to "sciences that go to the roots of human experiences and behavior" for its foundation. Despite becoming less practical, however, journalism education continued to come under attack during the late 1930s. Journalism education took the brunt of an attack on vocationalism at the university by Robert Maynard Hutchins, the chancellor of the University of Chicago. Hutchins (1936) gave journalism education as one example of the problems that vocationalism had brought to higher education. Two years later he stated that "the shadiest educational ventures under respectable auspices are the schools of journalism" (Hutchins, 1938, p. 20). Journalism education also was criticized by editors of smaller newspapers, who wanted a return to a vocational emphasis (Robb, 1941).

Dressel (1960) stated that the view that journalism education was a social science "led in some schools to greater concentration of the work of journalism students in the social sciences, to a demand for integration of social science and journalism and to the development of journalism courses which were in themselves distinctly social science in character" (p. 36). Wilcox (1959) wrote of these counterattacks against charges of vocationalism:

> While the problem was common to all professional disciplines it was especially critical to journalism because of the commitment of journalism education to a broad and meaningful background in the liberal arts as the essence of the educational experience. The problem was to remain one of journalism education's basic ones, although several universities later came to grips with the challenge by offering integrated "area" courses of considerable scope. (p. 6)

THE DEBATE OVER VOCATIONALISM IN THE EARLY YEARS OF SCHOLASTIC JOURNALISM EDUCATION

The first school newspaper is said to have been handwritten issues of *The Students' Gazette* at the William Penn Charter School in Philadelphia in 1777; however, no copies remain. *The Literary Journal*, published by the Latin School of Boston, dates from May 9, 1829, and copies of it do still exist (Arnold &

Kreigbaum, 1976). A course in scholastic journalism was offered in 1912, in Salina, Kansas. It was designed primarily to improve students' composition abilities (Knowles, 1974). Scott (1912) wrote about journalism's utility in improving students' writing, "One of the reasons for the effectiveness of the newspaper training is, of course, apparent to everyone. It is that the theme correction that goes on in the newspaper office is merciless and decisive. The young reporter cannot make the same mistake twice. He either learns and conforms, or he gets out" (Knowles, p. 28).

The same year that the first high school course in scholastic journalism began, what might be called the first college-level attempt to promote scholastic journalism was published. It was a 27-page book titled *Journalism for Teachers* that was produced by the University of Missouri. The author, Frank Martin, declared that teachers should have knowledge of journalism because:

> It was essential that they gather, supply and write school news for the town newspaper because parents want to know what is going on in the schools; they should write for educational journals; they should act as adviser for school publications; they should be able to direct the use of newspapers in the school; they should stir up opinion in favor of school improvements. (Scott, 1912, pp. 14–15)

The first scholastic journalism textbook was titled *Journalism for High Schools* (Dillon, 1918). According to Knowles (1974), the main purpose of such early textbooks was " 'how-to-do-it' in relation to publications—how to report, how to copy edit, how to write headlines . . ." (p. 26). However, the main purpose of scholastic journalism was not usually thought of as vocationalism but improving students' writing ability. As a 1922 journalism text stated about its purpose: "It does not purpose to train newspaper workers, but it aims to be a textbook and course outline for teachers who are using newspaper writing as a stimulus to student effort in composition" (Hyde, 1922, p. i). The author stated that journalists needed a broader education than mere practical skills. He wrote:

> Anything that tends to make a young man believe that he is ready to enter the journalistic profession without the broadest education that he can get will thwart the present tendencies in the newspaper itself and will launch the young man on his career without proper equipment to advance above the lower positions on the staff unless he is exceptionally gifted. (p. 3)

Willard G. Bleyer, the leading force in early college journalism education, also rejected the notion that high school journalism was primarily vocational and that writing for a high school paper was adequate preparation for someone to enter the journalistic profession. Bleyer wrote that vocationalism was but a secondary purpose of scholastic journalism:

> But what can we high-school teachers do as our part of this professional training for journalists? First, we may develop in our students habits of observation, thought, and expression that will be invaluable for them. . . . Secondly, we may use various types of journalistic writing and our school publications, not only to bring out in students whatever talent for journalism they may possess, but also to encourage them to take up journalism as a profession. (Bleyer, 1919, p. 193)

Grant Hyde was even stronger in his opposition to vocationalism in high school journalism. He wrote, "We must tell them what they can do after they have abandoned the vocational point of view" (Hyde, 1925, p. 5). He listed five purposes of scholastic journalism: to aid in teaching composition; to make better citizens; to develop habits of accuracy and carefulness; to aid the profession of journalism both by weeding out the weaker students and sending the better ones on to college and by training them to be intelligent critics of the press; and to teach young people how to read a newspaper (pp. 6–7). Later, Hyde (1928) added about vocationalism in high school journalism:

> Journalism must justify itself educationally. . . . [I]t must offer something of . . . value to the student who has no thought of entering the . . . profession. . . . High-school journalism is much larger than a school newspaper. . . . The schools which have brought the newspaper into the classroom must put it out again. . . . High-school journalism has no business to be vocational. . . . (Hyde, 1928, p. 716)

Gallop (1928) also set forth a larger purpose for scholastic journalism, stating that "the school or department of journalism if it is to make the most of its opportunities, must go beyond the mere practices of journalism—it must deal more in ideas and less in technique" (p. 35). A 1935 list of purposes for high school journalism placed vocationalism fourth, behind developing of initiative and responsibility, training students in written composition and developing an understanding and appreciation of newspapers (Casiday, 1935, p. 525). Five years later a college journalism instructor would write about scholastic journalism:

> There still exists a great deal of confusion as to aims and purposes; standards are not yet uniform. Some of the ideology is still blurred. Instructors who were content to include the work as part of the English program are disturbed when they note others are claiming it as a social science. High school journalism, as such, defies classification. (Stratton, 1940–1941, p. 284)

THE POST-WORLD WAR II GROWTH
OF JOURNALISM EDUCATION

Soon after World War II, journalism schools became the target of criticism again, this time by the Commission on Freedom of the Press, chaired by the nemesis of journalism education at the time: Robert Maynard Hutchins, president of the University of Chicago. The commission's report, *A Free and Responsible Press* (Commission, 1947), charged that most journalism schools "devote themselves to vocational training, and even here they are not so effective as they should be" (p. 78). It continued:

> The kind of training a journalist needs most today is not training in the tricks and machinery of the trade. If he is to be a competent judge of public affairs, he needs the broadest and most liberal education. The schools of journalism as a whole have not yet successfully worked out a method by which their students may acquire this education. (p. 78)

On the other hand, MacDougall (1947) called liberal arts education in the United States "almost a complete failure" (p. 2).

Soon after World War II, journalism schools achieved a period of major student growth, reaching a reported 14,567 students in 1948 (Emery & McKerns, 1987). They also greatly increased their curriculum offerings. A study of 40 of the country's top journalism schools found that seminars and research courses increased 496% between 1941 and 1951. Traditional professional courses grew to a lesser extent. Trade and technical journalism grew 195%, editorial and business administration and management 78%, feature writing and magazine writing 71%, current events and contemporary affairs 58%, copyreading and editing 56%, the community newspaper 56%, typography and printing 55%, reporting 54%, law of the press 53%, and teaching high school journalism 39% ("Herring Study," 1956).

With increased enrollments and a movement away from vocationalism, journalism education began to gain some grudging acceptance by more-established academic disciplines. Also, journalism began to emerge as a recognized academic discipline at research institutions. Steiner (1994) stated that after World War II criticism of journalism schools softened, and it shifted from what they were teaching to what they were not teaching. He wrote, "[B]oth professional career advisers and journalism experts have generally agreed that reporters benefit from journalism education—at least that provided by 'legitimate' journalism schools" (p. 52). The beginning of accreditation in the late 1940s began to make an impact on journalism education, though it brought with it controversy. Durham (1992) wrote about the beginning of the accrediting process: "Although it led to formalized criteria, the process of developing standards for journalism school accreditation in the 1940s initially created bitter political competition among the emerging schools and universities that sought legitimate status in the nascent discipline" (Durham, p. 16). An article in *Editor and Publisher* stated that initial conflict over accreditation had been overcome by the mid-1950s and that "[a]ccreditation is no longer a fighting word in journalism education." The article noted that "[o]nly two or three years ago anyone could spark a riot at a meeting of journalism teachers by leaping to a table top and shouting 'ACEJ'. . . . But now . . . a blessed calm prevails" (Farrar, 1993, p. 66).

Some critics of media education, however, continued to insist that the focus of journalism education should be on the liberal arts, with only a limited number of journalism courses allowed. For example, a 1951 study of Harvard University Nieman Fellows advocated basically a liberal arts approach with little time on technical skills. The curator of the Nieman program, Lou Lyons, stated: "My impression is that journalism programs are tending toward a greater concern for educational background and a lesser time for techniques, and this is, in most instances, good" (Serafini, 1984, p. 24). Dressel (1960) wrote about continuing criticism of journalism education in spite of a trend away from vocationalism that had begun at least 40 years earlier: "While the scathing criticism to which journalism education has been and still is subjected is perhaps beneficial, it does fail to take into account differences in quality on the one hand and difficulties in the way of achieving the ideal on the other" (p. 26).

Dressel (1960) listed four main conceptions of journalism education in practice by the end of the 1950s: technical journalism; journalism as a social science; journalism as a behavioral science; and journalism as liberal education. In the first view, he wrote, "liberal education tends to become a 'technical' field for the journalists, and professional journalism courses exist as an array of courses design to develop technical competencies in communication about this 'field' in one of the several medias" (p. 83). In the second view, social and political problems "are regarded as the major concerns of the present day, and the journalist who reports and interprets the developments to citizens and influences their point of view must be well grounded in the social sciences" (p. 83). The third conception assumes that a "[f]ull understanding of communication processes in a single individual requires knowledge of physical, biological, and psychological sciences" (p. 85). The fourth view assumes a journalist "is the broadly educated individual who becomes aware of many of the issues of his time, to the point where he personally feels that he must have deeper insight into these and must communicate to others his convictions as to the necessity of attention to them" (p. 87).

In the year of the 50th anniversary of the founding of the University of Missouri School of Journalism, Hochberger (1958) wrote that journalism education was "entering a period of maturity, a maturity notable, thus far, for introspective self-criticism and self-conscious striving toward improvement" (p. 2). He identified four groups that represented attitudes that endangered journalism education: (a) the *monopolists*, who "would centralize journalism education in the older, the larger, the more famous, the richer schools"; (b) the *deviationists*, who "would divert the journalism classes to becoming service courses for school publications"; (c) the *vocationists*, who "would reduce education to training"; and (d) the *indirectionists*, who "say, in effect, that the best way to prepare for journalism is not to prepare for it at all" (pp. 23–24). He concluded that journalism education, like professional education in law and medicine, had "survived the slings and arrows of the doubters." He stated that journalism education had had success in "winning acceptance from the profession and from any academic discipline's severest critics, its colleagues in other departments" (p. 3).

In addition to the four groups that Hochberger saw as threatening the status quo in journalism education in the late 1950s, the postwar growth of the field had led to other changes that were altering the very concept of what journalism education was and should be. The position of newspaper journalism, long the only major player on the field, began to be challenged for supremacy by a variety of programs that had developed within journalism education as it began to provide a home for all media-related education. Though the challenge wasn't evident when Hochberger wrote, within the next decade journalism education would face an identity crisis that continues to this day.

3

The Broadening of Journalism Education

The advent of new media, together with the demand for more precision in communications as the society grew increasingly complex, created pressures to broaden the program.

—Wilcox (1959, p. 7)

Journalism education before the 1920s essentially meant the news side of newspaper journalism as envisioned by Joseph Pulitzer, although journalism programs that followed Eliot's vision also offered courses in such things as newspaper advertising and business practices. Often, the only non-newspaper course to be offered was one in magazine journalism. Journalism education after 1920, however, began to expand its base as new types of courses were introduced. Some of the new courses were later to develop into full-fledged journalism sequences—a term first used at Wisconsin in 1927 (B. I. Ross, 1991). The first of the new sequences was advertising, seen in the beginning as an integral part of a number of journalism programs. As the field broadened in the 1920s to include public relations as well as radio broadcasting, the term *journalism education* continued to be used to represent the various media-related sequences, causing some confusion and, later, much irritation among faculty in those sequences.

According to the Herring Study (1956), the 10-year period from 1941 to 1951 saw a dramatic growth in the "all-media approach" to journalism education with "a new emphasis on mass communications generally in journalism education" (p. 363). Areas of instruction that developed during the 10-year period included public relations (as envisioned by Scott Cutlip), mass communications and society, and television news. Among existing nonprint journalism sequences, radio news writing and broadcasting courses increased 378% from 1941 to 1951 at 40 big programs surveyed in the Herring Study, news photography grew 90%, and advertising grew 71%.

As the other areas grew, newspaper journalism began to find itself in a minority position among media-related sequences, and some journalism educators worried that it might not remain the centerpiece of what was still called journalism education. Dressel (1960) noted about the broadening of journalism education into other media-related fields:

> Thus the development of radio and television, the increase in trade, business and technical publications, and the expansion of the fields of advertising and public relations required either an expansion of the conception of journalism or the acceptance of the existence of a number of different though related professions. (p. 31)

THE EMERGENCE OF ADVERTISING EDUCATION

Advertising has always had strong ties to journalism because of the importance of advertising to the financial success of newspapers. Prior to 1900, department stores often would hire experienced copywriters to train their employees to prepare newspaper advertisements. Entrepreneurs sometimes would set up their own training programs outside of department stores. For example, John Powers set up a mobile training program prior to 1890, and Charles Austin Bates held copy writing contests to locate men with ability he could train. According to Schultze (1980):

> Advertising instruction in the last decade of the 19th century was a combination of self-teaching and inchoate methods of formal instruction, including agency apprenticeships, on-premise retail advertising training and trade journal and textbook instruction. The business lacked any pedagogical principles or indeed any consensus as to what constituted practical or theoretical knowledge. (p. 4)

The rise in general interest magazines and an increase in newspaper circulation in the late 1890s led to increased expenditures on advertising and more formalized instruction through the development of correspondence schools, which "linked the social aspirations of young businessmen with the economic interests of advertisers" (Schultze, 1980, p. 4). The first such school, the Page-Davis Correspondence School of Advertising, began in 1896. Advertising practitioners, however, began to view such schools as detrimental to their desires to make the craft more professional. According to Schultze (1982), they "became preoccupied with the issue of professionalism" (p. 17) and considered ways to take charge of the training of copywriters.

The Chicago College of Advertising began operation in 1902 (Rotzoll & Barban, 1984), and Calkins (1905) proposed an "advertising college" that he hoped would do for advertising what law and medical schools had done for those professions. He proposed offering a dozen courses "devoted to a special study of some one of the departments of advertising, including business conduct, managership, commerce, mail order advertising and retail advertising" (Schultze, 1980, p. 9). Students would also take technical courses concerning printing and in the third year would take courses in such areas as psychology, statistics, and copywriting styles.

After some early opposition from practitioners, support for professional training grew with the forming in 1906 of the Associated Advertising Clubs of America, an umbrella organization for advertising clubs and the forerunner of the American Advertising Federation. Members thought that formal advertising education would help establish a body of advertising principles and that it might improve the profession by helping to control who entered it. Its Committee on Lectures developed a Standard Course for local clubs to provide instruction in advertising, which "effectively united public relations and vocational instruction" (Schultze, 1980, p. 15). Other advertising courses were offered by the YMCA, but they were criticized as being less professional. In 1910, Kennedy (1910) proposed "The Kennedy Plan," which suggested that professionalism could be improved through use of academicians. He proposed an Institute for Advertising Research to help establish advertising principles.

Advertising practitioners and experimental psychologists began collaborating in 1901 in an effort to make advertising a science. A leading exponent of that approach was Walter Dill Scott, later to become president of Northwestern University. In 1904 he established a course titled Advanced Experimental Psychology, the first academic course to be offered in the psychology of advertising. In 1912 the Associated Advertising Clubs of America set up the Committee on Standard Qualifications of an Advertising Man, which recommended that each advertising practitioner "study and understand psychology as it controls advertising" (B. I. Ross, 1991, p. 50).

Leaders of the Associated Advertising Clubs of America began to see that correspondence schools, business colleges, and YMCAs had done little to improve the status of advertising and that the academic route was the best route because of the increasingly vocational nature of higher education. The first textbook designed for an advertising course, Paul T. Charington's *Advertising as a Business Force*, was published in 1914; however, it was more oriented to business than psychology. Advertising education began to take two directions, usually toward journalism programs at land-grant schools and toward business schools at private institutions. Schultze (1980) noted that journalism schools were more likely than business schools to see advertising as an integral part of the program because of its link with the newspaper business.

Schultze (1982) noted that advertising education might have become firmly established in business schools had it not been for the desire of land-grant institutions to democratize higher education through vocational training. Instruction in advertising was a part of journalism programs before the turn of the century. Advertising was included in the University of Missouri curriculum at least as early as 1898 in a course titled Newspaper Making. The course description read as follows:

> Newspaper Making: Business management, cost and revenue, advertising, editorials, reporting, clipping from exchanges, methods of criticism. (B. I. Ross, 1991, p. 10)

New York University offered the first course titled Advertising in 1905–1906 in the business school, and the university developed an advertising program in 1915. The University of Missouri School of Journalism offered the first journalism-based advertising course, Advertising and Publishing, which was taught by John B. Powell, when it opened in 1908, and advertising was made a sequence along with news–editorial. Missouri gave its first advertising degree in 1910. Powell soon became a spokesman for practical education instead of education based upon the social sciences. The school hired the first instructor of advertising, Joseph E. Chasnoff, in 1911. It also offered the first graduate course in advertising in 1921.

Northwestern University offered a course titled Psychology of Business, Advertising, and Salesmanship in 1908. The University of Kansas and Indiana University each started an advertising course in 1909, and Iowa State University and the University of Wisconsin both began a course in 1910. Harvard, Dartmouth and Cornell followed by 1912. New York University began an advertising major in 1915, and Marquette University started one in 1916. The University of Wisconsin followed in 1917 and Northwestern University in 1919. An advertising program was started at the University of Oklahoma in 1919 in journalism (B. I. Ross, 1991).

Advertising teachers held a conference in 1915 to attempt to standardize curricula, but it "served only to accentuate differences in approaches" (Rotzoll & Barban, 1984, p. 5). The growth of advertising education in colleges and universities soon took away most of the advertising profession's role in developing the advertising curriculum. A 1917 survey of advertising practitioners found that the advertising business had gained little control over the content of advertising education. As Schultze (1980) stated, "The advertising business, by reaching out to the university for help in creating a profession, had mistakenly undermined its own desire for autonomy" (p. 25).

According to Rotzoll and Barban (1984), two contemporary characteristics of modern advertising education were already apparent by 1920: growth and ambiguity. They stated that "the ideal of a 'corpus' of scientific knowledge about the practice of advertising resulting from experimentation within the academic environment was never realized, as least to the extent anticipated by a status-seeking business" (p. 5). They added:

> Thus, with the exception of advertising efforts requiring some type of direct response, such as mail order, the nature of advertising "effects" are mysteriously intertwined with a host of both controllable (e.g., price strategy) and uncontrollable (e.g., competition and the incredible complexities of the human mind) factors.
>
> Given this fundamental element of uncertainly, then, it is not surprising that the university did not become the wellspring for truly "professional" practice that some practitioners had sought . . . If the university were to perform a gatekeeping function similar to the law schools, then there would need to be agreement about the corpus of knowledge to be passed on. Lacking that, what emerged were two fundamentally divergent approaches—the vocational emphasis of the journalism schools, and the managerial perspective of the business programs—both with their champions and detractors. (p. 6).

Fifteen advertising programs were begun during the 1920s. Among the earliest programs, advertising was first taught in journalism at 30 institutions, in marketing at 21 institutions, in business at 12 institutions, and in other departments in 5 institutions. Ninety percent of the 20 journalism schools in 1926–1927 offered advertising courses, and 93% of 32 schools offered them in 1936–1937 (B. I. Ross, 1991). Between two world wars, advertising education was seen as largely nonprofessional. Advertising courses in business schools were secondary to management and selling, and journalism schools focused on writing advertisements and selling ads. According to Rotzoll and Barban (1984), courses tended to reflect the teacher's area of interest rather than a standardized curriculum designed to pass on a particular body of knowledge. Typical courses were Typography, Copywriting, Advanced Copywriting, Retail Advertising, Illustration, Layout and Visualization, The Advertising Agency, Direct Advertising, Advertising Production, and Advertising Principles, as well as courses addressing the selling of advertising space and mail-order advertising. Two "basic ideologies" had emerged, however, "(a) a vocational, how-to-do-it emphasis, tracing its origins to Powell's prototype at Missouri; and (b) a 'why' philosophy, reflected in the principles-first approach, with its roots arguably reaching to the early 1900s quest for a 'corpus' of knowledge to achieve true professionalism" (Rotzoll & Barban, 1984, p. 8).

THE DEVELOPMENT OF THE MODERN ADVERTISING CURRICULUM

Rotzoll and Barban (1984) wrote that "[f]rom the initial quest for 'scientific' advertising in the early years of this century, through the present, practitioners have differed concerning the worth of advertising education as well as its ideal form" (p. 8). They reported a 1977 study in which 56% of heads of advertising agencies and corporate advertising departments stated that a college degree was "very helpful" and concluded from their research that "there appears to be a general consensus that advertising education is not a 'clinker,' but varying degrees of enthusiasm for what's there" (p. 11). They determined that executives who did not support advertising education thought that advertising skills are best learned on the job, that advertising education was inadequate for the needs of the profession, and that a broad-based, liberal arts education was the best preparation for the profession. They also determined that advertising executives who did support advertising education contended that advertising can be learned to some extent in the classroom, that advertising education was adequate, and that a broad-based advertising education was beneficial for students and the advertising profession.

Rotzoll and Barban (1984) noted two reasons for divergent conclusions about the form and content of advertising education: (a) Educators exist in a wide variety of different programs, serving different students for different purposes; and (b) educators differ on the appropriate "philosophy" from which advertising education should be pursued. They identified the two philosophies as a hands-on, "first job" approach that is specialized and basically inductive, and a theory-based, "last job" approach that is generalized and basically deductive. They wrote about the differences among educators:

> One way of understanding the divergence of educator opinions about the proper concerns of advertising education is, then, to understand it as an inevitable product of a field that is largely interdisciplinary by nature, and was shaped by an early dichotomy between research (to the ends of "professionalism") and vocational training (to the ends of democratized education). (Rotzoll & Barban, 1984, p. 12)

A number of studies have concerned the ideal curriculum. Sandage (1955) called for three levels of advertising education: (a) providing training in advertising as a craft, performed through night classes by the industry or universities in urban areas; (b) providing a solid foundation for future professionals; and (c) providing a basic understanding of research about advertising as a social and economic force as well as a craft. He proposed that no more than 12% of a student's courses should be in advertising, stating:

> Some training in skills would seem to be necessary, but only as an aid to communication and to problem solving—and to shape the rough diamond for future polishing by the buffing wheel of practice.
> Polishing is a job for industry to do. We should not expect universities to prepare skilled artisans for a first job. Let us help students to develop a philosophy of advertising, sharpen their powers of analysis, and give them enough training in specific skills so they will be apt pupils when we turn them over to their employers in the field of advertising. (Sandage, 1955, pp. 210-211)

Fryburger (1959) presented the Northwest University curriculum, which did consist of 12% advertising. It was 32% professional and 68% liberal arts. The professional 32% consisted of 12% advertising, 10% journalism, and 10% marketing and business administration. The 68% liberal arts consisted of 26% social sciences, 18% history, philosophy and art, 14% literature and composition, and 10% natural sciences and mathematics.

Link and Dykes (1959) found that the usual advertising curriculum in accredited programs at that time was 15 hours. The standard curriculum consisted of Advertising Survey, Copy (Writing) and/or Layout, Newspaper Advertising or Retail Advertising, Radio and Television Advertising, and National Advertising or Advertising Campaigns. C. L. Allen (1960) found that Principles (Survey) was most often taught, followed by Copy and Layout, Campaigns, Media, Problems (Radio or TV), and Retail Advertising. C. L. Allen (1962) studied advertising programs in journalism and in business at 35 institutions, omitting some larger programs, and compared the institution's requirements with recommendations of faculty. He found that catalogs required an average of 13.5 hours in advertising courses, 13.3 hours in journalism, and 6.1 hours in marketing. The advertising faculty surveyed, however, would have preferred more hours in advertising (a total of 15.5 hours) and marketing (7.3 hours) and fewer in journalism (10.8 hours).

J. S. Wright (1980) asked advertising programs to concentrate on training generalists instead of specialists. His proposed curriculum consisted of courses in marketing and communication, the behavior sciences, mathematics and research methodology, computers, business and economics, the fundamentals of advertising and the behavioral process, and problem solving. Johenning (1982) surveyed 445 advertising executives and compiled a list of the 10 courses that the executives thought were the most important for studying advertising. They were Marketing, Advertising Principles, English Composition, Advertising Copywriting, Advertising Media, Market Research, Advertising Management, Public Speaking, Business Writing, and Communication Principles.

The University of Missouri School of Journalism's Future Committee on Communication studied the needs of advertising education in the 1980s and 1990s and prepared an 80-page report titled *Communications 1990* (Doerner, 1984). The new curriculum increased the number of hours of marketing courses to 6 hours from 3 hours and created five new courses: Promotional Writing, Introduction to Selling for the Mass Media, Research in Advertising, Creative Strategy and Tactics, and Sales Promotion. Although the curriculum kept its requirement for 10 hours of journalism classes and 20 hours of advertising classes, it allowed more advertising electives. It required Ad Principles and Practices (3 hours), Graphics (2 hours), Ad Copy, Layout, and Production (3 hours), Introduction to Selling (3 hours), and Ad Electives (9 hours). The committee devised the following statement of objectives: "To provide journalism students with the principles, theories, and skills needed for a career in advertising, and an understanding of the social, economic and political order in which advertising operates . . ." (Doerner, 1984, p. 18).

The advisory group of advertising professionals at New York Institute of Technology surveyed 3,040 advertising executives in 1984 in an effort to redesign the NYIT advertising curriculum. Responses were received from 445 (15%), 40% of them from the New York City area and 29% more from the rest of the East. The respondents rated 47 courses on a 1-to-10 scale, with 10 meaning "The course should be required" and 1 meaning "The course has minimum value." Courses were listed in three categories: basic or general courses, communication courses, and advertising courses (Johenning & Mazey, 1984).

The highest rated advertising courses were Marketing, Advertising Principles, Advertising Copywriting, Advertising Media, and Marketing Research. The lowest-rated advertising courses were Advertising Print Production, Merchandising, Business-to-Education Advertising, Television Commercial Production, and Advertising's Role in Society. The lowest-ranked course, however, still had a mean rating of 6.71. Respondents who studied advertising in college rated courses in advertising as more important than respondents who had not studied advertising (Johenning & Mazey, 1984).

The highest rated communication courses were Communication Principles, Public Relations and Publicity, Writing for the Mass Media, Writing for Communication Arts, and Audiovisual Techniques. The lowest-rated communication courses were Television Production Workshop, Radio Production Workshop, Televising Program Production, Fundamentals of Filmmaking, and Broadcast History and Criticism. Communication courses generally were rated lower than advertising courses. The highest-rated basic or general courses were English Composition, Public Speaking, Business Writing, Business Management, and Psychology. The lowest-rated courses were Philosophy, World History, American History, American Government and Politics, and Life and Health Sciences (Johenning & Mazey, 1984).

Rotzoll and Barban (1984) stated that the challenge of the mid-1980s was "to be found not so much in securing business recognition of the viability of advertising education, but enhancing credibility" (p. 15). They noted that advertising still was seen as an "academic outsider" in journalism schools despite recent growth in advertising education. They concluded that "[s]ome of this ambiguity in relation to identity, as well as some latent feelings of inferiority on the part of advertising educators, stems, it may be argued, from the schism emerging in the first two decades of the century" (p. 15). Rotzoll and Barban (1984) proposed five components of advertising education: (a) the nature and organization of the advertising business; (b) the research function; (c) the creative function; (d) the media function; and (e) synthesis—"[c]ombining the functional elements in the marketing context of the advertising organization" (p. 16).

In 1989, B. I. Ross (1990) surveyed the 111 institutions offering an advertising major, 101 of them administered by journalism/mass communication units. He noted that the number of advertising programs had grown 44% since a similar study in 1964 (Ross, 1965). In his 1964 study, Ross identified 77 institutions offering advertising education, the largest number (24) being in the midwest, with about equal numbers in the east, southeast, southwest and west. Of the 111 programs he identified in 1989, 34 were in the midwest. The largest growth from 1964 was in the southeast, where the number of programs grew from 12 to 27.

Ninety institutions responded to Ross's 1989 survey. The most common requirement was five advertising courses or 15 hours (at 32 institutions). The number of advertising courses required ranged from two to nine. Ross found that the typical 15-hour advertising curriculum, based on the five courses most frequently required, were Principles/Introduction, Copy and Layout, Campaigns, Media Planning/Strategy, and Management/Administration or Advertising Research. Comparing his findings to those of Link and Dykes (1959), B. I. Ross (1990) noted that more emphasis was being put on research, strategy, and management in 1989 than was the case 30 years earlier.

THE EMERGENCE OF BROADCAST EDUCATION

In the early 1920s, colleges and universities began offering extension courses in various subjects by radio, and instruction in radio engineering began about the same time. The first broadcasting courses, however, were begun at the University of Southern California and Washington State University in 1929. According to Niven (1961), at least another 23 schools began instruction in the next decade. At least eight colleges and universities were offering bachelor's degrees by the end of the 1930s: Wisconsin (1931), Brigham Young (1932), Iowa State (1933), Washington State (1936), Syracuse (1937), Maryland (1938), and the University of Washington and Wayne State University (1939). Coursework was being offered at 300 or more colleges and universities. The number of programs offering degrees reached at least 81 in 1954–1955, 112 in 1962–1963 and 147 in 1967–1968 (Kittross, 1989).

In its first decade, broadcast education usually was offered in departments of English or speech. L. Smith (1964) found that radio engineering was the broadcast course offered the most in the early years. The second most offered broadcast course was Radio Speech (or Radio Speaking), followed in frequency by a survey course, Radio Scriptwriting, and Program Planning and Production. The purpose of Radio Speech was to help students develop announcing skills and to provide information about radio broadcasting. A typical course description for the course was this one from 1933:

> Radio Speaking—This course is taught four times during the year. It is a general course in the field of radio. Included in it is a study of (and then microphone practice of) announcing, advertising, public speaking, program building, continuity writing, voice training and interpretation, education and the writing or cutting and adapting of radio drama. (L. Smith, 1964, pp. 384-385)

Soon, radio drama was to become separated from more journalistic aspects of broadcast, and, as L. Smith (1964) noted, "Eventually the ill fit of the various components within the radio course led to the realization that radio was not just one aspect of some other discipline" (p. 385). Television began to have a larger role in the curriculum beginning in the mid-1940s, although by 1948 only 33 of 400 schools offering broadcast courses offered courses in television production and planning.

THE DEVELOPMENT OF STANDARDS
FOR BROADCAST EDUCATION

Armand Hunter, chair of Northwestern University's Radio Department, proposed in 1944 that the broadcasting curriculum be improved because of two major criticisms of broadcast education: that broadcasting courses lacked "content, stature and educational value, and . . . are used primarily as a device to build enrollment by capitalizing upon student interest" and because not enough broadcasting jobs existed to justify many colleges' broadcast curriculum (L. Smith, 1964, p. 388). He proposed six subject areas for the curriculum: an orientation and survey of the broadcasting field, work in the main professional areas of performance and production, teacher training for using radio in education, research, related courses in speech, and related and supplementary courses (such as journalism). The minimum requirements for a broadcast program, he stated, were "a competent and experienced teaching staff, standard broadcast equipment and studios, and a broadcast 'outlet' of some kind on which the student could acquire actual on-the-air experience" (Smith, p. 389).

The Council on Radio Journalism (CRJ) was organized in 1944 as a first step toward a system of accreditation for broadcast education, a role being filled for print journalism by the American Council on Education in Journalism (ACEJ). It was formed by the National Association of Broadcasters (NAB) and the executive committee of the American Association of Schools and Departments of Journalism (AASDJ) with support of the Committee on Radio Education of the American Association of State Universities (AASU), the News Committee of the NAB, the ACEJ, and the Radio Committee of the American Association of Teachers of Journalism (AATJ). Like the emerging print journalism standards, the broadcast standards strongly recommended that general education courses constitute the major portion the student's university coursework. The following are the 1944 curriculum standards proposed by the Council on Radio Journalism:

(1) The college or university preparation for radio journalism should be offered by means of a curriculum of at least four years, leading to a bachelor's degree. (2) At the completion of such a curriculum, the student should have gained a comprehensive background in the social studies. . . . (3) The student should have a thorough grounding in the broad field of communications, especially radio and the press. . . . (4) The student should be given sound specialized training in relevant skills and techniques. . . . (5) The student would have open to him technical courses in other fields: speech, radio announcing, radio production and similar or allied subject matter; elementary electronics. ("Council on Radio Journalism Planned," 1944, pp. 326–327)

Specialized training (standard 4) would include courses in Radio News, Radio Advertising, and General Script Writing. The communication courses (standard 3) would include such topics as the history of communications, government regulation of broadcasting, the social and legal responsibility of radio, radio's influence on public opinion formation, press and radio law, codes and practices in broadcasting, and public attitudes toward broadcasting, including a knowledge of audience measurement techniques. The liberal arts component (standard 2) would include government and political science, economics, history, geography and sociology; natural science and psychology, a reading and speaking knowledge of at least one modern foreign language, and a broad knowledge of English and American literature and English composition.

In 1945 the Federal Radio Education Committee published "Standards for College Courses in Radio Broadcasting." It proposed 18 to 30 credit hours for a major in one of eight areas: survey, program performance and production, music, news, writing (including continuity and drama), program planning, study of commercial radio, and radio as a public service. Majors in radio would not take courses until their sophomore or junior year, and they would be expected to obtain on-the-air experiences. According to L. Smith (1964), "Education for broadcasting was fast leaving the 'Radio Speech' stage to become a full-fledged discipline" (p. 389).

The National Association of Broadcasters continued to press the idea of accreditation in the fall of 1947. From these efforts, the University Association for Professional Radio Education (UAPRE) was established in 1948. Although, the National Commission on Accreditation did not give its approval for UAPRE to be the accrediting body for broadcasting, the Office of Education's *Directory* published UAPRE's requirements until shortly before the organization disbanded in 1955. When the University Association for Professional Radio Education was dissolved, its former members and members of the National Association of Radio and Television Broadcasters formed the Association for Professional Broadcasting Education in 1956. It became the Broadcast Education Association 2 decades later.

The Council on Radio Journalism conducted a study in 1948 of broadcasting course titles and descriptions at higher education institutions from 1946 to 1948 because of complaints about confusion and lack of consistency. The course most offered was Radio Speech. It was the radio course in 30 of the 51 institutions that reported having only one course. It was followed by Radio Production and Direction (107 of the 176 responding institutions), Introduction to Broadcasting (98), Script and Continuity Writing (87), Writing and Editing News for Radio (66), Radio Advertising (39), and Radio News Broadcasting (20). The council concluded that complaints over curricular confusion were justified and provided recommendations for names and content for the primary radio courses (Council on Radio Journalism, 1948).

During the 1950s, the major curriculum issue was whether broadcast should be basically a liberal arts program with some professional courses or a professional course with a few courses with liberal arts content (L. Smith, 1964). In 1956, the Council on Radio and Television Journalism of the Association for Education in Journalism updated the minimum standards for education for radio and television journalism set forth for radio in 1944 and called for broadcasting programs "to conform effectively to the general principles and specific goals" of the standards (Council, 1961, p. 161). The five principals were: (a) the basis of all education for radio and television journalism is sound general education; (b) students should be provided opportunity to acquire an understanding of the importance of broadcasting as a social instrument and of its relationship to government, industry, and the public; (c) students should be provided training of professional quality in the skills and techniques of radio and television journalism, together with an adequate understanding of other aspects of broadcasting; (d) teachers of radio and television journalism should be soundly equipped by practical experience, by education and by broad understanding of broadcasting's special values and implications; and (e) radio or television journalism programs should possess or have access to adequate laboratory equipment, library and other facilities (pp. 161–164).

The council stated that a 4-year plan of study should allow students to obtain "a comprehensive background" in the social sciences (government and political science, economics, history, geography and sociology); "a grounding" in natural science and psychology; at least a reading knowledge of one or more modern foreign languages; and "a broad knowledge" of English and American literature and composition (Council, 1961, pp. 161–162). The council also stated that students "should be thoroughly grounded in the broad field of mass communications," including such topics as the history of communication, government regulations, social and legal responsibilities of broadcasters, the media and public opinion formation, broadcasters' relationship to advertising and business, broadcasting standards of practice, public attitudes toward broadcasters, and techniques of audience measurement and surveying (p. 162). The council called for faculty members with "adequate professional experience to enable them to present courses at the professional level" (p. 163).

According to the Office of Education's *Directory*, slightly more than 400 colleges and universities provided broadcasting courses in 1948, 19 of them offering a major. By 1950, 420 institutions offered broadcast courses, and a broadcast degree was offered at 65 institutions. All but 11 were nonengineering degrees. In 1952 the *Directory* listed 361 institutions with two or more broadcast courses, with 60 of them having majors. Twice as many schools (136) offered courses in television in 1952 than was the case in 1950 (L. Smith, 1964). Niven (1961) counted 86 schools with a bachelor's degree in radio and television in 1956 and 97 schools by 1960–1961. The president of the National Association of Radio and Television Broadcasters (Fellows, 1957) asked about the variety of courses being offered in broadcast education: "Cinematography, television production, radio production, staging techniques, and various related specialized courses of study are offered. The question is: do these fit under the overall-all instructional umbrella, traditional and highly regarded I admit, called 'Journalism'?" (p. 216).

THE DEVELOPMENT OF THE MODERN BROADCAST CURRICULUM

Hudson (1981) surveyed 266 commercial broadcasters (235 radio and 31 television) in 45 states concerning entry level skills needed by new hires. He found that most entry-level news positions (80%) were at small- and medium-sized markets (under 300,000 population) and that the major skills desired were gathering, writing, and reporting news; however, they also wanted employees who had a broad background in the liberal arts, including history, economics, business law, and legal processes. Employers seemed to value new hires with a college degree in broadcasting, Hudson concluded. Stations in the largest markets were most likely to see the degree as very valuable.

The Roper Organization (1987) undertook a study for The International Radio and Television Society, The Radio–Television News Directors Association, The National Association of Television Program Executives, and the Gannett Foundation concerning preparation of students for careers in the electronic media. It was based on 514 telephone interviews with electronic media executives. Both educators and professionals named production skills and good writing as essential components of a good broadcast journalism curriculum. Nearly all respondents (91%) wanted stronger links between the electronic media and educators. The major complaint about new graduates was that they had a misconception of the broadcast industry because their professors lacked broadcast studio experience.

Executives in larger markets put more emphasis on liberal arts and cable courses than did those in smaller markets. Executives in smaller markets put more emphasis on marketing and sales, reading of industry publications, computer skills, and business management courses. Respondents generally expected new hires to know the basics needed to work in the industry. They were most often to name writing skills, the basics of broadcasting, knowledge of how to operate equipment, and communication skills as the most important skills or areas of knowledge.

In fall 1988 and winter 1989, a Broadcast Education Association Courses and Curricula Committee task force (Warner & Liu, 1990) undertook a study of 4-year schools belonging to the organization to update a 1985 study (Eastman, 1986). The 1988–1989 task force sent questionnaires to 258 4-year colleges and universities belonging to the BEA and received 128 responses, almost a 50% return rate. As in 1985, the largest percent of broadcast programs (40%) were in a communication(s) department. No other departmental title accounted for more than 9% of programs. The task force found that the broadcast sequences most often offered were broadcast news (39%), television (35%), production (33%), radio (31%), film (24%), management (24%), broadcasting (19%), advertising (13%), telecommunications (12%), sales (11%), video (8%), mass communication (6%), and performance (5%). All other sequences were offered by fewer than 5% of units.

A majority of broadcast units surveyed by the task force (Warner & Liu, 1990) had a core curriculum of between two and six courses. The course most likely to be in the core was Introduction to Media (in 35% of programs), followed by Media Law and Regulation (28%), and Introduction to Broadcasting (27%). Most units (60%) offered a bachelor of arts degree, almost one quarter (24%) offered a bachelor of arts and a bachelor of science, and slightly more than 12% offered only a bachelor of science degree. The rest offered degrees by a variety of names. More than 84% of the programs rated their professional orientation as moderate to high (3 to 5 on a 5-point scale), with the largest schools least likely to have a professional orientation.

The Jane Pauley Task Force (Society of Professional Journalists, 1996) surveyed executives at commercial TV stations and college faculty about their opinions of what broadcast journalism students should know. The task force determined that the four main needs were writing ability, a good attitude, knowledge and good work habits. It proposed the development of a model broadcast journalism curriculum. It also recommended that educators raise standards for admission and graduation, forge a better relationship between the industry and educators, emphasize performance characteristics valued by the industry, such as strong writing skills and a broad-based knowledge, and improve industry hiring practices through skills or knowledge tests in addition to tapes and writing samples.

Ketchum Public Relations (Ketchum, 1997) studied perceptions of broadcast executives about broadcast education as part of a larger study of print and broadcast for Virginia Commonwealth University and the Associated Press Managing Editors. It found that writing, reporting, ethics, and interviewing skills were deemed the most important skills (rated as very important by 94% or more of the broadcast respondents).

THE EMERGENCE OF PUBLIC RELATIONS EDUCATION

Public relations and journalism have long had close ties. Even though the profession of public relations didn't originate until the early 1900s, according to Cutlip (1961), public relations had its beginnings in North America in the work of Samuel Adams, Benjamin Franklin, and other revolutionaries. In addition, Bitter (1987) noted that early newspapers in this country were voices for various political positions and "were the equivalent of house organs" (p. 22). Public relations' modern beginnings have been traced to the 1900–1917 period. Although America's participation in World War I brought a wider understanding in this country of the use of publicity and propaganda, Cutlip stated that "in the first 20 years of PR's modern American history there was neither talk nor action in the matter of formal training for a rapidly growing vocation" (p. 363).

The first course in publicity techniques, titled Publicity Methods, was taught at the University of Illinois in 1920 by Joseph F. Wright, the university's publicity director. In 1922 Frank R. Elliott began a course in publicity at Indiana University. Cutlip (1961) noted that there "is no evidence that these courses resulted from practitioner or student demand for such training" (p. 364). Rather, they allowed publicity directors to gain faculty status and helped "bring respectability to publicity." The first course titled Public Relations was taught as a continuing education course for 1 hour of credit at the Department of Journalism at New York University's School of Commerce in 1923 by Edward

L. Bernays, who recently had written the first public relations book, *Crystallizing Public Opinion*. The same year, a course in social work publicity was taught at the New York School of Social Work (Cutlip, 1961).

A course in publicity was begun at the University of Oregon in the 1927–1928 school year, and the University of Minnesota offered a course titled Press Relations beginning in 1929. A course was begun at the University of Washington at about the same time, but was dropped after 2 years "under the gunfire of criticism from the state's newspaper editors and publisher organizations" (Cutlip, 1961, p. 365). In 1938, American University began a 2-year graduate program with hopes for "a national center of study of public relations in a democracy." The University of Texas also began a public relations course in 1938 because "leaders in the field of education for journalism were becoming conscious of an increased need for persons to do public relations work" (Cutlip, p. 366), and in 1939 a public relations course was re-introduced at New York University by Alfred McClung Lee. Kalman B. Druck began a course in public relations in 1940 at City College of New York. In 1941 Joseph E. Boyle began to teach a PR course at Columbia University's School of General Studies, and in 1942 Frederic E. Merwin started a course at Rutgers University. A public relations major was first offered at Bethany College in West Virginia in 1942. Alfred McClung Lee introduced a public relations course at Wayne University in 1942 as a liberal arts course.

By 1945, 21 colleges and universities reported offering courses in public relations (Grunig, 1989). In 1946, Alfred McClung Lee undertook a study of 59 colleges and universities (A. M. Lee, 1947). He found 47 courses with public relations titles at 30 institutions. All but seven of them were in schools or departments of journalism. The first School of Public Relations was organized at Boston University in 1947 around the Department of Journalism, but the next year it added "and Communications" to its name. Cutlip (1961) wrote about the growing trend toward housing public relations with journalism programs: "Many practitioners look askance at this. A few journalism educators share these doubts for different reasons" (p. 368). One of the practitioners who objected to the trend was Edward Bernays, who wanted public relations to become a field in the social sciences. Grunig (1989) stated about the situation, "Although Bernays tried to establish public relations as a social science discipline in the 1920s, most public relations practitioners came into the field after having experience in journalism. Thus, the academic field grew naturally as a subdiscipline of journalism" (p. 15).

SCOTT CUTLIP AND THE RISE OF MODERN PR EDUCATION

Although he didn't begin teaching public relations and journalism until 1946 (at the University of Wisconsin like Willard Bleyer four decades earlier), Cutlip rather than Bernays is usually seen as the "father of public relations education"

(D. K. Wright, 1991). As Wright put it, Cutlip "served as the major catalyst in moving public relations practice and education forward from the archaic, technical, skills-oriented, publicity mode of yesteryear into the respected field it is today" (p. 336). And, according to Grunig (1991), "Most of our research and most of our theories have been generated by the world view he gave us beginning in 1946" (p. 365). Grunig added:

> In contrast to the educators who came before him, Cutlip saw public relations as a management function, a two-way process of communication, as a symmetrical means of promoting social responsibility, and as an ethical profession encharged with a major portion of the system of public communication. (p. 364)

According to D. K. Wright (1991), at the time Cutlip began his contributions to the field of public relations education, "it was the illegitimate, bastard step-child of journalism education" (p. 335). Cutlip changed it "from a craft that taught people how to say things into a profession that shows people what to do and helps them do it" (p. 336). His book *Effective Public Relations*, coauthored with Allen H. Center, first appeared in 1952. According to Doug Newsom, coauthor of a competing book, the text "set the academic standards for the discipline through many years" (Wright, 1991, p. 339).

In a speech at a roundtable on "Education for Public Relations" at the annual conference of the Public Relations Society of America (PRSA) in November 1956, Cutlip laid out the plan for public relations education he had devised at the University of Wisconsin. He stated that his theory of public relations ruled out teaching "press agentry," "the techniques of rigging public opinion for unworthy causes or clients," "specialized training for publicity as such," and "instruction in the use of publicity in product promotion" (Cutlip, 1957, p. 69). He called for a "broadly-based liberal arts education oriented to a small core of basic courses in public opinion, public relations and communication." He noted that the Wisconsin public relations sequence had five courses: a general introductory course in public relations; an advanced course in case problems; a course in publicity media and methods; a course in public opinion measurement and analysis; and a course in media analysis (p. 70). He stated about the location for public relations:

> A meaningful preparation for public relations—consisting of studies in liberal arts, communications and public opinion analysis—is most logically centered in, but not confined to the school of journalism or communications.
> . . . What is taught and investigated in today's good school of journalism goes far beyond the teaching of press relations or publicity writing contrary to the erroneous notions you may have read. (p. 70)

An article in the *Milwaukee Journal* stated about the speech: "Professor Cutlip's talk met with mixed reaction" and "the applause was brief" (Cutlip, 1957, p. 68).

In August 1956, a few months before Cutlip's talk to the PRSA, the first organization of public relations teachers was founded. It was named the Council on Public Relations Education and was a unit of the Association for Education in Journalism. The PRSA set up an Educational Advisory Council in 1959. In 1960, Druck, who started teaching public relations at City College of New York in 1940, wrote that "in all the intervening 20 years there has been no basic change in the philosophy of what public relations is or how it operates" (Cutlip, 1961, p. 367). In 1961, Scott Cutlip stated that "[o]n the surface it would appear that the value of public relations instruction has been widely recognized, yet many of America's front-rank institutions still do not accord the subject recognition." He called for PR educators to undertake critical analysis of the impact of public relations on society. He added about other issues:

> There is, also, continuing debate as to whether public relations should be taught at the undergraduate level or exclusively at the graduate level to persons of experience; debate as to whether public relations teaching should be based in schools of journalism or communications, schools of business, or housed in its own departmental structure with a full-blown curriculum or highly-specialized courses. Likewise, there continues to be debate as to how best to teach public relations. (Cutlip, 1961, p. 370)

Cutlip also stated that "the pattern of education in this field remains fluid, experimental, somewhat fragmentary, and still quite controversial. There continues to be debate by both professional educator and practitioners whether it merits teaching" (p. 370).

THE DEVELOPMENT OF THE MODERN PUBLIC RELATIONS CURRICULUM

Two of the earliest published studies of the spread of public relations education in the post-World War II era were a 1951 study reported in the January 1952 *Public Relations Journal* and a 1955 study by Stewart Harral of the University of Oklahoma. Only 12 colleges and universities were thought to have a public relations program in 1951. In 1955, 66 institutions reported providing some instruction, and 28 reported a program or sequence (Simon, 1957). In 1955–1956, the Education Committee of the Public Relations Society of America (PRSA) conducted the largest study up to that point (PRSA, 1956). It was called the "first survey of public relations education in the United States" (Hiebert, 1971, p. 11) and the "most comprehensive survey of public relations education ever undertaken in this country" (Simon, 1957, p. 71). The committee surveyed more than 1,000 colleges and universities and received responses from 653 (65%). More than 20% of the responding institutions reported providing public relations coursework. A total of 136 of 653 institutions replying to the survey indicated they provided public relations training to some extent. Fourteen offered a PR major, and 29 offered two or more courses in a sequence.

Of those 136 institutions with coursework, 44 integrated PR principles into other courses or taught a single course not designed for those seeking a career in the field, and 92 provided career training. Of the 14 institutions that offered a major in the field, public relations was a school at one (Boston University) and a department at two (Bethany College and Nasson College). Other institutions with a major were Columbia University, the University of Maryland, New School of Social Research, New York University, Ohio State University, University of Oklahoma, Pacific Union College, Salem College, Syracuse University, Utica College of Syracuse University, and Youngstown University. Another 29 institutions offered two or more PR courses as electives, and 30 institutions offered a single course. Only 31 of the 236 business schools and departments in institutions responding to the PRSA survey (13%) offered PR courses (PRSA, 1956).

The PRSA study found that nearly all types of PR programs required 2 years of liberal arts courses. Journalism-related programs tended to concentrate on writing in the final 2 years, and liberal arts schools tended to emphasize the social sciences. More than one fourth of the institutions responding indicated interest in public relations at their institution. The committee found that 63% of the institutions offered public relations at the undergraduate level, and that the program was located in a journalism department or school in 36 of the 92 institutions offering career training. Two years later, Spevak (1959) found that the public relations courses at 69% of 121 institutions responding to his survey were located in a school of department of journalism, 27% in a school or department of business, and 4% somewhere else.

In 1964, the Public Relations Society of America Education Committee conducted a survey of public relations education (PRSA, 1964) that became the basis of a 1970 survey of all accredited colleges and universities in the country (Hiebert, 1971). In 1964, 280 institutions reported providing some instruction, and 43 institutions reported having a public relations major or sequence. By 1970, 303 colleges and universities reported providing some courses, and the number of programs or sequences had reached 89. Though the number of institutions with a major or sequence had increased from 43 in 1964 to 89 in 1970, public relations wasn't used in the name of any department in the country. Because of a decrease in degree programs from 1964 from 14 to 7 and almost a three-fold increase in public relations sequences (from 29 to 75), the 1970 study's author concluded that educators "now seem to view public relations not as a separate discipline but as an increasingly important adjunct to other fields" (Hiebert, 1971, p. 12).

Public relations was located in journalism or communications (other than speech) in 66.3% of the 142 programs responding to the 1970 survey, up from 57.5% in the 1964 study. It was in business administration in 14.2% (down from

15.5%), in education in 9.7% (up from 2.7%), in English in 4.3% (versus 3.7%), in speech in 2.2% (up from 0%), and in other disciplines in 3.3% of programs (down from 20.5%). Students spent an average of 52.2% of their coursework in theory-related courses (up from 48% in 1964) with the rest of the coursework seen as practical. Hiebert (1971) stated: "There is no longer much question about whether the child should be saved or what home should adopt it, but rather how it can continue to mature and make the best contribution to the profession and to society" (p. 9).

THE DEVELOPMENT OF STANDARDS FOR
PUBLIC RELATIONS EDUCATION

Scott Cutlip served with J. Carroll Bateman as cochair of the Commission on Public Relations Education in the mid-1970s. The commission's 1975 report, *Design for Public Relations Education* (Bateman & Cutlip, 1975), was "a first in the field and a milestone for the growing profession" (Commission, 1993, p. 2) and "may have been the single most influential document of its kind" in the field (K. O. Smith, 1982, p. 62). It proposed that five courses be the minimum number for a public relations program, the same number of courses the Public Relations Society of American in 1987 began to require for a college or university to have a chapter of the Public Relations Student Society of America (D. K. Wright, 1991). It looked at undergraduate studies as a series of three concentric circles. The inner circle consisted of core public relations courses, the middle ring of general communication courses, and the outer ring of liberal arts courses. It also suggested secondary areas of concentration for majors.

A 1978 task force chaired by William Faith and Dennis Wilcox sought "to probe the nature of continuing education as it currently engages PRSA members" (Walker, 1988, p. 20). The resulting report recommended courses in communication theory, attitude change and principles of persuasion for the beginner; continuing education in communication theory and attitude change, principles of persuasion, research methods, management techniques, issues management, and advanced topics for the junior practitioner; and futures planning and programming and seminars in decision making and problem solving for the senior practitioner.

Druck developed a "Public Relations Professional Development Matrix" for a 1980 task force. The matrix, which covered the accepted body of knowledge for the profession, recommended knowledge and skills for the beginning professional, staff professional, professional manager, and senior professional. The three categories in the matrix were management, communications, and knowledge of publics (Walker, 1988). Lesly chaired another 1980 task force, the Task Force on the Stature and Role of Public Relations, which published its report in the March 1981 *Public Relations Journal*. It noted the trend toward administrative skills as well as technical ability for public relations executives and a growing requirement for a "broad educational background and sensitivity to social and psychological forces" (Walker, 1988, p. 23).

The 1981 Commission on Public Relations Education (K. O. Smith, 1982), chaired by Kenneth O. Smith and Elias Buchwald, was asked by the Association for Education in Journalism (AEJ) Public Relations Division to review the recommendations of the 1975 Commission on Public Relations Education to try to design a model curriculum for graduate studies and to recommend support courses for public relations students. It also decided to look at the undergraduate core curriculum proposed by the 1975 commission. It concluded that accredited programs often included twice as many core studies courses as proposed by the 1975 study. It proposed merging core public relations courses and communication studies and recommended an updated PR program that would require the following courses: Introduction to Mass Communications, Principles of Public Relations, Public Relations Media, Public Relations Programs, Introduction to Research Methodology, Public Relations Case Studies, and Public Relations Internship. It also listed additional required courses that might be included: Advertising Principles, Introduction to Broadcasting, Graphic Design and Technology, Principles of Persuasion (Speech), and Advanced Media Writing. It also proposed a model graduate curriculum and discussed possible support courses.

The National Commission on Graduate Study in Public Relations, chaired by Michael Hesse and Paul Alvarez, issued its report in 1985. It recommended a master's degree curriculum consisting of research methods; communication theory and processes; public relations principles, practices, and theory; public relations management, programming, and production; a public relations specialty option; a sequence of minor courses; and a thesis or suitable graduate project. It also developed some broad proposals for a Ph.D. degree (Walker, 1988).

The 26-member Commission on Undergraduate Public Relations Education, cochaired by William Ehling and Betsy Plank, was established in late 1983 by the Public Relations Division of the Association for Education in Journalism and Mass Communication and the Public Relations Society of America. The committee was charged with a 3-year mission to develop and recommend a public relations program of study for undergraduate public relations in U.S. colleges and universities. Its report, *Design for Undergraduate Public Relations Education* (Commission, 1987), was later reissued by the Educational Affairs Committee of the Public Relations Society of America (Commission, 1993).

The commission differed from the 1975 commission in that it had representatives not only from the AEJMC and PRSA but also from the International Association of Business Communicators, the Foundation for Public Relations Research and Education, the American Marketing Association, the International Communication Association, the American Management Association, and the Speech Communication Association. Its goal was to find out what practitioners and educators thought the curriculum should be, not where it should be taught. Whereas the 1975 report made suggestions for specific courses, the 1987 report addressed the course content for a public relations program. It proposed that professional education courses, which should comprise 25% of the student's credit hours, would include two areas: Communications Studies (consisting of technical/production and historical/ institutions courses and communication process and structure courses) and Public Relations Studies (consisting of principles, practices and theory; techniques; research for planning and evaluation; strategy and implementation; and supervised work experience). Specialized advanced study also was recommended.

A 1988 study by the PRSA's Educational Affairs Committee (PRSA, 1988) found that 112 of 129 colleges and universities with chapters who responded to a survey reported offering at least the minimum five courses proposed by the Commission on Public Relations Education's 1975 study, with 59% of those institutions offering only five courses. Only 20 of the programs offered seven or more courses. It listed the following as important functions for PR graduates: being ethical and socially responsible, organizing and managing, communicating, building and changing relationships, cognitively processing information and influence, persuading (influencing) and informing, researching and analyzing, identifying publics and problems, planning and implementing strategies, designing messages, selecting channels, setting goals and objectives, and assessing pre- and post-campaign opinions.

Fitch-Hauser and Neff (1997) updated an earlier survey of public relations education in the United States and Canada (See Fitch-Hauser, Barker, and Barker, 1989; and Neff, 1989). The 1997 study was considerably broader than the 1989 study, which included only members of the Association for Communication Administration. The 1997 study also included the membership of the Association of Schools of Journalism and Mass Communication. The authors wanted to determine the extent to which recommendations of the 1987 Report of the Commission on Undergraduate Public Relations Education had been implemented and the types of administrative units where public relations programs tended to be located. Because the survey covered only institutions with administrators who belonged to the ACA or ASJMC, however, a number of public relations programs weren't contacted, the authors noted.

A total of 110 (85%) ASJMC administrators reported having a public relations program in their unit, and 68 (76%) of ACA administrators reported having such a program. Eighty-two of the programs (46%) were located in departments of journalism, mass communication, mass media, TV–radio, or telecommunication; 42 (24%) were in a combination or multidisciplinary departments; 36 (20%) were in a speech communication department; and 18 (10%) were located in such places as departments or schools of communication or communication studies, commercial arts, advertising, or public communication. Seventy-four percent indicated having a chapter of the Public Relations Society of America.

Concerning the recommendation of the 1987 Commission on Undergraduate Public Relations Education that public relations programs undergo periodic review, 94% reported undergoing a self-study on occasion. The commission also recommended that public relations courses be taught by full-time faculty with a combination of professional experience and a doctorate. Fitch-Hauser and Neff (1997) found that almost 80% of programs had public relations faculty with a doctorate, but 22% reported using part-time faculty without a graduate degree. The commission proposed that majors take at least 15 semester hours in courses identifiable as public relations. However, 63% of programs responding to their survey offered fewer than 15 semester hours a year of courses identified as public relations, and 69% required fewer than 15 hours of such courses for undergraduate public relations majors. (The authors counted only courses identified as public relations in the title.) The 1987 commission also had recommended that public relations majors minor in marketing or management, something that was allowed by about three quarters of the programs surveyed. In addition, the commission had supported the use of internships. Approximately one third of the programs responding required an internship, and two thirds of them allowed one as an option.

A new Commission on Public Relations Education was established in 1998 by a consortium of eight organizations to undertake a 2-year study of trends and issues in PR education and to recommend models for studying the field ("AEJMC plays," 1998). Members of the consortium were the Association for Education in Journalism and Mass Communication, the Association for Women in Communications, the International Communications Association, the Institute for PR Research and Education, the International Association of Business Communicators, the International Public Relations Association, the National Communication Association, and the Public Relations Society of America.

PRACTITIONERS' VIEWS CONCERNING
PUBLIC RELATIONS EDUCATION

VanSlyke Turk surveyed 2.400 PR practitioners in four states about the important skills needed by new graduates and received responses from 561. Oral and written communication skills were said to be important by nearly all respondents. Financial and budgeting skills were seen as the least important but the area of greatest need for improvement. In addition to communication skills, planning and organization, problem solving and decision making, goal setting and prioritizing, and time management were seen as important by 80% or more of respondents. "Public relations education successfully imparts communications skills at the expense of other skills and perspectives that also are essential to effective management," VanSlyke Turk stated ("Financial skills," 1988, p. 11).

Wakefield and Cottone (1992) surveyed public relations executives to determine what types of courses they recommended for public relations students. They sent surveys developed by Ed Burnett Consultants, Inc., of New York City to 500 public relations practitioners at public relations firms, advertising firms with a secondary focus on public relations, and public relations directors of corporations, government and not-for-profit organizations. They asked the respondents how important they thought particular course topics were. The researchers received 188 completed surveys. The top 20 choices were, marketing, advertising campaigns, public relations campaigns, speech communication, advertising and collateral pieces, business, basic public relations perspectives, management, organizational communication, basis advertising perspectives, publicity, case studies in advertising, journalism, case studies in public relations, graphic arts, ethical issues in public relations, ethical issues in advertising, survey research, economics, and computer science. Practitioners at agencies were significantly more likely than those in organizations to favor public relations campaigns and graphic arts. Organizational practitioners placed significantly more importance on management than did practitioners at firms. The authors concluded that the study "provides empirical support for previous literature recommending that public relations degree programs and professional development seminars should de-emphasize journalism in preference for emphases on marketing, advertising, public relations, speech communication, business, management, organizational communication, graphic arts, and research" (p. 74).

The Public Relations Student Society of America sponsored a study of 461 public relations professionals and chief executive officers of the top 50 public relations firms (Schwartz, Yarbrough, & Shakra, 1992). Practitioners were asked to list the four most important subjects or curriculum areas among 21 suggested and to rate each of them on a 5-point scale. "Writing skills" was rated among the top four areas by 86% of the practitioners and was the only one of the 21 areas to be rated among the top four topics by more than 35% of the practitioners. Only one area, international business trends, wasn't listed as quite or very important by half of the practitioners. The top areas (those for which two thirds or more of the practitioners rated it quite or very important) were: writing skills, internships and work experience, problem-solving skills, presentation-speaking skills, social trends and issue analysis, people management skills, media relations techniques, research skills, the psychology of persuasion/motivation, applied ethics training, and general liberal arts knowledge.

ISSUES FACING PUBLIC RELATIONS EDUCATION

D. K. Wright (1982) noted five major problems faced by public relations education at the time: enrollments were increasing faster than employment opportunities for graduates; a shortage of qualified public relations professors existed; some practitioners were questioning the abilities of some graduates of public relations programs; some practitioners continued to doubt that public relations education had any value at all; and despite its maturation and growth, public relations education still lacked the respect accorded other professional education programs, such as law, medicine, and accounting.

Grunig (1989) suggested four models of public relations that depict four typical ways public relations programs are conducted and the type of program in which they are normally housed. They are the press agentry model, the public information model, the two-way asymmetrical model, and the two-way symmetrical model (pp. 18–19). The first model, press agentry, stresses the role of the mass media as agents of publicity. It is not favored by most journalism schools, Grunig noted. The second, public information, stresses dissemination of "relatively objective information through the mass media and controlled media such as newsletters, brochures, and direct mail" (p. 18). It is offered usually at journalism schools with few public relations courses. The other two models are more sophisticated. The two-way asymmetrical model uses research "to develop messages that are most likely to persuade publics to behave as the organization wants" (p. 19). According to Grunig, this model is taught in departments of speech and marketing because of their grounding in rhetorical or social psychological theories of persuasion. He preferred the two-way symmetrical model, which "describes public relations efforts that are based on research and that use communication to manage conflict and to improve understanding with strategic publics" (p. 19). He concluded that existing public relations programs were not suited to teaching the two-way symmetrical model.

For the curriculum of the future, Grunig (1989) called for a minimum of 10 public relations courses. He also proposed a curriculum that, he noted, is similar to what was proposed by the 1987 Commission on Undergraduate Public Relations Education. He stated:

> At the undergraduate level, the department of the future should train students for entry-level jobs as communication technicians but also introduce them to the management of public relations, to communication theory and research methods, and to the ethics of the two-way symmetrical model of public relations. It would also offer a range of specialized electives in public relations programs such as employee, media, community, financial, or educational relations. It would offer advanced courses in campaigns, public affairs, marketing communication, history and law of public relations, ethics, writing, and gender issues and perspectives. (p. 23)

D. K. Wright and VanSlyke Turk (1990) attempted to identify and examine major issues facing public relations education in such areas as curriculum, program growth, faculty, research, relationship with practitioners, location of public relations programs, administrative support, continuing education, recruitment, and graduate education. They listed 10 problems that faced public relations education at the time. They included two things mentioned by D. K. Wright (1982): continued enrollment growth and a shortage of qualified faculty. They also noted the continued growth in the number of PR programs, especially within speech communication programs rather than in journalism and mass communication. Other issues were a lack of significant, seminal research, the imposition of requirements by PR professional societies such as the Public Relations Society of America, a possible need to move from a skills-based curriculum to one preparing graduates for midlevel positions requiring management and problem solving, pressure by practitioners to move public relations to business schools despite evidence suggesting such a move would be ill-advised, a lack of support by university administrators, a lack of interest in PR education at large research institutions, and the need for midlevel training for practitioners. They wrote about the situation:

> Public relations educators, like those who actually practice public relations, haven't even been able to agree upon a definition of what it is they do and how they're supposed to do it, much less achieve consensus about the parameters of professionalism that should guide their endeavors. Is it any wonder, then, that public relations education—and, indeed the entire public relations practice— faces a lack of credibility and fails to earn support, encouragement and understanding? (p. 4)

Heath (1991) listed five items for the 1990s agenda for public relations education and research: where it should be located, core theory and research, persuasion versus information, auxiliary disciplines, and the ideal curriculum. In response to a call by Grunig (1989) to move public relations to a business school or an autonomous PR program, Heath argued that "business administration is not inherently a natural disciplinary home" because many of the fields it serves "lack a commercial business management base" (p. 186). Instead, public relations is "a communication discipline that requires practitioners and scholars to be familiar with the humanities, fine arts, social sciences, government, and business management, as well as legal, scientific and technical issues" (p. 186). He stated that "fleeing to what seems to be a more 'respectable' home is defeatist" (p. 187). He called for an "issues management" approach, "which unites business and communication planning with concern for defining and meeting standards of social responsibility by being able to harmonize the interests of myriad stakeholders" (p. 187).

Heath (1991) concluded that the crucial question regarding curriculum was: "Has the field achieved the appropriate balance between a publicity model and a broader range of activities related to building effective relationships between organizations and stakeholders?" He added:

> The pragmatic test of the current pedagogy is that many persons who carry public relations in their titles are not competing successfully for management level positions in their organizations. As the discipline moves toward increased professionalism, curriculum may follow. But it is quite likely that curriculum needs to lead." (p. 193)

Schwartz, Yarbrough, and Shakra (1992) proposed the following areas on which public relations education should focus: writing and speaking skills, critical analysis ability, strategic communication planning ability, career orientation, and studies in communication science. They also called for a dialogue between educators and practitioners not to construct a required curriculum but to answer the following questions:

- What is the "short list" of critical skills and knowledge for entry into a public relations career?
- What skills and knowledge are best taught in a preprofessional, collegiate curriculum?
- If practitioners expect too much of collegiate public relations education, how can educational institutions and professional associations share curricular responsibilities and dovetail instruction?

The broadening of journalism education with the addition of such media-related fields as advertising, broadcast, and public relations changed the identity of the field considerably; however, traditional print journalists tended to accept the changes because the new sequences had a similar focus: preparing students for mass media careers. However, the post-World War II expansion also brought with it the hiring of a new breed of educator: faculty members without practical media experience who had obtained doctorates in the social sciences and who were interested in teaching about the media rather than in training students for media jobs. The hiring of these new faculty members, who were called "communicologists" by their more practical colleagues, was to lead to a growing schism within mass media education over the nature of the field. In addition, speech-based educators began to establish new media-related programs that crossed the boundaries between mediated and nonmediated communication.

4

The Development of Interpersonal Communication, Mass Communication, and Communication Studies

These new kinds of communication knowledge would eventually supplant—or at least supplement—the traditional skills-centered curricula."
—Schramm (1997, p. 157)

Mass communication emerged in journalism education in the late 1940s as a term that might better represent the burgeoning field of journalism education. According to Wilcox (1959), the term—which was used "to denote the anatomy, process, function and effect of the mass media and their audiences"—seemed to have the potential "to bring some sort of unity to a field hitherto considered in piecemeal" (p. 7). Because of its theoretical focus, however, mass communication was to come into sharp conflict with the more practical journalism subfields and was not soon to be accepted as an overarching term for the various sequences of journalism education or even to feel at home among them.

Under a similar influence from the social sciences, educators in speech education—which had emerged from a background of elocution, rhetoric, and public speaking—"found themselves teaching and researching areas that were previously unknown to them, or that they had regarded as outside their jurisdiction" (Cohen, 1994, p. 323). These diverse departments of interpersonal communication began to enter into communication studies and, in some cases, media studies, thus co-opting existing journalism and mass communication programs by developing communication management, organizational communication, and even public relations and broadcast programs.

Despite their later mutual concerns, the fields of mass communication and interpersonal communication developed separately, leading to what has been seen as "virtually a total separation" between the fields (Rogers & Chaffee, 1994, p. 37). McLeod and Blumler (1987) noted that "[t]he separation of mass communication from other forms of communication behavior was fostered by the division of academic departments into journalism, with its professional and social science roots, and speech communication, with origins in the humanities" (p. 286). Similarly, Rogers (1994) stated that when communication study—which soon evolved from mass communication in departments of journalism—moved into departments of speech, it changed them from "the humanistic study of rhetoric toward a scientific analysis of interpersonal communication." And, he noted, "This takeover of existing university units also divided the field of communication study into the two subdisciplines of interpersonal and mass communication" (p. 478).

THE FOUNDING OF SPEECH EDUCATION

Speech education evolved from programs in public speaking, which itself evolved from elocution and rhetoric, which—based on such classical authors as Aristotle, Cicero and Quintilian—were basic components of the curriculum of the American classical college. By the end of the first quarter of the 19th century, elocution was becoming separated from training in rhetoric. Elocution remained a required course in the classical college, though its utility was questioned as the classical college was being replaced by the elective system. The demise of elocution became assured in 1873 when it was dropped to elective status at Harvard under President Charles Eliot's plan for an elective system (Hochmuth & Murphy, 1954).

The traditional classical approach to rhetoric continued for a while, although late in the century it moved toward the belles lettres approach and often was found in departments of English. English departments, however, tended more and more toward the written rather than the spoken word. Hochmuth and Murphy (1954) stated about the transition:

> In the third quarter of the century speech training became linked with English literature, and departments of English assumed the main responsibility for training in rhetoric. Interest in elocution diminished, but the persistent urge of students to find artistic oral expression sought an outlet in intercollegiate speaking contests. In the last quarter of the century courses in public speaking and particularly in argumentation and forensic forms, because established. Speech as a field—the classical rhetorical tradition combined with the new concerns of vocal and physical training—became established clearly if not firmly. The base was supplied for the detailed structures which were to be erected in the twentieth-century Departments of Speech. (p. 173)

Gray (1954) called the period from 1890 to 1920 "a period of transition in the development of American speech education," and he called the changes during that period "perhaps more profound than in any other similar period since the founding of the first colonial schools." He wrote that during the 30-year period "the various aspects of oral communication were drawn together and integrated, under the common rubric of speech" and that by 1920 rhetoric had been "restored to its place as a substantial body of principles governing both oral and written discourse" (p. 422). Like journalism in a number of institutions, public speaking emerged from English departments in the early 1900s. Like the founding of communication studies several decades later, a major event was a rump session of its parent organization.

In 1912, the National Council of Teachers of English established an Oral English Committee to organize programs on the subject for its annual meetings. However, because committee members lacked an appreciation for the uniqueness of public speaking, "agitation was begun for the complete separation of the two disciplines" (Gray, 1954, p. 434). The first important call for a separation of speech from English departments was a resolution passed at the Public Speaking Conference of the New England and North Atlantic States at Yale University on March 25, 1913. It stated, in part, "[t]hat it is the sense of this conference that departments of Public Speaking in American colleges should be organized entirely separate from departments of English" (D. K. Smith, 1954, p. 455). James M. O'Neill, soon to be the first president of what eventually was to become the National Communication Association, presented a paper at the conference titled "The Dividing Line Between Departments of English and Public Speaking," what Gray (1989) called "a sort of academic Declaration of Independence" (p. 11). The need for a split was based on speech having a distinctive subject matter: both the classical field of rhetoric and the emerging scientific study of speech behavior.

In November 1913, O'Neill gave a speech to the annual dinner of the National Council of Teachers of English (NCTE). In the speech, he called for "independent departments (of public speaking), a professional journal, teacher training, and graduate work" (O'Neill, 1989, p. 3). He stated that "absorption of public speaking by department(s) of English is not to be thought of" (Gray, 1989, p. 11). On November 28, 1913, the results of a questionnaire sent to public speaking teachers were presented at the Public Speaking Section of the NCTE. They showed that 113 of the teachers were in favor of organizing a national association with 3 opposed. No action was taken at that time, however (A. T. Weaver, 1989).

James Albert Winans of Cornell noted at the meeting that there were "practical reasons for separation" because the spoken and written word could never be combined into a single discipline (Gray, 1954, p. 434). Cohen (1994) wrote that the decision to focus on the spoken word "was in fact rather rigorously observed by the profession in years to come," which "imposed limitations on the field for at least three decades as it concerned itself, in all of its branches, almost entirely with oral discourse. A reorientation of the field was necessary before the discipline began to deal with non-oral communication" (p. 49).

On November 27, 1914, at the next annual meeting of the NCTE, the teachers of public speaking voted 57–56 in favor of an independent association. It was followed by a proposal: "That a National Association of Academic Teachers of Public Speaking be organized" (A. T. Weaver, 1989, p. 13). The motion, however, was tabled on an 18–16 vote. A rump group of 17 NCTE members met on November 28 and voted unanimously to form a group to be called the National Association of Academic Teachers of Public Speaking (NAATPS) "for the purpose of promoting research work and more effective teaching" (Cohen, 1994, p. 32). According to Cohen, "The break from the parent group was clothed in ambiguity and was not really a clean break, let alone a revolution" (p. 36). In any event, the NAATPS was formed. In 1917, it became the National Association of Academic Teachers of Speech. It became The Speech Association of America in

1945, the Speech Communication Association in 1970 and the National Communication Association in 1997.

The 17 original members were called by the NCTE "some of the more aggressive of the teachers of public speaking in the colleges" (D. K. Smith, 1954, p. 455). Like the first organization of journalism teachers, the first president of NAATPS, James O'Neill, was from the University of Wisconsin. And, like journalism, the new field was focused in the midwest. All but two of the 17 original members were from colleges or universities in the midwest. And, like Andrew Dickson White and Charles Eliot in journalism, founders who were not from the midwest were from Cornell and Harvard. Nine of the 15 members from the midwest were from large state-sponsored universities following the model of the German research university. Because the field was founded by educators at such schools, its founders realized that their programs must foster research. As Cohen (1994) stated, "Not only were universities to be judged by the quality and quantity of their research; the same criteria also applied to departments and disciplines. Thus if the new discipline was to be accepted in the modern university, it had to establish itself as a discipline capable of undertaking and carrying out research" (p. 37). However, Cohen added that "it appears that the founders had no clear idea of what sort of research they should pursue, or, for that matter, exactly what constituted research" (p. 37). Because they knew little about research, they borrowed from other disciplines.

The association organized a committee (Research Committee, 1915), which agreed on a structure for the field by developing a "classification of titles" to be used for a bibliography of books on public speaking. They consisted of Elocution and Expression; Public Speaking and Oratory; Debate and Discussion; Expressive Reading and Reciting; Reading and Literature; teaching of Physiology and Psychology, Tone Production and Phonetics, Gesture and Pantomime, Spoken Language, Written Language, Psychology of Social Groups, Sociology of Communication; and the history of each of the foregoing subjects (Cohen, 1994). Cohen noted that the proposed bibliography included some topics that were carried over from elocution (Elocution and Expression, and Expressive Reading and Reciting) but that the addition of Reading and Literature "seemed to anticipate the development of oral interpretation as a division of the discipline" (p. 41). Like journalism education's founders, the founders of speech education saw a tie between the new field and the social sciences. Cohen stated about the founders' plan:

> The vision of the founders called for a discipline broader and more inclusive than the title "public speaking" would connote. Moreover, the importance of the social sciences was, even then, visible to the founders. Psychology and sociology are mentioned three times in the list of topics and we find only one reference to literature and one to history. It is worth noting that in its classification, the committee saw the need to research the pedagogy of 'performance' areas and to investigate the histories of the more theoretical aspects of the field. (p. 42)

Cohen noted that "[t]he committee apparently foresaw that research would result in specific outcomes. Not surprisingly, much of the early research in the field could be characterized as effects research" (p. 43).

PUBLIC SPEAKING: SPEECH SCIENCE OR HUMANISM?

A. T. Weaver (1989) called James M. O'Neill (of Wisconsin), Charles H. Woolbert (of Illinois) and James A. Winans (of Cornell) public speaking's "triumvirate." He termed O'Neill "the sparkplug of the rebellion," Woolbert "the dynamo of the revolution," and Winans "the balance wheel of the movement" (p. 16). It was Woolbert who proposed the term *speech science* for the fledgling field. Rather than being humanistic as was the case in English programs, he declared, the new field would be scientific. Woolbert (1916) stated that public speaking was related to the "pure sciences" of physics, psychology, and anatomy (D. K. Smith, 1954, p. 456). He proposed 10 divisions to speech science: Phonology, The Technique of Expression, The Psychology of Expression, The Application of Laws of Expression, Acting Drama, Extempore Speaking, Argumentation and Debate, Persuasion, The Pedagogy of Oral Expression, and The Aesthetics of Speaking, Interpreting, and Action.

Woolbert (1916) stated that subdivisions of speech science and arts that were independent of other disciplines were Stage Craft, Stage Art, Speech Art, Persuasion, Debating, Argumentation, Expression, Elocution, Rhetoric, and Phonology. According to Cohen (1994), "The Woolbert taxonomy was significant in the history of the discipline because it predicted in general form, but not in specific detail, much of the form that Speech Communication would assume over the years." He added:

> Woolbert described a discipline which was dependent on other disciplines for its theoretical foundations. The subject matters which he regarded as indigenous to speech were the applied and performance aspects of the discipline. From the outset Woolbert conceived of the new science as a derivative or perhaps a synthetic discipline. Whether it could truly be regarded as synthetic would depend on the discipline's ability to integrate the materials drawn from outside into a unitary discipline with distinctive focus and with autonomy which would free it from the excessive theoretical and methodological dependence." (p. 53)

A competing vision came from Hunt (1916), who concluded that a discipline that drew from other fields would not become a science because it was not creating its own knowledge. He proposed emphasizing what was distinctive to public speaking and its role in synthesizing and applying knowledge. According to Cohen (1994), Hunt "visualized Public Speaking as the grand synthesizer of all the liberal arts, if not all of human knowledge" (p. 56). Cohen added:

Woolbert, probably correctly, argued that he and Hunt represented dissimilar historical and intellectual conceptions and different academic settings. The emergence of the German modeled research university, of which Illinois was by 1916 an example, served to explain the divergences of their orientation to the new profession. To some extent the differences were dependent on the respective situations of Hunt and Woolbert but they were also representative of two conceptions of the academic enterprise which reflected views of the academy which were strikingly unlike. In contrast to Hunt's humanism, Woolbert presented a picture of what he saw as the new world of higher education. (pp. 56–57)

Woolbert did not think the new discipline could rely on other disciplines and remain independent. In addition, Cohen noted, Woolbert "was adamant that the teacher of Public speaking could not be solely, or largely, responsible for the general education of students. That task must fall to the specialist—not to the 'general specialist' " (p. 57).

A third vision of the new field was presented by Mary Yost of Vassar College in the April 1917 issue of *The Quarterly Journal* in an article titled "Argument from the Point of View of Sociology." Yost, one of the first members of the field to obtain a doctorate, contended that argumentation theory was based on logic and that sociology would provide a better foundation for speech education. Cohen (1994) stated about her vision:

The shift from logic to sociology meant that the focus of communication was now not on the logic of the argument. The new focus was now centered on . . . 'communication between the members of a social group, a society in the sociological meaning of the term.' Yost's sociological approach was fundamentally concerned with the characteristics of social groups, which, in most cases, constituted audiences, and the response of those groups to arguments. (p. 67)

Cohen (1994) argued that Yost's article was "one of the very earliest models of human communication" but was ignored for years. He continued, "It is worth noting that she used the term 'communication' more often than 'argumentation,' Whether knowingly or not, Yost had opened a new way of examining communication, and in so doing had offered what amounted to a new research paradigm" (p. 68). Her proposal would have shifted the focus from the individual to the group. Cohen noted that Yost's plan could have laid the foundation for group communication. However, he stated, "Sadly, such an effect seemed not to happen. When the discipline turned to 'group discussion' a few years later the conceptual base was altogether different from Yost's. The social–psychological orientation of Yost was not considered; instead close attention was paid to the more logic based idea of 'Reflective Thinking' derived from the work of John Dewey" (p. 68).

Instead of taking Hunt's or Yost's path, however, the new field followed that of Woolbert and experimental psychology. By 1918 Woolbert's position had become the framework for the new field. Gray (1954), for example, stated, "Although Woolbert's books did not appear until 1920, after that date scarcely a textbook on speaking was written that did not take into account many of the principles that he had advanced" (p. 439). Cohen (1994) posited the lack of interest in Yost's article partly to the fact that it was more abstract and theoretical and Woolbert's writing was more specific and concrete. Also, Woolbert was a prolific writer, and Yost published only one article on the subject.

Cohen (1994) suggested that if Yost's road had been taken instead of Woolbert's, "it might have given a different, less rigid perspective to research" (p. 70). He noted that Woolbert had a strong behavioral bent and that his concept of psychology was "one of a science with irrefutable laws" (p. 71). He called Woolbert the instigator of the conflict between "empiricists" and "rhetoricians" and argued that the field likely would have been broader if the methodologies from the "more flexible social sciences, such as anthropology and sociology had been available" (p. 72). Cohen stated that the lasting influence of Woolbert, himself a professional psychologist, was to make the young field "overly dependent upon a single discipline to provide a theoretical and methodological base" (p. 77). He continued:

> Charles Henry Woolbert's name may not be widely known to present day members of the discipline, but, without question, he must be regarded as the founder of an important and durable conception of what the new discipline should be, what its central concerns should be, and how its research should be conducted. Disputes between "humanists" and "scientists" have arisen from time to time in the history of the discipline; the grounds of the disagreement, however, were established in the confrontation between Woolbert and Hunt. (p. 77)

Although Woolbert's writings were the most influential, two other educators— Arthur Edward Phillips and James Albert Winans—also had been influenced by a psychological model. Phillips' *Effective Speaking* was published in 1908 and Winans' *Public Speaking* in 1915. According to Cohen (1994), "Winans upheld what has continued to be a practice in much communication pedagogy. He acknowledged that conviction and persuasion were really inseparable but, 'for convenience,' he treated them as if they were separate entities" (p. 81). He added: "The early writings of Phillips and Winans combined with the prolific output of Woolbert may have insured the dominant influence of psychology on the new profession. At the same time, they may have minimized the possibility of influence from other social sciences" (p. 82). Cohen (1994) added that "the initial concerns with public speaking and persuasion have remained as central issues in the profession" (p. 84). And, according to Cohen, the debate begun by Hunt and Woolbert over whether its orientation would be toward the humanities or the social sciences has endured—as has the debate over whether to teach students about speech or to speak.

WILBUR SCHRAMM AND THE BIRTH OF
MASS COMMUNICATION AND COMMUNICATION STUDIES

According to Chaffee, the advent of radio and then television "led people to conceptualize mass media and mass communication back in the late 1930s" (Rogers & Chaffee, 1993, p. 129). That conceptualization, which was to be called *mass communication*, came into its own in the 1941–1951 period ("Herring Study," 1956). The title of founder of the new area of study is given to Wilbur Schramm. Schramm (1981) identified four founders of communication studies: Paul Lazarsfeld, Kurt Lewin, Harold Lasswell, and Carl Hovland. However, Paisley (1984) wrote "that it was because of Schramm more than anyone else, that communication could become a field of study in its own right" (p. 2). Likewise, Tankard (1990) stated that Schramm "is perhaps himself a better candidate than any of the four men whom he named be the 'founding father' of communication theory" (p. 248). And Rogers (1994) stated: "Laswell, Lewin, and Hovland were definitely forerunners, not founders. They did not give up their primary identification with political science, social psychology, and psychology, respectively" (p. xiii).

Schramm went to the University of Iowa to work on a Ph.D. in American Literature and stayed as a faculty member in the English Department. From 1943 to 1947 he was director of the School of Journalism at Iowa. His vision of communication study was born during World War II when he worked for 15 months at the Office of Facts and Figures and the Office of War Information. When he returned to Iowa City, he began to pursue his vision of communication studies in the School of Journalism. His plan included beginning a communication-based Ph.D. program. According to Rogers (1994), offering the first communication Ph.D. program in a school of journalism led directly to the division of the communication field into mass communication and interpersonal communication. Doctoral programs in communication study were later to be offered in speech departments; however, they stressed interpersonal communication rather than mass communication.

In 1947, Schramm left Iowa for the University of Illinois, where he founded the Institute of Communications Research. The purpose of the Institute was:

> to apply the methods and disciplines of the social sciences (supported, when necessary, by the fine arts and natural sciences) to the basic problems of press, radio, and pictures; to supply verifiable information in those area of communications where the hunch, the tradition, the theory and the thumb have too often ruled; and by so doing to contribute to the better understanding of communications and the maximum use of communications for the public good. (Tankard, 1990, p. 240)

Schramm edited what became the first text for the emerging field, *Mass Communications* (Schramm,1949). The founding of mass communication as an autonomous field, however, usually is traced to the publication of *The Process and Effects of Mass Communication* (Schramm, 1954), which he also edited. It became the manifesto that gave mass communication a legitimacy of its own.

Dressel (1960) wrote that the concept of mass communications "further affected the nature and content of journalism by injecting more principle and theory and implying a concept of journalism as evolving into a behavioral science" (p. 36). He added:

> By identifying as a focus of concern the process of communication basic to all the specialties subsumed under or associated with journalism, a logical basis for the continuing association of what were threatening to become diverse fields, unrelated except by common emphasis on the liberal arts, has been found. Perhaps even more important, the concept of mass communication opens the way to study of new ways of relating or integrating elements from traditional disciplines in connection with the problems of communication. Finally, the communication process and its effects on the views and behavior of people becomes a new and, for the present and future eras, especially significant area of research. (p. 36)

Journalism education was slow to accept mass communication as an equal, let alone an overarching term. According to Durham (1992), the terms *communication* and *mass communication* came into use by independent social science research centers in the 1950s. Educators who thought of themselves as teaching mass communication rather than journalism tended to have a greater interest in research. A number of them took their doctorates in other academic fields and had no practical media experience. Thus, the rise of mass communication education did little to tie the field together. Instead, it began a debate between journalism and mass communication educators as to whether they should teach their students about the media or teach them how to get a media job.

Though some departments of journalism added "and Mass Communication" to their title in the 1960s and 1970s, it wasn't until 1982, more than 30 years after the field was born, that the acceptance of mass communication became formalized among journalism educators. That year, the Association for Education for Journalism became the Association for Education in Journalism and Mass Communication. Further legitimization of the term was accomplished in 1995 when two of the AEJMC's major journals, *Journalism Quarterly* and *Journalism Educator*, added "and Mass Communication" to their titles.

COMMUNICATION STUDIES AND
MASS COMMUNICATION DIVERGE

The terms *communication, communications,* and *communication studies* soon began to be used by the social science researchers who first located in journalism schools and departments to indicate that their research interests were not limited to the mass media. Communication studies first took root at Illinois, where Wilbur Schramm moved in 1947, established a doctorate in communication, and became the world's first educator to gain the title "professor of communication." It also was early to bloom at two other large midwestern universities, Wisconsin and Minnesota. All were headed by administrators trained by Willard Bleyer. As Rogers (1994) put it: "Bleyer's strategy was to help schools of journalism survive in U.S. research universities by training a cadre of directors for these schools ('the Bleyer children') who had Ph.D. degrees in a social science and shared his vision of journalism as a social science" (p. 19).

Schramm took communication study to Stanford, where he took a position in 1955. Rogers (1994) called Schramm's moving to Stanford and the beginning of a doctoral program there "the key event in gaining acceptance of communication study in American universities" (p. 477). However, communication study in journalism programs still tended to be called mass communication. Rogers and Chaffee (1994) noted about the choice of the term *mass communication* over *communication studies*: "One might dismiss this naming as a minor variation on a theme, but we find that it masks a tension between the Bleyer approach and the Schramm approach that has yet to be resolved" (p. 5).

In his memoirs published posthumously, Schramm (1997) wrote that young Ph.D.'s in the social sciences who were interested in the study of communication in the late 1940s and early 1950s found a place in schools of journalism and broadcasting. In addition, cooperation between the professional schools and academic departments allowed "new opportunities for research on the mass media, controls on them, and their effects on society" (p 19). Schramm assumed that communication study would bring media education and speech education closer together in schools of communication. However, as Rogers (1994) noted, the idea of communication study was threatening to the journalism educators who taught practical courses and weren't interested in theoretical research. The educators who weren't interested in research and theory called the research-oriented educators *communicologists* or *chi-squares*. The educators who taught practical courses began to be called the *green-eyeshades* for the visors that old-time editors used to wear.

In 1955, the year after Schramm's *Process and Effects of Mass Communication* was published and the year he went to Stanford, an event took place that Rogers (1994) called "a key turning point in the acceptance of Schramm's vision of communication study by journalism educators" (p. 462). A group of scholars decided to try to open annual meetings of the Association for

Education in Journalism (AEJ) to research sessions. In May 1955, the heads of half a dozen larger journalism programs got together during a meeting of the American Association for Public Opinion Research (AAPOR) and decided to hold a rump session that summer following the annual meeting of the AEJ for the presentation of research. Seven papers were presented, and the "rumpers," as they called themselves, decided to hold another such session the following year. The group evolved into the AEJ's Communication Theory and Methodology Division. By 1958, research sessions had become part of the regular AEJ program (Emery & McKerns, 1987). By 1963 George Kienzle, director at Ohio State University, could charge that " 'communicology' papers have dominated" recent meetings of the Association for Education in Journalism (Highton, 1967, p. 10).

Rogers (1994) wrote about the incident, "Their actions amounted to organizing the Chi-Squares, who were then a minority in the AEJ, against the Green-Eyeshades" (p. 463). The rumpers were all "Bleyer children"—people who had studied under him. Rogers wrote: "Thus, Schramm's vision of communication study rested on a base laid down some decades previously by Daddy Bleyer, and it was the Bleyer children who implemented Schramm's vision through schools of journalism" (p. 463). However, Schramm's and Bleyer's children went further than did Bleyer, who wanted only to establish journalism as an academic, nonvocational program tied to the social sciences. Stated Rogers, "There always was a tension between these two visions, and there still is" (p. 467).

Schramm had predicted an integrated social science of human communication. Journalism and speech programs would be merged into one unit, which would provide professional training for undergraduate and master's students and doctoral study into processes and effects of communication. Graduate students would teach entry level skills for such communication-related professions such as print journalism, persuasion, and broadcasting. In Schramm's memoirs, editors Rogers and Chaffee noted that "Schramm imagined something akin to the history of other scientific disciplines, which had gradually upgraded and differentiated themselves by building a specialized knowledge base" (Schramm, 1997, p. 157).

COMMUNICATION STUDIES FINDS ITSELF WELCOME IN SPEECH DEPARTMENTS

During the 1950s and 1960s a number of communication departments were formed around journalism programs with a focus on a behavioral science approach because their faculty were trained in the social sciences (Rogers & Chaffee, 1983). The movement toward communication studies wasn't universally popular among journalism educators, however. Medsger (1996), for example, noted that by the mid-1950s, "a new force was taking root in some journalism education programs. Eventually it would permeate most programs."

She added, "This new force—communication studies—would radically rewrite the rules governing who should teach journalism, and it would lead to changes and confusion that dog journalism education even today" (p. 54). Likewise, MacDougall charged that "college and university administrators are combining journalism under an umbrella called communications along with drama, radio, linguistics and a lot of other things. That is demeaning the importance of journalism, reducing it to just another way of transmitting information and gossip" ("Curtis D. MacDougall," 1983, p. 27).

Though Schramm expected schools of communication to include both journalism and speech, few of the journalism schools that took up the name communication in the 1950s and 1960s included speech communication. According to Rogers, "This separation is seen in the existence of different departments ('mass communication' and 'speech communication') in the same universities, divisions within and among professional associations, and even in the character that has been taken on by professional journals that seek not to make any such distinction" (Rogers & Chaffee, 1983, p. 24). Reardon and Rogers (1988) called the division between interpersonal and mass communication a false dichotomy.

Despite journalism programs' head start in communication studies, speech departments were more amenable to the idea than were journalism schools. Rogers (1994), for example, wrote:

Communication study would infect existing schools of journalism, at least in an initial era, rather than be implemented in newly created departments of communication. Later, more gradually and without the Green-Eyeshades versus Chi-Squares conflict that occurred in journalism, communication study also invaded departments of speech, turning them away from their humanities emphasis on rhetoric to become, in essence, departments of interpersonal communication with a strong orientation toward psychology. (p. 476)

Like journalism education, speech education grew to include a number of subfields. Some of them, such as theater and communications disorders, grew to the point where they broke away from the parent. Marlier (1980) noted the problem of identity that has plagued speech communication because of its varied subfields. "We in speech communication are too often perceived as being content to view speech communication as a disunified field rather than as a discipline with an agreed-upon focus which unites us," he wrote. "Unfortunately, this perception of our academic self-concept is also too often an accurate one" (p. 324). He added, "What speech communication has lacked, that other disciplines have and which is the basis for their disciplinary identity, is a general agreement, both within and outside the discipline, as to *the kinds of questions* which are properly addressed by the practitioners of those disciplines" (p. 324). He argued that speech communication not only is a distinct discipline, but "it is also a distinct *kind* of discipline" (p. 326).

When he was president of the Speech Communication Association, Zarefsky noted that specialization had replaced the generalist nature that once characterized the field. He wrote that the "1940's or 1950's model of the 'generalist' who could teach broadly across the curriculum is often the object of either nostalgia or ridicule" (Zarefsky, 1990, p. 2). He added:

> The joke may be on us. Some of the most exciting recent developments in communication not only have occurred in total disrespect of our disciplinary substructure but make much of that substructure irrelevant. Unless we can become as good at transcending our differences as we are at recognizing them, we may miss out on keeping abreast of these issues and leading the field into the future. (p. 2)

Zarefsky also noted that the growth and specialization of speech communication meant that several distinctions "now are questionable." Two such distinctions related specifically to the relationship between speech and mass communication. He noted about the distinction between rhetoric and mass communication that "mass media are increasingly recognized not to be neutral transmission vehicles; they have rhetorical effects." About the distinction made between interpersonal and mass communication, he wrote that as changes in technology and economics of the mass media that favor "narrowcasting" over broadcasting, "the concept of 'mass' in our theories and research becomes more problematic and consumption of media appears to be more of a para-social interaction" (p. 2).

THE FUTURE OF COMMUNICATION STUDIES: INTERDISCIPLINARY SUBFIELD, FIELD OR DISCIPLINE?

In the 1990s, a department, school, or college of communication might include anything from a professional unit composed of journalism, advertising, and public relations to a broad hybrid unit including both interpersonal and mass communication to a specialized unit that consists only of interpersonal communication. Communication studies remained an interdisciplinary study, though more at home in interpersonal communication.

Shoemaker (1993) stated that communication-related studies were in a "crisis of legitimacy" because it had no home. She wrote, "One could say that communication is both everywhere and therefore nowhere, a status that has potentially disastrous consequences for communication departments as they battle for their slice of an ever-smaller university budget pie" (p. 146). Shoemaker presented a view of communication as an interdisciplinary discipline located not only in such academic units as (interpersonal) communication, journalism, communication arts, and mass communication but also in sociology, political science, economics, history, law, and other academic departments. She called for lowering or elimination of the walls between communication-related sequences. She also called for the establishment of a common core of classes for all students in the department and then the development of the sequence skills courses—what she termed "zero-based" curriculum development (p. 151). She set forth the following vision of communication as a liberal education based on Dennis' vision of journalism education set forth in the "Oregon Report" (Project, 1984):

> We must give our students a general communication education with a large conceptually based core of courses. There will still be a place for classes that give students technical skills for entry-level jobs, but these must be subordinate to classes that teach critical thinking, law, history, mass media and society, international communication, and so on. . . . Our graduates must leave campus with the ability to train themselves when changes in the field require it, to work effectively with others to solve problems, and to think critically about the world around them. (p. 151)

Swanson (1993) stated that communication is a field whose subfields "are connected politically by the organization of communication programs and historically, but not intellectually" that share an interest in the communication "each in its own terms and for its own purposes" (p. 169). He argued that communication is not a discipline, "at least in any traditional sense, and it will be helpful to discard the contrary view once and for all." Despite not being a discipline, he wrote, "communication nevertheless is quite central, both in terms of demand for instruction and in its growing intellectual exchange and partnerships with disciplines across the humanities and social sciences" (p. 169) He added:

> The reasons for our existence as a field do not depend on clinging to the fiction that we are a discipline. It does not follow from recognizing our status as an interdisciplinary field that, therefore, our various subfields should break apart and seek independent status. Something like the present organizational structure of the field, shaped and elaborated by whatever new subfields come along, ought to be retained. (p. 170)

Rogers (1994) stated that fitting communication study into existing speech and media programs had both positive and negative results. A negative aspect was that "the discipline of communication was bifurcated into mass communication versus interpersonal communication and perhaps into a third wing of information science" (p. 480). On the positive side, the occupational fields supported by media-related education provided jobs for graduates of communication studies, which requires that students also take practical courses and gives communication study an applied perspective that "is a cause of certain strains, but it can also be advantageous" (p. 481). He called communication studies "mainly empirical, quantitative, and focused on determining the effects of communication" (p. 491). He added:

> Wilbur Schramm ended his final book manuscript, *The Beginnings of Communication Study: a Personal Memoir* (Schramm, 1997), by forecasting that communication study would pass through a near-future stage of consolidation and reidentification in which university units, now called journalism, speech

communication, cinema, mass communication, and information science, combine into larger units (schools and/or colleges) called simply "communication." . . . Such future unification will put the communication-related units on the same campus together in a community of interest rather than in competition with each other, as is now the case at most large universities. (p. 494)

Educators from the fields of journalism, mass communication and speech communication met at the University of Texas at Austin on June 16–17, 1994, to discuss common concerns and perhaps form alliances at what was billed as the State of the Field of Communication Conference ("State of the Field," 1994). Wartella (1994) wrote that the conference was designed "to refocus and refine communication education to shape a field coming of age." She noted that colleagues often ask, "What is communication? What do you study? What do you do?" She stated that there is "little meshing of journalism and communication study with the undergraduate core curriculum" and that educators have "overlooked our responsibilities as public scholars to articulate communication's centrality to society and the university." Additional problems, she wrote, were "internal fights—professionals versus academics, differences across subfields, and differences across communication units on campus [that] reduce coordination and worsen the problem of isolation" (p. 1).

The conference delegates noted five areas of concern for communication education: centrality and vision, building bridges, structure and location, outlining a vision, and a common purpose ("State of the Field," 1994, p. 11). The conference approved a resolution for establishing a commission of communication educators drawn from all major communication associations to "analyze, synthesize and recommend directions for communication education in the 21st century." The resolution stated that the role of that commission would be "to generate a series of communication competencies necessary for the future." Issues addressed by the commission would include "the role of communication programs in delivering the general education requirements in the modern university" and "a consideration of the core knowledge claims that are central to the communication discipline." In addition it would look at "communication as a practical discipline, with a set of skills that we can share with our students and a delineation of those skills" (p. 19).

A group of 85 speech communication administrators and professors representing the Speech Communication Association and the Association for Communication Administration attempted to define the field of communication at a meeting July 28–30, 1995, in Alexandria, VA. They came up with four definitions of communication that were submitted to a committee, which reached a consensus definition: "The field of communication *focuses* on how people use messages to generate meanings within and across various contexts, cultures, channels and media. It *promotes* the effective and ethical practice of human communication" (Berko, 1995, p. 12). As a result, the members of the Association of Schools of Journalism and Mass Communication at their annual business meeting in early August passed a resolution that stated: "Regarding the definition of communication that was arrived at during the ACA meeting in Alexandria, Virginia in July 1995, ASJMC has serious reservations about the definition and about the possible consequences of its inappropriate use. ASJMC does not endorse this definition" (Rowland, personal communication, Sept. 29,1995).

In a letter to Merritt, the president of the ACA, Willard Rowland, president of the ASJMC, noted that the ASJMC concerns were threefold:

1. Communication is best thought of [as] a field, not a discipline.
2. The ACA definition reflects too much of a singular, speech communication approach, failing to convey the true breadth and interdisciplinarity of the field.
3. Any such definition ought to contemplate the possibility of multiple definitions, reflecting the considerable variation of approaches and types of programs in the field. (personal communication, Sept. 29, 1995)

The dispute showed no signs of being resolved, however. The Speech Communication Association followed the example of the Association for Communication Administration and made speech education's transformation official in 1997 when it dropped the word *speech* from its name and became the National Communication Association. In the spring of 1999, the Association for Education in Journalism and Mass Communication staked its claim to the word *communication* without a modifier when it changed the name of *Journalism & Mass Communication Monographs* to *Journalism & Communication Monographs*.

The growth of the theoretical components of the field was viewed with alarm by some educators with a practical inclination. The development of mass communication and communication studies had led not only to a blurring of the boundary between mass media education and interpersonal communication, but it had also led to a bifurcation within media education. Media professionals usually joined in the debate on the practical side (the green-eyshades) as they decried what had happened to journalism education because of the rise of the communicologists and chi-squares.

5

Mass Media Education's
"Split Personality"

A great part of that problem [mass media education's "General State of Mental Health"], in my view, is rooted in another of our ongoing maladies, our split personality—now academic, now professional.

—Budd (1985, p. 25)

Though the founders of journalism education were primarily interested in providing well-trained and well-educated graduates for jobs in the media industries, they and media educators who followed them also have thought of journalism schools not only as professional schools but as academic enterprises producing well-educated graduates. Because of its divided loyalties, Sloan (1990) called journalism education "schizophrenic." He stated, "It has not known which way to go: Should it become primarily professional, or should it be a traditional academic discipline? Possessing a sense of inferiority to both professional journalism and academia, it has tried to prove itself to both." And, he added, "Traveling in two directions, it has never decided on, much less obtained, its destination" (p. 4).

With the advent of mass communication and communication study in the late 1940s with their emphasis on theory and faculty with doctorates, journalism educators with professional experience but no doctorate began to feel threatened in many media programs. Some began to think that their contribution was less valued than that of new faculty with Ph.D.s but little or no professional media experience who were hired to teach the new mass communication courses. Also, along with the growth in the number of faculty with Ph.D.s came an increased emphasis on research, some of it practical but much of it increasingly theoretical.

Despite its attempts to connect with the liberal arts in general and the social sciences in particular, media-related education continued to be seen by people outside of the field as vocational, however. Schweitzer (1985) wrote that journalism educators "lack the respect of their colleagues in the academic community" (p. 38) because they are seen as teaching a trade. And, according to Parisi (1992), "Journalism education suffers from the stigma of being a narrow, practical training that oversimplifies the very intellectual complexities that disciplines such as literary study, philosophy, sociology, psychology, and anthropology seek to explore" (p. 4).

THE GREEN EYESHADES VERSUS THE CHI-SQUARES

The debate over whether journalism education was practical or academic was particularly spirited in the 1960s as communication studies grew within journalism schools. In his presidential address to the Association for Education in Journalism in 1967, Harold L. Nelson stated that "some of the best-known critics have in recent months let fly with such balderdash as the following: 'There is a death struggle going on between academic communicators and those who believe in teaching pragmatic journalism.' " He concluded, however, that "both . . . are thriving as they have not before" (Nelson, 1967, p. 745). He noted that Malcolm MacLean had stated in 1964: "There is an 'either–or' character to journalism education today. You must be on the side of the great professionals and of experience in the field, or on the side of what is disparagingly called 'the communicologists' " (Nelson, p. 746). In response, Nelson stated:

> Hogwash. The best and greatest schools and departments of journalism today reflect the fact that journalism education has two phases, paralleling each other and depending on each other: One phase is teaching the best possible understanding of and practice in our field; the other is discovery of new knowledge, which is research. (p. 746)

Despite Nelson's conclusion that the academics and the professionals were both at home in journalism education, the debate continued unabated. Budd and MacLean wrote the following in a paper presented at the 1967 Association for Education in Journalism convention at which Nelson gave his speech: "Though we pay lip service to the need for liberalizing influences, we often seem to act as though the most important purpose of a student's journalism education is to please the boss on his or her first job" (Budd, 1985, p. 24). Taking the other side of the debate, Highton wrote that same year in an article titled *Green Eyeshades vs. Chi-Squares*: "Newspapering is becoming a sidelight, if not an afterthought, of many journalism schools" (1967, p. 10).

One of the leaders of the "green eyeshades," Curtis MacDougall, presented his vision of journalism education in a paper presented at the 1973 AEJ convention. MacDougall (1973) charged that for "more than a half century journalism education has fallen short of what it should be" because it had emulated the liberal arts college instead of schools of medicine or law, which are self-contained professional schools. He added:

> Long freed from being just a part of English departments, journalism courses and curricula today are being swallowed up by colleges and schools of communications, most of whose directors are more ignorant of and/or less sympathetic toward journalism than was true of the English professors who were the principal bottlenecks before World War II. (p. 1)

He stated that all journalism faculty needed a minimum of 5 years of professional experience. He called for use of "step-by-step exercises (drill)" and stated that a "journalism student's entire training . . . should be planned as a continuous relayed experience, not as an opportunity to meet all-campus standards by acquiring credits in a specified number of unrelated courses" (p. 2).

MacDougall (1973) stated that journalism "cannot be taught effectively as a mere major within a liberal arts college which presumably provides a versatile life view for students with no definite occupational goal in mind" and that the "[e]xecution of a vocationally motivated curriculum is dependent upon the highly qualified journalism faculty that knows what the finished product should be like" (p. 2). He also noted the difference between research in journalism, which begins with an open mind, and research in the social sciences, in which the researcher has a set hypothesis in mind. "The journalistic approach to knowledge is much sounder," he wrote, "and professors of journalism should crusade to persuade their campus colleagues to emulate it" (pp. 8–9).

A meeting of media professional and education organizations was held in February 1976 at the headquarters of the American Newspaper Publishers Association in Reston, VA, to discuss efforts to "upgrade the standards of education on the campuses" (L. Smith, 1977, p. 26). The focus of discussion was a proposal by the Journalism Education Committee of the National Conference of Editorial Writers. Its objectives were: (a) to provide greater independent status for journalism education, approximating that of medical schools; (b) to require professional experience, preferably no fewer than five years, for all instructors in skill-course areas; (c) to curtail emphasis on communications faculty advancement; (d) to update curriculum requirements to insure a core of liberal arts background courses; (e) to assure general survey courses in the sciences and social sciences for students not planning to major in those disciplines; (f) to schedule undergraduates' skill-writing courses earlier than their third year; (g) to provide full-time advisers to supplement the advisory role of faculty members wherever budgets permit; and (h) to explore two-track programs, one in skills courses for career-oriented journalism majors and one in "service" courses with consumer orientation for students not planning careers in journalism. The NCEW achieved no consensus for their proposals. Smith noted that the first three proposals caused more controversy than the remaining five.

The academic–practical debate continued to be heated going into the 1980s to a large extent because of the continuing assumption that journalism school graduates were headed toward media jobs and, thus, needed practical experience taught by experienced practitioners in order to get that first job. Roosenraad and Wares (1983) tried to determine whether grades or practical experience was more important for new hires. They conducted a random survey of editors of 114 newspapers with more than 50,000 circulation and received responses from 74, a 65% response rate. They concluded that the "experience vs. academics question was settled strongly on the side of experience" (p. 18). Of the six factors listed, experience was seen as the most important factor in getting the first job, followed by interviews and published articles ("clips"), with grades, college attended, and company test scores trailing far behind. Twenty-eight editors listed journalism as the best preparation; however, despite the findings concerning experience, 20 editors stated that the type of major was not important and 18 editors listed a liberal arts major as the best preparation. Business, law, and foreign languages also were mentioned.

Dennis (1987a), however, questioned whether the practical approach was the best alternative for journalism schools. He charged that journalism education "appears to be on the ragged edge of being so hopelessly outdated that its usefulness may soon be severely questioned" (p. 80). Dennis argued that course titles and course descriptions in a 1928 journalism school catalogue were not noticeably different from modern ones. He also stated that few schools were offering courses that went beyond the basics of professional practice. He proposed that media programs add more courses about the changing media industries themselves or begin to be seen as irrelevant. In response to Dennis' article, Bagdikian (1987) continued the call for hiring faculty with practical experience in order to train future journalists:

> Journalists cannot be competently trained by teachers whose only expertise is in theory, any more than surgeons or concert musicians can. Communication theorists cannot be competently trained by teachers whose sole expertise is in journalism. Communications-theory faculties are designed to produce promising teachers and researchers in communications theory. Journalism faculties are designed to produce promising journalism practitioners. Combining the two curriculums produces poor theorists and poor journalists. (p. 83)

The lightning rod for the academic versus practical debate in the early 1980s was the Oregon Report by the Project on the Future of Journalism Education (1984, 1987), the most in-depth study of journalism and mass communication curriculum up to that point. The project, headed by Everette Dennis, dean of the School of Journalism at the University of Oregon, found areas of concern for journalism educators and concluded that "[t]he general state of journalism and mass communication education is dismal" (Project, 1987, p. iii). It predicted that the "rapid infusion of new knowledge and pace of technological change will push journalism/mass communication programs away from industry-oriented sequence programs and toward more generic mass communication study" (Project, 1987, p. 1). Specialized courses would be pushed to the student's senior year and into graduate school or continuing education, according to the report.

In 1985, Dwight Teeter, then president of the Association for Education in Journalism and Mass Communication, called the question of journalism education versus journalism training one of the three "demonic questions" facing journalism education (Teeter, 1985, p. 12). Decrying what he called the "split personality" of journalism education, Budd (1985) stated: "We have and continue to manifest an unhealthy dependence upon and a timidity inspired by practitioners, making us susceptible to a variety of pushes and pulls. . . . Many criticisms of journalism education consider our schools parts factories forced to design their curricula through rear view mirrors" (p. 25).

As part of a symposium of prominent journalism educators, Peterson (1986) concluded that "a professional program in journalism is part training, part education, and both parts are essential to the whole. The trick is to strike a happy balance between the two parts, and that's where the trouble starts, because the terms we use to describe the two wind up as something either pejorative or tendentious" (p. 4). He added: "Without teaching the craft, we are simply teaching *about* journalism. And without the other, we are divorcing ourselves from the university itself and we are drifting into a narrow vocationalism" (p. 5).

Dennis (1988) noted that by the early 1980s, the structure of journalism schools was basically unchanged from the 1940s and that they were beginning to feel the "strains of their own success" caused by growing enrollments. He noted that scholarship in the field had made little impact on the journalism curriculum or on the media industries. Dennis charged that "many professionally-oriented schools were training what could only be regarded as media-illiterate students: journalists-to-be with little knowledge of the legal, regulatory, or intellectual history of the field they were about to enter" (p. 16). At the same time, he noted the effects of the new technology on the media industry, resulting in the elimination of barriers between the print and broadcast media and between the news and nonnews side of media organizations. But, he wrote, "few journalism schools moved with dispatch to acknowledge these changes" (pp. 16–17).

Supporters of a practical approach to journalism education continued to fight for their cause with fervor. In a response to Dennis' 1988 article, Mencher (1990b) wrote that Dennis "finds a distinction between the trade school offerings of the craft courses and the intellectual others. In demolishing what he calls myths about journalism schools, he perpetuates the trade-school myth and advances another: *'The trade-school curriculum is simple-minded and anti-intellectual'* " (p. 5). He added about the academic, research-oriented approach to media education:

> The change promises, as administrators see it: A contented faculty; a high output of publications in the refereed journalism, which leads to status within the journalism education brotherhood; an end to budget woes caused by declining craft majors and expensive practitioner-teachers; a steady flow of students taking journalism courses that are cross-listed with courses in the established disciplines.
>
> In this new curriculum, the professional-turned-teacher has a diminished role. Craft courses, shoved into a lesser role in all but the few schools that continue to emphasize professional training, are themselves being altered so that the nonprofessional can teach some of them. (p. 5)

He continued, "Isn't it possible, (some professionals) ask, that some of the courses the academy offers are best taught by others trained in the traditional disciplines?" And, he questioned, "Beyond the introductory mass media courses taught by a journalism faculty member, why not push students into the other disciplines and let the journalism school do its job of training people for the practice of journalism?"

In support of comments on journalism education by Mencher (1990b), Talbott (1990) stated that he was "appalled at the notion of the 'book learned'—folks with little or no professional news background—calling the academic shots in journalism programs." He predicted "a major flurry of libel suits and a downslide of public confidence in the news media in the next few years as a result of such soft and pompously directed education" (p. 36). Kittross (1990), however, wrote that "if Mencher really wants to improve the professional teaching of journalism, I suspect that dropping the sour grapes in favor of trying to open a dialog that might bring together academicians and practitioners in a common endeavor would be a better use of his time and ours" (p. 12).

Other academicians continued the call for lessening the practical approach to the media curriculum. Dates (1990), for example, called for a focus on theory to "lessen dependence upon media industry shifts and changes" (p. 10). Blanchard and Christ (1990) stated that the "first essential outcome of a broadcast or communication curriculum is to contribute to undergraduate, liberal education." They added, "We should see ourselves as more than broadcasters, more than journalists, more than production technique teachers. We are educators in the University tradition" (p. 8).

In her study on print and broadcast journalism education, Medsger (1996), continued the attack on the "communicologists," whom she accused of fostering the view that practical journalism education was little more than vocational training. She wrote, "The term 'occupational training' is intended to disgrace journalism in the university. If journalism education is mere occupational or 'trade school' training, then no self-respecting university would want to support it and journalism should be submerged within communication studies" (p. 12).

THE THEORY VERSUS PRACTICE DEBATE IN ADVERTISING EDUCATION

The split personality exhibited by newspaper journalism programs was also evident in advertising sequences. Rotzoll (1985) stated that advertising education's initial mission was "to help turn advertising into a profession by providing a standardized curriculum formed around a corpus of knowledge essential to the thought and practice of the business." He added, however, that it was "an aspiration soon to be thwarted by what can, in reflection, be considered the path of least resistance—and avoidance of the rigors of a principles-first approach and a reliance on teaching existing advertising practice." Thus advertising education soon "evolved its ongoing educational dichotomy: the inductive/practice-specific approach and the deductive/principles-first approach" (p. 37). He noted that the "educational dichotomy" in advertising programs in journalism schools continued as advertising entered a period of extensive growth in the 1950s and 1960s.

Although advertising was taught in slightly more business schools than journalism schools before 1950, two studies in 1959 that criticized advertising education in business schools—one by the Carnegie Foundation and the other by the Ford Foundation—led to a trend for advertising programs to abandon business schools for journalism schools. The two reports were conducted in response to criticism that "instead of teaching the liberal arts, (business) schools were offering too much 'how to' or professional work" (B. I. Ross, 1991, p. 24). Of 13 institutions whose business schools dropped advertising from 1955 to 1963, nine began offering advertising programs in journalism as business schools changed their course content "away from 'how to' and toward the teaching of advertising as a tool of marketing management" (Ross, p. 27). By 1990, the migration was almost completed. Of the 111 institutions offering advertising programs that year, 98 were in journalism and mass communication units, 11 were in business or marketing, and two were joint journalism–business programs.

Rotzoll (1985) stated that the movement of advertising programs away from business schools following the Carnegie and Ford reports' attacks on specialized and practical programs gave the "practice-specific" model in place in most journalism schools "a jolt" (p. 38). Some educators had began to push for the "principles-first approach" even before the reports. Sandage (1955), for example, argued that advertising courses should be kept at a maximum of 12% of the student's hours and that "such work be heavily weighed with the why and philosophy of advertising and that training in specific advertising skills be minimized" (pp. 210–211). A 1959 study, however, found that the usual advertising curriculum in journalism schools was practical. A typical 15-hour curriculum consisted of Advertising Survey, Copy (Writing) and/or Layout, Newspaper Advertising or Retail Advertising, Radio and Television Advertising, National Advertising, or Advertising Campaigns. A 1960 study found that Principles (an advertising survey course) was most often taught, followed by Copy and Layout, Campaigns, Media, Problems (Radio or TV), and Retail Advertising (B. I. Ross, 1991).

The nature of advertising education in most journalism schools continued to be mainly practical. Twenty years after the Ford and Carnegie studies, Schultze (1980) could say that "it is worth noting that advertising education at universities has progressed little beyond the form it took in the early years of the century; it remains a hybrid of applied social science, common-sense craftsmanship and professional aspiration" (p. 26). Some journalism educators continued to call for the principles-first approach, which had become the model for the remaining business schools with advertising programs. For example, J. S. Wright (1980) stressed the importance of a general, broad-based course of study. He called for advertising students not only to have advertising skills but also to be knowledgeable about such things as marketing, communication, and computers and to have a background in the behavioral sciences and research methods.

Rotzoll (1985) argued that "advertising education has generally been a tentative discipline, unsure of its identity, as it has looked both to commerce and the academy for role models and rationale" (p. 37). Rotzoll added:

> It is to some extent an identity crisis shared by many dimensions of professional education, but seems particularly acute with advertising due primarily to its core subject matter.
>
> Simply, advertising is generally unloved. It may be tolerated, but it is rarely championed. It is the giver of jokes and the target of them. . . .
>
> All of this, of course, makes it difficult to take advertising seriously . . . . (p. 37)

He predicted that advertising education would continue "to reflect existing advertising practice" no matter whether the inductive (practice-specific) or deductive (principles-first) philosophy of education was followed because the advertising business "seems destined to retain many of its basic institutional arrangements" (p. 40).

Rotzoll (1985) stated that other options were available, however. One was that advertising education could mature through concentration on the deductive, principles-first approach. Rotzoll stated that advertising has functional (research, creative, media), synthesis (management, campaigns), and institutional (social and economic dimensions, ethics) areas about which research has been undertaken and theory developed. He noted that focusing on that body of knowledge using a deductive, theory-first approach "can, to some degree at least, free the advertising educator from the tyranny of the immediate, while better serving students, who emerge with principles rather than particulars" (p. 41). On the other hand, Schweitzer (1988) called for a practical education for the majors. However, he also warned of using a trade school approach.

Like Rotzoll (1985), Lancaster, Katz, and Cho (1990) concluded that advertising programs in journalism schools offered a vocational approach that contrasted with the "managerial 'why' focus adopted by business departments." They added:

> Advertising programs in journalism schools favor an inductive, more practical and specialized approach—training students for their "first" job—while those situated in business colleges prefer a more theoretical, deductive and generalized strategy to prepare students for their overall career, or "last" job. (p. 10)

MEDIA EDUCATION'S QUEST FOR
ACADEMIC RESPECTABILITY

Ever since media educators determined that their programs had to be academic instead of vocational if they were to earn respectability within the academy, they have sought the proper balance between practical and theoretical coursework. In recent years, they have seen an added urgency in the endeavor because of the fear that programs that are seen as too vocational by the administrator or are seen as not central to the institution's mission face possible elimination. That point was made by Beasley, then president of the Association for Education in Journalism and Mass Communication, who asked, "Are journalism/mass communication programs becoming an endangered species?" (Beasley, 1994, p. 2). As Iorio and Williamson (1995) stated, "The challenge this involves is how to implement cohesive courses of study that train students for communications professions, and, at the same time, are fused with the core principles of academe" (p. 16). They found "threads of liberal arts and sciences content running through curriculum that iterate communication studies as central to the university mission"; however, they found "those threads to be fragile links" (p. 24).

The fragile links with the academy were noted more than 20 years ago by J. W. Carey (1978) in his presidential address to the Association for Education in Journalism. He said that "there is an inherent tension between the university tradition and the professions the modern university serves" (p. 847). Carey stated that journalism education "must extirpate much of the professional spirit of our curricula" in order to "reassert the university tradition" and "to reassert the general ethical and intellectual point of view against all the claims of specialism that would overwhelm it." He added:

> We must recognize that we are not merely training people for a profession or for the current demands of professional practice but for membership in the public and for a future that transcends both the limitations of contemporary practice and contemporary politics. Our client is more a re-vitalized public than it is consumers of the professions. . . . That is, we must be concerned with the limitations of journalism as a practice. (pp. 854-855)

Likewise, Birkhead (1985) wrote: "Journalism educators, in effect, are responsible for teaching the limitations of the craft." He added, "Many journalism departments operate in intellectual isolation, closer in spirit to the media they serve from a distance than to the university community in which they reside" (p. 35).

Blanchard and Christ (1985) stated that "[b]y the 21st Century, two major revolutions will have converged to profoundly affect higher education in journalism and mass communication (JMC)" (p. 28). They identified the two revolutions as the communication revolution and the reform movement in higher education. Blanchard and Christ stated that the two revolutions required media educators to reexamine their curricula and ask basic questions about their role in higher education, their relationship to liberal arts and sciences, and their relationship with fundamental and general education. They wrote:

> It is possible that JMC units could lose the campus political struggles that are sure to accompany reforms. JMC offerings could be perceived—if they are not already—as being too vocational or specialized and, as a result, not appropriate to the reform movement back to the "basics" of general and liberal arts and sciences education. (p. 28)

Newsom (1985) mentioned several reasons why media education has not been well accepted in academe as a legitimate area of study. She noted the tendency for the young discipline to borrow from the theories of other disciplines, the split between journalism/mass communication and speech communication, a failure for the discipline to establish a solid theoretical base and its inability "to replicate . . . , to codify and to originate." On top of the problem of lack of acceptance within academe, she noted "the failure of the mass communication components with ties in specific industries to establish themselves as professions." She said that a failure to remedy such problems "clouds the future of the entire field of journalism/mass communication" (p. 23).

Henningham (1986) wrote that one problem with media education's reputation in academe is that the best college students in other fields of study become scholars but that the best journalism students usually become journalists. He noted that the gap between the practical and theoretical approaches in journalism education seems further apart than in other disciplines and stated that the "common focus—mass media, and in particular news—seems too broad to be a unifying concept for academic theorizing and skills-training" (p. 8). Henningham also noted that the establishment of journalism schools has not been as advanced as the establishment of schools in other professions. The academic aspects of journalism are fairly recent developments, he wrote, and "are still regarded as irrelevant by many practitioners" (p. 9). He stated, however, "The tragedy for journalism educators in willingly identifying themselves as simply the teachers of practical skills to would-be journalists is that they become largely irrelevant to journalism the occupation" (p. 10).

In the Oregon Report, Everette Dennis concluded that the journalism/mass communication curriculum should "do more to help students make sense out of the rest of their education" what he called a "linchpin" function. He stated that media "faculty members need to know and understand quite specifically how the courses they teach fit into the student's larger general education" (Project, 1987, p. 50). Likewise, Dennis and DeFleur (1991) proposed the use of linchpin essays in the introductory mass communication course to help tie course content to other fields that they are studying in general education.

Ernest Boyer, then president of the Carnegie Foundation for the Advancement of Teaching, wrote about the issue of professional education within higher education in much the same terms as the Oregon Report (Project, 1984) and Dennis and DeFleur (1991). Boyer (1990) warned "against making too great a distinction between careerism and the liberal arts, between self-benefit and service." He added:

> The aim of education is not only to prepare students for productive careers, but also to enable them to live lives of dignity and purpose; not only to generate new knowledge, but to channel that knowledge to humane ends; not merely to study government, but to help shape a citizenry that can promote the public good. Thus higher education's vision must be widened if the nation is to be rescued from problems that threaten to diminish permanently the quality of life. (pp. 77–78)

Cooper (1993) called the academic discipline of communication a *corpus callosum*: a bridge between two hemispheres within the liberal arts. He saw the centrality of communication as a bridge on three levels: (a) the universal level because it is essential to all disciplines; (b) the academic level because it is a place where "many academic languages are spoken and translated"; and (c) the pragmatic level because all teaching and research depend on forms and technologies of communication (p. 85). He concluded that "[w]ithin the vast sea of subconscious storage, our understanding of communication at all levels becomes a priority and *a priori*" (p. 87).

Christ (1993) stated that the "first object, or star if you will" that can help position media education within the university and guide it into the future is a broader, redefined mission. He stated that "[o]ne of the 'traditional' stars that many in media education have followed instead is the personnel training needs of the mass media industries" (p. 2). The second traditional star is an "isolationist" mission. Such a mission, he said, moves media education in the wrong direction because "it suggests that liberal arts education comes exclusively from other departments, from other disciplines" and it "has led to inbreeding within sequences, majors, and divisions" rather than providing cross-disciplinary majors, minors, or electives (p. 2).

Blanchard and Christ (1993) called for building bridges within the academy by "reaching out to the nonmajor; seeing media courses as central to students' general education; building bridges among departments and disciplines; and providing extra- and cocurricular activities for the academy as a whole." They stated that such reaching out to nonmajors was good for media programs as well as majors. Blanchard and Christ noted that media programs involved in general education have developed both skills (writing) and studies (introduction to mass media) courses. They urged that "programs that feature writing in their major should move to integrate their writing courses into the general education program. Equally important—we would say more important—is the need for mass communication units to make media studies central in the academy." They also noted that "media educators should be providing media studies courses for the general student—in the social sciences and the humanities; in theory, economics, history, criticism, and effects—that integrate disciplines and methodologies" (p. 105).

The AEJMC Vision 2000 Task Force (AEJMC, 1994b) urged faculty and administrators "to undertake a vigorous, explicit, consistent campaign to demonstrate the value, mission, and accomplishments of journalism education and of journalism educators." It added:

> In particular we urge administrators to explain clearly the role of communication skills as well as of the understanding of mass communication institutions within the education of the undergraduate degree, that is, to demonstrate the integral role journalism and mass communication programs have within liberal education and to distinguish clearly the undergraduate and graduate programs. (p. 23)

The latter point also was made by Soloski (1994), who called for the need "to clarify the distinction between M.A. programs and undergraduate professional programs" (p. 7). Both share a mutual need, however. He stated, "At the heart of my argument is the need to better integrate our graduate programs into the academy and to better prepare our students for their chosen careers. Above all, we need to make our programs central to the educational mission of universities" (p. 4).

Mencher (1994b) stated the need for print and broadcast journalism education to achieve a place of honor within media education and within higher education in general through invigorating it and providing a renewed direction. He stated that journalism undergraduate training was being devalued at a time during which higher education was reaffirming the mission of service that arose after the Civil War and the demise of the classical college. He urged journalism education to return to its roots of service as set forth by Joseph Pulitzer and others through providing service to the public. Mencher stated, "The recognition of the essential role the journalist plays in making democracy work may yet save professional journalism education from its pallbearers" (p. 71).

Mencher (1994b) cited the work of Ernest L. Boyer and the Carnegie Foundation for the Advancement of Teaching's call for the "New American College, an institution that celebrates teaching and effectively supports research, while also taking pride in its capacity to connect thought to action, theory to practice" (p. 72). He added:

> While the critics of professional journalism training denigrate it as "vocational education," Boyer and others are charging the university with the task of preparing what Donald Schon of the Massachusetts Institute of Technology describes as the preparation of "reflective practitioners." These advocates of change within the university want it to be in the forefront of "service to the nation," as Boyer puts it. (p. 72)

To respond to society's need, he called for journalism schools to adopt higher admission standards, an emphasis on community-oriented instruction, and course-specific liberal arts requirements.

Carter (1995) asked rhetorically whether one reason media programs appear vulnerable to cuts in funding was because the "mass media have become too important not to be analyzed and criticized" (p. 4). He noted that an almost equal division existed between practitioners over whether a journalism degree or a liberal arts degree was better preparation for a media job, ". . . hardly the hallmark of a profession" (p. 5). He also suggested a new focus for media education, one not oriented toward the media professions. He set out a path for media education he hoped would help it move from field to discipline and, thus, earn it an improved academic status that was not based on professional education. He stated that such a path requires that media education become as much a behavioral science as a social science. He commented that a number of authors agree that to become an academic discipline, a field must have "methods that are responsive to the distinctive nature of its concerns." Thus, he asked:

> Is the study of mass communication not yet a discipline because this point has not been realized in an appropriate behavioral science? In what respect is mass communication behavioral, and how is it behaviorally distinctive? For it is most definitely behaviorally distinctive, and because of this distinctiveness we should take a much different view of where the study of mass communication belongs in higher education. (p. 6)

Carter noted that media education is not the only academic field needing new methods but that it probably needed them the most. He concluded, "For our contributions, we might reasonably expect a difference in academic status." He added that "[p]roperly understood as an essential contribution to collective behavior, mass communication should stand at the very center of elementary and higher education—especially of public education" (p. 10).

The AEJMC/ASJMC Task Force on Missions and Purposes of Journalism and Mass Communication Education was established for several reasons, among them difficulties of some media units to persuade their administrators of the centrality of media programs to the institution. The task force undertook a benchmark study in the mid-1990s to look at mission statements of journalism and mass communication schools and departments. The task force concluded that the study was the first "systematic compilation, analysis and publication of mission statements from a large selection of JMC programs" (AEJMC/ASJMC Task Force, 1996, p. 1). It surveyed 419 media programs and received responses from 248 (59%). It received 176 mission statements. The task force found areas common to a number of mission statements that had to do with the unit's centrality to the institution's mission. They included citizen and consumer preparation and skills, the relationship to the nonmajor or general student, and linkages to the community. The task force stated:

> JMC programs in this sample of mission and purpose statements tend to articulate their unique contributions to their universities in the specialized knowledge, values, skills and objectives of the program, the special publics or stakeholders they are concerned with, and/or a particular environment they are part of or are trying to create. (p. 6)

Wartella (1996) noted the role of communications programs—both speech communication and mass communication—in providing a service function to nonmajors as a means of furthering the mission of the university and, thus, helping those programs survive. She argued that "if we think of universities as institutions committed to preparing future citizens with the tools of citizenship, an appreciation of our cultural heritage and history, useful skills to be productive contributors to our economic and material life, and critical thinkers to help solve the social and human problems facing our society and indeed the world, then the study of communication should be central to any university curriculum" (p. 150). However, she noted that a number of such programs are consolidating or being closed down.

Wartella (1996) suggested three reasons that communications-based programs might not be seen as central to the university's mission. First, the name *communication* is ambiguous and the term *journalism* is exclusionary, making the broader field look incoherent.   Second, communications-based programs are located in a variety of different places on campus with in-fighting between professionally oriented programs and speech or communication studies, and their faculty members often are isolated from those in other academic departments. Her third point was that "our curriculum and our literature is not addressing the public questions about communication practice in the world." She concluded:

> In short, the question of whether or not communication study is central to the mission of a university masks other questions about the fractured nature of our field, our naive role in campus politics and our inattention to [a] wider teaching mission within the university. It is attention to these other issues which should occupy our disciplinary leaders. (p. 152)

Fedler, A. Carey, and Counts (1997) were interested in finding out what faculty members in other disciplines thought of the importance of media-related education. They surveyed a random sample of 225 nonmedia faculty members to determine which of 37 academic programs they would likely eliminate if they were institution administrators and had to cut programs. Ranking sixth was advertising/public relations, candidate for elimination by 32% of respondents. Broadcasting ranked seventh with 26% of respondents proposing elimination, speech ranked 19th with 5% proposing elimination, and journalism ranked 24th with 3% proposing elimination. The authors noted that a number of respondents proposed that the communication fields be merged into a single school.

Fedler, A. Carey, and Counts (1998) concluded that the situation of the communication fields was not unique, however. Instead, they stated, "their problems reflect widespread changes within academia: changes that affect most departments" (p. 38). They listed eight strategies that media programs might adopt to improve their position at their institution: (a) making themselves more central to the mission of their institution; (b) serving larger numbers of students;

(c) recruiting more talented students; (d) doing more to help their students find jobs; (e) improving their record of scholarly activity; (f) developing unique programs; (g) emphasizing intellectual rather than vocational training; and (h) seeking accreditation.

THE DEBATE OVER THE IMPORTANCE
OF ACADEMIC RESEARCH

In order to be seen as academic by their colleagues within academe, or because they see the merit of research, most media-related programs require faculty to undertake academic research in order to be promoted or tenured. Medsger (1996) concluded that the "requirement for tenure-track and tenured educators to engage in research is an issue that has been confusing—and defeating—to many journalism educators" and "is at the heart of why the place of the experienced journalist in journalism education has diminished over the last few decades" (p. 45). Medsger (1996) stated that the research requirement was the result of the emergence of communication studies. She wrote:

> As communication studies professors took over journalism education after the middle of this century, in-depth journalistic research—the type in which most master journalists have expertise—was no longer recognized by many schools as acceptable. These professors had used their scholarly research about communications as a way of taking over journalism education. . . . and convincing university administrators that journalists were not serious academics.
>
> On top of that some journalism educators who had been journalists were stubbornly resistant, for various reasons, about doing research. (p. 45)

A similar point had been made years earlier by George Kienzle, then director of the journalism program at Ohio State University. He sounded the alarm against the "trend away from professional instruction in journalism" in a 1963 speech at the Associated Press Managing Editors convention in Miami. In the speech, in which he charged that " 'communicology' papers have dominated" at AEJ conventions (Highton, 1967, p. 10), Kienzle stated:

> Some schools of journalism—big ones—admit they are not primarily interested in preparing students for careers in the journalistic media. They stress something they call 'research.' It isn't research designed to help the profession examine its problems. It is sociological and psychological study referred to by Jacques Barzun (of Columbia) . . . as 'teasing the obvious and trivial' in the name of research. (Highton, 1967, p. 11)

Instead of hypothesis-based research, Kienzle called for critical analysis, which "ultimately is fact-finding, like a reporter going anywhere and everywhere with no preconceived notions" (Highton, 1967, p. 12). Ironically, Kienzle's call for research to help the profession echoes one made by communication theorist

Wilbur Schramm, who wrote in an article published the same year, "The basic task of journalism research is that of all research: to contribute to the knowledge which is the common property of men everywhere. But journalism research . . . has at least one obligation of a restrictive and special nature: to serve the profession's needs for research knowledge" (Schramm, 1963, p. 25).

Highton (1967) called the research articles presented at the 1966 Association for Education in Journalism convention "masterpieces of murky prose" (p. 10). He quoted Curtis MacDougall of Northwestern University as stating that journalism schools "have gone in for quantitative analysis and theorizing regarding the communications process which produce statistical tables and philosophical gobbledygook which few understand" (p. 12).

The importance of research has continued to be an issue in recent years. In 1985, the American Society of Newspaper Editors' Committee on News–Editorial Education (CONEE) issued what was called the "CONEE Statement." It urged that schools of journalism and mass communication allow "analyses and critical review of professional subjects," "professional achievement of an original nature," or "meritorious work of a demanding nature in professional positions with the media" as acceptable professional contributions toward promotion and tenure (Brock, 1993).

Henningham (1986) noted that, in other disciplines, what is taught is a "subset of what is researched and theorized." In journalism, however, much of the curriculum is based on the practices of media professionals—"who may have mastered their skills without academic assistance." He noted that for journalism educators, "scholarship is to some extent a byproduct, an activity to justify their status as academics. As a paradigm, therefore, journalism is in an ambiguous role" (p. 8).

Lovell (1987) argued that the main reason for a journalism educator to have a doctorate is to undertake research, but that the research often is irrelevant. He charged that "many of the best schools of journalism throw greater human resources into research than into teaching." He argued that research in journalism is different from that in other fields, stating, "In other professional schools, even the most pristine of 'pure' research may eventually lead to insights and techniques that may, in turn, help practitioners in those fields do their jobs better. However, such claims cannot be easily made about academic research in journalism" (p. 22). He concluded that the "communicologists" had triumphed. He wrote, "The battle has been fought quietly for more than 20 years and the Chi-squares appear to be winning, largely because of the peculiarities of higher education where publish or perish is still a way of life" (p. 23).

Despite achieving some degree of academic legitimacy, academic research by media educators continued to come under attack. For example, Weinberg (1990) gave a critique of the 1990 AEJMC convention reminiscent of Highton's critique of the 1966 AEJ convention. Weinberg concluded that journalism professionals would not read much of the research presented at the convention because "[m]any of the papers discussed obscure or thumbsucking topics, were poorly organized, boringly written, and filled with grammatical, spelling, and factual errors." He noted that some experienced journalists earn doctorates. However, he stated, "Overall, though, the trend toward journalism faculties dominated by research-oriented Ph.D.s is depressing to professionals in newsrooms" (p. 27). Likewise, Corrigan (1993) stated about the 1993 AEJMC convention: "To an alarming extent, (academia) has strayed from its primary mission of training students to perform well in entry-level positions." He added:

> To an alarming extent, professors either have succumbed to working out personal agendas in their research or to conducting research that has a semblance of sophistication but that has little real-world value.
> . . . [W]hat is alarming is that none of the professors' scholarly research papers directly addressed the classroom crisis of kids now in journalism school who can't spell or write much less cover a story. (p. 34)

STUDIES ABOUT RESEARCH
BY MASS MEDIA FACULTY

The ongoing debate over the importance of research caused Haskins (1970) to survey 253 newspaper publishers to determine what types of research they thought were most needed. Publishers' greatest needs concerned mechanical, production, and technology issues and personnel matters, both listed by 70% of respondents. That was followed by newspaper image (53%), journalism education (52%), reader research (48%), and editing, content, and selection (42%).

The debate caused by Highton's 1967 article criticizing academic research also led Sanders (1972) to survey newspaper editors to determine what they thought about such research. He sent surveys to editors of 135 newspapers of all sizes in a national study to find out their attitudes about research and received responses from 105 editors. Out of the 51 usable surveys from those he received, only one editor indicated an obvious negative attitude about journalism research. Sanders concluded that the sample was not representative because editors who did not have a positive opinion about academic research about newspapers likely did not respond. He concluded that a "communication gap" existed between researchers and editors over academic research for four reasons. Editors stated that (a) the research writing style was "full of jargon and difficult to understand"; (b) researchers "fail to explain adequately the importance and possible applications of their research"; (c) "most of the potentially useful research isn't getting to them"; and (d) they want researchers to consult "more closely with newsmen in selecting research problems and in mapping research designs" (p. 529).

G. Stone and Norton (1980) surveyed 22 participants at the Journalism Education Administrator workshop in 1979 to determine how they defined *faculty research*. All administrators disagreed with the statement that "It is impossible to do research without a Ph.D. in mass communication," and all but one disagreed with the statement that "It is impossible to do research in only an undergraduate program." Nearly 60% disagreed with the statement that "There are 'teaching' faculty and 'research' faculty, and they should be evaluated separately." The same percent disagreed with the statement that "Writing a column for the local paper should be considered equivalent to producing one refereed publication each semester." The authors concluded that "journalism program administrators believe their faculty members can and should do 'research,' but these administrators define research as something other than merely the number of refereed journalism articles professors hang on their belts" (p. 40).

Despite the assumption that research is valued and necessary for promotion, Fedler and Counts (1982) concluded that journalism media educators weren't too productive. They found that 22% of media faculty had not published even one article in the previous 5 years, and 54% had not published in a national refereed publication. Fedler and R.F. Smith (1985) surveyed all 147 members of the American Society of Journalism School Administrators to find out what types of research they considered most valuable. They received responses from 94 (64%). The researchers found that all administrators responding agreed that 6 activities of the 33 activities listed were legitimate scholarly research: writing a scholarly book, presenting a paper at a refereed national convention, coauthoring an article for a refereed national journal, writing an article for a refereed regional journal, writing an article for a journalism magazine such as *The Quill*, and presenting a paper at a state or regional convention. All but 14 administrators said grant applications were research. The researchers concluded that administrators favored traditional research, such as refereed national journals, rather than nonrefereed local publications and favored journals over convention papers. They found that several administrators were attempting to change their institution's definition of research to allow credit for professional journalism activities.

D. Weaver and Wilhoit (1988) found that research and publication activity of media educators "appears to match that of the [teaching] profession at large" (p. 28). They found that 26% of media educators had never published an article, compared to 22.3% of all faculty at 4-year institutions in 1985. Also, 49.4% of media faculty had never written or edited a book, compared to 54.8% of all U.S. faculty. One quarter of media faculty responding had published more than 10 articles, compared to about one fifth of faculty overall in 1975. About 16% had published three or more books, similar to the figure for all U.S. faculty. More than one third reported publishing no articles during the previous 2 years, with the median response being two articles. That was somewhat higher than in other professional fields. Half of education and business faculty and 70% of applied professional faculty reported in 1975 that they had not published anything in the previous 2 years. Media faculty were slightly more likely than faculty overall to prefer teaching to research (65.9% vs. 63.0%). As Cole and Bowers (1975) had determined earlier, Weaver and Wilhoit concluded that graduate training was associated with higher publishing productivity. They added:

> Faculty with doctorates report a research grant and publication record that is more than double that of their colleagues who do not have doctoral degrees. That should *not* be interpreted as suggesting that non-Ph.D.s are less valuable faculty members. These faculty enrich journalism education in other ways. (p. 29)

Lancaster, Katz, and Cho (1990) found that advertising educators who belonged to the American Academy of Advertising spend an average of 23% of their time doing research versus 48% teaching, 10% each to administration and service, 7% to consulting, and 2% to other activities. They found that the average respondent had published 39 articles on advertising in his or her career. Dickson and Sellmeyer (1992a) asked administrators of media units about the importance of research in their unit. A minority of administrators (41%) stated that more emphasis on research was a high or very high priority. Administrators with a news–editorial background were least likely to favor research. Whereas 31% of those administrators thought emphasis on research was a priority, 41% of administrators with a broadcast or public relations background and 65% of administrators with some other media specialty favored emphasizing research.

The joint Association for Education in Journalism and Mass Communication and Newspaper Association of America Foundation Cooperative Committee on News-Editorial Education (CONEE) undertook research in 1992 to determine how well its so-called 1985 "CONEE Statement" concerning the use of practical research for promotion and tenure had been implemented. The committee sent questionnaires to media units at nearly 300 institutions in the fall of 1992, both to remind administrators of the CONEE Statement and to determine whether its suggestions were being implemented. Brock (1993) noted that despite the fact that most schools reported that professional writing was given equal weight with scholarly writing, the committee concluded from written comments and telephone interviews that traditional scholarship in practice was weighted more heavily. At only one of the 72 schools responding (South Dakota State University) was professional writing rated higher that academic research. Some schools reported that faculty could follow two tenure tracks: either Research and Teaching or Professional Experience and Teaching. The rank of professor, however, often was reserved for those in the research track. Brock stated that cooperative ventures between academe and practitioners would be advanced if faculty were rewarded for "contributing to the editorial pages, participating in job exchanges, critically reviewing media performance, developing new technology uses and policies, or otherwise enhancing practitioners' performance and knowledge" (p. 51).

Medsger (1996) found that print and broadcast journalism educators were most likely to favor requiring in-depth journalistic research and writing as a way of meeting research and writing requirements. Just over three quarters (77%) of her respondents agreed with that option, with 41% agreeing strongly. A strong majority (64%) also agreed with requiring either traditional academic or in-depth journalistic research and writing, with 39% strongly supporting that option. Almost half (48%) favored requiring traditional academic research and writing, with 21% strongly supporting that option. When asked to state what type of research should be used for hiring, tenure and promotion decisions, 79% of her respondents agreed that either traditional academic research or in-depth journalistic research and writing should be used, with 54% agreeing strongly. She found very little difference between respondents based upon numbers of years taught, amount of media experience, or whether they had a Ph.D. She concluded that "faculty members expressed opinions that do not match current policy and practice trends" (p. 47).

Fedler, Counts, A. Carey, and Santana (1998) looked at the charge that every faculty member is required to conduct research and determined that "[t]he evidence, however, suggests, otherwise" (p. 9). They surveyed 598 members of the AEJMC and received responses from 279. They concluded that faculty members who taught reporting/editing courses conducted less research than other media faculty members but "were among JMC's most experienced and successful" (p. 12). Faculty members who taught reporting and editing were most likely to do no research. Whereas 18.4% of reporting/editing faculty members reported doing no research, the average for all media faculty was 5.4%. The only other specialties in which more than 7% of faculty members did no research were media law (11.9%) and ethics (10.5%).

Fedler, Counts, A. Carey, and Santana (1998) found that 43.7% of faculty members teaching reporting and editing had not presented a paper at a convention in the previous 5 years. The specialty with the next highest percent of faculty with no presentations was law (34.9%), followed by ethics (31.6%), history (28.6%), and radio/television (27.7%). News/editorial faculty were also most likely to have published no refereed journal articles during the previous 5 years, with 41.7% reporting no articles. They were followed by law (37.2%), radio/television (34.0%), and history (32.7%). Faculty members teaching theory and methodology had the most publications, with 40.1% reporting four or more articles within the previous 5 years. They were followed by faculty teaching mass communication and society (35.0%), media law (34.9%), and media history (32.7%). Faculty with the highest number of papers (11 or more papers during the previous 5 years) taught theory/methodology and advertising/public relations, both with slightly over 22% of faculty.

Fedler, Santana, Counts, and A. Carey (1997) also looked at the value of research for faculty members. Only 5.4% of the respondents stated they did no research. They were most likely to state they did research to become a better teacher, an answer given by 70% of respondents. Two thirds of respondents (66%) stated that they did research because they enjoyed it, slightly more than those reporting they did it because it helps in obtaining tenure and promotion (65%) or because it is of value to students and other faculty members (64%).

Just over half (53%) reported they did research because it was a job requirement, and 53% also reported they did it because it is of value to professionals working in the field. Faculty members with a doctorate were more likely to enjoy research and to believe that it resulted in their being better teachers. Faculty members in academic units offering a doctorate tended to be more productive than other faculty. The authors concluded that many faculty members apparently were able to undertake other activities rather than do research, that most faculty (two thirds) enjoyed research, and that nearly all found it valuable—all but four respondents saying they used others' research. They stated, "Although they may not use it themselves, even academia's most vehement critics can no longer claim that faculty research is of little or no value" (p. 19).

As media educators struggled with the academic–practical nature of the field and how to achieve a central place within their academic units, media education was almost constantly under attack by media practitioners, who questioned the value of media-related education and the hiring of faculty with doctorates and with little professional experience. The practitioners, educators charged, either did not understand the role of media-related education or misperceived what educators were doing not only to expand the depth and breadth of the education being provided to their majors but also, in most cases, to prepare them for jobs within the media-related industries.

6

The Debate Between Media Educators and Practitioners: A Dialogue of the Deaf

If there is a dialogue about the purposes and prospects of journalism education, it is a dialogue of the deaf. The same issues and problems have been inventoried and debated for years, yielding little agreement and much confusion. Industry leaders denounce and denigrate journalism schools at one moment—and eagerly hire their graduates the next.

—Dennis (1988, p. 4)

Professional journalists have been skeptical of the value of college programs in journalism since the first one was established briefly at Washington College following the Civil War. None of the 27 leading journalists profiled by Wingate (1875) supported the idea of academic training in journalism, and a decade later newspaper professionals were saying that the idea of journalism education had "always been a dire and utter failure" ("The Amateur School," 1888, p. 8). More than four decades after the founding of the first school of journalism in 1908, it was apparent that a number of journalists still did not value journalism education much. A 1951 survey of past participants in Harvard University's Nieman Fellowship program for professional journalists found many of them had strong reservations about the value of academic training for journalism (Serafini, 1984). Throughout the rest of the century, media-related education was to come under attack from media professionals.

Dennis (1987a) cited three major complaints against mass media education. One is that the pure liberal arts education without journalism courses is far superior to the journalism–liberal arts balance advocated by the journalism schools. Another says journalism schools teach too much theory and not enough practice. Still another says journalism schools are too vocational (p. 85). He also noted that almost 85% of new hires at U.S. newspapers were journalism school graduates, but that "many leading editors openly scorn journalism education" (p. 85). Cowdin (1985) cited two reasons practitioners give as to why they are dissatisfied with journalism graduates: "They can't write, and they don't know enough about fields that they are going to be writing about . . ." (p. 18). He stated:

> Concerning the first, the complaint is that not enough time is spent on instruction in writing, mainly because journalism faculties are loaded up with "communicologists" who have Ph.D.s but lack professional experience and who would therefore prefer to teach "theory." Concerning the second, the complaint is that too much time is spent teaching writing (which, they say, probably can't be "taught" anyway) and other techniques that the student would be better off spending

97

that time learning about economics, science, business, international relations, and so forth. Journalism educators would be much obliged—perhaps even grateful—if the critics would get together and reconcile these contradictory positions. (p. 19).

Mabrey (1988b) noted the two criticisms mentioned by Cowdin and added several more: that editors think journalism school graduates "do not or will not read, . . . do not have an urgent sense of accuracy, including spelling and grammar, . . . do not know how to ask questions, or, at least, the right questions, and . . . do not have a love of news" (p. 41). He added, "There is no argument that journalism educators, by and large, and editors, by and large, want the same thing: young reporters and editors who read, inquire, write, spell, and have an inner sense of cause. The problem here may be in the rhetoric. And it may be the editors with strong voices and journalism educators with inferiority complexes" (p. 42).

Bagdikian (1990) found three problems with journalism schools. The one that he found to be the most serious was an "increasing fuzziness in the lines that separate sequences in journalism from those in public relations, advertising and mass communications theory" (p. 32). The second was "irrationality in faculty appointments": the "silly" requirement that faculty have a Ph.D. rather than professional experience. The other problem was not a problem with journalism schools as much as it was a problem with publishers: the low salaries paid by newspapers, which make it difficult to get people into journalism.

Dennis (1990) wrote that "[f]or disgruntled professionals there are two major complaints: they do not like what is taught in the communication schools, and they do not much like or trust those who teach it" (p. 9). Fedler (1993) listed the following eight major demands of media professionals: (a) faculty members with more professional experience; (b) a greater emphasis on good teaching; (c) a greater emphasis on the practical skills needed to prepare students for work in the newspaper industry; (d) a greater emphasis on the liberal arts; (e) more rigor; (f) less emphasis on communication theory courses; (g) less emphasis on techniques that can be learned on the job; (h) less emphasis on Ph.D.s and research as requirements for the J-School faculty members.

Dennis (1987b) noted that educators felt that a number of media practitioners "have trouble understanding that journalism educators are just that—educators" (p. 86). He stated that even if they have practical media experience, practitioners are no longer reporters or editors when they enter the classroom. Dennis noted that educators charge that "many leading editors simply won't listen to them and attempt to understand what the modern journalism school is all about." In response to the charge that "journalism graduates can't spell, punctuate or write," he noted that journalism educators spent considerable time in "literacy training" and that outside evaluators such as law school admissions committees applaud journalism schools for that training (p. 86).

Both Lovell (1987) and Dennis (1988) called the debate between media educators and media professionals over the content of and need for media education "the dialogue of the deaf." Dennis noted that the same issues and problems have been discussed for years but that the debate has yielded "little agreement and much confusion" (p. 4). Dennis (1994) stated that "the same tired debates continue decade after decade. These range from whether communication and journalism schools should exist at all to the relative balance between theory and practice. The debate is deeply class-conscious and apparently unending" (p. 8).

BRIDGING THE GAP BETWEEN MEDIA EDUCATORS AND PRACTITIONERS

The National Center for Business and Economic Communication of American University stated in 1984 that "in the largest sense, the education of journalists after 75 years has been a dismal failure" and that "journalism schools are sneered at as mere trade schools" (Cowdin, 1985, p. 16). Also in 1984, the Project on the Future of Journalism and Mass Communication Education (Project, 1984) concluded that "the general state of journalism and mass communication education is dismal" (Project, 1987, p, i). In addition to those attacks, in an article in *The Quill*, the publication of the Society of Professional Journalists/Sigma Delta Chi, Anthony Serafini asked, "Does, in fact or theory, the very concept of a 'school' of journalism make any sense?" (p. 24). He answered his question by stating, "There is no need for journalism education in its present form" (p. 28). Those statements came just 1 year after Dennis (1987b) stated that he had noted signs of a thaw coming in the "longstanding love–hate relationship between journalism educator and journalistic professionals" (p. 86).

Despite the attacks on journalism education, Copple (1985) stated that "the communication age is pushing the practicing professionals and journalism educators closer and closer together." He added, however, "Can we stand the proximity? Or are we going to rush out for more academic deodorants?" (p. 20). Lovell (1987) suggested some common ground from which to commence dialogue. He wrote that although "more relevant journalistic research and a greater commitment to professors with experience" wouldn't stop the decades of bickering between journalism educators and media professionals, "it could serve as a start and perhaps, in time, put an end to the present dialogue of the deaf that serves no one" (p. 24). David Weaver, then president of the Association for Education in Journalism and Mass Communication (AEJMC), noted that only 40% of media faculty keep contacts with media professionals. He stated, moreover, that "it is terribly important to keep some conversation going between the university and the professional world of mass communication, even if it results in only disagreement" (Lindley, 1988, p. 18).

Signs, however, were suggesting that the gap was still wide. The *Electronic Media Career Preparation Study* (Roper Organization, 1987) concluded that broadcast education fell "far short in providing practical knowledge for the real world" (p. 5). In response to the report, McCall (1990) stated, "Many academics have a sense that the criticisms lodged in the report simply demonstrate broadcast industry misconceptions of what a college education should philosophically (and reasonably) be expected to accomplish" (p. 9). He stated that a "purely skill-driven approach to media education diminishes the utility of the student both for the non-media, and eventually media-related careers" (p. 9) and that the "industry should also grow to recognize that the academic setting is a place to engage in criticism and research, and not simply train entry-level employees" (p. 10).

Mabrey (1988b) noted that a survey of 1900 journalism faculty by the Associated Press Managing Editors Association that year found that around half of the educators felt there was "antipathy or estrangement between themselves and the working press" (p. 42). Hartman (1990) wrote, "Many editors are mad at journalism units, be they colleges, schools, departments or sequences" (p. 5). He stated that editors, "unhappy with an 'alleged drift' " toward communication education, had set up a quasi-accrediting body. Van Ommeren (1991) reported that the March 1990 Texas Associated Press Managing Editors Convention in El Paso featured attacks on journalism education. The major focus of the attack was the hiring of faculty with doctorates, who they thought tended to give research and publication a priority over teaching.

Dennis, Romm, and Ottaway (1990) suggested that the gap between journalism educators and the media professions could be narrowed by collaborative efforts built around press criticism. They stated, "Perhaps out of such mutual cooperation would emerge mutual respect between people who often have been suspicious and distrustful of each other, but who should be exchanging useful ideas and information" (p. 4). Likewise, Finney (1990) called for critical study of the media to be built into the curriculum. Weinberg (1990) concluded that some educators did want to narrow the gap between academe and the newsroom, but he noted that "many newsroom professionals are far less optimistic than I, seeing not a glimmer of hope in the evidence I have presented. For the sake of journalism's future, I hope they are mistaken" (p. 28).

Concern over journalism education led the American Society of Newspaper Editors in late 1989 to undertake a national study. In the introduction to the report about the study (ASNE, 1990), Robert Giles, editor and publisher of the Detroit News, stated: "Looking at journalism education through the eyes of editors . . . one finds signs of dissatisfaction that should be troubling to both ASNE and the educators" (p. 1). The study found that only 4% of editors gave journalism schools an A for the quality of training received by their new hires, and half of the editors stated that they didn't care if their new hires had a journalism degree or a degree in the liberal arts, and editors rated journalism school graduates lowest in the skills they thought were most important: reporting, spelling and grammar, and journalism ethics. Giles wrote: "Of most immediate concern to ASNE is the decline in the proportion of news–editorial majors in journalism/mass communication programs and the rising bias against tenuring experienced journalists who do not have doctorates" (p. 2).

Wyatt (1991) noted that the ASNE report was the subject of heated discussion at the 1991 meeting of the Colorado Press Association. Mazingo (1991) stated that a press seminar with executive and managing editors that she attended had "an atmosphere charged with more vitriol toward journalism schools as any I have seen" (p. 48). She wrote that

> a blanket indictment of all journalism faculty as "incompetents" is an unthinking, arrogant, and inaccurate statement that insults thousands of knowledgeable, highly qualified journalism   educators. It is obvious that some editors and other newspeople subscribe to the motto that "those who can, do; those who can't, teach." (p. 40)

Jim Willis of Ball State University stated that academicians and professionals do not admit that they need each other. He wrote that close ties that exist in other professions are not found between journalism educators and media professionals. "Instead," he wrote, "working journalists are fond of declaring that media researchers are out of touch with reality, while researchers accuse the working media of striking the classic ostrich pose—head in the sand—and refusing to advance with the times." Willis concluded, "The situation is unlikely to improve unless universitywide and journalism school administrators understand what their academic mindsets are doing to the craft" (Weinberg, 1990, p. 28).

The publisher of *Electronic Media* continued the attack on journalism schools, calling on journalism schools to "close the reality gap that separates journalism schools from journalism itself." He suggested that journalism schools might fall victim to "academic Darwinism" if they don't "make themselves more relevant." At the root of the problem, he wrote, is faculty without significant practical media experience, and he laid the blame on college administrators who require that faculty have at least a master's degree, preferably a doctorate. "It doesn't take Woodward and Bernstein to figure out that something has gone awry in academia," he wrote. "Where there's smoke there's often an old geezer who went to sleep holding his cigar" (Alridge, 1992, p, 30).

Rayfield (1992) wrote that loss of relevance to the industry is a "ticket to oblivion." He noted that most of the Association for Education in Journalism and Mass Communication's activities would not take place if it were not for financial support from publishers. Moreover, he said that if what is taught in journalism schools goes "far enough out in left field, what we teach will no longer be relevant to journalism and mass communication careers, which would take away our *raison d'etre*" (p. 5). Likewise, Tonda Rush, chief executive officer of the National Newspaper Association, charged at the 1993 convention of the AEJMC that journalism educators were ignoring industry needs and that journalism schools were "soaking up tremendous resources and intelligent people's time writing things that the industry doesn't need" (Corrigan, 1993, p. 44).

Journalists continued their attack on journalism schools throughout the 1990s. For example, in a report on classes he attended at the Columbia University School of Journalism, the school established with Joseph Pulitzer's bequest, Lewis (1993) reported that "the desperate futility of journalism instruction becomes clearer the closer one gets to the deed" (p. 23). He stated that "[t]hose who run, and attend, schools of journalism simply cannot—or don't want to—believe that journalism is as simple as it is" (p. 23). Lewis added: "Journalism schools are not alone in their attempts to dignify a trade by tacking onto it the idea of professionalism and laying over it a body of dubious theory. After all, McDonald's Hamburger U. now trains Beverage Technicians" (p. 27).

Although some media educators were concerned that the gap between them and media professionals was widening, the AEJMC Vision 2000 Task Force in 1994 concluded that "the separation of journalism and mass communication units from their industrial moorings" was becoming "increasingly defensible" (AEJMC, 1994b, p. 21). It said such a position was defensible because:

1. More students explicitly express an interest in learning about journalism and mass communication in the context of liberal education, rather than wanting job-focussed training in journalism and mass communication.
2. Fewer students find jobs in the traditional mass media, regardless of their original career expectations and aspirations.
3. The nature of the so-called traditional jobs changes in the direction of a "new professionalism." (pp. 22–23)

The Task Force concluded that media education was preparing students only for entry level professional jobs and that the emphasis on skills courses was keeping media-related programs from developing academically.

Journalists tended to agree that journalism schools were not needed to teach the craft of journalism. In an attack on the Columbia School Journalism, for example, Whitelaw (1996), reported a comment by the media critic for the *Washington Post* and a graduate of the school, Howard Kurtz, who said only that "It can't hurt" when comparing a master's degree in journalism and eating chicken soup for a cold. Whitelaw added, "But given the cost, it is a much more expensive remedy than the kind Grandma used to make" (Whitelaw, 1996, p. 100).

In another attack on media education, Ledbetter (1997) reported that "American journalism schools are in the midst of a years-long crisis, struggling to define their very purpose" and that "journalism educators are foundering, brooding, unsure of how, and what, they should teach or whether they should even exist" (p. 74). Ledbetter noted that the study of journalism had been eclipsed by the study of advertising and public relations. He wrote: "Once, journalism classes taught students how to investigate misconduct within American corporations; currently, a journalism school is just as likely to be taking money from corporations and offering up its students to help conduct market research" (p. 74). Discussing the broadening of journalism education, he wrote:

It is little more than a historical accident that beginning after World War II, many universities teamed their journalism schools or departments with the upstart "communication studies," programs that use social-science tools to analyze the practice of mass communications. That accident multiplied as dozens of schools added instruction in marketing and public relations, in the 1960s and '70s; now those fields are primed to take over the entire discipline.

    Sober-minded journalism teachers find themselves asking whether their positions have any purpose at all, whether it makes any more sense to train people to write stories for newspaper jobs that don't exist then it does to teach them how to run a pony express or send Morse code. (Ledbetter, 1997, pp. 74, 76)

The debate over whether journalism schools were necessary for the training of entry-level journalists was eclipsed by an actual threat to that mission when Thomson Newspapers stated in early 1999 that it would begin to train its own journalists. Thomson announced plans to establish a training center in Oshkosh, Wisconsin, to provide 12 weeks of training in the basics of journalism to people interested in becoming entry level reporters for its small dailies (Romell, 1999). The Connecticut-based chain announced that the training center would be located in the building that houses the *Oshkosh Northwestern.* Though most recruits were expected to be college graduates, some were expected not to have a college education. The training would include actual reporting for the *Northwestern* and seven other Wisconsin newspapers owned by Thomson. The company planned to recruit people who had ties to their community and who would stay at a small newspaper rather than use it as a stepping stone for a better-paying job at a larger newspaper.

    The proposal was based on the British practice of training high school graduates for six months in shorthand and the basics of governmental operations before sending them to work as reporters. Trainees at the Oshkosh center would be paid minimum wage plus travel money and housing assistance. The center, which would train 20 recruits at a time, was expected to open in August 1999. Stuart Garner, president and chief executive officer of Thomson Newspapers, stated that the center would ensure that "new journalists bring a passion for readers to their work, unencumbered by lofty preconceptions of what journalism is all about" (Romell, 1999).

RESEARCHING THE GAP BETWEEN
MEDIA EDUCATORS AND PRACTITIONERS

Several studies have investigated differences in how educators and media professionals perceive journalism education. Jones (1970) surveyed editors at 104 daily newspapers in Pennsylvania and educators at seven institutions offering journalism or communications degrees. He concluded that editors and educators agreed closely as to what a good daily newspaper employee's competencies should be. Ryan (1978) looked at the gap between professionals and editors on the issue of press criticism. He surveyed deans of 66 journalism schools with at least one accredited sequence, 66 faculty members, and 61 newspaper editors. He found that the three groups were in substantial agreement about the role and responsibilities of journalism schools regarding press criticism; however, some differences were statistically significant.

Mills, Harvey, and Warnick (1980) surveyed editors at 666 daily and weekly newspapers and received responses from 277. The editors urged that the number of journalism hours be increased, that educators put more emphasis on grammar and spelling, that internships be required, and that journalism training be broadened. The authors concluded that the editors were "disgusted" at journalism school graduates' lack of grammar, punctuation and spelling skills. They urged journalism school directors "to appraise their own programs and, where necessary, work toward providing students with training more in line with professional expectations" (p. 19).

Gaddis (1981) looked at differences between journalism educators and editors over journalism education. He surveyed 327 editors of daily newspapers with less than 100,000 circulation and heads of the 63 accredited news–editorial (print journalism) sequences. A total of 127 editors and 32 educators responded. He found that journalism educators were more likely than editors to state that the skills of new graduates were adequate for a beginning reporter. However, he found a number of areas in which editors and educators were in agreement. Responses of educators and editors differed significantly on slightly less than half (46%) of the items relating to his two hypotheses.

Nearly all respondents (88%) in the Electronic Media Career Preparation Study (Roper Organization, 1987) stated the need for closer ties between the electronic communications industry and educators. "More professionals lecturing/teaching" was listed most often (by 40%) as the best way to improve the industry's relationship with academia. "Courses taught by people who work or have worked in the broadcasting and cable industries" was rated as the area most deserving of "more emphasis" by higher education by 91% of respondents. It was followed closely by "lectures and other instructional participation by people who work in the broadcasting and cable industries" (87%). The area where higher education was rated lowest was "practical knowledge," listed by about one third of respondents. It was followed by "hands-on experience," listed by just over one fifth of respondents. They were most likely to give higher education a C, with 45% giving that grade as compared with 2% giving an A.

Crawford and Sabine (1958), Richard (1979), and J. S. Wright (1980) concluded that a gap existed between advertising and marketing education and advertising practitioners. The Advertising Task Force of the Task Force on the Future of Journalism and Mass Communication Education (Task Force, 1989) surveyed the presidents and education chairpersons of 420 local professional advertising associations affiliated with the American Advertising Federation as well at the entire membership of the Advertising Division of the AEJMC to investigate the gap. It received 407 usable responses from AAF members and 116 from AEJMC members and achieved an overall response rate of 80%. The survey found considerable agreement between advertising practitioners and advertising educators on the advertising curriculum. Educators and practitioners were in substantial agreement about the importance of particular coursework. Both groups rated advertising, marketing, and English composition as the most important areas of study for advertising majors, followed by psychology, journalism writing, and economics. Computer science and literature were in the middle of both lists. However, professors rated sociology slightly higher than did practitioners (7th vs. 10th). Also, practitioners listed management higher (5th vs. 10th).

Practitioners and professors also agreed on most statements concerning the value of advertising education. They agreed about the importance of a broad education for graduates, that graduates of accredited programs were preferable to those from unaccredited programs and were better prepared, and that a master's degree in advertising was not becoming more important in gaining an entry level position. Professors were somewhat more likely to agree with the statement that "Most programs I am aware of seem alert to the implications of changes in the structure and function of the advertising industry." The task force concluded: "This survey showed considerably more agreement between the academic community and the advertising community about the importance of various components of an advertising program than some observers might believe" (Task Force, 1989, p. A-12).

Lancaster, Katz, and Cho (1990) also examined the perceived gap between advertising educators and practitioners. They sent surveys to the 692 members of the American Academy of Advertising (AAA) and obtained responses from 349, 282 of whom taught a college course in advertising. They concluded that "[a]s a group, advertising educators do appear to be attempting to bridge perceived gaps between advertising education and the industry" (p. 20) and that the gap wasn't as wide as expected. For example, they found that more than half of the respondents did consulting work regularly and had been consulting for more than 5 years. They determined, however, that the results might not be representative of all advertising educators because the AAA membership list was used.

The American Society of Newspaper Editors Committee on Education for Journalism (ASNE, 1990) surveyed 600 editors—200 each from newspapers over 100,000, between 25,000 and 100,000, and under 25,000—concerning journalism education and received responses from 381. They rated "more media professionals on the faculty," "more emphasis on the nuts and bolts of journalism," and "more visiting professionals" as the three things that would most help journalism schools. The lowest-rated factor was "more emphasis on research." Two thirds of editors rated journalism school graduates either as strong (4%) or somewhat strong (62%) overall. Just over two thirds of editors (68%) were opposed to or were skeptical of the idea of journalism schools "taking a broad approach" to curriculum with courses that look at all media. Only 17% favored it.

Dickson and Sellmeyer (1992a, 1992b) compared attitudes of heads of media units with attitudes expressed by editors in the 1990 ASNE study. They surveyed 380 heads of media programs, 271 of whom responded. Dickson and Sellmeyer found that responses by editors and administrators of media programs differed significantly on 15 of 21 issues. The greatest differences concerned whether mass communication was a priority for journalism education, whether advertising and public relations belong in journalism schools, whether the media should be seen as interrelated, whether media history and media law were priorities, whether more nuts and bolts courses were a priority, and whether media sequences should be eliminated. They were most alike on whether media economics and media management were priorities, and whether tougher grading, research, better students and marketing research were priorities. In all cases, editors were more likely to want practical courses. Administrators with a news–editorial background were more likely to agree with the editors. For example, whereas 35% of editors and 31% of administrators with a news–editorial specialization agreed that research was not a priority, 55% of administrators with another specialty area stated that is was a priority.

Schwartz, Yarbrough, and Shakra (1992) surveyed 461 public relations professionals and chief executive officers of the top 50 public relations firms for the Public Relations Student Society of America. Only one fourth of the practitioners responding recommended a public relations major as the best preparation for a public relations career. Fourteen percent of practitioners did not like the idea of public relations as a university program of study, and 10% did not think public relations programs should be offered at the undergraduate or graduate level. Just over half (52%) of practitioners stated that they were not sure how good public relations education was.

The authors of the study noted several inconsistencies in the responses. They noted, first, that both practitioners and CEOs stated that a minor in public relations is the best approach for students, but there is no way educators could put all of the 19 subjects they rated as very important into six courses that normally make up a minor. Second, journalism was a favored major to be taken with the public relations minor; however, media production skills, usually seen an important component in a traditional journalism program, was not seen as an important subject. Third, if public relations were only a minor, they wondered how it could obtain the political clout necessary to obtain sufficient funding from the university. Fourth, the authors were unsure why internships were seen by practitioners to be important. They wrote: "Is it the skills and knowledge that students are expected to obtain? Or is it the dose of 'career reality' one might encounter? In our opinion, the last is a more predictable, and useful, outcome" (Schwartz, Yarbrough, & Shakra, 1992, p. 24).

The Associated Press Managing Editors (Bullard & McLeary, 1994) surveyed recent journalism graduates to have them grade their journalism schools and to determine the areas in which students thought they were best and worst prepared. Graduates were most often to state that they needed more training on cutting through red tape and handling detailed beat reporting. That was followed by a greater need for an emphasis on interviewing skills, more emphasis on practical experience, more emphasis on story research and investigative reporting techniques, and more emphasis on copy editing, layout, and design. A large majority said they were best prepared to write soft features and general assignment reporting and that they had learned to write well. In responding to the APME survey, Mencher (1994a) stated, "This study, like others before it, indicates that both editors and young reporters believe journalism schools can do a better job of preparing men and women for covering the community." However, he warned that "professional journalism education will continue to wind down" unless the media professionals are more aggressive (p. 18). He noted that many students are not prepared for college work, particularly writing and basic arithmetic. He suggested a greater emphasis on reporting skills, which, he said, were slighted because of the need to teach writing, and he proposed screening out students who shouldn't be there.

Dickson (1996) analyzed the 1990 ASNE study. He concluded that opinions of editors about journalism schools and their graduates differed based on whether the editors were journalism schools graduates or not and on the size the editor's newspaper. The size of the editor's newspaper was related to how editors rated the abilities of journalism school graduates, what editors were looking for in regard to new hires' skills, how editors rated the abilities of their new hires, and editors' opinions of what the curriculum of journalism schools should be. Editors at smaller newspapers were more interested in graduates with basic journalism skills and were more likely to hire journalism graduates. Editors at larger newspapers were more interested in new hires with a more broad-based background than were editors at smaller newspapers. Editors at larger newspapers were less likely to state that basic journalism skills were important, and they were less likely to list most media-related courses as being important courses. Editors at larger newspapers tended to have no preference between journalism school and nonjournalism school graduates and tended to hire a smaller percentage of journalism school graduates. Interestingly, however, they rated journalism graduates higher on most competencies. Editors at larger newspapers also were less likely to be journalism school graduates, something also noted by Bales (1992). Dickson concluded that journalism schools have at least three diverse newspaper constituencies (small, medium and larger newspapers) and a likely fourth—weeklies.

The Jane Pauley Task Force on Mass Communication Education (SPJ, 1996) was established because of the broadcast journalist's concern that "journalism programs place too little value on knowledge and too much on skills training" (p. 4). The task force sent a survey to news directors of 1,131 commercial television stations and received responses from 394. It also sent surveys to program heads at 195 colleges and universities with broadcast journalism programs, 108 of whom completed the questionnaire. News directors were most critical of graduates' writing abilities, with 45% citing it as a weakness, followed by general knowledge and unrealistic expectations (16% each). Graduates were rated highest by news directors on "enthusiasm/eagerness" (37%), "willingness/ability to learn" (20%), "good attitude/personality" (17%), and "willingness to work hard" (15%). Only 2% mentioned "ability to communicate," and only 5% cited "general technical skills." Educators and news directors agreed that writing abilities were most important, though educators were more likely to think so (64% vs. 42%). The second most important area mentioned by educators was technical skills, listed by 29%. However, only 8% of news directors stated that they were seeking new hires with technical skills. Instead, news directors put good attitude/personality second, listed by 31%. The task force concluded: "For the most part, educators evaluate their graduates more favorably than the news directors" (SPJ, 1996, p. 10).

The Survey Development Task Team (Stacks, 1998) surveyed 1500 public relations educators and practitioners concerning PR curriculum, outcomes, assessment, and pedagogy and received responses from 258 (20%). They concluded that educators and practitioners strongly agreed that students were learning what they needed. Just under 20% of educators and just over 14% of practitioners disagreed with the statement that "PR education is keeping up with current trends in the profession." Also, only 18% of practitioners and 21% of educators disagreed or strongly disagreed with the statement that "Most PR practitioners have a very positive attitude toward PR college graduates."

Practitioners and educators closely agreed on the content of PR curriculum, differing significantly concerning the importance of only 5 of 90 items. Practitioners saw courses in journalism, radio/TV/film, and film-making as more important than did educators, and educators saw courses in communication theory and graphic design as more important than did practitioners. On the other hand, both practitioners and academicians were dissatisfied with the actual skills of graduates. Only graduates' "good attitude," word processing/E-mail skills, and typing skills received a score above 5 on a 7-point scale. The executive summary of the report stated: "Although the data is by no means definitive, survey results indicate public relations educators may be focusing too much on mechanical skills (e.g., typing and word processing) and not enough on the half dozen entry level skills that are more important in the eyes of practitioners: being a self starter ($M = 6.61$), writing news releases ($M = 6.53$), critical thinking and problem solving skills ($M = 6.49$), and flexibility ($M = 6.44$)" (Botan, 1998, p. 2).

MEDIA EDUCATION'S RESPONSE
TO CRITICISM BY PRACTITIONERS

Mencher (1990a) stated that the attack on journalism education was coming from four directions: from editors who do not like the quality of graduates, from colleagues in other fields who consider journalism schools as trade schools, from journalists who state that journalism education is not relevant to the practice of journalism, and from other journalism faculty. He concluded that the most vocal attacks against media education, however, had been from media practitioners. He mentioned, for example, television's Ted Koppel's call for journalism schools to close down and the usual statements by editors that they prefer to hire graduates with liberal arts degrees.

Mencher (1990a) stated that the attack on media education by media practitioners was based on contradictions. Whereas media professionals have charged that journalism education is too broad and theoretical, academic critics charge it is too narrow and trade-oriented. He wrote that media professionals, although complaining about media graduates' technical skills, usually admire journalism students for their thinking and working habits. Mencher concluded that media educators are trying to educate students who have been "victimized by a failing educational system" and then blame themselves when they can not overcome those deficiencies (p. 67). Instead of being defensive when attacked by critics, journalism educators should speak out about the importance of media education to society, he wrote. Mazingo (1991) also defended journalism schools' record. She noted, first, that both newspapers and journalism graduates were better then than a decade earlier and that it "did not happen by accident" (p. 48). She also stated that some programs are more theory-oriented, but a number of programs were moving toward a more practical, skills-based curriculum. In addition, she noted that the quality of a program's graduates depends on the intelligence and abilities of its students.

Fedler (1993) evaluated articles attacking media education over a 20-year period to determine the nature of the complaints. He concluded that editors complain that students can not write or spell, do not read, and do not know much about government, current events, technology, or how newspapers work. Instead of what they are getting, they say they wanted graduates that "are more highly motivated, dedicated, imaginative, precise, and curious" (p. 2). Like Mencher (1990a), Fedler concluded that media professionals' criticisms of media education were inconsistent. In his critique of *Journalism Education: Facing Up to the Challenge of Change* (ASNE, 1990), he noted that some editors want students to have taken more liberal arts, others complain that students do not have the technical skills they need, and still others say new hires can learn techniques on the job.

Fedler (1993) also stated that media educators do not think they should be held responsible for every flaw in their graduates and that, instead, societal problems, students' family situations, and problems with elementary and secondary education were more to blame. He laid much of the blame for the quality of hires in the newspaper industry on problems within the industry itself. He said the best media graduates often do not go into the newspaper field "because of their notoriously low salaries and difficult working conditions" (p. 4). Fedler noted that research refutes professionals' charges that media faculty members lack practical experience, that media graduates are not as capable as earlier graduates, that too much emphasis is put on communication, and that media professionals prefer liberal arts graduates who can be better trained while on the job. Concerning the last two points, he noted that many media education units do not even offer a communication theory course and that most new hires are journalism school graduates because little on-the-job training is provided new hires.

Professionals' charges that emphasis is put on academic research and publication in academic journals are accurate, Fedler (1993) concluded. However, he also found that critics exaggerate media faculty members' interest in research and the amount of time they spend doing it. He noted that creative activities and writing for nonacademic publications often are acceptable for promotion and tenure and that the pressure on faculty for academic publications varies significantly between media programs based upon whether they have a graduate program. Fedler also concluded, however, that research supports media professionals' claims that media faculty with doctorates do not have the amount of professional experience that faculty with only master's degrees have and that faculty with doctorates are more likely to be granted tenure and promotion. In addition, he concluded that media educators have failed to show whether: (a) their research makes them better teachers; (b) their research is valuable enough to justify the emphasis placed on it, and all the resources devoted to it; (c) research helps faculty members remain current in their field; (d) research expands everyone's knowledge of the field; (e) research is of some real value; and (f) their colleges and universities require and reward good teaching (p. 15).

The AEJMC/ASJMC Joint Task Force on Professional Alliances (Self, 1994) surveyed journalism and mass communication programs and members of the Newspaper Association of America and made recommendations to increase professional–academic cooperation. It received 163 responses from a mailing to 407 media-related programs. Self, chair of the task force, noted that previous studies had found a lack of cooperation and even hostility between educators and media professionals. The task force study of educators, however, found close cooperation on a number of areas, several indirectly related to curriculum.

Self noted surprise at finding that 99% of the schools reported that media professionals speak to classes, that 99% of units provided academic credit for student field experiences such as internships, that 98% encouraged undergraduates to seek field experiences, that 93% reported faculty attended media conferences, and that 89% stated that media professionals serve the unit as adjunct or part-time faculty. In addition, 61% of the media units reported that faculty had worked in the media in the previous 3 years. On the other hand, only 51% of the units reported that they had an advisory board that included media professionals. Self noted about the close ties found despite only moderate use of media advisory boards, "Still, what emerges is hardly a picture of disengagement between faculty and professionals. Instead, intense interaction between these academic programs and their professional constituencies is reported" (p. 35).

THE DEBATE OVER THE NEED FOR A PH.D.

For decades, a major point of contention between media practitioners and educators, as well as among educators, has been whether faculty needed practical experience and, if so, how much. For example, Myers (1926) stated, "Teachers of journalism should combine in proper proportions practical experience in newspaper work, knowledge of teaching practice, and inspirational qualities, whatever that last may mean" (p. 12). He declined to give the proper ratio; however, he concluded that someone could teach history of journalism without newspaper experience and possibly editorial writing.

The issue became a national one when Allen Sinclair Will introduced a resolution at the a meeting of the American Association of Schools and Departments of Journalism at the University of Iowa in late December 1927 concerning newspaper experience as a qualification for teaching journalism. It proposed that "teachers of professional journalism employed after July 1, 1928, . . . shall be required to have five years of versatile experience on a newspaper or newspapers of high standing" (Will, 1928, p. 18). He said he proposed the resolution because "[i]n many cases teachers who knew little or nothing of journalism yielded to urgency by presidents or deans of important institutions of education to 'start a department of journalism.' " He charged that "[n]on-journalistic teaching of journalism will no more be tolerated by public opinion than non-engineering teaching of engineering or non-medical teaching of medicine or non-architectural teaching of architecture" (p. 18). In 1935 the American Association of Teachers of Journalism set 5 years of practical experience as the minimum acceptable for a journalism educator (Sloan, 1990).

Following World War II, graduate education in the United States expanded, increasing the supply of Ph.D.s dramatically. By the late 1950s, the idea was in place in higher education "that while young faculty were hired as *teachers*, they were evaluated primarily as *researchers*" (Boyer, 1990, p. 11). A survey by the Carnegie Foundation for the Advancement of Teaching in 1969 found that 21% of faculty strongly agreed that tenure was difficult to achieve without publications. By 1989, 42% of all faculty gave that response. From 1969 to 1989, the number of faculty at research institutions giving that response increased from 44% to 83%, and at comprehensive colleges (which have no doctoral programs) it increased from 6% to 43%. As Boyer noted, "The emphasis on undergraduate education, which throughout the years had drawn its inspiration from the colonial tradition, was being overshadowed by the

European university tradition, with its emphasis on graduate education and research" (p. 13).

Since the rise of communication studies and a dramatic increase in the 1950s in the numbers of faculty with communication Ph.D.s, some media professionals and media educators have charged that media professionals were losing out to Ph.D.s in job searches. Sloan (1990), for example, stated that "by 1960 schools were lowering their expectations" and were decreasing the standard of 5 years of experience set in 1935 by the American Association of Teachers of Journalism. He noted that journalism professionals "greeted these changes with suspicion" (p. 17). As late as the mid-1960s, however, research showed that a Ph.D. wasn't necessarily required in journalism programs. An Association for Education in Journalism survey reported by Highton (1967) found that 51 of 54 journalism schools stated that they didn't require the doctorate and that experience was more important.

MacDougall (1973) called for the American Council on Education in Journalism to restore the minimum of five years of professional experience for faculty members "if journalism schools are to continue to be journalism schools" (p. 17). Good (1984), however, attacked the practice of staffing journalism programs with former journalists, who "train young people for careers [they] have abandoned." He also charged that journalism education "tends to be schizoid" because faculty must teach "nuts and bolts" courses as well as such things as history, law, ethics, and theory. He called for inviting nonjournalists to teach such courses and to leave instruction in technical skills to newspapers in order to "get journalism programs out from under the shadow of the newspaper industry, where they have clung half-apologetically, half-defiantly to the values of their trade school" (p. 27).

The Oregon Report (Project, 1984) stated that "faculty members should be capable of intellectual, academic and professional leadership." It noted that the most common situation at that time and in the future was the "scholar/teacher with modest professional experience." However, it added:

> There should be room for the professional teacher who comes from the media professions as well. Both the scholar/teacher and the professional teacher should be given clear directions about productivity demands and expectations. There should be greater use of professionals in residence and short-term appointments and more opportunity for scholars with little professional experience to get greater exposure to industry experience. (Project, 1987, p. 2)

Likewise, Copple (1985) stated that the need for faculty members to do research eventually would make journalism education like other disciplines in that there would be "no place for the professional with significant experience but without research credentials." He added, "I know. We have argued experience versus degrees for years. Strange, that we never learned that there is no 'versus.' We need both" (p. 21).

Critics have predicted dire consequences because of the rise in the number of media educators with a Ph.D. For example, Jerry Ceppos, managing editor of the San Jose Mercury News, questioned whether new faculty members with doctorates in mass communication would have strong enough backgrounds to teach most journalism courses. In addition, he questioned whether universities were refusing to recognize scholarly qualifications "in research, writing, critical thinking, clear expression and visual aesthetics—of highly skilled journalists to teach the courses that constitute the heart and major substance" of media education (Ceppos, 1990, p. 17). Robert Giles, editor and publisher of the Detroit Press, wrote, "The trend toward hiring Ph.D.'s in communications further undermines the principle that distinguished experience as a journalist is the equivalent of a doctorate" (ASNE, 1990).

Weinberg (1991) reported that "[a]dministrators across the country are under pressure from their university bosses to hire only faculty members with Ph.D.'s." He stated that most administrators of media education units fail to understand that few top journalists hold doctorates or want to earn one in order to teach. He also stated that many academics with doctorates in journalism have little or no newsroom experience, which makes it difficult for them to teach students the skills they need to function in news operations. He added, "The wrong-headed push to fill journalism schools with Ph.D. holders will undermine the quality of journalism programs." Weinberg charged that it would lead to students who were ill-equipped for writing "clear, meaningful, fair, and accurate stories," that the media would increasingly hire liberal arts majors for entry level positions, that enrollments in journalism schools would likely decline, that journalism professionals would be less interested in gaining mid-career training on campus, and that "[t]he public will be starved for comprehensible, balanced news" (p. B1).

Some educators applauded the trend toward Ph.D.s, however. For example, the AEJMC Vision 2000 Task Force (AEJMC, 1994b) noted that the "evidence is that faculty members must—both to get jobs and earn tenure, and for the sake of the field itself—now have doctorates" (p. 22). It noted that the same situation exists in the traditional liberal arts. In reporting on a 1993 study by DeFleur predicting that not enough new Ph.D.s are being produced to fill the need, the task force's report stated, "This may significantly limit the options for flexible responses to the changing environment at American universities" (p.23).

Other educators agreed with outside critics that the trend was harming journalism education. Medsger, then chair of the Journalism Department at San Francisco State University, said the tendency to hire Ph.D.s "is moving the teaching of journalism even farther from the journalists who have the most experience and knowledge to offer students." She added that it was threatening to undermine a basic principle "of journalism education that has been supported by ASNE but not widely accepted by the academy: Journalism itself is a scholarly activity that merits evaluation and acceptance by the academy as a qualification for teaching" (ASNE, 1990, p. 15). Medsger (1996) wrote that "the question about degree is having a great impact on who teaches journalism—and probably on quality and basic content of journalism education" (p. 41).

When reporting on his assignment to cover the AEJMC convention in Minneapolis, Weinberg (1990) commented on the phenomenon of journalism schools being dominated by Ph.D.s by noting that it leads to an "us versus them mentality." Weinberg, a freelance writer and a professor at the University of Missouri School of Journalism, added:

> At some large journalism schools that question is of little concern. Their faculties contain a mix of both Ph.D.s and long-time newsroom practitioners. The theorists tend to teach the theory courses, and the practitioners teach the writing and editing courses.
> But many, probably most, journalism programs have smaller faculties where Ph.D.s predominate and try to tie theory and practice, no matter how unprepared they may be to teach the latter. Preparation time is limited anyway if they want to attain tenure. (p. 27)

Despite such fears, research by Weaver and Wilhoit (1988) found that the percent of media faculty with doctorates has historically been quite low compared to other fields. They found that fewer media faculty held a doctorate as compared to college faculty overall—approximately half compared to 80% in some other fields in 1980. Seventy-one percent of media educators who were full professors had a doctorate, compared to 54% of associate professors. They noted, "Most advertisements for faculty positions in journalism and mass communication seek a combination of media experience and the Ph.D. or other graduate degree" (p. 16).

Fedler, Counts, A. Carey, and Santana (1998) found that the percentage of faculty with Ph.D.s differed considerably among specialties. Advertising/public relations faculty members had the fewest Ph.D.s (67.2%), followed by reporting/editing (69.3%), and radio/television (76.6%). In contrast, more than 80% of faculty members in ethics (81.1%), mass communication and society (83.8%), media law (84.6%), theory and methodology (88.6%), and international media (88.9%) had a Ph.D. In only one nonpractical area—media history—did less than 80% of faculty have a doctorate (75.5%). Fedler et al. stated that their findings did not support the findings by Medsger (1996) that faculty who had taught 10 or fewer years were twice as likely to have a doctorate than faculty who had taught more than 10 years. They found instead that the longer the faculty members had taught, the more likely they were to have a doctorate. The percent of those with doctorates rose from 68.8% for faculty with under 6 years of experience to 74.6% for those with 6 to 10 years, to 76.3% for those with 11 to 15 years, and to 88.5% for those with 16 or more years.

RESEARCH ABOUT PROFESSIONAL EXPERIENCE
OF MEDIA FACULTY

Despite fears to the contrary, research has found that the requirement for a Ph.D. has not resulted in faculty without practical experience. Fedler and Counts (1982) determined that the average journalism educator had 12.5 years of practical media experience. G. Stone (1982) reported that the difference in the amount of professional experience of journalism faculty with Ph.D.s and those without the degree was not particularly wide. His study of 68 programs headed by members of the American Society of Journalism School Administrators found that faculty with doctorates averaged 5.9 years of professional media experience to 7.2 years for other faculty. The greatest difference in experience between the two groups was for photojournalism (3.6 years), followed by newspapers (2.6 years), magazines (2.4 years), and advertising (2.1 years). However, Stone found no difference for radio–TV production experience, and faculty with doctorates had slightly more experience in three areas. He also found that faculty with doctorates tended to have such mass communication areas as law, history, and theory as their primary area, rather than practical courses. He concluded, "The message seems clear throughout the survey that 'communicologists'—if doctorate faculty can be so classified—aren't diluting the traditional journalism skills areas" (p. 4).

Weaver and Wilhoit (1988) concluded that "[m]edia experience is valued especially in faculty members who teach classes focusing on the journalistic skills of writing, reporting, and editing." They found that only 1.5% of media educators surveyed had no professional media experience and that faculty with Ph.D.s had an average of 6.5 years of media experience versus 12 years for faculty without a doctorate, a finding "offering no support for the often-heard charge that Ph.D.s in our field have little or no media experience" (p. 16). Similarly, Lancaster, Katz, and Cho (1990) found that just over two thirds (69%) of the 283 educators surveyed, all members of the American Academy of Advertising, had received a Ph.D. or an Ed.D. and another 6% were working on a doctorate. On the other hand, two thirds of the educators averaged 11 years of experience or more as advertising practitioners.

Dickson and Sellmeyer (1992a) found that 74% of the 271 administrators of media units who responded to their survey stated that having a high proportion of media professionals on the faculty should be a high or very high priority. Just under half of the administrators (46%) stated that having more doctorates on the faculty in relation to faculty without doctorates was a high or very high priority. They found differences based upon the specialization of the administrator. Whereas only 34% of respondents with a news–editorial specialization stated that having more faculty with doctorates was a priority, 61% of respondents with a broadcast or a public relations specialization and 68% of those with some other specialization gave that response.

Medsger (1996) found that only 17% of print and broadcast journalism faculty she surveyed had never worked full-time as a journalist and that 47% had 10 years of professional experience or less. She found that 21% of print and broadcast journalism educators with doctorates had no full-time professional experience, compared to 11% of journalism faculty without a doctorate. In addition, 66% of journalism faculty without a doctorate, compared to 28% of faculty with a doctorate, had worked more than 10 years as a journalist. She concluded, "Extensive professional experience, though diminished in importance by current practices, is highly regarded by journalism educators" (p. 48). She found that 14% of respondents agreed somewhat and 80% agreed strongly that journalism faculties should include faculty with extensive journalistic experience.

Fedler, Counts, A. Carey, and Santana (1997) asked, "How much professional experience is enough?" They answered, "Critics often suggest a minimum of 10 years, but rarely explain or justify that figure (or acknowledge the possibility that different faculty members with different specialties may benefit from different types of experiences)" (p. 18). They challenged the notion that media educators with a Ph.D. have little practical experience and, thus, are harming the quality of journalism education. They cited three reasons to question the statement by Medsger (1996) that "The future of journalism education is jeopardized by college and university hiring policies and philosophies of journalism education that have led to a decline in hiring faculty with significant experience and expertise in journalism." The reasons they gave were: "First, other studies have found that faculty members in journalism and mass communication (JMC) have more professional experience [than Medsger found]. Second, Medsger's response rate was low, only 22%. Third, Medsger and other critics generalize, perhaps unfairly" (p. 1).

Fedler, Counts, A. Carey, and Santana (1997) noted that results of the studies by G. Stone (1982), Fedler and Counts (1982) and Weaver and Wilhoit (1988) all reported higher response rates than Medsger's study. They noted that faculty members teaching professional courses need and have more professional experience than those who teach more theoretical courses and that faculty members' teaching interests were changing because fewer students were taking the traditional news–editorial (journalism) sequence—less than 12% of media students in 1996. The authors surveyed almost 600 members of the Association for Education in Journalism and Mass Communication and received responses from 279. Faculty with 10 or fewer years of professional media experience usually taught such courses as theory and methodology (59.8%), mass communication and society (54.2%), media law (51.3%), and international media (48.6%), as well as radio/TV (48.9%). Those with the more than 10 years of professional experience usually taught reporting/editing (61.4%), media history (55.3%), media ethics (54%), and advertising/public relations (52.4%). Overall, 53% of faculty in the skills areas had 11 or more years of professional experience, compared to 44% in the concept area. Only 22.5% of faculty in skills areas had less than 6 years of professional experience, and none of the 103 skills faculty responding reported no experience.

Similarly, the report of the Survey Development Task Team (Botan, 1998) concluded, "Practitioners and educators share far more working experience than most think" (p. 2). Whereas the respondents to their national survey of PR practitioners averaged 17.42 years of experience, PR educators responding averaged 10.35 years of professional experience and 7.79 years of teaching.

MEDIA EDUCATION'S ROLE
IN DEVELOPING CITIZENSHIP

A number of educators and practitioners see journalism education as being distinct from other media-related fields, such as advertising and public relations, because journalists represent the public rather than special interests. As Medsger (1996) put it, journalism students "are asked to think—carefully, critically, precisely—and to do so beyond their own interests, to think of the public's interests and needs" (p. 9). She noted that the principal visionaries of journalism education—Joseph Pulitzer, Willard Bleyer, and Walter Williams—were interested in more than educating journalists and making newspapers better. Medsger stated, "The larger goal to which they aspired was to produce a more-informed citizenry through better journalism" (p. 54).

Likewise, Hachten (1998) noted that such things as the "growing stress on professionalism, the role of investigative reporting as a regular feature of serious newspapers, and even claims made for special treatment such as *shield laws* (protecting confidential news sources) suggest that the media perceive themselves today as serving the public interest" (p. 39). Like Medsger (1996), he wrote, however, "More than any other sequence such as advertising, PR, communication, or media studies, journalism has the greatest claim on being a profession" (p. 163). Moreover, he added, "By objectively and dispassionately gathering all the important news of the day and making it available to the public, journalism performs an essential public service for our democracy. Advertising and PR do not meet this test and could just as easily be taught in business school" (p. 163).

The essential public service role of journalism certainly was understood long before there was journalism education. On Sept. 25, 1690, Boston publisher Benjamin Harris noted about his editorial policy in the first—and last—issue of what is seen as the first colonial newspaper, *Publick Occurrences Both Foreign and Domestick*, which was suspended by Massachusetts authorities because of its content:

> That which is herein proposed, is, First, That Memorable Occurrents of Divine Providence may not be neglected or forgotten, as they too often are. Secondly, That people every where may better understand the Circumstances of Publique

Affairs, both abroad and at home, which may not only direct their Thoughts at all times, but at some times also to assist their Businesses and Negotiations.

Thirdly, That some thing may be done towards the Curing, or at lest the Charming of that Spirit of Lying, which prevails amongst us, wherefore nothing shall be entered, but what we have reason to believe is true, repairing to the best foundations for our Information. And when there appears any material mistake in any thing that is collected, it shall be corrected in the next. (*Publick Occurrences*, 1690, p. 1)

Benjamin Franklin also thought the press had a role in improving public affairs, particularly public virtue. He wrote that "nothing is more likely to endanger the liberty of the press than the abuse of that liberty by employing it in personal accusation, detraction, and calumny" (Frasca, 1995, p. 5). Franklin thought that "published defamation only detracted from the press' role of purveyor of republican enlightenment, useful education and moral teachings" (p. 8). In the *Pennsylvania Gazette*'s first issue on October 2, 1729, Franklin defined the ideal editor as follows:

He ought to be qualified with an extensive Acquaintance with Languages, a great Easiness and Command of Writing and Related Things clearly and intelligibly, and in a few Words; he should be able to speak of War both by Land and Sea; be well acquainted with Geography, with the History of the Time, with the several interests of Princes and States, the Secrets of Courts, and the Manners and Customs of all Nations. Men thus accomplish'd are very rare in this remote Part of the World. . . . (Altschull, 1990, pp. 106-107)

In "An Apology for Printers," published in the *Gazette* on June 10, 1731, Franklin wrote that "when men differ in Opinion, both Sides ought equally to have the Advantage of being heard by the Publick" because "when Truth and Error have fair Play, the former is always an overmatch for the latter" (Altschull, 1990, p. 107. According to Rivers and Schramm (1969), "news was usually filtered deliberately through the biases of the newspaper that carried it" until the start of World War I. They credited the transformation to objectivity to the rise of the wire services, "which found it prohibitive to try to prepare a story to suit the slant of each of its clients" (p. 151). Bybee (1999) wrote about the debate over the role of the press in a democracy following the rise of objectivity:

There is a long held and often repeated assumption within liberal pluralist theories of the press that modern democracy rests on the foundation of the informed citizen who makes decisions based on rational, objective criteria and that the news media are perhaps the most crucial source of this information. The citizen, the media, and democratic government are neatly stitched together in this civic trilogy. And it is this assumption that has been eroding as we appear to have moved into a post-factual age where the border between fact and fiction, news and entertainment, information and advertisements has increasingly blurred. (p. 29)

The defining event in the advent of an objective press was the publication of *Public Opinion* in 1922, in which Walter Lippmann argued for a "sweeping rejection of traditional theories of democracy and the role of the press" (Steel, 1980, p. 182). In his book, Lippmann wrote: "For the troubles of the press, like the troubles of representative government . . . go back to a common source: to the failure of self-governing people to transcend their casual experience and their prejudice, by inventing, creating, and organizing a machinery of knowledge" (Lippmann, 1922, pp. 364-365). He stated that an intellectual elite should make the important decisions. Taking an opposing view was John Dewey. In *The Public and Its Problems*, Dewey (1927) wrote about the elite: "It is impossible for high-brows to secure a monopoly of such knowledge as must be used for the regulation of common affairs. In the degree in which they become a specialized class, they are shut off from knowledge of the needs which they are supposed to serve" (p. 206).

Bybee (1999) wrote about the contrasting philosophies of Lippmann and Dewey:

> Ironically, Lippmann, often heralded as one of the founding figures of modern journalism and media studies, substantially downgraded the role to be played by the press in democracy. In Lippmann's scientistic view of the press and democracy, the press was ill-suited to inform the public and the public was ill-suited to be informed. Scientifically informed experts would, for the most part, substitute for the phantom public in the act of governing.
>
> Dewey, on the other hand, saw an intimate relationship between science, the public, and government. He believed communication is central to democracy not only in a mechanical role linking citizens together, but also in an epistemological role helping to define what will be taken as truth, as well as in a moral role providing an everyday answer to the apparent contradiction between the interests of the individual and society. (p. 55)

Merritt (1998) concluded that "when Lippmann's views eventually prevailed in the debate, the courses of democracy and journalism were set for decades; courses only now being challenged by a restless and cynical populace" (p. 14).

Dewey's ideas about journalism having an important role in promoting democratic values were not forgotten by educators, however. Some media scholars, such as Carey (1989), wrote of journalism as "conversation"— interpersonal communication rather than a transfer of information to the public. Likewise, Anderson, Dardenne, and Killenberg (1996) argued that "journalism's practical strength . . . can provide a better forum for intellectual excitement, civic conversation, and public debate" (pp. 13–14).

Mencher (1994b) noted that at a time when journalism education as practitioner training has been diminished, universities are reaffirming the service mission of higher education and discussing ways to prepare "reflective practitioners." He called for invigoration and a renewed direction for the professional curriculum through a recognition of "the essential role the journalist plays in making democracy work . . ." (p. 71). Mencher proposed three essentials for meeting society's need for able journalists: (a) higher admission standards; (b) emphasis on community-oriented instruction; and (c) course-specific liberal arts requirements (p. 73). He wrote that journalism programs should admit only the best prepared students and require more of students and that all courses should have a writing component and stress public service and community reporting.

Astin (1995) wrote about the university's obligation to develop students' understanding of the role of the media in society:

> Our educational system should help students to become better critics and analysts of contemporary mass media and of the political information they produce. Most faculty members put a high premium on the development of students' "critical thinking" skills, but we still have a long way to go before we can say that we are producing graduates who have sufficient critical understanding of the media and the motivation to demand better information. (p. B2)

Astin suggested that universities establish an interdisciplinary freshman seminar contrasting democratic theory with the role of the media in informing or misinforming citizens or a required seminar that focuses on the media's impact on public political thought and the public's involvement in public issues. He stated that such a "citizenship curriculum" would address the point that the media are large businesses run for a profit and are not critical mavericks but an integral part of the business community, and that the news media do not make money if they offend advertisers or alienate the audience. He stated:

> Our students, then, need to be taught how to inform themselves so that they can formulate the right questions. How about taking a hard look at our journalism-and-communications programs with this idea in mind? . . . How much emphasis does each of these programs put on training its students to understand the most important questions citizens should ask concerning public issues—as opposed to training them to pursue the most obvious or sensational facets of a story? (p. B2)

THE DEBATE OVER PUBLIC JOURNALISM

Lambeth and Aucoin (1993) noted that journalism education had risen to meet the challenge of producing journalists skilled in public service. They wrote that a "new standard of excellence in public affairs reporting" was emerging in newsrooms. They called the movement the *new community journalism*. They said it has four key elements: (a) enterprise reporting based on a more deliberate assessment of community needs and interests; (b) commitment of significant newsroom resources; (c) mastery of story content at the level of an expert; and (d) virtually assured connection and impact within a community. They suggested that the new community journalism would help preserve journalism's public service values and would help journalism educators prepare students for the profession. They stated, "Perhaps the success with which we help students understand and report on communities will be the best measure of the leadership journalism educators are able to exert from the classroom" (p. 12). They added, "Unlike some other disciplines, journalism education has good reason to be directly connected with not only professional but with community life. By teaching students how to understand communities, we can keep not only students but ourselves abreast of the news media and the society they serve" (p. 18).

Because the term *community journalism* had been in existence for years to mean reporting on the small community rather than the big city, several other names began to be used in the early 1990s to refer to the concept outlined by Lambeth and Aucoin (1993): *public journalism, civic journalism,* and *communitarian journalism*. Public journalism began as a movement within the media industries to actively promote efforts to strengthen citizenship and improve the quality of public debate in order to revive public life and, in the process, increase circulation. According to Bybee (1999), public journalism follows the path suggested by John Dewey, "although the term public journalism as it is being used today contains much less than what Dewey was calling for" (p. 32).

Davis "Buzz" Merritt, editor of the *Wichita* (Kansas) *Eagle*, is considered the founder of the public journalism movement. Disgusted with the coverage of the 1988 presidential election, he decided to change the way his newspaper covered the 1990 elections. He stated that the news media did not fulfill their First Amendment mandate when they "ignored our truer and far more valuable franchise: The essential nexus between democracy and journalism, the vital connection with community and our role in promoting useful discourse rather than merely echoing discontent" (Merritt, 1998, 14).

According to Rosen (1996), Merritt changed the focus of the election by replacing "covering the campaign" with "a new principle: making the campaign 'cover' what mattered to citizens. The Eagle vowed to give readers 'the opportunity to understand in great detail the candidates' positions on every major issue Kansas faces' " (p. 35). James K. Batten, chief executive officer for Knight-Ridder Inc., which owned the *Eagle*, saw what he called *community connectedness* as a means of increasing newspaper readership and citizenship while using the journalistic tradition of public service and began to promote the movement (Rosen, 1996). In 1993, Batten persuaded the Knight Foundation to donate $513,000 to set up the Project on Public Life and the Press with Jay Rosen, a journalism professor at New York University, as director, to promote public journalism (Shepard, 1996).

The movement evolved during the 1990s into a major movement of educators and media practitioners aimed at revitalizing journalism as well as democracy and public life by setting the agenda for public debate. In doing so, the proponents admitted that the media were major players in the disintegration of public trust in the political system. The movement received a major boost in 1993 in addition to the Knight Foundation grant when the Pew Charitable Trusts, which provide $180 million a year in grants, decided to become involved by providing an initial grant of $3.6 million to establish the Pew Center for Civic Journalism, which would provide money to news media to promote citizen involvement in community affairs (Shepard, 1996).

Whereas some supporters of public journalism, such as Merritt, say public journalism is just an extension of what journalists have always done, other suggest it goes well beyond that. Opponents argue that it threatens to replace journalistic objectivity with a political agenda. For example, Max Frankel, former executive editor of the *New York Times*, stated about the movement: "I've never understood it." He added: "I've read all the theory on it. Some of it sounds like good old fashioned reporting. Some of it sounds like getting in bed with the promotion department, and that's unfortunate. Some of it sounds downright political" (Shepard, 1996, p. 28). In a talk to the 1995 convention of the Investigative Reporters and Editors in Miami, Jay Rosen, director of the Project on Public Life and the Press, noted these differences:

> Traditional journalism believes that people need to be informed so that they can participate effectively. In public journalism, we believe that people have to participate effectively so they'll want to become informed. Traditional journalism assures that democracy is what we have, and information is what we need; in public journalism, we think that the reverse is true, information is what we have—we live in a sea of information. Democracy is what we need. Public journalism is about forming the public, as much as informing the public. The assumption that the public exists, and always will, is a complacent one. (Corrigan, 1995, p. 9).

The movement soon gained the support of other academics. For example, Dennis (1995) wrote: "If public journalism is truly an effort to improve information and news reaching the public, it deserves the highest commendation. If, on the other hand, it pushes the media toward a quasi-governmental role, one more appropriate for the community organizer, people should know it" (p. 36). He added, however, that "[i]n the end, if the effort inspires greater public awareness about the content of all of our media, it will have served a noble public purpose" (p. 36).

The response from journalists was mixed. Public journalism was soon to draw criticism from such journalists as Leonard Downie, editor of *The Washington Post*; Max Frankel, former executive editor of the *The New York Times*; and Tony Marro, editor of *Newsday*. One journalist wrote about the critics: "Any good thing that does come out of a civic journalism initiative, they can be counted on to contend, is plain old traditional journalism, nothing new. Proponents, meanwhile, complain bitterly that the critics erect and bash straw men, skewering examples that are aberrations or arguing against tenets that civic journalism just doesn't hold" (Hoyt, 1995, p. 28). Journalist David Broder said he welcomed the public journalism experiment "because frankly, the nightmare of my life is that it will be written at some future point about my generation of political reporters that we covered everything, but we didn't notice that support for representative government and democracy was collapsing" (Hoyt, 1995, p. 32).

Determining whether public journalism is the solution depends to some extent on agreement as to what the problem is. McMasters (1997) noted that two fundamental assumptions behind public journalism are that "democracy is disintegrating" and that "the press is in peril of extinction." He questioned whether either was the case and whether the situation at the end of the 20th century was worse than at other times in the past. He wrote, "To concede that the press has problems is not to say that those problems are unprecedented or even unequaled" (p. 189). He added:

> But, for the moment, let's accept these assumptions at face value and ignore other factors possibly contributing to the decline of both public life and the press—changing society, changing technology, or changing cycles. We still must confront a third issue: whether the problems of democracy and journalism are inextricably—or even materially—entwined. (p. 189)

McMasters (1997) argued that the ambiguity used in defining the concept "provides an opening for those who see public journalism as a vehicle for separate agendas, some of which may not be all that friendly to good journalism" (pp. 189–190). In response to the comment by Rosen (1995) that "Public journalism is about forming as much as informing a public" (p. 7), McMasters responded that the "First Amendment adventurism implicit in such statements sounds a warning for proponents and critics alike to proceed carefully" (p. 191) and concluded that "the value of the press rests largely on its independence, its detachment, its need to report from a vantage point above and beyond the fray . . . in order to inform the citizenry" (p. 194). Dickson (1998) concluded that the issue is more than a debate over alternative theories of the press. He stated: "How the issue is resolved in the next decade will have important ramifications not only for the media and journalism educators but for the role of the public in a democratic society" (p. 114).

Public journalism projects continued to spread around the country throughout the late 1990s and remained a topic of discussion among educators, as well. Though newspaper editors had begun to ask readers for feedback in an effort to increase circulation before the advent of public journalism, some editors experimenting with public journalism began to asking readers and potential readers what the news was. Gil Thelen, executive editor of the *Tampa Tribune* in Tampa, FL, stated about the process, "This is a very threatening process for journalists. It's throwing the robes off and letting the people into the clergy" (Harper, 1999, p. B4). Marshall Lobe, editor of the *Columbia*

Journalism Review, challenged the experiment, stating: "This is not a popularity contest. The primary role of the journalist is to report on subjects that the audience didn't know they wanted to learn about" (Harper, 1999, p. B4). Reese Cleghorn, dean of the College of Journalism at the University of Maryland, said that editors "can learn something from people without it swaying [their] decisions." However, Michael Delli Carpini, chairman of the political science department at Barnard College in New York, countered: "Sometimes this is all just a public-relations tool. Readers either have no power or lack the professional judgment necessary to make real decisions" (Harper, p. B4).

RESEARCH ABOUT PUBLIC JOURNALISM

Ketchum Public Relations (Ketchum, 1997) undertook a study of print and broadcast journalism executive (news managers, publishers, editors, and radio and television executive producers) about, among other things, civic/public journalism for Virginia Commonwealth University's School of Mass Communications and the Associate Press Managing Editors (APME) in the summer of 1997. It received responses from 554 executives from a mailing to 2,335 (24%). The study found substantial support for civic/public journalism.

A total of 56.1% of respondents agreed with the following statement: "For many news organizations, 'civic journalism' has become an important means of enabling them to 'reconnect' with their alienated communities by paying much more attention than they have in the past to what people think." One hallmark of public journalism has been the use of focus groups to determine what the public sees the issues are. A total of 51.1% of media executives agreed that "Having newspapers sponsor and conduct 'citizens' forums,' at which those in the community can discuss issues of importance to the public, usually results in better reporting of community issues." In addition, only 24.0% of respondents agreed that " 'Public journalism' is little more than boosterism; it's a gimmick to make publishers feel better about themselves." Also, 29.2% agreed that "Those who practice 'civic' or 'public' journalism unfortunately cross the line between reporting and advocacy—putting journalism's ebbing credibility in further peril" (p. 7).

Dickson and Brandon (1998, 1999) surveyed a random sample of 332 members of the Broadcast Education Association (BEA), 383 members of the Association for Education in Journalism and Mass Communication (AEJMC) Newspaper Division, 294 TV station news directors, and 501 newspaper editors. Respondents were asked whether they agreed with the statement that "A major charge against civic/public journalism is that it reduces a media organization's objectivity because it becomes closely involved in public issues." They responded based upon a 1-to-5 scale with 1 meaning disagree strongly, 3 undecided, and 5 agree strongly. Educators and practitioners overall were undecided on the issue; however, TV news directors were significantly more likely than AEJMC members to disagree with the charge (TV news directors, 2.31; editors, 2.69; BEA, 2.72; AEJMC, 2.99; $M = 2.68$).

Supporters of public journalism assert that it provides a means for increasing reader/viewer interest in the news media (and thus boosts advertising and revenue). Respondents in the survey by Dickson and Brandon (1998, 1999) agreed that civic journalism does increase audience interest. No difference between practitioners and educators was statistically significant (BEA, 3.46; AEJMC, 3.56; TV news directors, 3.60; editors, 3.74; $M = 3.59$). Supporters of public journalism also state that the practice helps the news media improve their credibility in the community. Practitioners agreed somewhat that it does improve media credibility, though AEJMC and BEA members were undecided overall; however, differences were not statistically significant (AEJMC, 3.38; BEA, 3.47; editors, 3.60; TV, 3.79; $M = 3.56$).

Though educators and practitioners have found some agreement over the nature of the public service role of journalism and the usefulness of civic/public journalism, the "dialogue of the deaf" continues on other issues. Despite what research has found, attacks from media practitioners over the value of media education in training future media practitioners and over the need for faculty with a doctorate show no signs of easing. Moreover, media educators also have found themselves at odds with practitioners, as well as at odds with each other, over the role of the liberal arts in media education. Though it might be assumed that media practitioners would favor practical coursework, many of them have charged that a liberal arts degree would be a better preparation for future practitioners than a media degree. They also have shown little sympathy for educators who would require social science-based media studies courses to replace liberal arts courses in other departments. Such challenges to media education have even called into question the need for media education as it currently exists.

Mass Media Education and the Liberal Arts

One of the most fundamental questions addressed by JMC missions and purpose
statements concerns the relation of the programs to the liberal arts and sciences.
—AEJMC/ASJMC Task Force on Mission and Purpose (1996, p. 11)

The conclusion that students in media-related fields need to obtain a liberal as well as a practical education can be traced to the start of academic training in journalism—Robert E. Lee's abortive plan for college training of journalists following the Civil War. In his attempt to determine the most important liberal subjects, Camp (1888) found that leading journalists of the day recommended that education in journalism should contain not only courses in political science, history, and economics, but also courses in journalism that involved news recognition and analysis as well as news presentation. The six men who were most responsible in establishing the foundation for the field of journalism education—Lee, White, Pulitzer, Eliot, Bleyer, and Williams—all proposed a liberal education for journalists.

Beginning with Willard Bleyer's 4-year "Course in Journalism" in 1909, journalism educators came more and more to conclude not only that journalists needed a liberal arts background, but that journalism education had strong ties to the liberal arts overall and social sciences in particular. Through much of the first two decades of the 20th century, however, vocationalism was seen to be the dominate model of journalism education (for example, E. W. Allen, 1924; Dressel, 1960; Flint, 1924; Wilcox, 1959). By 1920, though, "there was evident a trend toward thinking of journalism education as a broad liberal education with a minimum of attention to techniques" (Dressel, 1960, pp. 24–25). Dressel noted that "the development and acceptance of the various social sciences in higher education have to some extent paralleled the development of journalism," leading to a "more cordial acceptance among social scientists" (p. 26).

In spite of the practical nature of media-related sequences and majors, media educators long have attempted to produce broadly educated practitioners by requiring that students be well grounded in liberal arts fields. By the 1930s, however, many journalism educators were becoming concerned about the specialized nature of the liberal arts courses their students were getting, particularly in the social sciences, and began to devise more social science-based courses within their curriculum (for example, Hyde, 1937, and Dressel, 1960). Thus, the issue within media education became not whether students should be grounded in the liberal arts and sciences, but to what extent media education itself was a liberal art. Some media educators concluded that their courses helped students put their general education courses into perspective. In addition, media

126

education was seen as having something to offer the liberal arts themselves. For example, Parisi (1992) stated: "Just as the liberal arts can deepen the study of journalism, the study of journalism can draw the liberal arts away from mere theorizing" (p. 10). And because media-related courses began to make their way into the general education curriculum, media educators began to argue that the accreditation standards should be changed to allow media courses to be counted as liberal arts courses.

SPECIALIZATION AND FRAGMENTATION
OF THE LIBERAL ARTS

As some media educators gained an appreciation for the idea that the field had much to offer the social sciences, uncertainty developed not only as to how journalism education could best achieve its mission of integrating the other social sciences but also over the meaning of the term *liberal arts* in general and the term *social sciences* in particular. Dressel (1960) wrote of this situation:

> Not only have the social sciences been very broadly interpreted in discussions of journalism, but their role has taken on a double meaning. The social sciences are viewed almost as an essential part of the professional preparation and also as providing a general background. For some years, the social sciences as interpreted and offered by the departments of the liberal arts college were uncritically accepted as filling both roles. As liberal arts subjects became more fragmented and specialized, it became more difficult for the embryo journalist to obtain an integrated view of the social sciences. (p. 27)

Dressel (1960) noted that the breadth requirement of most journalism programs meant that students must take a number of introductory liberal arts courses, which "have tended to become tools or techniques courses considered by their teachers as bases for advanced study rather than as courses broadly introductory to the respective disciplines" (p. 28). At the same time, he noted, the "liberal education aspect of journalism courses has been on the increase, though in practice probably lagging behind the optimistic statement of philosophy" (p. 30). He wrote that the "integrative demands of the communications, behavioral science conception of journalism has given new impetus to thinking about the relationship of professional courses in journalism and the liberal arts" (p. 99). He added, however:

> The large proportion of liberal arts taken by journalism students and the element of choice involved tends to diffuse the liberal education aspect of journalism so widely over liberal arts departments that any attempt to inform liberal arts faculty about the interests (of) . . . professional education would be difficult if not impossible. (p. 100)

Dressel (1960) also concluded that "journalism students too commonly have a superficial contact with many disciplines and insufficient contact in depth with some one or two" (p. 100). Similarly, Budd (1985) noted that he had written, in a paper presented at the 1967 Association for Education in Journalism convention, that journalism education's attempt to give its students a liberal arts-based professional education was being thwarted by specialization in the liberal arts disciplines:

> We have sent our students to other departments—very much encouraged by our accrediting system—to get smatterings of history, literature, psychology, economics and political science, assuming that these brief immersions would prepare them well for interpreting the world. In this, we have been caught up in what we consider an education-wide problem: too much concern for fact storage, too little for learning processes of learning, too little for contemplating purposes, too little for basic philosophical matters, too little for exercising our precious intellects. (p. 24)

The goal of how best to broaden students intellectually in a professional program was to remain elusive and the subject of much debate throughout the final three decades of the 20th century.

The problem with fragmentation and specialization also became a national issue in the last 20 years of the century. Liberal arts education came under attack for much the same reason journalism educators gave for criticizing it in the 1930s: an apparent lack of liberal content in many cases. Bloom (1987), for example, wrote that higher education "has lost its unity and is in crisis" (p. 262). One reason for the crisis, he stated, was the state of liberal education. "Most professors are specialists," he wrote, "concerned only with their own fields . . ." (p 339). Similarly, Mullins (1987a) noted that the Carnegie Foundation for the Advancement of Teaching (Boyer, 1987) described higher education in the 1980s as driven by careerism and professional education. He stated that the Carnegie Foundation's report made at least two points that were pertinent to the role of liberal arts in media programs:

> First, the study cites a "disjointed" curriculum whose disciplines have fragmented into smaller and smaller pieces, unrelated to a student's education as a whole. Second, some traditional liberal arts departments have themselves become "professionally oriented" in order to attract majors or have narrowed their focus in order to carve out a research niche that may bring peer recognition but is irrelevant to nonmajors. Such departments may have traditional liberal arts names, but they do not provide the balance we need for our students. (Mullins, p. 6)

Likewise, Blanchard and Christ (1993) concluded about the liberal arts disciplines, "There is little liberal arts 'there' " (p. 5). In their analysis of critiques of undergraduate education, they found three major areas of criticism: (a) that "undergraduate education lacks integrity and purpose"; (b) that "its content especially the liberal arts 'canon,' needs revitalization"; and (c) "that it is too vocational, narrow and fragmented, and needs integration and unity of knowledge." They added, "Interconnected with these criticisms in an intense debate over the relationship between liberal and professional education" (p. 4).

On one side of the issue, some media educators called for a continued emphasis on external liberal arts courses because future journalists needed to have a broad-based education. At the same time, some of them argued that even practical journalism courses were broadening. For example, Medsger (1996), wrote that "some of those (skills) emphasized in introductory journalism courses—research, critical thinking, organization of material and clear expression—are among the key skills the university tries, but often fails, to teach all students as essential parts of their liberal education" (p. 12). On the other side, media education task forces continued to call for accreditation standards to change to allow media students to take more social science-oriented media courses in addition to their professional courses. Williamson and Iorio (1994) said of that debate, "The primary issue is the institutional and scholarly legitimacy of communication studies" (p. 1).

THE 75/25 LIBERAL ARTS CURRICULUM STANDARD

The Accrediting Council on Education in Journalism and Mass Communications (ACEJMC), the organization that the Council for Higher Education Accreditation (CHEA) and the U.S. Department of Education recognize as the accrediting body for journalism and mass communication in colleges and universities, was formed in 1945 by educators and professionals from the newspaper industry as the American Council on Education in Journalism (ACEJ). Other disciplines that began accreditation at about the same time include chemistry, architecture, art, theology, and some medical fields (Harcleroad, 1981). In 1978, the ACEJ began to accredit entire media units rather than individual media-related sequences (Garrison, 1983), and in 1980 it took its present name (Davis, 1991).

Until 1989, the ACEJMC had a curriculum rule (Standard 3) stating that 75% of the media student's hours should be in the liberal arts and sciences and 25% in the professional major. The 75/25 standard was based on Willard Bleyer's 1906 proposal that from two thirds to three fourths of a journalism student's coursework should be in the liberal arts and sciences. Under the 75/25 standard, all media courses were seen as professional courses and could not count as liberal arts. Dressel (1960) noted that few accredited programs were meeting the standard and that it was unlikely that the standard would be met "until a core program common to all sequences is instituted and joined with a ceiling requirement on professional courses, including those offered in other departments and schools in the institution" (pp. 100–101). He also called for the development of a "sequential, integrative approach in advanced journalism courses" so journalism courses could "be brought into the most meaningful relationship to each other and to the liberal education upon which the courses should depend" (p. 101). He added:

> This philosophy can be meaningful only as it is spelled out in more significant terms and as it becomes accepted by the journalism professors and the students advised by them. As yet, this is not the case in many schools, but there is evidence that individuals and even entire faculties are beginning to think in these terms. If they are successful in convincing their "how-to-do-it" oriented colleagues, journalism education could become the model for a synthesis of liberal and professional education in contrast with the mere juxtaposition of professional and liberal education now characteristic of most journalism programs and even to a greater extent of other professional and technical programs. (p. 102)

Everette Dennis, director of what was then the Gannett Center for Media Studies, noted that in the 1970s the accrediting system found itself in the middle of the practical versus theoretical debate over the role of liberal arts courses in media-related education. He said of the period:

> Originally designed to train well-rounded reporters and editors, journalism schools had developed into complex centers for a wide range of professional media training. There was intense debate about educational standards, and to what extent the "article of faith"—that all undergraduate majors should take 75 percent of their course work in the liberal arts—needed to be honored. The volatility of this debate, which is not yet over, has often threatened to end the 40-year pact between educators and professionals. (Dennis, 1988, p. 15)

The ACEJ also continued to draw criticism for not enforcing its standards. Trayes (1973) found that the 75/25 standard was not met by half of the accredited programs, and he found evidence that a number of programs deviated from other standards, as well. In addition, a study committee of the American Association of Schools and Departments of Journalism (AASDJ) criticized the accrediting body for (a) procedures that wasted financial and human resources; (b) inadequacy of standards and the way they were applied; and (c) a violation of due process of some applicants ("AASDJ Committee Recommends," 1973).

During the early 1980s, the ACEJMC came under scrutiny because of battles over accreditation at Northwestern University and Boston University. Both decided not to seek accreditation, though Northwestern later was to become accredited. Boston University took its battle to the U.S. Department of Education, asking that the ACEJMC's accrediting authority be taken away. The accrediting commission instead received a probationary 2-year renewal. Stanford also decided against accreditation and remains unaccredited. In 1983, the University of Michigan decided not to seek reaccreditation and remains unaccredited.

Dennis (1983a) noted, "In the midst of these conflicts on campuses, there have been vigorous debates within journalism education over professional–academic control of accreditation and various procedural issues that deeply divide educators" (p. 87). One such debate was at the 1983 convention of the Association for Education in Journalism and Mass Communication. A panel member, Charles W. Duncan, stated, "In my opinion, the journalistic accreditation process as it now operates is overly cumbersome, time-consuming and expensive" ("Accreditation issues debated," 1984, p. 6). He stated that the 75/25 rule "is related to most of the complaints about ACEJMC" (p. 10).

Hampden Smith III noted three areas of dissatisfaction that he had found from interviewing ACEJMC members and heads of accredited and formerly accredited programs:

- First, "cookie-cutter," numerical standards have been emphasized and tightened in the last few years, meaning some accredited schools must alter their programs, which they see as both successful and outstanding, if they are to remain accredited.
- Second, the broadly stated general principles outlined in the accrediting standards are applied with nearly absolute rigidity in the accrediting process, despite the statement that "it is the policy of ACEJMC to encourage experimental and innovative educational programs."
- Third, professionals have two distinct, and probably mutually exclusive, concepts concerning the nature of undergraduate journalism education, but ACEJMC's members and standards support and accredit only one of those approaches. Most recent surveys involving the opinions of professionals about the training of entry-level employees show strong support for increasing the number of journalism courses. ACEJMC is effectively increasing the non-journalism component of the undergraduate program. ("Accreditation issues debated," 1984, pp. 11-12)

Smith noted that, despite such findings, "it has been the professional members of the ACEJMC who have been most adamant about narrowly defining the 25 percent rule and imposing the internship limit (of 10% of the hours in the major)" ("Accreditation issues debated," 1984, p. 12). He urged a "careful, detailed look" at the accrediting process and proposed that courses be categorized as liberal arts or professional training "on their merits rather than their labels." He added:

If ACEJMC continues to adhere solely to the standards accepted by the large professional organizations that are relatively unconcerned about professional training, it does a disservice to the smaller ones, which need entry-level employees ready to perform, and to the vast major of journalism school graduates, who expect to be employable. On the other hand, if it succumbs to a trade-school mentality, then journalism programs would be unlikely to provide either the well-rounded, literate citizens and employees everyone wants or the excellence and leadership in the graduates that, five or 10 years out of college, are demanded for promotion and management. (p. 12)

Serafini (1984) stated that the 75/25 standard was "on target" because journalists must write about a wide variety of subjects and need a broadly based education. However, he added, "But in being on target, they implicitly argue for their own self-destruction. There is no need for journalism education in its present form" (p. 28). Instead, he suggested that students interested in journalism take a 4-year liberal arts major, to be followed by 4 years as a working journalist before returning to a major university "to sit in on courses of their choosing." He suggested that the young journalists attend periodic seminars with distinguished visiting scholars. Universities would spend money previously spent on journalism schools to attract scholars in *other* fields who had a research interest related to journalism. Journalism would then be a shared responsibility. He stated, "The emphasis would still be on a broad liberal-arts education for journalists, but the existence of such scholars would help future journalists by providing a staple of courses that would help bridge the gap and show the connections between journalism and other fields" (p. 28).

In addition, Serafini (1984) charged that allowing only 25% of a student's courses in journalism courses—or "technical" training—with the rest outside of journalism in "the liberal arts" gave evidence to journalism education's lack of content. However, he compared journalism schools, which are an undergraduate experience nearly everywhere, to schools of medicine and law, which are postgraduate enterprises, in making his point against the 75/25 requirement:

> That alone is provocative, inasmuch as a similar distribution in any other field would strike one as preposterous: Imagine the reaction if, say, medical schools suddenly required that no more than twenty-five percent of course work should be in medicine? What if law schools demanded that most course work be in fields other than law?
>
> If, *per impossible*, such a distribution could be justified, it would be tantamount to admitting that there really ought not to be medical schools or law schools. It would be a tacit admission that there was simply not enough substance to warrant a program or school in the field. (p. 26)

Somewhat less provocative, Cole (1985) argued that "the sacrosanct 25–75 rule . . . needs some enlightened breathing room. The philosophy is excellent, but reasonable flexibility should exist (maybe up to 30 percent in journalism in certain cases)" (p. 7).

Despite the lukewarm support for the liberal arts curriculum standard by media educators, studies continued to show media practitioners strongly supported the standard. In 1987, for example, the Journalism Education Committee of the American Society of Newspaper Editors, "in a meeting with educators tinged with mutual suspicion," proposed withdrawing the organization's support for the ACEJMC, but the ASNE board changed the proposal to state that if the ACEJMC did not continue its "full and vigorous support" of the liberal arts curriculum standard, the ASNE would withdraw its support (Mabrey, 1988b, p. 42).

THE 75/25 ACCREDITATION STANDARD
BECOMES THE 90/65 RULE

After years of debate over the inflexibility of the fixed 75/25 percentage, the ACEJMC adopted the 90/65 rule in the 1985 and made it mandatory in 1989 (Leatherman, 1991). It required undergraduate students in accredited units at institutions requiring 120 semester hours for graduation to take a minimum of 90 semester hours in courses outside the major area of journalism and mass communications, with no fewer than 65 semester hours in the basic liberal arts and sciences. The standard was amended in September 1992 to allow units at institutions requiring between 120 and 124 semester hours to count up to 6 hours of media courses that are liberal arts in nature as part of the 90 outside hours but not the 65 liberal arts hours. Units at institutions requiring between 125 and 128 hours, however, were allowed to count only 3 hours of media liberal arts course toward the 90 outside hours.

In 1991, the University of Wisconsin—the home of Willard G. Bleyer, to whom credit is given for the ACEJMC curriculum standard—decided not to seek reaccreditation, which was to take place in 1993, because the new 90/65 rule would limit the number of hours its majors could take to 30 rather than the 40 hours it had required (Leatherman, 1991). In explaining the decision, Drechsel (1993) said complying with the standard would either limit Wisconsin students to 30 hours in the major and "thereby dilute the skills-concepts–theory balance and liberal arts emphasis within the School" or require more credits for graduation. He added: "Valuing the spirit of the curriculum standards more than its letter, and not wanting the curriculum standard to be the tail that wagged the dog, we chose to withdraw" (p. 68). Drechsel gave three reasons why Wisconsin didn't seek accreditation even when the ACEJMC decided to allow some media courses as part of the 90 outside hours:

> First, freed from the constraints of accreditation, our faculty has been intrigued by the opportunity to design an alternative form of external review, a process that is leading us fundamentally to rethink and articulate our goals, to reconsider our curriculum and to devote our attention to developing new and better ways in which our program can be evaluated. . . .
>
> Second, the existing reaccrediting system, though paying lip service to differences in institutional missions, seems to remain largely inflexible, too often adversarial, and oriented more toward quantifying program characteristics rather than assessing fundamental quality. . . .
>
> Third, and perhaps most important, the ACEJMC system continues to be based on the assumption that journalism and mass communication is itself not among the liberal arts. (p. 68)

Drechsel stated that denying journalism and mass communication courses are liberal arts "denigrates journalism education, reinforces its insularity, and stultifies the growth of journalism and mass communication as an academic discipline" (p. 68). He said the move was not planned to "incite revolution against ACEJMC" but to stimulate "beneficial change in the curriculum standard" (p. 69).

Ceppos (1992) said that the Wisconsin decision not to seek accreditation because of the liberal arts requirement was difficult for him to understand. Ceppos, chairman of the Associated Press Managing Editors Journalism Education Committee and APME's representative to the ACEJMC, said he wished he had taken more economics, history, politics, "and maybe ecology so that I'd have a real understanding of the fire in the Oakland hills" (p. 4). He quoted Bob Giles, then the American Society of Newspaper Editors' representative to the ACEJMC, as stating, "We used to say the real rub was that kids couldn't spell or write. But the real rub will be that kids don't know enough about the world they live in. If they don't begin to present us with graduates of more all-around academic competence, we're going to begin to turn to the liberal arts schools" (p. 4).

MASS MEDIA EDUCATION:
REDEFINING THE LIBERAL ARTS

The debate over the liberal arts curriculum standard gave some media educators an opportunity to make their case that many of their courses were liberal arts courses or that media education itself was liberal education. De Mott (1984) called such attempts by media educators to gain acceptance for the field as one of the humanities or social sciences as "semantic nonsense," but, he added, "a persistent strain of nonsense." However, he did call for media educators to promote a course in mass communication and society as "an indispensable course in every college student's education" (p. 31). He asked, "What's more 'liberalizing' and 'humanizing' than an appreciation of the contribution that mass media have made and continue to make to our culture; and what's more relevant to effective living in a democratic culture than a sophisticated knowledge of its mass communication network?" (p. 31). He added: "Certainly, numerous journalism/mass comm courses can be described, accurately, as 'liberalizing.' There is no need, however, because understanding mass communication and its role in a democratic social system transcends the concept of 'liberal education' " (p. 33).

Similarly, Mehra (1984) noted, "A liberal arts professional program would not only equip students with professional skills, but also develop in them a critical awareness of historical, social, political, cultural and economic forces at play in society that impinge upon the profession." He stated that students need to understand economics of the media, have a knowledge of the "social, historical, political and judicial" forces shaping modern media, understand the impact of the media on society, and, above all, be aware of the "inadequacies of the profession" (p. 34). He concluded, "The value of university education even in skills courses . . . lies in their ability to develop a conscious appreciation of the art of writing, the cultural context of their reports, the philosophy of their profession" (p. 35).

Responding to the attack on journalism education by Serafini (1984), Cowdin (1985) took the position that journalism education was a liberal education. He stated that "journalism education exists primarily for the good of students, not primarily for the good of the media industry" (p. 16). He wrote that the needs of students are served because not only the writing-based courses but also the conceptual courses "are at the very heart of a liberal education." In addressing the ACEJMC liberal arts accrediting standard, Cowdin argued, "But if the conceptual courses and the craft courses related to writing and visual communication are themselves liberal-arts courses, then what is the point of making a distinction at all between 'liberal-arts' courses and courses in journalism and mass communication?" (p. 18).

Cowdin (1985) also argued that journalism schools are not like schools for doctors or lawyers because fewer than one fourth of journalism graduates become journalists but, instead, go into other fields. He stated, "This is the nature of liberal arts, and this is the nature of journalism education, which most often is located within colleges of liberal arts because it is considered by the academic community to be one of them" (p. 18). He proposed that the distinction between journalism and the liberal arts should be eliminated for accreditation purposes "because it is a distinction without a difference." He added:

> Since the primary concern of the ACEJMC members is, appropriately, that journalism majors receive a substantially liberal education, then the major function of professional accreditation should be to make sure that there are not so many non-liberal craft courses being taught (for example, broadcast production courses and technique courses in advertising and public relations) that the program has come to resemble a technical community college or professional institute—but that there are enough craft courses being taught to enable the program to accomplish its stated objectives. (p. 18)

Cowdin called for more journalism education, not less, particularly in media ethics and responsibility, and suggested that it was time that all universities deal with mass communication as part of their core offerings in the liberal arts.

McCall (1987) noted that agreeing on a common definition of liberal arts is necessary before the decision can be made as to what is a liberal art. He suggested that a consensus could likely be achieved on a definition by Eastman (1986):

> A traditional liberal arts education should teach students (1) to learn how to learn, (2) to evaluate, and (3) to communicate. Subject matter content should function primarily as vehicles for learning how to understand, measure, evaluate, utilize and convey concepts, factual material, creative insight and methods of analysis.

McCall argued, "It is wrong to assume a future mass communicator is liberally educated just because that student takes a certain amount of coursework outside of the major discipline. Indeed, that approach simply tosses the liberal arts burden into the laps of colleagues in other departments on campus" (p. 18).

McCall (1987) also stated that liberal arts colleges were playing an important role in the movement toward incorporating liberal arts into their mass communication programs. He suggested that opposition to media-related programs because they are seen as too vocational can be met in two ways:

> First, the study of mass communication must be approached like any other liberal study, with concepts, critical insight and discussion and analysis of issues. Media courses must deal more with "why" than simply "how to."
>
> Second, the media system must be viewed for what it is—a pervasive means of touching and affecting every individual in contemporary society. Given this pervasiveness, knowing and understanding the media in American society is as important to every citizen as is an awareness and appreciation of political science, literature, history, sociology and the arts. (p. 19)

Roberts (1988) noted, "There has been considerable debate about what constitutes an arts and sciences course and whether certain courses, such as ethics, should be counted as professional courses or liberal arts." He concluded that the curriculum rule was useful because it "has been able to ensure a broad liberal arts education in the face of mounting pressure for greater specialization and hands-on training" (p. 18). Hoskins (1988) stated, however, that he had heard little discussion concerning the question "What are 'the basic liberal arts and sciences'?" (p. 1) and concluded that the terms " 'liberal arts' and 'liberal education' are terms that defy precise definition" (p. 2).

REFORMING THE MASS MEDIA
CURRICULUM

Blanchard (1988) argued that the accrediting council was dominated by professional organizations and that, instead, it should represent the concerns of the educators. "However well-intentioned and sincere," he wrote, "it is up to the academic representatives of the council to tell the professional representatives that curriculum design and implementation are the final judgment call of the officers of instruction in higher education—the faculty" (p. 50). He charged that the policy of not counting any media courses as liberal arts was the result of the dominance of newspaper organizations, which "have taken a rigid, anti-intellectual, illiberal position on the issue which can only result in a confrontation between the newspaper groups and journalism and mass communication educators—unless some flexibility is inserted into the issue" (p. 51). He added about the ACEJMC that "programs that voluntarily subscribe to an organization that defines their function as entirely vocational or preprofessional and not capable of contributing to the liberal education of all students, will soon lose out" (p. 51). Blanchard (1988) also stated that the liberal arts had become less liberal because of "rampant specialization and even vocationalism" (p. 51), whereas communication has emerged as "an academic discipline . . . (that) represents a new synthesis of older disciplines, just as modern history, sociology, political science, and other liberal arts disciplines emerged in their day in response to new knowledge, technology, and institutional systems" (p. 52). He called for two or three media courses to count as part of the 65 hours of liberal arts required.

Blanchard and Christ (1988) tied curriculum reform in media education to national developments in higher education and argued for the idea of an "enriched major" proposed by Boyer (1987). Boyer stated that an academic program is "liberal" if it has "a legitimate intellectual content of its own" and has "the capacity to enlarge, rather than narrow, the vision of the student" (Boyer, 1987, p. 109). Blanchard and Christ argued that media education must become part of what Boyer called the "integrated core," the basic general education program. "In other words," they stated, "JMC education can provide intellectual leadership by demonstrating how media studies can revitalize and liberate liberal education in the 21st century" (p. 10). They proposed four steps: that media programs (a) "evaluate themselves and their course offerings in light of what is fundamental and common to the field of mass communication"; (b) "articulate just how and why mass communication should be included in the general education program"; (c) "be more forcefully and effectively articulate to media professionals their liberal and general education role"; and (d) "join with the business, engineering, education, computer science, and other educators in appropriate pre-professional fields to determine points of commonality" (pp. 13–14).

While supporting the idea of accreditation, Mullins (1991) called the curriculum standard the "litmus test of accreditation" (p. 33). He noted that accredited programs tend to be at large, state-supported institutions and that no private liberal arts college was accredited. The only private institutions that were accredited were large universities, and no Ivy League institutions were accredited or had even applied. He noted that one problem that remained was getting large broadcast-oriented programs to apply. However, he concluded that "the most divisive issues of the past are gradually giving way to a more ecumenical philosophy that will eventually embrace all professionally oriented members of the mass comm family under a common accreditation structure" (p. 35).

The opposite view was taken by Davis (1991), who noted that accreditation was a matter of concern to programs in broadcasting, film, and other forms of mediated communication as well as communication studies. He wrote, "No matter how much has been said about accreditation before, the issue is not settled nor is the debate likely to grow less heated." He noted that there is no organization to accredit communication programs that have no professionals programs in journalism. And like Blanchard (1988), he argued that the curriculum, policy, and personnel matters should be "the responsibility of the academic faculty and not an outside agency" (p. 36). He concluded that ACEJMC accreditation might be appropriate for professionally oriented programs in journalism and related disciplines; however, he stated that "it is neither desirable nor appropriate for the ACEJMC to serve as the accrediting agency for academic programs in other communication fields" (p. 42).

The Associated Press Managing Editors (APME) developed an "Agenda for Journalism Education," which it presented to journalism educators in December 1993. The organization asked members to rank 11 skills that today's journalists need in addition to the fundamentals of journalism. Several were in professional skills areas, such as "presenting information well," "writing concisely," "understanding numbers in the news," "storytelling," and "desktop publishing." Others were broader, liberal arts concepts, such as "our multicultural society." Members listed "thinking analytically" as most important. Jerry Ceppos of the San Jose Mercury News and director of APME, noted that the Gannett newspaper group also had focused on the importance of critical thinking in its News 2000 project and developed a road show "that involves brainstorming with the staff specifically about analytical, critical thinking" (Ceppos, 1994. p. 4).

Williamson and Iorio (1994) stated that as a result of the ferment in the field concerning the liberal arts, "communication units in colleges and universities have been challenged to redefine and more coherently focus their curricular efforts" (p. 1). In an effort to do just that, representatives from 21 of the largest schools and colleges of journalism and mass communication met with representatives of the Association for Education in Journalism and Mass Communication, the Accrediting Council on Education in Journalism and Mass Communications, the Freedom Forum, the John S. and James L. Knight Foundation, and the Poynter Institute for Media Studies on Feb. 16–18, 1995, at the University of Maryland for what was called the Deans' Roundtable. The major topic of the conference was "Professional Education as Liberal Arts: Building on Strengths," and the major question before the group was "What should journalists know, and where should they be taught?" The subtopics covered included: (a) What is needed for a mature professional school; (b) What competencies graduates should have; (c) What partnerships should exist with the professions in the field; (d) Accreditation; (e) Private support; (f) The need for better exchange of information between the 21 schools.

Trevor Brown of Indiana stated at the conference that it had become harder to identify non-journalism courses that were essential for journalism students. David Rubin of Syracuse questioned the continued specialization in the liberal arts. "Do political science departments teach government or do they teach political science?" he asked. He suggested that students were not learning enough about government. Willard Rowland, Jr. of Colorado suggested that participants had tended to "idealize" external arts and sciences courses. Instead, he said, "We ought to celebrate what we see in the mirror, our own strengths. We've been too defensive" ("What Makes a Great Journalism School," p. 5).

Robert Giles, president of the ACEJMC, announced at the conference that the 12 accrediting standards were being reviewed for the first time in a decade. "Too many universities seem more comfortable with the idea of mass communications as a research-based discipline," he said, "while the industry wants graduates who can do journalism but is not willing to make a full commitment of support" ("What Makes a Great Journalism School," p. 6). The participants discussed whether to establish a two-tiered accreditation system with a separate tier for the best programs, but no consensus was achieved.

The AEJMC Curriculum Task Force (AEJMC, 1996) proposed that the ACEJMC replace the accreditation system with one that allowed for "creativity and experimentation" (p. 105). It proposed a tiered system that would allow nonprofessionally oriented programs to be evaluated. It would have four levels: affiliated, certified, accredited, and elite. It also proposed that the AEJMC prepare a self-rating system by which units could rate themselves as to the extent they were preparing their students for media careers and to publish the self-ratings. The scale would range from "professional schools with few theoretical courses to academic units with few skills courses, and from units with sequence-oriented structure to units with an integrated structure" (p. 106).

The AEJMC Curriculum Task Force (1996) concluded that "the liberal arts can and do exist inside as well as outside media education" (p. 108). It stated that as media students find ways to look at issues and problems in the courses they take throughout the institution, "they will broaden their education and be able to see how their major is important in obtaining a liberal education." It also noted that media educators already do many things to help develop students' higher level, critical-thinking skills but that they need to put more of their efforts in that direction "rather than retrenching and selling themselves as nothing more than trade schools" (p. 108).

Medsger (1996) noted that those who want internal courses to count as liberal arts argue that doing so would give media students a stronger liberal arts background. She stated that "[w]ith the liberal-arts seal of approval, they reason, the added theoretical communication courses can be justified as required for the major. The liberal-arts label, they say, also would enhance a communication course's reputation on campus." She rebutted such arguments, however, by stating:

> This view ignores the fact that on many campuses journalism has been considered part of liberal arts for many years. It also ignores the fact that the accrediting standard that limits the number of journalism units a major can take was created not because of the failure of journalism courses to be liberal arts but to force students to study extensively outside the major—to stretch their minds and build their knowledge. (p. 12)

STUDIES CONCERNING ACCREDITATION
AND THE LIBERAL ARTS

Research by VanderMeer and Lyons (1978) found what they determined was weakening support for the liberal arts. They compared the results of a 1976 national study about attitudes held by faculty members in various professional programs concerning the liberal arts with a similar study conducted in 1958. The authors noted that journalism faculty were much more oriented to liberal studies than any of the other eight professional faculties surveyed. A majority of all nine professional faculties indicated a preference for reducing the size of the liberal arts component at their institution, a tendency that was the strongest among journalism faculty. Sixty-nine percent of journalism respondents had what the researchers deemed to be a pro-liberal arts orientation as compared to 73% in 1958.

About a third of the journalism educators in the study by VanderMeer and Lyons (1978) stated that the liberal arts requirements should be met by taking courses related to the major; however, the authors noted a trend since the 1958 study for faculty to want liberal studies courses to have greater relevance to journalism. Three of five respondents preferred that half or less of their students' time be taken up with liberal studies, which the authors took to indicate that most respondents disagreed with the accrediting council's 75/25 standard. Less than 10% of respondents stated that their students had to take too many liberal arts courses. The liberal arts disciplines that half or more of journalism faculty would require students to take courses in were English composition (94%), history (75%), political science (70%), economics (66%), literature (61%), and sociology (51%). The authors noted a trend since the 1958 study for journalism faculty to favor social science courses more as liberal arts courses and to favor natural sciences and humanities less. They concluded from their study:

> The trend toward professionalism that has characterized higher education in the United States for at least fifty years is apparently continuing, and the faculties that offer professional programs in Journalism are in step with this trend. At the same time, there is a trend toward taking the interests and aspirations of individual students into account in establishing academic requirements for professional programs. . . . Consideration for individual students' interests and aspirations is manifest in an increased reluctance to retain extensive lists of required subjects, and a corresponding press toward making both the selection and the time of scheduling of specific liberals arts subjects at the option of the student and, presumably, his/her academic advisor. (p. 4)

G. Stone (1984) compared opinions of administrators of accredited journalism programs and members of the ACEJMC and its accrediting committee to determine the extent of agreement as to which journalism courses were and were not liberal arts courses. He concluded that "there is substantial difference in interpretation of the 25 percent rule" and that the study indicates that "some tightening of the guidelines, or at least greater clarity of the guidelines, be considered" (p. 16).

The Oregon Report (Project, 1984) supported the existing 75/25 plan with almost no discussion. However, the Task Force on Liberal Arts and Sciences of the AEJMC/ASJMC Task Force on the Future of Journalism and Mass Communication Education (Mullins, 1987a) attacked it. Although it opposed "any dilution of the liberal arts emphasis in JMC education," it objected to "classification of liberal arts and other courses based solely on the name of the course and the name of the administrative unit in the university offering them." The task force added:

> [Willard G.] Bleyer's observation about the prominent place of liberal arts in JMC education is still valid, but "liberal arts" are taught throughout the university—even in colleges of home economics, business schools, agriculture schools, and, yes, in journalism schools. . . . Simplistic definitions of liberal arts fly in the face of the makeup of the modern universities. . . .
> Simplistic classification of courses leads to the absurdity of mass comm ethics courses that are liberal arts for non-majors but must count in the professional total for majors. (p. 5)

The Liberal Arts Task Force also urged that media units and ACEJMC accreditors become responsible for classifying outside courses in departments such as communication, telecommunication, art, and business that actually are communication skills courses. It noted that few guidelines existed for classifying courses.

Mullins (1987b) noted that the accreditation system was a major concern of Liberal Arts Task Force members in that it "gives no overt credit for the liberal content in many standard JMC courses." He added:

> In this view there is as much liberal arts in such courses as mass communication history, law, ethics, public opinion, theory and research, and to a lesser extent in more practical courses like editorial writing and depth and public affairs reporting. These critics of accreditation bookkeeping point out that many of these courses are indeed classified as liberal arts for non-majors. (p. 12)

In answering the question of whether journalism and mass communication education is a liberal arts discipline, two of the subcommittees making up the task force said it was and three said it probably was not. Mullins concluded, therefore, that the dominant view of the task force was: "Journalism/mass communication is a professional discipline *allied* with the liberal arts" (p. 13). In its final report (Task Force, 1989), the Liberal Arts Task Force concluded about its curriculum proposals concerning the liberal arts: "There will be some who view these recommendations as opening a pandora's box leading to anarchy in JMC curricular matters. That's a risk we may have to run in order to improve our curricula and accreditation procedures" (p. A-8).

Hoskins (1988) surveyed administrators at 87 ACEJMC-accredited programs concerning how they interpreted the ACEJMC's liberal arts standard and received responses from 61 (70%). He listed seven statements about how they identified liberal arts courses. Forty eight percent of them responded that they would assume that any course taught in a liberal arts and sciences unit was acceptable as liberal arts. One quarter had no procedure for deciding whether a course was acceptable as liberal arts and sciences. At 30% of the programs, the unit head made the decision. At two, outside groups or faculties advised them as to which courses were liberal arts. Hoskins also asked administrators to rank (on a 1-to-6 scale, with 1 being most important) the best way to make the determination as to which courses were liberal arts. Ranked first was the course description (2.65), followed by the course syllabus (2.76), knowledge about the department or college in which the course was taught (2.85), whether a course fulfills general education requirements (3.25), talking with an instructor of the course (3.96), and reviewing the textbook used (4.53).

In his study, Hoskins (1988) also asked administrators to classify a list of courses as arts and sciences or not. Courses listed as arts and sciences by more than half were: Dance History (College of Fine Arts), 89%; Fundamentals of Music Theory (College of Liberal Arts), 74%; Police–Community Relations (College of Arts and Sciences), 72%. Such courses as Reference and Bibliography (College of Education), National Agriculture Policy (Economics), and Remote Sensing (College of Arts and Sciences) were rated liberal arts by from a third to a half of administrators. Telecommunications Law and Regulation (College of Arts and Sciences) was rated arts and sciences by 10%. Hoskins concluded that classifying liberal arts was "a complex, highly subjective undertaking" (p. 8).

RECENT STUDIES ABOUT THE LIBERAL ARTS
AND MEDIA EDUCATION

A study by the American Society of Newspaper Editors (ASNE, 1990) found that 75% of editors stated that recent job candidates would have been better off if they had taken more work in other fields. Most editors (81%) thought that having a broad background in the arts and sciences was important or very important. Nearly two thirds of editors thought that the liberal arts and sciences education of entry-level hires during the previous 5 years was strong (5%) or somewhat strong (57%), and only 43% percent of editors thought it was important or very important for journalism schools to educate students in mass communication concepts as well as the fundamental of journalism.

Dickson (1992) surveyed media administrators at 380 institutions concerning the importance of the liberal arts. He received responses from 71% of the administrators. A majority of them (55%) favored the 90/65 curriculum rule, compared to 24% who liked the 75/25 rule. Another 9% had no preference, and 12% disliked both rules. Administrators at accredited programs were significantly more likely than those at unaccredited programs to favor the 90/65 rule (69% vs. 49%) and significantly less likely to favor the 75/25 plan (13% vs. 28%). Overall, 64% of the programs required less than 27.5% of students' hours to be in media courses, and 10% of programs required more than 32.5% of the students' hours to be in media courses. Unaccredited programs were significantly more likely than accredited programs to require 36 or more media hours for a major (49% vs. 15%). Three fourths of the programs required 65 or more hours in liberal arts and sciences (65 hours being the minimum number for accreditation), with 52% stating that 70 or more hours were required in the liberal arts and sciences and 24% stating that 65 to 69 hours were required. A larger percentage of unaccredited programs than accredited programs (54% vs. 48%) required 70 or more hours in liberal arts. Administrators at 71% of the institutions stated that the media unit had some control over which liberal arts courses students took. Nearly two thirds of the respondents (63%) stated that some media non-skills courses should be allowed to count toward the 65 hours of liberal arts. Dickson concluded that the issue of what a liberal arts course is might be the source of continued conflict. He stated, "The curriculum pandora's box has been opened, but it is too early to tell if it will lead to anarchy or just be a can of worms for journalism educators" (p. 14).

Carter (1995) commented that when the university and the country look at mass communication, they find a "social science of sorts." He said the reason media education is a social science instead of a behavioral science is "because we equate mass communication with mass media. Difficulty arises because we thereby attempt to understand the problem of the collectivity's need for mass communication by addressing only one kind of solution for it: the mass media" (p. 5). He called for broadening mass communication education to gain the best of both social and behavioral sciences. Carter concluded, "If we are to become both behavioral science and social science, then we need a behavioral foundation that is different from what is now available from any existing academic field in the behavioral sector" (p. 7).

Iorio and Wiliamson (1995) investigated what liberal arts courses and components were being taught across the curriculum at three types of programs: accredited media programs, unaccredited media programs, and programs that combined instruction in mass communication and speech communication. They looked specifically at three types of liberal arts components: history, theory, and philosophy courses. The authors found the three liberal arts components throughout the curricula of all three types of the communication programs; however, of the three types of programs studied, combined mass and speech communication programs had the highest percentage of all three types of liberal arts courses. They also found considerable differences as to whether such courses were required or elective; however, in all three types of media programs, courses interrelating history, theory, and philosophy were more likely to be required for all majors than were separate courses. They found liberal arts components in the introductory course, but they did not find a wide range of interrelated liberal arts components in the rest of the curriculum. Iorio and Williamson concluded that the curricula were "infused with liberal arts and sciences components," but they also found a "fragmented curricula that may be more reflective of the vestiges of separate traditions than the evolution of liberal arts studies" (pp. 24–25).

In his analysis of the 1990 ASNE survey, Dickson (1996) determined that editors of small newspapers were significantly more likely to want graduates to have taken more journalism courses rather than more courses in fields such as history, the arts, the social sciences, and the physical sciences than were editors of medium-sized newspapers (48% vs. 26%) or editors of large newspapers (48% vs. 4%). Editors of small newspapers were significantly less likely to want new hires to have a broad arts and sciences background than were editors at medium-sized newspapers (69% vs. 81%) and editors at large newspapers (69% vs. 89%). Editors of small newspapers were significantly less likely to rate their recent entry level hires as strong or somewhat strong in the liberal arts and sciences than were editors at medium-sized newspapers (51% vs. 55%) and editors at large newspapers (51% vs. 78%). Also, editors at small newspapers were significantly less likely than editors at medium newspapers (82% vs. 93%) and editors at large newspapers (82% vs. 97%) to want journalism schools to provide a fundamental knowledge of journalism but keep the present level of commitment to the liberal arts and sciences.

The AEJMC/ASJMC Task Force on Missions and Purposes of Journalism and Mass Communication Education (AEJMC/ASJMC Task Force, 1996) found that 36% of the mission statements of media units they received and analyzed stated that their program was designed to impart critical thinking or analytical skills. Another 44% stated that the program was designed to impart practical skills. Nearly half (45%) of the mission statements mentioned such things as the role of media in society and rights and responsibilities of the media as being a focus of the unit. Though only 89% of the mission statements indicated that part of the unit's mission was to prepare students for jobs in media industries, the task force concluded that it may have overlooked some references to that purpose because of the level of abstraction of some statements. Nearly half (47%) stated that they offered a fairly equal balance between professional preparation and a liberal arts and sciences background. Another 18% listed a liberal arts orientation as their primary focus, and 11% noted that a liberal arts and sciences background was a secondary mission. Only about 16% did not mention a liberal arts and sciences role.

As media educators were wrestling with the issue of the content of their professional curriculum and its relationship to the liberal arts, they also had to deal with other major issues. The most contentious of those was whether media education was to continue as a field under a journalism umbrella or whether it would follow some other vision: either the path to greater integration with interpersonal communication and communication studies or the path to fragmentation, a path that would require journalism education to spin off some or all its allied sequences and narrow its focus.

8

The Future of Mass Media Education: Integration or Fragmentation?

If the communication and media-related disciplines do not hang together, they will hang separately.

—Blanchard (1991, p. 13).

Mass media education could follow one of a number of directions based on different visions of its future. Newsom (1985) suggested three possible futures for mass media education: (a) the re-absorption of studies in journalism/mass communication into classical disciplines; (b) the establishment of a few large umbrella mass communication schools that are primarily research oriented but tied to industry; and (c) fragmentation. Under the first option, mass media education would become a subset of sociology or go piecemeal into political science, history, sociology, or possibly English. Under the second option, the few large schools of mass communication would provide graduates for the larger publications rather than provide entry level graduates for smaller publications, who would have to look elsewhere than journalism schools for their new hires. About the third option, fragmentation, she wrote:

> Some schools will specialize in various areas like newspapers, magazines, photojournalism and broadcast, with the management of all these in one school. Advertising in all media, and the management of advertising wherever it is practiced, agency or in-house, may be in another school either mixed with public relations or not. PR may exist apart in still another school teaching all facets and the management of PR agencies, in-house and in counseling. In this case specialists will be teaching and will be moving in and out of industry and academe. (p. 23)

She concluded, however, "It could be (that) without securing our role as an academic discipline, we will have no future." (p. 44).

Other scenarios also might be envisioned in the 21st century. A type of integration other than media education's absorption into an older discipline is the integration of interpersonal communication and mass communication to form a communication discipline. Another type of integration is one in which media-specific sequences are abolished or reduced significantly in favor of a generic media curriculum or a curriculum with a broad core requirement. A more limited vision of integration is the merger of advertising and public relations into a subfield of media education called integrated communication or

146

integrated marketing communication. Such a move might accompany a movement toward greater integration of print and broadcast journalism.

Integration also could lead to the emergence of a broad communication discipline. Heckhausen (1972) stated that a discipline has a (1) a material field; (2) a subject matter; 3) a level of theoretical integration; (4) methods of examination; (5) analytical tools; (6) applications to a field of practice; and (7) historical contingencies, i.e., the background and development of a field of knowledge. Using that definition, Paulson (1980) has argued that speech communication itself met the criteria of a discipline. Whether or not Paulson is correct, such an argument for media education is somewhat less plausible at present because of its apparent lack of theoretical integration but could be made if the two communications fields were merged.

Competing with those visions of integration is the vision of disintegration or fragmentation noted by Newsom (1985). In one variation of that vision, journalism education would spin off one or more subfields, likely advertising and/or public relations, as autonomous fields of study. While suggesting that print and broadcast journalism are more or less equals, Medsger (1996), for example, has argued that "the nature and mission of journalism are different from those of other fields of communication." She also stated that print and broadcast journalism differ from advertising and public relations in that journalism works on behalf of the public interest "rather than by representatives of special interests, as happens in advertising and public relations" (p. 7). Fragmentation, however, could include loosening ties between print and broadcast journalism, as well.

A less drastic form of fragmentation of media education might be a change in the role that journalism plays. Some educators still see journalism education as taking a starring role among the media-related fields. For example, Medsger (1996) called journalism "a star in the mass communication education constellation" (p. 12). Print journalism may not remain the jewel in the crown, however. In fact, some critics would suggest that enrollment shifts toward public relations and other specialties have already removed it from that position. Welke (1985), for example, argued that advances in technology "may now be forcing such units to recognize that journalism is a subset of mass media and not the other way around" (p. 21). He suggested that broadcasting appears to favor "a broader 'telecommunication' umbrella," whereas print journalism "appears to be leaning backward to a 'mass media' concept." He added, "All of this illustrates a 'journalism equals mass media' fallacy" (p. 22). He urged a curriculum redefinition "that moves forward, encompassing mass media *and* telecommunication concerns" and "avoids a narrow position where the journalistic function is dominant" (p. 22).

THE COMPOSITION OF MEDIA-RELATED
EDUCATION TODAY

In their 1997 annual survey of media education, Kosicki, Becker, Watson, and Porter (1998) counted 141,006 journalism and mass communication undergraduates in 443 programs (of 450 programs identified), up more than 3,000 from 1996. Another 10,041 were in master's programs and 1,148 in doctoral programs. A total of 31,374 undergraduate degrees were granted in the 1996–1997 school year along with 3,649 master's degrees and 125 doctorates. Journalism graduates comprised 26.2% of the journalism and mass communication enrollments, slightly more than the combined totals for public relations (12.1%) and broadcasting (11.7%). Advertising students comprised 8.7% of the total, and other specializations accounted for 41.3%. Females constituted 61.3% of undergraduate majors and 59.9% of degrees granted. Whites comprised 71.0% of students, Blacks 13.5%, Hispanics 8.5%, Asians 2.7%, Native Americans 0.5%, and other 3.9%. A total of 4,845 full-time and 3,343 part-time faculty were reported. They concluded that an increasing number of media students were graduating with specialties other than journalism, broadcasting, advertising, and public relations.

The AEJMC Curriculum Task Force (Dickson, 1994b) found that the greatest area of structural change reported by media-related units in the previous 5 years was an increase in the number of components (sequences, majors, or programs), with 37% of units responding that they had increased the number of media components. Units at institutions with fewer than 15,000 students were more likely than those at larger institutions (41% vs. 27%) to have increased the number of media components. Units located somewhere other than a journalism department or a journalism school were more likely to have increased the number of media components (43% vs. 20%). Twelve percent of media-related units had added a media component through consolidation or merger, and the same percent had reduced the number of media-related components through consolidation or merger. Another 9% had eliminated a media component by other than merger.

Becker and Kosicki (1997) reported that "traditional journalism sequences remain at the heart of the journalism and mass communication programs" (p. 63). They found that 87% of journalism and mass communication programs offered at least one traditional journalism sequence. The most popular journalism sequences were news–editorial (in 58.1% of the 446 academic units reporting), followed by broadcast news (43.9%), journalism (34.3%), photojournalism (13.2%), and magazine journalism (8.3%). Other journalism specialties were offered by 2% of units. Public relations was the nonjournalism sequence that was most offered (50.9% of units), with radio/TV or telecommunication offered by 36.3% of the units and advertising by 30.3%. Among nonjournalism media-related sequences, mass communication was offered most often (by 17.7%), followed by advertising and public relations combined (13.7%), film/cinema (7.4%), and mass media (7.2%). In addition, 26.2% of the units offered speech, 10.1% offered theater, 9.9% offered organizational communication, and 49.1% offered other types of programs.

Becker and Kosicki (1997) reported that their data did not support the findings of Medsger (1996) that journalism education "is at the margins, rather than the core" of media education. They concluded that their data for 1996 suggests that "this notion is quite at odds with the data on what journalism and mass communication programs actually offer" (p. 67). Noting her criticism of a shift toward mass communication as a field of study at the expense of journalism, they reported that 75.9% of units with a mass communication sequence also offered one or more journalism sequences and that 90.6% of units with a mass media sequence also offered journalism. In addition, media units offering speech as well as public relations and advertising also had journalism sequences, causing the authors to state, "Basic journalism remains the core of these and other journalism and mass communication programs" (pp. 68–69). They added:

> In fact, what these analyses show is that mass communication and mass media specialties are not taking over journalism and mass communication programs from basic journalism offerings. Rather, these are most often offered in large programs that are above average not only in size but also in the number of sequences dedicated to basic journalism instruction. (p. 69)

WHERE DO MEDIA-RELATED PROGRAMS BELONG?

Dressel (1960) argued that affiliation with a college of arts and sciences was "not necessarily the best organization pattern for the development of a strong program of journalism education, since it tends to relieve the journalism faculty of responsibility for careful planning of the liberal education experience of journalism students" (p. 99). He added:

> An independent faculty, in accepting full responsibility for the total education of its students, has greater incentive for developing a truly integrated program in which professional and liberal education are indistinguishably merged to produce a liberally educated person with some skill in and full realization of the responsibility involved in the communication process. (p. 99)

Likewise, the Oregon Report (Project, 1984) concluded that "the journalism/mass communication unit should ideally be a freestanding professional school reporting to the highest level of university leadership, not subsumed in a liberal arts college structure unless that is the clear preference of the local institution" (p. 1). Also, the Vision 2000 Task Force (AEJMC, 1994b) stated:

Although it is difficult to generalize, it may be that self-standing schools of journalism or mass communication or colleges of communication may compete better for university resources than do schools and departments of journalism and mass communication that are part of colleges such as letters or science or social and behavioral science. (p. 10)

Wartella (1994) noted that journalism, mass communication and speech communication programs were "sometimes considered not central to the university's mission—adding to the field's isolation and complicating the issue of organizing its study" (p. 1). Dennis (1994) warned that university budget-cutting would lead to "reorganization, retrenchments and downsizing" that would leave communication and journalism programs vulnerable "because they lack clout in the university, often have little prestige and are not well understood" (p. 4). He added, "There is still considerable debate about where communications belongs in the university—whether in colleges of arts and sciences, professional studies, performing arts, business or in freestanding units such as holistic schools of communication" (p. 7). He added:

There is, of course, no one-size-fits-all formulation for communication education, any more than there really is for apparel. If the structure is troubled, so is the field's internal identity, which is often marked more by conflict and hostility than by cooperation and collaboration. Different cultures, institutional histories and jealousies seem at odds with any serious notion of common ground or working together. (Dennis, 1994, p. 7)

The model of the autonomous school of journalism is the image usually projected of media-related programs because the term "journalism school" often is used to describe all types of media-related education. The reality is that only a small percentage of media programs fit that model. Instead media units tend to be located in a college of arts and sciences or arts and letters. The AEJMC Curriculum Task Force (Dickson, 1995) looked at the structure of media-related units. It received responses from 289 institutions with journalism and mass communication programs. As to a departmental breakdown, the task force found that somewhat over one third (37%) of the administrative units housing media-related programs were departments of communication. Nearly 20% were journalism departments, and just over 16% were departments of mass communication. Slightly over one fourth were some other type of administrative unit.

The Curriculum Task Force (Dickson, 1995) found that nearly 41% of media units were in a college of arts and sciences and another 17% in a college of arts and letters or humanities. Just under 10% were located in a college of communication, and just over 5% were located in a journalism school. Other configurations accounted for 27% of the programs reporting. Likewise, Becker and Kosicki (1997) also noted that the liberal arts college was the most common home for journalism and mass communication programs, something "that has become even more pronounced in the last three years" (p. 63).

VISIONS OF A UNIFIED DISCIPLINE

If media education follows the route of an integrated discipline of communication, it would be following the path envisioned by Wilbur Schramm, the founder of mass communication and communication studies. Such an integrated communication discipline could legitimately claim to be a discipline. Schramm's vision did not transpire, Chaffee noted, because "Schramm's new paradigm for communication study was added to existing academic traditions of speech and journalism, which never lost their separate intellectual roots" (Rogers & Chaffee, 1993, p. 126). Rogers, however, stated that despite the lack of integration in the communication–relation fields, Schramm did create a new discipline. Rogers wrote:

> By creating books and curricula in communication, the humanist Schramm founded a new social science. It is the first one to be widely accepted in American universities since the five traditional social sciences—psychology, sociology, economics, political science, and anthropology—were established around the turn of the century. (Rogers & Chaffee, 1993, p. 127)

Like Schramm (1997), Blanchard (1991) argued for integrating the communication discipline. He stated that intellectual ferment in the discipline would "either destroy or merge the historic division in our fields based on the distinction between interpersonal [speech communication, et al.] versus mass media channels [journalism, mass communication, et al.]" (p. 13). He noted the statement by Chaffee (Rogers & Chaffee, 1983, p. 24) that the division is "an instance of functional autonomy in our field, one that doesn't make much sense in the light of current theory and research." Blanchard concluded, "If the communication and media-related disciplines do not hang together, they will hang separately" (p. 13).

Likewise, Rakow (1993) stated that the curriculum for the future will need to "integrate what are now fragmented subfields of speech, interpersonal, organizational, and mass communication, all of which are further fragmented into specializations" and suggested that "communication studies should serve as a model in breaking down the disciplinary walls" (p. 157). She noted that divisions were becoming less sustainable because of the development of new technologies that straddle the boundaries between interpersonal communication and mass communication. In addition, she stated that educators "owe it to our students and to ourselves to make sense of our field of study." She concluded, "We must find the commonalities, the patterns, the maps, if we expect our students to leave us with anything more than a collection of disparate courses" (p. 158).

THE INTEGRATED/GENERIC/FUNCTIONAL
CURRICULUM

Perhaps the most controversial recommendation of the report of the Project on the Future of Journalism and Mass Communication Education—called the Oregon Report (Project, 1984)—was its call for a "generic model of journalism/mass communication education" to replace the "industry model." The report stated:

> Essentially, the problem is that journalism schools tend to operate on an industry model. That is, students are taught the entry-level skills they will need to secure their first jobs in a single, specific communication industry such as newspaper or broadcasting. Reliance on the industry model, however, does not give students the sufficient understanding of the media as a whole that they will need to advance later in their careers. An alternative approach would be to use a generic model of journalism/mass communication education. . . .
> In substantive terms, the generic model will enable students to develop a better understanding of the fields in which they wish to work. (Project, 1987, pp. 9–10)

Toward that end, the Oregon Report called for merging conceptual/theoretic and craft/professional courses in many cases and for conceptual courses (such as media and society, media economics, etc.) to be organized as "linchpins to the liberal arts" (p. 1).

A number of task forces and commissions beginning with the Oregon Report have suggested that media education is too fragmented and should become more integrated through what has been called alternatively an *integrated*, *generic*, *functional*, or *holistic* curriculum. The curriculum would provide a broad-based introductory course, such as a course in media writing, instead of introductory courses in print, broadcast, advertising, and public relations writing. The resulting integrated media classes began to be called *generic* courses because they represented a variety of subfields. Proponents of such a curriculum argued that media education has been dominated by the media industries and that it must reform itself to serve students better.

Blanchard and Christ (1985) proposed that media units develop a universal undergraduate curriculum core: courses taken by all media majors. They noted three rationales for the common media core: (a) utilitarian (the idea "that some skills and knowledge are so useful that all students should acquire them"); (b) introduction/orientation (courses that contain "substantial orientation and introductory functions," those in which the "subject matter is wide-ranging and integrative rather than specialized and atomized," and those that are "more conceptual than applied"); and (c) integrative (courses that "seek connections and commonalities among both conceptual and applied specialties") (pp. 29–30). They stated that units that reorganize as integrated units without a common core "can shield and sustain old divisions and specialties" (p. 30). They wrote, "It is our contention that undergraduate students will best be served in the 21st century by JMC units that offer curricula which emphasize the commonalities of the communication fields—regardless of the diversity of delivery systems and career labels" (p. 31). Welke (1985), on the other hand, stated that the generic/integrated curriculum "could become the most significant threat to the academic quality and integrity of broadcasting/telecommunication programs in the 1980s." He added, "The generic idea would appear to be more than the isolated musings of obscure educators or professionals. This has the ring of an unfriendly corporate take-over" (p. 21).

Other reports were to call for an integrated curriculum, however. One was the ASJMC/AEJMC Task Force on Liberal Arts and Sciences in Journalism and Mass Communication. Its report (Mullins, 1987a) stated that figures showing entry level media jobs made up for only 8% of the jobs taken by print and broadcast graduates "show us the folly of narrow, industrial-based training of our students." Therefore, in its most controversial recommendation, it suggested a "functionalist (or integrated) rather than a fragmented or segmented approach to curriculum planning and evaluation" (p. 4). In its final report (Task Force, 1989), which was part of a larger report by seven task forces, the Liberal Arts Task Force defined a functionalist approach as "a specification of how all components of the curriculum interrelate in addressing explicit goals and objectives of the unit." It stated that such an approach "would not categorize courses simply on the basis of where they are taught" (p. A-5).

THE NEW PROFESSIONALISM

Blanchard and Christ (1993) saw an integrated/generic/functional/holistic curriculum as a means for strengthening the field's relationship with the "new Liberal Arts" and for helping create what they called a *new professionalism*. They stated about the challenges and opportunities facing media education because of ferment taking place in higher education:

> We believe that for the survival of the field, the revitalization of the liberal arts and the benefit of society, these challenges should be met with a restructuring of undergraduate curriculums in media education toward a New Professionalism that replaces the uniformity and expediency of the occupational ethos of today's media programs with the diversity of a liberal ethos more reflective of the university tradition and community values. (pp. 3–4)

Blanchard and Christ (1993) noted two forces making major changes in media education essential: the lack of study in depth or unity of knowledge in the undergraduate liberal arts experience and the technological revolution that is causing major changes in the U.S. media system. In their review of critiques of undergraduate education in the 1980s, they identified three related criticisms: (a) "undergraduate education lacks integrity and purpose"; (b) "its content, especially the liberal arts 'canon,' needs revitalization"; and (3) "it is too vocational, narrow and fragmented, and needs integration and unity of knowledge" (Blanchard & Christ, 1993, p. 4). The challenge of the new technologies, they stated, "calls for flexible, integrated, and innovative media courses and curricula. . . ." Moreover, they added,

> it means a movement away from narrowly conceived media-specific sequences based on industrial configurations toward broad-based, cross-media, integrative models; the teaching of ideas and skills that transcend the narrow occupational focus of specific, entry-level, job-related protocols; "de-massifying" the concept of communication to incorporate the study of intrapersonal and interpersonal communication and their relationship to "mass" forms of communication distribution; and, finally, rethinking how people teach and how learning environments can be enhanced with the use of technologies. (p. 22)

They predicted that the new professionalism they envisioned would result in more diversity of undergraduate media education as occupational-based media sequences would be replaced by "integrated communication and media education curricula" and that communication and media programs would move into the "campus academic and intellectual mainline" (Blanchard & Christ, 1993, p. 35). However, they saw two main obstacles to reform: fragmentation of communication education into mass communication and interpersonal communication and "the apparent unwillingness of leaders in the field to develop courses and curricula in communication and media for the general student or nonmajors" (p. 44). The curriculum for the new professionalism would consist of "the conceptual core, a conceptual enrichment component, and an experiential learning capstone or media workshop emphasizing familiarity and understanding with, rather than technical proficiency in, media technology" (p. 46). The curriculum would be designed to produce a "liberally educated media professional," that is, someone with "a self-directed cultural self-consciousness and a high degree of control over one's field" in addition to a dedication to public service and an ethical commitment (p. 62).

The Association for Education in Journalism and Mass Communication's Vision 2000 Task Force (AEJMC, 1994b) noted that media professionals tended to criticize mass media education but, at the same time, hire media graduates. It predicted that, eventually, the media professions will be filled with college graduates "with the interests of providing both a liberal education and a 'new professionalism.' " It added,

> Ironically, in some sense that more modern understanding looks more like the "original" definition of journalism education: to prove an ethical foundation for work to provide the historical and theoretical bases for launching reasonable, useful, intelligent critiques of social and economic institutions. (p. 22)

The Vision 2000 Committee on Journalism/Mass Communication Curricula concluded that the "notion of 'sequencing'—preparing students for specific jobs in journalism—appears to be increasingly unsound" (AEJMC, 1994b, p. 28). Like the Oregon Report, the committee proposed that students concentrate on core subjects that prepare them generally for journalistic practice in a wide variety of careers. It proposed that the core offerings be "broad, inclusive and interdisciplinary" and include history, law and ethics, current practices, communication theory, and the social role of communication. All media students would also take a skills minor.

The Association for Education in Journalism and Mass Communication Curriculum Task Force (AEJMC, 1996) proposed that media education has at least five purposes: (a) to provide students the competencies they need for successful careers in media-related professions; (b) to educate nonmajors about the role of the media in society; (c) to prepare students to become teachers or to undertake graduate education; (d) to prepare liberally educated graduates to become media analysts and critics; and (e) to provide midcareer education for media professionals. It concluded that "media education has a larger role than producing media professionals, though that is its primary responsibility" (AEJMC, 1996, p. 106).

The Curriculum Task Force proposed that media units establish a core curriculum for all majors that would include "an overview of the philosophy and practice basic to the particular media areas for which the unit offers courses." The overview would consist of "cross-media synthesis courses or . . . media-specific courses, whichever is determined most appropriate by the unit's assessment procedures" (AEJMC, 1996, p. 107). It also proposed that students gain multiple competencies so as not to be tied to finding a job in only one media area. Media units would be expected to provide graduates with "an advanced level of competency in a major emphasis area and a basic level of competency in a second media subspeciality." It added:

> Competency could be accomplished in two subfields in a single major field (such as an advanced competency in news-editorial and a basic competency in photojournalism), in two media fields (such as an advanced competency in public relations and a basic competency in advertising), or in an integrated field and a professional field (such as an advanced competency in media studies and a basic competency in broadcast journalism). (pp. 107–108)

In a study titled *Winds of Change: Challenges Confronting Journalism Education*, Medsger (1996) dismissed the idea of an integrated/generic/holistic media curriculum. She wrote:

> The strongest winds of change promote removing journalism education as a separate academic discipline and merging it into communication courses designed not to prepare journalists—people with a mission to stimulate public

discourse and serve the public interest—but to prepare generic communicators who could be hired to serve any interests. (p. 5)

She charged that such an approach "often involves increasing the number of communication courses required of students and decreasing the number of courses they take outside their major" (p. 5). She saw the integrated approach as being in conflict with the vision of journalism education established by the Accrediting Council on Education in Journalism and Mass Communications, which requires that only about one quarter of a student's hours can be in journalism and mass communication. Most of the rest (65 hours) must be in the liberal arts and sciences.

Medsger (1996) argued that proponents of the ACEJMC's approach "believe that the journalism curriculum should not dominate the education of journalism majors." She said the approach is designed "to prepare the minds of journalists, but, in fact, it sharpens minds in ways that are useful in any number of professions." She charged, on the other hand, that the integrated curriculum or new professionalism would "[p]ermit or require students to take 50% or more of their units in journalism/mass communication, reduce the number of writing courses they take, and require them to take a very large portion of their major courses in communication theory." She added that proponents of the generic model "want communication studies to be generally accepted as a liberal arts field" (p. 11).

In her report, Medsger (1996) stated that a "generic communication" curriculum would mean journalism students would be spending less time on promoting the intellectual skills necessary for practicing journalism. She wrote that journalism students "are asked to think—carefully, critically, precisely—and to do so beyond their own interests, to think of the public's interests and needs" (p. 9). She stated that the "apparent failure to understand the nature of journalism skills has been expressed repeatedly in histories of communication studies and in recent studies of journalism/mass communication education" (p. 12). She stated that integrated approach "would mean that the number of units in the communication major would increase considerably while the skills courses would decline in number and value" (p. 12).

Medsger (1996) specifically attacked the AEJMC Vision 2000 Task Force, Blanchard and Christ's new professionalism and the AEJMC Curriculum Task Force. She suggested, for example, that the Curriculum Task Force's proposal to allow some media courses to be counted as liberal arts and to allow students to take a minor as well as a major in a media-related field "would, in large measure, eliminate journalism as a star in the mass communication education constellation." (p. 13) She stated, "To those who believe in limiting the journalism content of a major in order to guarantee a wide liberal-arts education, the integrated-communication approach would erase the possibility of the major graduating with a rich and diverse liberal-arts education, let alone a menu of challenging skills courses" (p. 12).

STUDIES CONCERNING THE
INTEGRATED/GENERIC/HOLISTIC CURRICULUM

Dennis noted 3 years after the Oregon Report's proposal that "journalism and communication schools make their programs more holistic and more unified" and that "[b]y the fall of 1986, a large number of universities and colleges could accurately be described as heavy users of the Oregon Report, which became a catalyst for change but not a precise patter(n)" (Project, 1987, p. 62). In their research, Weaver and Wilhoit (1988) found broad support for the plan. Though twice as many media educators surveyed favored an industry-based sequence approach as favored a "generic" or "holistic" approach to curriculum, almost half of them favored some sort of combination. The two researchers found no significant difference based on whether the faculty member's institution was accredited.

A large majority of newspaper editors surveyed by the American Society of Newspaper Editors (ASNE, 1990) were opposed to eliminating sequences and replacing them with generic communication courses. Editors were asked: "Some journalism schools have opted to eliminate sequences such as news–editorial, broadcasting, public relations, etc. Instead, students heading toward different career goals take courses designed for everyone (e.g., newswriting). Do you favor such a trend?" Only 20% of editors with an opinion favored such a move. However, when they were asked "Some journalism schools are taking a broad approach in their curriculum with courses that look at all media, including newspapers, as interdependent and interrelated. Do you think this is a good idea?," 48% of editors with an opinion thought it was a good idea and the rest thought it was not.

Dickson and Sellmeyer (1992a, 1992b) surveyed 380 heads of media programs and received responses from 271 (71%). They found that 77% of the institutions responding were organized by media sequences. About 62% of administrators having an opinion opposed eliminating industry-based sequences and offering courses designed for everyone. About 80% of administrators favored courses that looked at all media as interdependent and interrelated, and those with a news–editorial background were significantly less likely than other administrators to favor such courses. Only a minority of the units (43%) had an introductory writing course aimed at several media. Forty-one percent of administrators stated that their program had been moving toward a more integrated curriculum during the previous 5 years, 36% stated that their program had made little or no movement in relation to an integrated curriculum, and 23% stating that their program had been moving toward a more segmented, industry-based program. They concluded from their study:

> If the measure of the successful implementation of the Oregon Report is based upon a movement toward elimination of industry-based sequences and addition of generic courses, then the success of that report appears limited. However, if the measure of the acceptance of the report is based upon a movement toward

more interrelationships between sequences, that success is more evident. (1992, p. 35)

The New Configurations Subcommittee of the ACEJMC Long-Range Planning Committee (Hynes, 1993) surveyed 426 media programs listed in the AEJMC directory concerning changes in structure and curriculum relating to program integration. It received responses from 202 programs (47%) with accredited programs being slightly overrepresented. Just over 16% indicated that they would be consolidating with another communication unit within the next 3 to 5 years, and seven programs reported recent consolidation. Nearly 72% stated that professional journalism and mass communication should be merged with media studies into a single administrative unit. Whereas two thirds of programs had specialized sequences and another 9% included a combination of sequences and integrated programs, only 52% stated that media sequences were the ideal program structure. Though only 17% of programs had an integrated curriculum, nearly 22% stated that the integrated curriculum was the ideal approach, and another 16% preferred a combination of sequences and integrated programs. Just over one fourth of the programs had a nonprofessional media specialty, and 17% had an emphasis in communication theory. Almost one fourth had a specialty in speech communication. The committee concluded:

> The dissonance reflected in the survey results between the current curricular organization based on sequences/tracks and the ideal preference for more generic or combined curricula may be particularly worthy of the ACEJMC's attention Such intellectual unrest with current curricular structures may be a harbinger of changes to come that are not yet even fully articulated. (p. 3)

The AEJMC Curriculum Task Force (Dickson, 1994b) investigated the extent to which the integrated curriculum had become a part of media education. It sent surveys to administrators of 575 administrative units thought to offer media-related degrees. A total of 289 administrators (50%) returned surveys. Just over half (53%) of the units offered only specialization in professional media sequences or tracks, and another 26% offered a combination of sequences and integrated mass communication or media studies. Nearly 14% offered only an integrated mass communication or media studies degree, and almost 7% listed other types of degree options. Units at institutions with more than 5,000 undergraduates were significantly more likely than those at smaller institutions to have specializations in professional media sequences or tracks (56% vs. 46%). Units that were accredited were more likely to offer specialization in media sequences (67% vs 42%), as were units with graduate programs (56% vs. 50%). The fewer the number of undergraduate students at the institution, the more likely speech communication was part of the unit, and unaccredited units were more likely than accredited ones to include speech communication (56% vs. 16%).

The Curriculum Task Force (Dickson, 1994b) also found that 37% of the units had increased the number of journalism and mass communications components (sequences, majors, or programs) in the previous 5 years, and 12% had added a component through consolidation or merger. Another 12% had reduced the number of components through consolidation or merger. Just under 9% had eliminated media-related components by other than merger. "Proposals that journalism and mass communication education break away from training for specific media professions" was ranked sixth among factors influencing media-related programs during the previous 5 years. Ranking higher were changes in technology used by media-related professions, changes in technology used in the classroom, changes in the job market requiring graduates to look outside traditional media-related fields to gain employment, and shifts in the employment needs of the various media-related industries.

INTEGRATING ADVERTISING EDUCATION AND
PUBLIC RELATIONS EDUCATION

During the late 1980s, advertising and public relations educators began to debate the value of what has been called integrated marketing communications (IMC), integrated communications: advertising and public relations (ICAP), or just integrated communications (IC). The terms referred to the merging of communication roles in advertising and public relations, something begun by practitioners as they began to take a multidisciplinary approach to planning. By the early 1990s, Rose and Miller (1993) noted that advertising professionals were bigger supporters of integrated communication than were public relations practitioners; however, they concluded that "there is a perceived need for integrated communications by many corporations and agencies and that IMC is here to stay" (p. 21). The debate among educators, however, was far from being concluded. Rose and Miller noted that public relations educators charged that public relations has little or nothing to do with marketing and called the movement toward IMC "imperialist and an encroachment on the field" (p. 20).

Rose and Miller (1993) hypothesized that advertising and public relations practitioners in smaller markets would have similar roles and, thus, the educational needs of students preparing for those markets would be similar. They surveyed 822 advertising and public relations practitioners in southern Florida and received responses from 308 (37%). When presented a list of 33 courses, advertising and public relations practitioners differed significantly on the importance of only eight courses. Five of the eight courses were distinctly oriented toward public relations (advanced public relations writing, crisis management, international public relations, issues management, and speech writing) and one was distinctly oriented toward advertising (international advertising). The two groups of practitioners also had a similar interest in areas of study involving communication skills. They concluded that their findings supported their hypothesis that there was little difference in the type of educational background needed by practitioners in advertising and public relations in a small market.

The Advertising and Public Relations divisions of the AEJMC established the Task Force on Integrated Communications at the 1991 convention. In its report (Duncan, Caywood, & Newsom, 1993), the task force concluded that "advertising and public relations students must be offered a more conceptually unified and integrated program of communication study" (p. I). The task force noted that in 1988 only 18% of public relations majors found jobs in their field, and in 1989 the figure fell slightly to 16%. The total for advertising majors was 27% in 1988 and 23% in 1989. The task force also noted, concerning a review of the literature by Donnelly (1992), that "when an advertising major actually landed a job in advertising it was the exception rather than the rule" (p. 15). The task force determined that an integrated communication degree would increase the likelihood that students would get a job and remain in the field.

The task force report proposed two curricular models, one designed around subject areas and the other around courses. The subject-oriented curriculum model consisted of three types of courses: personal development, professional development, and integration. The course-specific model offered the following course content: survey of integrated communication; stakeholder and customer behavior; organizational analysis; persuasive communication; message strategy and design; message delivery and evaluation; campaigns; and internship (Duncan, Caywood, & Newsom, 1993, pp. 20–21).

To determine what educators thought of IMC, Griffin and Pasadeos (1998) surveyed 600 advertising and public relations faculty members. They received responses from 259 (43%). As expected, they found much stronger support for IMC from advertising faculty. Almost two thirds (64%) of advertising faculty reported that proposals or actual IMC-related program changes had been made; however, just over one third (34%) of public relations faculty reported such a movement toward an IMC-related program. They found considerable differences in other areas, as well. Whereas most advertising educators responding stated that IMC provides students sufficient in-depth instruction, most public relations educators stated that it did not. Though 67% of advertising respondents noted their colleagues were interested in moving to an IMC-oriented curriculum, 62% of public relations respondents noted their colleagues were not interested. Both groups agreed that the advertising and public relations practices had become more interrelated. However, advertising educators were significantly more likely to state that advertising and public relations practices were becoming more interrelated. Also they were more likely to state that the two subfields should be combined in the undergraduate as well as the graduate curriculum.

The two researchers also found a generation gap between younger and older faculty. Younger faculty were more interested in incorporating management courses and were more likely to want to agree that advertising and public relations should be integrated at the graduate level. The authors concluded that they had found among public relations faculty "a pattern of philosophical and logistical barriers to integration that are not found among the advertising set" (Griffin & Pasadeos, 1998, p. 16). They stated that some critics charged that merging advertising and public relations with business/marketing coursework would tend to cause students to be less able "to become fluent in any single discipline" (p. 6). Also, they noted that some public relations educators did not see IMC as a "catalyst for change" and "seem reluctant to limit their options for improving the quality of instruction their programs provide" (pp. 6–7). However, they noted, other educators saw little need to be concerned. Because public relations practitioners tend to have more of a management role than a marketing one, they concluded that "an IMC approach is not perceived to have the same universal application for public relations practice—a practice where marketing components may not always be involved" (p. 17).

THE MOVEMENT TOWARD FRAGMENTATION
OF MASS MEDIA EDUCATION

At the same time that media educators were pushing for integration of media-related disciplines or integration of media education with interpersonal communication, other educators were pushing for more fragmentation, much of it centered around public relations. Though part of the push came from print and broadcast journalism educators wanting to cast off advertising as well as public relations (Mabrey, 1988a), much of the impetus came from public relations educators. Walker (1988) noted that the first person to teach public relations, Edward Bernays, stressed the need for a social and behavior sciences basis for public relations education from the 1920s onward and deplored "the partnership between journalism and communication and public relations" (p. 20). Others shared Bernays' distaste for the alliance with journalism education. Walker (1989) noted that Dr. Donald Krimel of the University of Maryland, one of the few full-time public relations faculty in the country in the early 1950s, wrote an article for *Public Relations Quarterly* in 1955 suggesting that public relations was a "campus orphan." After weeks of discussion, the journal decided not to run it. It was not long, however, before the topic became widely discussed.

Westland (1974) noted that the then recent determination that public relations students needed management skills in addition to communications skills called into question whether they should be in a journalism school. He wrote that public relations often had not been able to "earn the respect of newspaper people or teachers of newspaper journalists" (p. 49) and that its leaders were looking increasingly to business schools for a home. He suggested two solutions: to put greater stress on management techniques in all areas of journalism education and to remove the "stepchildren" label from public relations students. "With these two changes in viewpoint," he wrote, "journalism education can continue to provide the pathway to careers in public relations" (p. 50).

Bernays (1978), the "godfather of public relations education," continued his argument that public relations was a social science and that public relations students weren't well served by an emphasis on writing skills. He proposed that accreditation of public relations be moved from the American Council on Education for Journalism to the Public Relations Society of America or "some group like the Society for the Psychological Study of Social Issues." He added, "Public relations, in its own interest and the public interests, needs a new deal in higher education" (p. 18). Moreover, Bernays (1980) stated: "Public relations education is hampered by too close affiliation with journalism programs and control by sometimes unsympathetic media-oriented deans" (p. 18).

Mader (1980) asked rhetorically, "Why all the present clamor about where or why public relations should be taught? Shall it be in schools or departments of Journalism, in schools of Commerce or Business Administration, in divisions of Political or Social Science, in the Humanities, or in Seminaries?" He stated that an answer to where public relations should be was obtainable. "Key to it, so it seems to me," he wrote, "lies in cooperation, integration and good will . . ." (p. 17). On the other hand, Haynes (1981) argued that public relations—whether it be called organizational communication, public affairs, public information, public relations or corporate communications—is "distinctly different from mass communications and journalism as traditionally taught in American universities" (p. 24). After listing the pros and cons of public relations being located in a department of advertising, a college of business administration, and a department of journalism versus being located in an independent department, he concluded that public relations should be given departmental status. If that weren't possible, he stated, the next best option was for public relations to be a "strongly identified sequence" within journalism and mass communication.

K. O. Smith (1982) noted the "lively ongoing debate regarding the value of training in primarily print-media skills" (p. 66). Kalupa and Allen (1982) suggested that the "relationship between public relations sequences (subsystems) and journalism schools and colleges (suprasystems) could approach a state of conflict in a struggle over curricular revision." They wrote that a "potentially unstable situation thus exists where the subsystem is the largest within the suprasystem" (pp. 41–42). Newsom (1984) emphasized that two main concepts of public relations existed: that is was a social science or that it was a management tool. If it is the former, she wrote, it belongs in a communication unit in the arts and sciences or humanities. If it is just a management tool, it should be in a school of business, "but the discipline as a management program is unusual" (p. 15). She noted that public relations can be taught in a variety of places, and it can be accredited by the ACEJMC wherever it exists.

Wakefield and Cottone (1986) stated about threats by PR educators to leave journalism schools, "Unfortunately, these are mostly idle threats." They argued that public relations "is literally carrying the department while other departmental programs, with their numerous tenured professors, are waning." They added:

> Compounding the problem is the fact that departments containing public relations degrees—usually journalism departments—naturally tend to employ individuals trained in their own "mother" discipline to teach in the public relations program. How likely is it that those faculty are going to press the point that public relations is a very separate and distinct field of study? (p. 43)

They added that if public relations educators would say "that public relations is a distinct academic discipline deserving its own separate and unique accrediting body, many of the problems presented in this article should be resolved" (p. 44).

Gibson (1987) attempted to demonstrate the desirability of speech communication for the home of public relations programs. He stated that "current public relations programs overemphasize journalism and neglect necessary instruction in social science theory and techniques as well as management training" (p. 25). He noted that the "need for improvement in public relations education has been alleged so frequently that it has attained an aura of common knowledge" and that "over-emphasis upon the study of journalism as the emphasis of public relations curricula has been decried and cited as the major deficiency in public relations academic training today" (p. 30).

The issue of where public relations belongs was aired before a wider audience when David Weaver, president of the Association for Education in Journalism and Mass Communication at the time, was quoted in the *Chronicle of Higher Education* in October 1987 as saying that both public relations and advertising belonged in a school of business rather than in a school of journalism or mass communication. In his discussion of Weaver's proposal, Grunig (1989) responded:

> I have no data on public relations programs in speech or business, but my observation is that they fare no better than in journalism schools and usually fare worse. What incenses public relations educators, therefore, was that Weaver seemed to be endorsing efforts of administrators to restrict resources given to public relations in the university home where they had the strongest foothold—precarious as that foothold may be. (p. 14)

Walker (1989) warned against public relations faculty being duped by a move toward a generic curriculum, as proposed by the Oregon Report (Project, 1984), which, he noted, "is just another name for 'news–editorial' "(p. 23). Walker noted that an advantage for a public relations program in a journalism and mass communication program that is accredited is the focus on the liberal arts and the limit on the number of departmental courses that can be used for the major. However, he noted that the ACEJMC liberal arts standard has a downside. The Public Relations Student Society of America requires that public relations programs at institutions with a PRSSA chapter offer five public relations courses, which is approximately half of the major. The ACEJMC requirement for 65 semester hours in the liberal arts also may limit the number of business school courses the public relations major can take, Walker stated. In addition, Walker noted that a problem with public relations being in a journalism school is that most of the faculty are from the news–editorial sequence and "it is by majority vote of the faculty that decisions are made regarding what shall be taught" (p. 23). He argued, however, that it would be preferable for public relations to be within a journalism school rather than in a speech communication department or business school because of the writing requirements. He added:

> The real solution to the dilemma, however, is not offered by a home college or department, but by a faculty majority or plurality to represent a public relations student majority or plurality. This will not happen as long as public relations faculties turn over their majors to the news faculty for the writing and editing skills courses. The price is control over the curriculum by the news faculty. (p. 25)

Grunig (1989) determined that although public relations could be taught in journalism, speech or business, it would best be centered in a college of communication as a separate department along with journalism, speech, advertising and broadcast. If that was not possible, he stated, an alternative would be a "comprehensive" school of journalism or communication. Like Walker (1989), he opposed the idea of a generic program designed to serve the various media-related specialties because such a program "is little more than an excuse to dump public relations students into a news–editorial program—as journalism schools have done for years" (p. 22). If autonomy for public relations was not possible, then he proposed moving public relations to schools of business and management.

Editors surveyed by the American Society of Newspaper Editors (ASNE, 1990) were fairly evenly split over whether advertising and public relations belonged in schools of journalism and mass communication. Of those with an opinion, half thought advertising did belong. Editors were slightly more likely to state that public relations belonged elsewhere. Of those with an opinion, 48% thought it belonged, and 52% thought it did not. Big city editors were less likely than small city editors to think both advertising and public relations belonged.

Wylie (1990) called public relations education a "stepchild of an orphan." He noted that journalism education, an orphan in the academic community, adopted public relations education because early PR practitioners had begun in the newspaper business. Journalism did little to foster it, however. Public relation's position with journalism was reinforced, Wylie noted, when the Accrediting Council on Education in Journalism and Mass Communication (ACEJMC) was named as the accrediting agency for public relations education, which "came as a blow to many PR educators who claimed they could never prosper there" (p. 62). He concluded, however, that the "claim that PR and journalism cannot work together is specious; there are too many successes to support that argument" (p. 63). Likewise, D. K. Wright and VanSlyke Turk (1990) concluded that public relations "can be (is being and probably will continue to be) taught effectively in the academic venue of journalism/mass communication as well as in speech-communication."

Falb (1991) proposed what was soon to be suggested by the Task Force on Integrated Communications (Duncan, Caywood, & Newsom, 1993): that public relations and advertising separate themselves from journalism and business schools and become linked "as separate but equal components of a separate academic area that would take advantage of an opportunity of basic preparatory courses in Liberal Arts, Mass Communications, Business/Marketing" (p. 42). He said the problem with staying in journalism schools is that "the rest of the curriculum is essentially media oriented and tends to fall within the science, literature and arts area" and that advertising and public relations "really fall half-way between mass communications and business marketing but are fully neither" (p. 42).

Similarly, Falb (1992) suggested that neither public relations nor advertising were best served by being situated in schools of mass communication or business "where courses are often relegated to media or business types who don't really believe in advertising and/or public relations" (p. 98). Because of that organization arrangement, he charged, advertising and public relations "have been inhibited in their growth in academic and as true professional areas" (p. 100). He proposed that both fields must be autonomous in order to take advantage of business/marketing and mass communications courses that fit the needs of students.

Wakefield and Cottone (1992) proposed that public relations curricula be revised toward an interdisciplinary emphasis, as recommended in the report of the Commission on Undergraduate Public Relations Education (Commission, 1987). They concluded that their study

> provides empirical support for previous literature recommending that public relations degree programs and professional development seminars should deemphasize journalism in preference for emphases on marketing, advertising, public relations, speech communication, business, management, organizational communication, graphic arts, and research. (p. 74)

They also challenged the Accrediting Council for Education in Journalism and Mass Communication to change its accrediting standards dramatically "to reflect development in the public relations field" and "to include public relations programs housed in academic units other than journalism and mass communication" (Wakefield & Cattone, 1992, p. 77).

Bovet (1992) stated that journalism schools have not wanted to part with public relations because its students have become "cash cows" for the program in which they are housed. Medsger (1996), however, stated that journalism education should disassociate itself from advertising and public relations education because their graduates served as "representatives of special interests" (p. 7). Fitch-Hauser and Neff (1997) stated that the model of an independent department of public relations had not yet become widespread, but they found that speech communications programs appeared to be making inroads into the position of dominance that media-related programs had had as the umbrella field for public relations education.

The University of Maryland sent shock waves through media education in 1998 when it phased out its advertising program in a budget-related decision and its College of Journalism faculty voted to eliminate public relations. "A journalist's mission is to tell the truth," College of Journalism Dean Reese Cleghorn told the *New York Times*. "It's not to sell something, it's not to sell people on something – it's to find out and disseminate the truth in a responsible manner." He added, "We should be able to deal with the complex questions that arise from that particular mission all the way through our curriculum" (Rosenberg, 1998). The public relations program, whose students accounted for 32% of the college's majors, moved to the College of Arts and Humanities into a newly created Department of Communication built around interpersonal communication.

As the end of the 20th century approaches, educators in media-related field are still debating what the future structure of media-related education should be. Though the integrated/generic/holistic model of media education was proposed in the early 1980s, the industry-related sequence remains the basic model. Media-related units are following a number of different patterns, however. A merger between mass communication and interpersonal communication appears unlikely unless required because of budget considerations, but the movement toward fragmentation of media education by jettisoning advertising and/or public relations has gained momentum. With so many uncertainties, however, the answer to the question of what path media educators will take as the 21st century dawns is uncertain.

9

Questions Facing Mass Media Education

The founders of journalism and mass communication education . . . could not have predicted the complexity of today's mass media. Yet, their collective legacy of liberal education, social science research, and public service in journalism and mass communication education remains relevant. No new development in the field could erase such fundamental mandates.

—Durham (1992, p. 19)

A number of questions concerning media education endure after years of debate and appear likely to remain for future educators to ponder and debate for years to come. The following are some of the major questions that still face media education at the end of the 20th century.

Is there a unifying focus that can bind the various components of media-related education at the start of the 21st century?

A focus on the media industries is not broad enough, even if the focus is both preparation for media-related careers and the study of the media industries. An apparent unifying focus for media education is mediated communication. That focus, however, still does not cover the breadth of current media subfields, public relations in particular. Moreover, the rise of the Internet has caused educators to rethink what mediated communication and even the media industries are. The mass media themselves, however, remain a unifying focus. Three unifying emphases also remain: the importance of a liberal education, social science research, and public service. Though debate continues concerning how they should be implemented, they are still at the heart of mass media education.

Is there an appropriate name for the field?

One accepted name for the field, *journalism and mass communication*, is dated and carries too much baggage. It suggests a field with more than one focus. To some people, it means journalism versus the rest of the field. To others, it means practical education versus theoretical education. Either way, it suggests a bifurcated field. Return to the use of *journalism* alone isn't likely to be acceptable to most mass media educators because it is a distinct subfield. Also, the term *mass communication* is seen by media educators who have a practical background as being theoretical and not practical. The terms *communication* and *communication studies* are too broad for the field. Not only do they suggest a broader discipline, but they also have been taken over by interpersonal communication. Wilbur Schramm's vision of a united communication discipline consisting of mass communication and interpersonal communication might be realized some day, but the movement toward unification has been slow. Use of the term *media studies*, like *communication* and *communication studies*, would suggest the field is basically theoretical instead of practical. The terms *mass media education* and *media-related education* come closest to covering the range of activities comprising the field.

Is a mass media degree necessary?

Critics of media-related education still suggest that a generic liberal arts education is the best preparation for a media career; however, evidence suggests otherwise. Though some college graduates are extraordinarily talented, extremely bright, and particularly adept at learning quickly on the job can succeed with only a liberal arts degree, the nature of a media-related career is such that some level of preparation for the field seems necessary. Some critics likely will not agree, but mass media education provides at least the necessary minimum background required of entry level practitioners and a solid academic base for someone pursuing an advanced degree.

Is the best model for media education the liberal/theoretical one or the vocational/practical one?

Even though DeMott (1982) concluded that "by 2001 the distinctions of the 1980s between 'liberal' and 'vocational' education will have become as obsolete as they were destructive . . ." (p. 54), it appears at this time that DeMott overestimated the ability of media educators to agree on the purposes of media education. Most educators, however, likely would agree that the debate has been destructive. While eschewing the term *vocational training*, mass media educators have debated for decades whether the practical model is better preparation for a media career than the theoretical model. However, neither is the best model for all mass media programs, whether it be print journalism, broadcast, advertising, or public relations education. The purposes of media education are too diverse, as are the needs of the various media industries. A vocational/practical model might produce graduates who are better at their first jobs, whereas a liberal/theoretical approach might produce graduates who are quicker to advance to better positions. Some combination of the two approaches is needed. The best solution is for students to have a balance of practical and theoretical media coursework to be best prepared for whatever situation arises, whether it be media job, nonmedia job, or graduate school. However, some institutions may wish to follow one model or the other because it best meets the needs of faculty and the nature of the program.

What is the appropriate balance of professional experience and academic credentials that mass media educators should have?

As no one model of mass media education fits all types of programs, so no one set of credentials is appropriate for all media educators. All media programs should have a place for the faculty member with practical experience and the one with an advanced degree. Preferably, they are the same person. Most medium-sized to large media programs should have a place for the career media practitioner without an advanced degree serving as lecturer or practitioner in residence, and a place for the academic with little or no professional experience to teach conceptual media courses. The determination of where along the practical–theoretical scale each faculty member should fall depends on both the available candidate pool and the practical–theoretical orientation of the program. Certainly, every program with more than one or two faculty needs people with practical as well as theoretical backgrounds.

Is mass media education too broad and theoretical or too narrow and trade oriented?

Critics who charge media education is too broad or too narrow are themselves making charges that are too broad. It likely is neither on most campuses. Breadth is something to be sought throughout the curriculum. By far the dominant model of media education is the practical one, which is certainly what accreditation requires. Most media students take some theoretical courses, though it is to be hoped that a number of practical courses are as much academic as practical. If there is a failure of media education on this point, it is that programs are too trade oriented. The irony of that situation is that many surveys of practitioners show they are more interested in personal characteristics of applicants than they are in specific media-related competencies. If media education is to overstress one type of course, it is better that it do so on the side of courses promoting analytical thinking, the ability that topped the Associated Press Managing Editors agenda for journalism education over skills that can be picked up on the job.

Is research by mass media faculty of value?

Despite what critics say, research shows that most faculty members make use of academic research. That most practitioners don't make much use of research results from their not having the time or inclination to read the research and from its lack of availability to them as much as from a paucity of practical research that could be useful to them. Media research has more than one purpose. Ideally, it is useful for improving media practice and media education. It also should push forward the frontiers of the known into the previously unknown. It has intrinsic value for the researcher, too, providing a sense of accomplishment as well as intellectual stimulation. Research is of value if it does any of those three things. Media educators more than most other researchers tend toward research with practical ends, which is good; however, their research doesn't have to be of use to media practitioners to be of value.

What can be done to increase the regard that media practitioners have for mass media education and media educators?

Some media practitioners have little regard for mass media education and educators because they themselves do not have an academic background in a media field and do not understand the goals of media education. Although they might be proud of their success despite not having a media-related degree, such practitioners are also likely to feel a little inadequate. Research has shown that media practitioners with a media-related degree tend to believe that their degree was beneficial. As more media practitioners with media-related degrees take their places in media industries, the closer the potential ties between mass media education and the media industries will be. In the meantime, media educators should be making connections with practitioners in their vicinity in order to build alliances that will improve not only media practice but also media education.

To what extent might mass media education provide professional development courses as continuing education for midlevel professionals?

The Oregon Report proposed that media education provide such midlevel training, but research shows that few mass media programs do offer such training. Part of the need is met by the Poynter Institute and the American Press Institute, which may be better organized to conduct skills training. Two areas on which media educators might wish to focus their attention in continuing education are media ethics and responsibility and media law, areas where practitioners might want further education. Another likely area in which media educators can be of service is in working with practitioners to improve the practices of the media industries. For example, they should take the lead in the development of new concepts, such as civic/public journalism.

Are mass media educators on the "cutting edge" of professional practice and, if not, should or can they be?

Just as media practitioners without a media degree tend to feel somewhat inadequate around media educators, media educators without significant practical experience feel similarly around media practitioners. It is difficult for media educators to stay on the "cutting edge" of professional practice because of the increasing pace of changes in technology. As critics have stated, most of the innovation in media industries comes not from academe but from the industry itself. To stay current, faculty should spend a significant amount of time each year working in the industry. Likely, public relations practitioners have the closest connections with the related industry because of the consulting opportunities. It is more difficult in other media fields, although some good programs do exist for faculty interested in retooling and refreshing their knowledge by spending time in the industry. It would be ideal if media educators who teach practical courses would spend their summers in the pertinent media industry; however, that is not likely to happen in many cases. If such faculty don't make those connections with the industry, they may fall behind current practice, particularly because of rapid changes being brought on by technology. It is to be hoped that academicians who write texts are able to keep up with industry trends. If not, students stand a chance of learning outdated techniques from faculty behind the times.

Is Willard Bleyer's vision of journalism education on the decline or at the center of mass media education today?

Both the practical, career-oriented side and the theoretical, research-oriented side of journalism education claim Bleyer as one of their own. Those with a practical orientation argue that Bleyer's vision was to turn out well-trained professional journalists and that his vision is in a state of decline because of the rise of Ph.D.s with their orientation toward research (e.g., Hachten, 1998; Medsger, 1996). The social science research-oriented side argues that Bleyer was a strong supporter of the doctorate and research and that "Bleyer's children" were at the forefront of the mass communication and communication studies movements within media education (e.g. Bronstein & Vaughn, 1998; Rogers & Chaffee, 1994). It is a tribute to Bleyer that he is claimed by both sides. Bleyer was interested in journalism education, and he might not have approved of the idea of a "generic" media practitioner. Certainly, he didn't envision the integration of mass communication and speech communication, though it is not certain that he would have disapproved of the idea. He realized that journalism education could not be solely practical and exist within a research university. And like Robert E. Lee, Andrew Dickson White, Joseph Pulitzer, Charles Eliot, and Walter Williams, he was interested in improving journalism and, with it, citizenship and democracy. Rather than being dead or on the decline, the basic concepts shared by Bleyer and other founders remain at the heart of mass media education today.

Has hiring of research-oriented Ph.D.s and the requirement for research undermined career-oriented mass media education?

Some critics of mass media education seem to suggest that having the doctorate should disqualify someone from teaching future media practitioners and that practical experience and academic credentials are somehow incompatible. Certainly faculty with doctorates are more interested in research, academic research in particular, than are faculty without the degree. However, to suggest that faculty holding doctorates somehow undermine career-oriented media education is an exaggeration. Practically oriented media programs at nonresearch universities may wish to hire experienced practitioners without an advanced degree. However, few comprehensive universities or research universities will tenure a practitioner without an advanced degree. There is no question that faculty members who teach practical professional courses need to have had the practical experience themselves, and that is the situation at most institutions. However, there is little validity in the argument that educators who are teaching conceptual rather than practical courses must have had 5 or more years of professional media experience. Lectureships, practitioner-in-residence positions, and per-course positions are normally available to allow media programs to hire practitioners without an advanced degree if needed.

Does mass media education have a sufficient theoretical base to be taken seriously as an academic field of study?

Certainly, it should be taken seriously academically; however, the practical nature of most mass media education has resulted in an insufficient theoretical base. The risk media education takes in spurning faculty with a doctorate with limited practical experience in favor of the experienced practitioner without an advanced degree is that it won't be taken seriously as an academic field. Mass media education has begun to develop a theoretical base only with the hiring of faculty with doctorates and research interests. Though practitioners may complain that academic research is always boring and often "thumb-sucking," being an academic field requires that its faculty expand its theoretical frontiers as well as its links with the media industries. In addition, media educators must fulfill their obligation to the media industries by providing practical research.

Which is of greater concern for mass media education: loss of relevance to the media professions or being seen as a trade school by academic colleagues?

Mass media educators face a real dilemma if these are the only options. Neither option is an acceptable one. Being seen as irrelevant to the media professions would spell doom for media education because it would take away the basic reason for its existence. However, the risk media education takes if it follows the advice of some practically minded critics to become mainly or totally practical and eschew theoretical development is to risk its place within academe. Though it may never be taken as seriously as it would be if it were more academic and less practical, media education provides students the best of both worlds. It can provide them with both a practical, salable degree and a broadening educational experience. Media education's future existence lies in combining theory and practice.

Should mass media educators be preparing their students for entry level positions, or should they be preparing them for management and leadership roles in the media-related professions?

Mass media education can and should do both. It owes it to students who intend to seek a media career to provide them with entry level skills for one or more media jobs. However, it cannot stop there. The problem with the concept of providing students only with a practical education is that such an education is too limiting. Though some people may have the inherent ability to obtain an entry level position in a media industry without having taken media skills courses, most don't. Some media graduates have the inherent abilities to progress within or between media industries to management and leadership roles only having taken basic skills courses, but most don't. Though most practical media courses do involve the analytical thinking skills that media practitioners require, those skills can be enhanced not only by external liberal arts classes but by more-theoretical media classes as well.

To what extent should mass media educators stress development of students' analytical, creative thinking skills in addition to their practical skills?

It can be argued that the development of students' analytical, creative thinking skills is more important than the development of their practical skills; however, both are important. By their very nature, even practical media courses are designed to improve students' analytical skills. Thus, to call practically oriented courses vocational is doing a disservice to media education. However, media educators also should be looking for ways to increase the analytical components of not only theoretical/conceptual courses but also practical courses. If media graduates are going to hold the edge over nonmedia liberal arts graduates, they not only are going to have to outshine them in the area of practical skills, but they also are going to have to outthink them. That is a goal that all media educators should strive to reach.

To what extent should there be an integrated curriculum among all media-related subfields?

Use of the term *generic curriculum* by the Oregon Report and later reports did considerable harm to the concept of an integrated curriculum and was the cause of much misunderstanding. That a generic communicator with one or two courses in each media subfield can take his or her place in any media-related field is not a reasonable expectation. However, the concept of a broad media core as the heart of an integrated curriculum is not only useful but also essential. Whether such a core is 6, 9, or 12 semester hours or more depends on each program's structure and needs. Whatever the program's structure, a core that is a preponderance of the major (including such things as mass media and society, media history, media ethics, media law, and media analysis and criticism) is essential for producing well grounded graduates who have not only the competencies required for an entry-level media job, but also the broad-based understanding of the field necessary for advancement.

Should existing media-related subfields, such as advertising and public relations or broadcast and print journalism, merge into integrated degree programs?

The concept of partial integration among closely related media subfields is a practical solution to the "convergence of modes," discussed at least since the Oregon Report. Partial integration makes sense because of the high likelihood a media graduate will take a job someplace other than in his or her area of emphasis, another issue discussed at least since the Oregon Report. Whether it is called *integrated communication* (which is too broad), *integrated marketing communication* (which is too narrow), or something else, a partially integrated advertising and public relations curriculum makes sense. *Journalism* remains an appropriate term for a partially integrated print and broadcast journalism curriculum. Under a partially integrated curriculum, advertising and public relations students would share a common core in addition to the media core, as would print and broadcast journalism students. The advertising and public relations core could consist of an introduction to methods of audience research, persuasive writing, and message presentation and analysis. The journalism core could consist of an introduction to journalism, writing for print and broadcast, and public affairs reporting. The extent of integration and the total number of media hours required would be determined by the number of hours in the media core and the maximum number of hours of media courses that the program's faculty or the accrediting agency sees as appropriate.

Would an integrated approach to mass media education keep majors from graduating without either a sufficient number of challenging skills courses or a diverse liberal arts education?

Critics of an integrated curriculum have argued that providing students with both a common core of media studies courses and common skills courses would impoverish graduates by reducing the upper level skills courses they could take. Or, they argue, it would require an expanded major that would cut into the external liberal arts courses a student could take. Certainly, something has to give whenever courses are added and the maximum number of hours isn't increased. Several task forces have proposed allowing media studies courses to count as liberal arts courses. The accrediting council has allowed some inside courses to count as "outside" nonliberal arts hours, which helps somewhat. Media units desiring ACEJMC accreditation must follow its mandates; therefore, they might have to cut back on the number of skills courses in order to have a common core. Conceptual courses that promote critical thinking skills should be kept, however. If they want a professional program but are unwilling to risk loss of accreditation, media units will have to undertake course assessment to determine how best they can teach the desired practical skills along with having a common core.

Was journalism education taken over by communication studies and, if so, was it to the detriment of either or both?

The Cassandras of the last 40 years who have called the takeover of journalism education by communication studies an established fact have been premature. In fact, it can be argued that most journalism schools have all but banished communication studies—to the detriment of both of them. What remains of communication studies within many journalism schools, usually called media studies, often has been relegated to an inferior status. Although media studies has found a niche in most comprehensive journalism schools, it is the dominant force in only a few. It could be the glue that helps bind the plethora of practical media-related programs. If journalism education cuts itself off from the broader academic study of the mass media and communication in general, it will be to the loss of both.

Is journalism education distinct enough from other media-related subfields that it should have a separate identity and curriculum?

Certainly, journalism education has a different focus from advertising and public relations and should have a separate identity. In most mass media programs, it does. However, some journalism educators are bothered by any association with programs that prepare students for professions whose goals don't seem to be as lofty as those of the profession of journalism. Likewise, some print journalism educators want to keep a firm line between it and broadcast journalism, which seems more like entertainment than straight news. Yes, journalism education is a distinct subfield. That does not mean, however, that journalism majors should not have the options of taking courses in other media-related subfields, something some journalism educators seem to find objectionable.

Should journalism programs spin off their advertising and public relations sequences?

The growth of advertising and public relations within journalism schools occurred somewhat by happenstance; however, those programs have grown to a point where they rival or surpass broadcast and even print journalism in number of majors at some institutions. Advertising and public relations programs have not always felt welcome in journalism schools, however. Often they have felt like orphans or outcasts. Journalism programs might disassociate themselves from the other media subfields and opt for a separate identity without much impact on their curriculum. Likewise, advertising and public relations education might find a friendlier home elsewhere. Journalism schools might be "purer" if it spins off the other media-related subfields, but they would be the poorer for it.

Should preparation of students for a particular media-related career be the sole or even the main goal of mass media education?

There is little doubt that preparation of students for careers in the media-related industries will continue to be the major role of media education for some time to come, unless the growth of the Internet or other technological advances lead to major changes in the media industries sooner than expected. Certainly, media education cannot dissociate itself from the existing media industries. However, media education also has other responsibilities. The most important of those is providing courses for nonmajors, especially for the institution's general education program. All students need to understand the role of media in society and how to be savvy media critics. At some institutions today, those responsibilities overshadow the role of preparing media practitioners, and the number of such institutions likely will grow in the future. Until then, the twin roles will go hand in hand at most institutions. Most other institutions also have the obligation to prepare students for practical as well as theoretical graduate programs. Though this role is of lesser importance, it is a valuable one nevertheless and is reason enough for undergraduate programs to assess the number and type of media studies courses they offer.

Should mass media education aimed at preparing future practitioners be focused mainly on the undergraduate or graduate level?

Though a few institutions have respected practical graduate programs in media-related fields, practically oriented graduate instruction solely at the graduate level does not appear to hold promise as being the dominant model for media education. As long as media education remains as an undergraduate professional program, however, it will continue to have to struggle to polish its image as a professional rather than a vocational school. It is possible for an undergraduate professional school to be seen as a quality professional program, though, as is the case for many schools of business. Whereas journalism educators have been wont to compare themselves to professional schools of medicine or law and to rue the fact that they fall short, media educators surely realize they are on an uneven playing field because media education is an undergraduate program. It would improve the quality of media graduates if they completed a liberal arts education before enrolling in a professional program. However, it makes little economic sense for most future practitioners to spend an extra year or two in a media-based graduate school only to have to accept the paltry salaries available in the field. It would be better for schools of media-based education to try to emulate undergraduate business schools, which are practical but also respected, by improving the scope of their curriculum and the quality of their students. Once again, however, the economic reward of a media career is not an incentive to draw in the brightest and best students. Though it might be seen as pejorative by some, a media career is a vocation—a calling. Most media practitioners undertake media careers in spite of the money, not because of it.

How best can mass media education become central to the mission of the academic institution?

Media education can become central to the mission of the academic institution by focusing on its liberal arts and social sciences aspects as well as its professional nature. That is not to say that a professional program cannot be seen as an important part of many, if not most, colleges and universities. In most institutions, the need exists for practical, career-oriented programs. To become central to the mission of the institution, media programs need to reach out to the entire institution through contributions to the general education program and through other offerings for nonmajors. In the information age that will continue as we enter the 21st century, it is not a difficult argument to make that mass media education is an essential component of every student's plan of study.

To what extent should mass media education merge with interpersonal communication?

The merger of mediated and nonmediated communication at an institution most likely will be caused by economic exigency, something that has already occurred at a number of institutions, or because the institution doesn't have a large enough student population to support two separate units. The transition to a merged program wouldn't be easy, and political squabbles likely wouldn't stop after the merger. A major problem would be what to do with the media-related programs that have formed within programs of interpersonal communication—public relations, broadcast, and communication studies in particular. It would be a fairly easy move at some institutions and a major battle at others. However, if mass media education and interpersonal communication education continue to evolve in the same direction, merger seems inevitable. And, in the long run, it could be beneficial for both.

To what extent is mass media education itself a liberal art?

Courses with liberal arts and social sciences components are essential in any type of media-related program, practical or theoretical. The close relationship between the liberal arts and social sciences and media education was seen beginning with Robert E. Lee's experiment at Washington College. The social science and liberal arts nature of media courses themselves have been identified at least since Willard G. Bleyer began to teach to the University of Wisconsin early in 1905. Journalism educators' assurance that the field was a social science seems to have peaked in the 1930s and early 1940s, however. Though mass media educators began to feel more self-assured about the liberalizing nature of their courses in the 1960s and 1970s, more media educators began to again embrace the idea following the Oregon Report in the 1980s. Today, few media educators doubt either the liberalizing nature of most of the nonskills courses in their curriculum or the usefulness of most skills courses to increase students' analytical and critical thinking skills.

Should mass media courses be allowed to count as liberal arts courses?

The ACEJMC curriculum rule (Standard 3) calls for a balance between mass media courses and courses outside the discipline, as well as a balance between skills courses and theoretical/conceptual courses within the discipline. The standard states that the balance should be heavily in the direction of outside courses: The student at the average program must have 84 to 90 hours outside the program, 65 of those hours being liberal arts courses. The standard does not state what the balance between practical and theoretical/conceptual courses should be, however. It assumes that any course offered by a traditional liberal arts discipline is broadening. If the purpose of the liberal arts standard is to force students to sample other disciplines to a larger extent than the general education curriculum requires, it succeeds. If the purpose is to ensure that media students' education will be as broad as possible, it does not succeed. All media units should determine the relative balance between skills and concepts in their courses. Moreover, media units should track students' external hours to ensure that their outside courses are indeed broadening. Assuming that any course in a liberal arts discipline is more broadening for a student than any media course is demeaning to mass media education.

Is ACEJMC accreditation something that all or most mass media units should seek?

Having an outside evaluating agency can be a useful tool for program assessment and improvement. The problem with ACEJMC accreditation is not necessarily its goals, but its focus. Accreditation is designed for undergraduate and graduate programs designed to prepare media practitioners. Although that is a noble enterprise and the major preoccupation of most mass media programs, it is not the only purpose of media education. Accreditation forces all programs that want outside validation into the professional mold. At the graduate level, the ACEJMC does not even evaluate programs that are not professionally oriented. Not seeking or not achieving accreditation suggests a program is not a quality program, but that often is not the case. Though professional accreditation is valuable, it is not enough. Media educators need to devise some other method to evaluate their programs based on academic standards, rather than on standards based on the presumed needs of media industries.

Are complaints that media graduates are insufficiently prepared in the basics to undertake specific media-related careers valid?

Practitioners in all media-related fields continue to criticize the quality of media graduates for a variety of reasons: because they don't know the basics of grammar and spelling, because they aren't broadly educated and well read, because they don't know the basics of the industry, and because they don't have the skills that a beginning practitioner needs. To the extent practitioners are correct about the abilities of media graduates, much of the blame goes to the entire educational system and not just media education. Secondary education has failed students, as has undergraduate general education—particularly English departments. Holistic grading and a lack of emphasis on grammar and punctuation over the years have led to elementary and secondary school English teachers who themselves don't know the basics. The situation is self-perpetuating. Of course, the problem is more acute in print journalism and public relations, where a good understanding of the written language is essential. Many media programs cannot or will not fail students for lack of competency in English grammar or hold them back until they can pass a competency test, and whether such students should be denied admission to a media major is open to debate. The charge that media graduates are not as "broadly educated" as graduates in liberal arts fields, has little merit, in most cases. It is the best and brightest liberal arts graduates who are most likely to apply for media positions and who are most likely to be hired. The charge that media graduates don't know the basics of the field may be a more accurate charge. Part of the problem is the limited number of media courses that majors are allowed to take. Moreover, media employers' expectations may be unreasonable.

How does the development and growth of the Internet affect mass media education?

Like the development and growth of radio in the 1920s and 1930s and television in the 1940s and 1950s, the growth of the Internet provides media education with an opportunity to expand because of changes in technology. Whether the Internet will be just another voice, like cable and satellite television, or whether it will have a dramatic impact on media curriculum, like radio and television did, is yet to be seen. At the end of the 20th century, it seems likely that the Internet will become a major component of the media industries and will change them considerably, bringing in new corporate players as well as bringing the print, broadcast, cable, and telephone industries closer together. What makes the Internet unique and important for media education not only is its usefulness as a teaching/research tool but its ability to be a vehicle for both mass communication and interpersonal communication. It offers a medium that could blur distinctions between the two types of communication and as well as between the media industries.

Should mass media education take the lead in influencing the way journalism professionals see their responsibility to improve citizenship and public life?

Yes. At few times in media education's history has it had an opportunity to have a major impact on the practice of media industries, and critics charge that media education doesn't often take the lead when it has the opportunity. Such an opportunity exists at the start of the 21st century with civic/public journalism. Although it originated in the industry itself, some educators were involved from the early days in merging democratic theory with media practice. Though few educators or practitioners question that journalists have a role in promoting democratic values, some of them question civic/public journalism because in its extreme it appears to threaten the ideal of a journalist who is a detached and objective watchdog. Educators have a major role to play in developing theory for the movement and reconciling journalism's ideals with public journalism's promise. Public journalism is controversial now, much like interpretive reporting (the concept that journalists not only should report what their sources say but also present the news in a meaningful context) was during the 1930s and 1940s. However, in a decade or two, public journalism, like interpretive reporting, may be seen as what all journalists should do. Whether public journalism is the salvation of journalism—and whether the practice of journalism as we know it is itself imperiled—is yet to be seen. However, media educators should be taking a leading role in determining what public journalism becomes.

To what extent should media educators be critics of professional practice and try to improve the media industries?

Mass media education is returning to its roots when it attempts to improve professional practice. Public service is the cornerstone of mass media education. It is something that media education does daily by inculcating particular values in future practitioners. It also is something all media educators can do as their contribution to the field through their writing and personal contact with the media practitioners. One major need of media industries is the promotion of ethical professional practice. Another is to determine how best to invigorate the media industries' role in public service. Media educators can provide an essential service to the public and the media, whether the media will admit it or not, by analysis and criticism of media practices and through educating a new generation of savvy media consumers as well as ethical media practitioners.

10

Visions of Mass Media Education

It is this central character of the communication disciplines, in both their human and mediated forms, that presents such opportunity for the field as media technology converge and the larger academy seeks the means to prepare the well-rounded student for life in the 21st century.

—Pease (1992, p. 9)

A number of mass media educators, media practitioners, and friends of media education were asked to respond to two questions about the future of media education: What do you see at the major issues facing media-related education at the end of the 20th century? What direction do you think media-related education should take in the first decade of the 21st century? The following are their visions.

MAURINE BEASLEY

Maurine Beasley is a professor of journalism at the University of Maryland, College Park. She holds a Ph.D. in American civilization from George Washington University. Her professional experience includes 13 years of newspaper reporting, 3 at the Kansas City (MO) Star, where she was education editor, and 10 as a staff writer at the Washington Post. Professor Beasley is a past national president of the Association for Education in Journalism and Mass Communication. She is the author/coauthor or editor of seven books, including Taking Their Places: A Documentary History of Women and Journalism (with Sheila Gibbons).

The foremost issue before us is to redefine our mission in the midst of a communications revolution. The question implies, correctly, that journalism programs already are changing into media studies programs. We must ask ourselves what this means not only in terms of course offerings but of philosophical rationale. It is insufficient to merely tack new classes onto the curriculum without addressing their broader implications in terms of the scope and purpose of our programs. As educators we cannot continue simply to react to changes outside and inside our campuses. We must take a visionary look at the communications revolution that surrounds us and see how we can articulate a new mission that incorporates the best of what we have done in the past with socially desirable goals for the future. Journalism and media programs must take more of a leadership role in emphasizing the importance of both globalized and multicultural communications.

Traditionally, journalism programs had a specific and socially worthwhile rationale. In both our skills courses in writing and editing and our theoretical courses in history, law and ethics, we presented journalism as a professional field with a mission to promote the public good, primarily by educating newspaper reporters and editors. Walter Williams, who founded the world's first school of journalism at the University of Missouri in 1908, put it this way in his Journalist's Creed, which all students had to memorize: "A public journal is a public trust." Obviously, in this era of competing media, diversified publics, and declining newspapers, this creed no longer suffices. For years, however, it gave our programs balance, cohesion, and purpose. Under it, we taught aspiring journalists to think in terms of serving the public, even though they went to work for profit-centered employers.

As journalism education has merged with mass media programs, the overriding vision of journalism as a public trust has become obscured, particularly on the graduate level, to be replaced by theoretical constructs drawn from cultural and critical studies. These concepts may make us more at home in the academy where deconstruction is the prevailing motif, but they don't serve us well as the foundation for professional education. We need to develop a positive new paradigm that will justify our continued existence as separate programs. In this day of low public esteem for the media, we should offer well regarded programs for the preparation of ethical communicators. We need a new creed that updates and expands our mission in an age of globalization, but still bases it on the idea of educating professional communicators to serve society.

Our programs should be the keystone of media literary education throughout the college curriculum to increase public understanding of mass media as an exceedingly powerful social institution capable of both good and ill. We must recognize that much of the current public disenchantment with journalism and related fields stems from lack of knowledge of media history, economics, processes, and practices. We should be strong advocates of student media of all types and in all levels of the educational system to give young people an opportunity to learn for themselves the strengths and weaknesses of various means of communication.

One of the strong points of our programs traditionally has been the fact that they are experiential. Our skills courses, with their emphasis on writing for publication, have been offering a type of interactive experience for decades. We now are rapidly broadening them to incorporate new technologies and to prepare students to enter new communications professions related to online publishing.

As we widen hands-on components of the curriculum, however, we must make sure that we are teaching the theoretical differences between various forms of media. Students need to ponder the question of whether or to what extent different forms of media offer different representations of the world. They also need to understand both historical developments and comparative media systems to gain a clear picture of the interaction between political, economic, and cultural trends and the means of communication.

Insisting that our programs remain bastions of liberal arts education, we must guard against inaccurate perceptions of ourselves as purveyors of vocational training. Our emphasis must remain preparation for life, not jobs. The strength of our programs always has been the fact that they offer a breadth of general knowledge as well as practical experience in journalism or a communications-related specialty. Many of our students do not find or even seek employment in a media field. That's not necessarily bad, as long as they have gained a good knowledge base of the importance of communications in society today.

Nevertheless, if we are to continue to operate as professional programs, we must seek closer alliances with communications industries old and new. Recognizing that educators and media practitioners share common interests, we need to hold more industry–education conferences, seek more industry support, and develop more cooperative research agendas. But, we must not lose our separate identity. As educators, we ought to speak out against the exploitation of our graduates in the form of unpaid internships and low starting salaries. We should give our views on ethical lapses by practitioners. Even though we seek greater rapport with communications industries, we must remain independent voices in a communications-driven world, spurring better media performance at the same time we explain its rationale.

JERRY CEPPOS

Jerry Ceppos has been executive editor and senior vice president of the San Jose Mercury News since 1995 and is on the executive committee of the Associated Press Managing Editors. He was a Pulitzer Prize juror in 1996 and 1997. In 1997, the Society of Professional Journalists named Ceppos one of three winners of its first national Ethics in Journalism Award. He was elected president of the Accrediting Council for Education in Journalism and Mass Communications in 1998. He serves on the Board of Visitors of the College of Journalism of the University Maryland, from which he was graduated in 1969.

The major issue in journalism and media-related education today is the loss of public confidence in our reporting. It is not television or the Internet that will kill newspapers and other media. It is the loss of trust. After all, if you don't trust what you read (or hear or see), why would you waste your time with newspapers, radio, or television?

It seems to me that educators can turn the trust dynamic on its head: Have students look for unfair material in the local or college paper. Call the subjects of news stories and see what they think. Debate whether journalists really lose anything by allowing printed responses from the subjects of stories—even when we think we've been fair. (After all, what's wrong with permitting the subjects to frame their responses rather than letting us frame them?) Change the value system so that reporters who suggest corrections for their own work are rewarded rather than penalized; any newspaper needs to run more than one or two corrections per day if it's honest with its readers.

For that matter, students and educators probably will have much better ideas than these. Let's face it: My generation of editors hasn't exactly scored a grand success in pioneering new ways to achieve fairness and accuracy.

Closely related to that, the direction that journalism and media-related education shouldn't take is a love affair with new media. Ask the director of any newspaper-related Web site, and you'll learn that those sites have become more conservative over time. The traditional journalistic values are very much being embraced at newspaper-related Web sites. Thus, I would concentrate on the traditional values of fairness and accuracy for all students, including those interested in new media. Sure, all students should learn how to navigate the Web, but if there's a choice between teaching traditional values and HTML, the traditional values must win out. (Consider: How many of us were taught in school to use front-end systems? None of us—but we've succeeded in the business because we understand traditional values and are smart enough to learn how to use new tools. Today's kids, who have been brought up on computers, will have no problems learning HTML. They can learn that skill anywhere. What they can't learn anywhere is the importance of accuracy and fairness.)

WILLIAM G. CHRIST

William G. Christ, Professor and Chair in the Department of Communication at Trinity University, has a Ph.D. from Florida State University. He has served as chair of the National Communication Association's Mass Communication Division and as chair of the Broadcast Education Association's Courses and Curricula Division. He was cochair of the AEJMC/ASJMC Committee on Missions and Purposes of JMC Education. He serves on the Editorial Board of the Journal of Broadcasting and Electronic Media. He was a coeditor for the Journal of Communication's symposium on media literacy. He also headed a group that developed media literacy standards and competencies for the National Communication Association. He has three edited books on assessment and leadership. His coauthored book, Media Education and the Liberal Arts: A Blueprint for the New Professionalism (with Robert O. Blanchard), calls for the reform of media education in the United States. He presented much of his argument below in Christ (1999).

Mass media education does not take place in a vacuum. The major issues we will face in the 21st century are directly tied to the issues facing higher education in general, including decreasing federal and state revenues and resources; increasing tuition costs; loss of access to schools by diverse class and racial groups; deferred building maintenance; increasing equipment and salary costs; faculty morale; lost public trust; disconnects between what is taught and what is learned; lack of clear focus and mission; and limited links between universities, their communities, business, and K–12 education. The challenges are daunting.

In 1993, we (Blanchard & Christ) identified three challenges facing media educators in the late 1980s and early 1990s: calls for the reinvention of undergraduate education, the convergence of communication technologies, and the philosophical and theoretical ferment in the communication and media field. We suggested that the reinvention of undergraduate education called for a *new liberal arts* that combined elements from both traditional and newer fields and disciplines. We argued for a new commitment from programs to the nonmajor, general student. We called for the centrality of media studies in the common curriculum of all students.

We saw the convergence of communication technologies and the philosophical and theoretical ferment in the communication and media field leading to a *New Professionalism* that educated students to become broad-based communication practitioners. We argued for a strong core of courses that would provide a foundation for all communication students and a flexible series of second-tier and elective classes that would allow students to build broad, personalized programs of study. Our call for a broad approach to media education has been both praised and attacked (cf. Dickson, 1995; Duncan, Caywood, & Newsom, 1993; Medsger, 1996).

Later, building on the earlier argument (Christ & Blanchard, 1994), we suggested a second aspect to the challenges facing undergraduate higher education, when we wrote that there are "at least two major interrelated forces impacting today on higher education: a reemphasis on undergraduate education and a movement toward assessment" where "the concern about the first has led to the second" (p. 32).

Two recent studies both confirm and extend these analyses and suggest new areas that will have direct impact on media education (Council for Aid to Education, 1997; Kellogg Commission on the Future of State and Land-Grant Universities, 1997). These new studies suggest the need to reinvent undergraduate education and respond to technological innovation. Moreover, and perhaps most importantly, one of the studies suggests the need to realign universities' missions and governance structures.

The Kellogg Commission on the Future of State and Land-Grant Universities (1997) released their first of several planned "open letters" entitled "Returning to Our Roots: The Student Experience," in April 1997. The Commission, comprised of 25 presidents and former presidents of state and land-grant universities and an advisory council, argued that "State and land-grant institutions must again become the transformational institutions they were intended to be" (Kellogg Commission, 1997). Although aimed at state and land-grant universities, what they said was in keeping with many other institutions of higher learning. The Commission suggested "three broad ideals":

> (1) Our institutions must become genuine learning communities, supporting and inspiring faculty, staff, and learners of all kinds. (2) Our learning communities should be student centered, committed to excellence in teaching and to meeting the legitimate needs of learners, wherever they are, whatever they need, whenever they need it. (3) Our learning communities should emphasize the importance of a healthy learning environment that provides students, faculty, and staff with the facilities, support, and resources they need to make this vision a reality. (pp. v–vi)

The move from universities being conceptualized as teaching institutions to learning institutions requires a paradigm shift that has profound implications for higher education (cf. Christ, 1994, 1997). As universities become more focused on student learning than on teaching, more concerned with the outcomes of education than the "inputs" into education, then at least two things become evident. First, outcomes assessment of learning becomes critical and, second, the classroom is seen as only one part, and sometimes one small part, of the total learning environment.

The paradigm shift from teaching to learning communities, from teacher-centered to student-centered approaches to education, changes the role of the classroom teacher and the university administrator. If it is, as the Kellogg Commission (1997) suggested, that learning communities should be committed "to meeting the legitimate needs of learners, wherever they are, whatever they need, whenever they need it" (pp. v–vi), then it is clear that teaching and learning can no longer be confined to the classroom. And, as the costs of higher education have escalated, as more people lose access to traditional higher education opportunities (CAE, 1997), the idea of a 4-year residential university or college, where lectures are delivered in huge classrooms, will become an anachronism.

Among all the other things that media educators are held accountable for, they will also be judged or rewarded on how well they foster learning in their units or how well the students in their units learn or perform. This call for outcomes assessment linked to resource allocation is already taking place in a number of states and programs and should intensify as limited resources bump up against increasing costs. Specifically, the Kellogg Commission (1997) suggested that state universities and land-grant colleges should:

- Revitalize partnerships with elementary and secondary schools.
- Reinforce commitment to undergraduate instruction, particularly in the first 2 years.
- Address the academic and personal development of students in a holistic way.

- Strengthen the link between education and career.
- Improve teaching and educational quality while keeping college affordable and accessible.
- Define educational objectives more clearly and improve our assessment of our success in meeting them.
- Strengthen the link between discovery and learning by providing more opportunities for hands-on learning, including undergraduate research. (pp. vi–vii)

Beside concerns about undergraduate education, we (Blanchard & Christ, 1993) suggested that the technological communication revolution (including computers, fiber optics, satellites, and new uses for the telephone) was changing how people and corporations communicated; how they received, processed, and used information. Long gone were the days when the city paper or the network affiliate held the privileged position as the only news, information, and advertising source in town; when interpersonal communication could be solely conceptualized as face-to-face communication without a mediating technology involved; when organizations could successfully function without understanding how technology impacted small group dynamics, organizational communication, and public relations. We suggested that media educators needed to account for these changes by developing programs that were fundamental, flexible, and broad-based. Again, we called this kind of integrative, broad-based approach the *new professionalism*, suggesting that if nothing else, communication programs should be studying and teaching the impact of communication technology on such issues as culture, texts, politics, community, family, privacy, and identity.

With multimedia and the Internet, the whole mediated world can become a classroom. How will we use multimedia in our courses and how will multimedia transform the ability of colleges, universities, and governments to deliver an educational experience to students? What will become the roles of the teacher and curriculum in a multimedia educational world? Multimedia will have a profound impact on how and what we teach and the perceived relevance of our profession (cf. Christ, 1998). Along with the Internet, multimedia promise to change the university learning experience itself in a number of ways.

What is clear is that technology is changing media not only, and how and what is studied at the unit level (Blanchard & Christ, 1993; Christ, 1995), but also how institutions deliver education and create learning communities. Although the educational promise of distant learning is not new, changes in telecommunications technology suggest radically new ways of delivering interactive learning experiences. Technology, however, is a two-edged sword. Anderson (1997) suggested that one of the greatest challenges facing administrators was "integrating new technology" (p. 18). He suggested: "Journalism–mass communications administrators and their schools are confronted with technology-related challenges on three levels: first, finding funds to purchase and maintain needed equipment; second, determining the most appropriate ways to integrate it into the curriculum; and, third, devising ways to keep faculty members current in its use." (p. 19). Even with the problems and challenges, the bottom line is that the new communication technologies give media educators the opportunity to take leadership roles in their colleges and universities.

Beside the issues of what constitutes an appropriate media undergraduate education and the need to integrate new communication technologies, university governance is another important issue. In 1994, the Council for Aid to Education, a subsidiary of the Rand Corporation, created a Commission on National Investment in Higher Education to "examine the financial health of America's higher education sector" (CAE, 1997, p. 1). They argued that access to higher education was central to our democracy and our way of life. They suggested that by 2015 there will be a crisis in higher education due to increased pressures for classroom space and higher prices. The CAE report called for

> a two-pronged strategy: increased public investment in higher education and comprehensive reform of higher education institutions to lower the costs and improve services. The second of these, institutional reform, is in fact a prerequisite for increased public funding. Unless the higher education sector changes the way it operates by undergoing the kind of restructuring and streamlining that successful businesses have implemented, it will be difficult to garner the increases in public funding needed to meet future demands. (p. 3)

What the CAE (1997) was suggesting is a business model for higher education that would make educators, colleges, and universities more accountable. Although the CAE call is not new, it clearly intensifies the drum beat of criticism aimed at higher education, and media educators should take heed. What makes the CAE call troublesome is its direct attack on faculty governance. In the dominant U.S. business model of the 1990s, workers might be considered partners in some companies, but the reality is that management calls the shots. Academic protections, such as tenure, will be considered impediments to the streamlined, efficient university business model of the CAE. Free-standing colleges and schools with their own resources make little sense in this new model. As calls for accountability continue to grow, media educators need to be prepared.

As we join together in honest debate about media education's current issues and future directions, it is important to remember that our conversations take place within a dynamic context where the missions, purposes, and organizational structures of higher education are being questioned. We need to work together to develop answers.

ROBERT DARDENNE

Robert Dardenne, associate professor in the School of Mass Communications at the University of South Florida at St. Petersburg, holds a Ph.D. in journalism and mass communications from the University of Iowa. He is coauthor of The Conversation of Journalism and has written numerous book chapters. He worked for 12 years as reporter, feature writer, and editor on newspapers in Baton Rouge, LA, Mexico City, Mexico, and Rochester, NY, and for Broadcasting Magazine in Washington, D.C. He contributes to and edits Public Life, a new Tampa Bay publication/Website devoted to neighborhood and community issues and voices.

News organizations have been criticized for about as long as news organizations have existed, and much of the criticism is familiar. By nature, they intrude, irritate, sensationalize, and entertain as well as inform, comfort, and afflict. I think much of the press may indeed be less relevant now than it has been in the past, in part because people have many more choices as to where they can go for information and entertainment.   The choices may not all be good, but that doesn't stop people from seeking them out.

I don't think the press can afford to keep doing things the way it has always done them, and I think the so-called civic or public journalism is at least a partial recognition of this. A problem is that too many people have too many "definitions" of public journalism, and too many journalists and educators condemn it based on what they think it is (or what they like to think it is). I see it simply as an effort to connect to communities, in ways that are different for every news organization.

Media managers like models. From hit TV shows to news set design, to newspaper makeovers, executives seem to want to copy others. Asking reporters and editors to join community organizations may be a wonderful idea somewhere, but it's not a wonderful idea everywhere. Leading voter registration drives may be exactly what one news organization needs to make a positive impression and lasting contribution in its community, but it's not what every news organization needs. Writing narrative style about everyday people might dramatically improve the relationship between one newspaper and the people in its circulation area, but it won't improve the relationships in every area. I can say the same thing about virtually all the kinds of practices associated with public journalism. Picnics and pizza parties and focus groups and forums and all the other gimmicks that public journalism haters so glibly trash as "not journalism" or being "subjective" or "overstepping the bounds" all represent efforts that news organizations have made to bridge credibility gaps, to learn more about communities, to invigorate citizenship, to get more citizens involved in the news by giving them voices, or simply to reach beyond the same old sources to get new perspectives on persistent problems.

It's true that some organizations have been more sincere than others about their goals. But public journalism is not a set of rules, or, to my mind, even guidelines. It is an attitude. It goes well beyond the usual lip service journalists give to how important the reader is. Saying that public journalism is just the same "good journalism journalists have always done" may be true at the finest, most public-spirited newspapers in the country some of the time, but it's a poor criticism of public journalism. I think every newspaper and news organization should come up with the most innovative approaches they can to get people excited about what's happening (or not happening) in their communities.

Forums and focus groups aren't for everybody, and they should not be part of some kind of inclusive definition of public journalism. But if people in your newsroom could benefit from sitting around 3 or 4 hours with groups of citizens talking about what's important to them, then why not do it? If they could learn about the people in various neighborhoods through informal settings in which the news organization supplied the pizza, then why not do it? Every community and every news organization is different, and what works at one may fail at another. Concentration on one neighborhood through door-to-door interviews or surveys might be great in one town, but not right for another. Why should any news organization limit itself to what others have done? Why should any news organization not do something because no one else has done it first?

Some strong reactions against public journalism come from journalists who have a kind of contempt for people who don't have power, which includes most of us. They follow the people who make the decisions, who wield the power, who have the influence, who control the money. It is essentially traditional journalism. I'd argue that journalists can't afford to ignore the authorities, leaders, and experts, but that they can no longer ignore the 99% of the rest of the people. A problem is, of course, that including what some journalists call the "great unwashed" in other than crime or novelty news is a messy proposition. It takes time, skill, patience, knowledge, perhaps even some kind of wisdom. It's not the journalism we are used to (and, I'll note, it's not the kind of journalism most other people are used to either) and it costs. It also requires a redefinition of news. Perhaps the essential qualities aren't timeliness, proximity, and importance; perhaps they are context and perspective, even timelessness.

All this means that journalism schools can't stay in their comfortable ruts. No matter what you call public journalism—that the news should include more people in more ways—it means that schools have tremendous opportunities for innovation and creativity, the very things so many students have said journalism lacks. If we as faculty don't recognize this, and foster that innovation and creativity, we'll likely find ourselves out of step with news organizations that seem to be searching for means to reach a public that is on the verge of having even more news, information, and entertainment choices.

The Internet combines technologies to such an extent that some journalists will no longer be able to think of themselves as print or broadcast. Often what keeps the walls up between the sequences is school or departmental politics. I'd argue that they, like most news organizations, have to do something they aren't particularly good at doing: change. And not all of them the same way. Like news organizations, they have to figure out their constituents' needs and where their own strengths lie and try to mesh the two.

Older professors whose experience, like my own, is more than a few years back need to reorient themselves in both professional practice and academic research (and now is as good a time as I've seen to combine the two in rich and rewarding ways). Good leads and multiple sources and important facts first and concise writing will always have a place in organizing and presenting news, but we can't sit back in our walled-off sequences and do what we've been doing forever and say we're sending out students prepared for this news/information environment.

Nor can we do everything. But we can teach students how we got here and what "here" is through history and issues courses, and we can encourage flexibility and innovation and creativity. Yes, I think it's good for a student to be able to quickly write an inverted pyramid article. But they need to be just as conversant with whole other languages, other ways of seeing and presenting the world. These may or may not include links, or sections, or chronology, or sidenotes, or lists. They may tell a story or offer a snapshot, or provide a virtually infinite amount of information. Their "sources" may write essays or provide oral histories or poems or short stories. It's difficult to think of scenarios that aren't possible or appropriate under some circumstances.

I'm not sure how many of us as journalism educators are used to or even comfortable in this kind of environment, and I think a major problem for many of us is that we face an unlimited horizon with limited vision.

DONALD GILLMOR

Donald M. Gillmor is Silha Professor of Media Ethics and Law Emeritus at the University of Minnesota and founding director of the Silha Center for the Study of Media Ethics and Law. He holds a Ph.D. degree from the University of Minnesota. He is the author of a number of books on media law, including Free Press and Fair Trial; Mass Communication Law: Cases and Comment; Power, Publicity, and the Abuse of Libel Law; and Fundamentals of Mass Communication Law. Professor Gillmor is a former reporter and editor for the Winnipeg Free Press and worked for newspapers in Fargo and Grand Forks, ND.

It is my suspicion that there has been in this last 50 years of the television age a serious erosion in basic language skills and in the exercises of critical reading, writing, listening, and speaking that develop those skills. Computer technologies and their Internet and Web site outgrowths may recoup some of our lost literacy and the reverence for words that we depend on for meaningful communication between persons and publics, but technology also permits us to sit in silence and to communicate with one another anonymously and without accountability. Vocabulary, grammar, spelling, punctuation, crucial to effective criticism and commentary, cannot be left to chance and, obviously, not to high schools. It seems a rare occurrence in the late 20th century for a faculty member predating the age of television to encounter a well read undergraduate, and it is discomforting when students from China and Russia are more familiar with present and past classics of our written language than are North American students.

I also suspect that our best graduates reached the pinnacles of their profession by reading, reading, reading, just as one, it is said epigrammatically, gets to Carnegie Hall through practice, practice, practice. In journalism I am thinking of Wisconsin's Ed Newman, Minnesota's Carl Rowan, Ohio State's Leonard Downie, Northwestern's Andrew Malcolm, Missouri's Haynes Johnson, South Carolina's Jim Hoagland, Stanford's Ted Koppel, and Columbia's Gail Sheehy, to mention only a few. Every program has its stars. Nor am I concerned about those studious high achievers who enroll in our MA and Ph.D. programs. They have for the most part found and nurtured the written word, and their writing and thinking will reflect it.

I am concerned about undergraduates who choose this profession of words with only a rudimentary knowledge of the art and artifice of words: the successful college newspaper editor/journalism grad who can't pass the AP's basic writing test; the advertising copywriter who monumentalizes bad grammar; the public relations practitioner who seems to be speaking English as a second language.

Whatever startling new technologies the 21st century may bring, our civilization, our democracy, and much of our artistic success will ultimately depend on meaningful communication between persons and on written and oral language used in such a way that it says what it intends to say clearly, concisely, and with precision. If there is a crisis of content in a media world of abundance, then there is also a crisis of meaning in human communication. On the edges of every vacuum of misunderstanding and nonsense, there lurks the Orwellian prevaricator, the despot, the flim-flam man. In a world seeming to go mad, those privileged to tell others about it must keep their bearings and their verbal composure and forever hone their communication skills. I am talking about basics. The medium is NOT the message: if it is, we are doomed.

ARNOLD H. ISMACH

Arnold H. Ismach has a Ph.D. in communication from the University of Washington. He worked for newspapers in Walla Walla, WA, and San Bernardino, CA. A specialist in public opinion research, Professor Ismach served as a consultant to news organizations and political campaigns for more than 20 years. In 1985, he became dean of the School of Journalism at the University of Oregon, a position he held until 1994. He is the coauthor of three books on journalistic practice and has written extensively on the use of scientific research methods by journalists. He has served as a director of the Oregon Newspaper Publishers Association and the Oregon Association of Broadcasters. Professor Ismach retired in 1997.

It may be trite, but it's true: convergence is the principal issue confronting journalism educators in the 1990s. There are other issues, of course. They include:

- A shift in student interest away from traditional news media careers to other fields in the communication galaxy;
- Declining financial support for higher education in tax-strapped states;
- Dilution of professional emphasis in journalism and communication programs caused by mergers with speech communication departments;
- The growing chasm between traditional communication research methodologies (legal, historical and social–scientific) with the newer a-theoretical or "critical theory" approaches.

However, these are largely administrative, internal challenges. The convergence question transcends all of them in depth and complexity. It first appeared in the 1980s, this question of the blurring of traditional boundaries between the fields of mass communication study. The appearance of new media channels was one factor that produced this phenomenon. The expansion of media companies across single-media boundaries was another. The situation intensified in the early 1990s as the growth of the Internet and the World Wide Web produced even greater demands for trained personnel who could meet the demands of the convergence of the media industries: providing simultaneous services to print, broadcast and digital channels.

Media industries are placing this demand on their own staffs. Journalism educators must now decide how to prepare graduates for the increasing demands bound to come in an age of increasing convergence.

Whither journalism education in the next decade? This is the $64,000 question and one that almost defies rational, logical analysis. That's because of the relatively weak influence of the accrediting council on journalism curricula and programs, and the rather large gulf between the media industries and most journalism programs.

Accreditation, while expanding in the past two decades, is not often seen as essential to the success of journalism programs. Several notable programs have chosen to withdraw from accreditation, with no noticeable penalties.

Media industries, particularly in the current age of convergence, have not demonstrated a commitment to or a dependence on graduates of journalism programs. With technical skills becoming increasing essential, however (from computer graphics to web page development), it is clear that journalism programs have a new opportunity to create and solidify linkages with the media industries. The programs that capitalize on these needs, making the new skill areas a part of their core curricula, will be the pace-setters of the decade ahead.

LILLIAN LODGE KOPENHAVER

Dr. Lillian Lodge Kopenhaver is professor and associate dean in the School of Journalism and Mass Communication at Florida International University in Miami. She spent 6 years as a daily newspaper reporter and editor in New Jersey and 3 years as public relations director of FIU. She is coauthor of College Media Advising: Ethics and Responsibilities (with J.W. Click). She became president of the Association for Education in Journalism and Mass Communication in October 1998. She served for 10 years as chair of the Professional Development Committee of the Society of Professional Journalists, and currently chairs the society's International Journalism Committee. She is a past president of College Media Advisers, the national Community College Journalism Association, and the Student Press Law Center in Washington, DC, and has been a member of the SPLC corporate board since 1976.

There is no doubt that the biggest challenge facing us in journalism/mass communication education at the end of the 1990s is the whirling growth of technology that is taking us at an unprecedented pace toward reevaluating what we are teaching and how we are teaching it.

We are now seeing students who are more technologically literate and capable than many instructors and who have expectations of us that often exceed what we are able to provide because of a dearth of the kind of funding necessary to keep up with the rapidly evolving equipment advances.

The challenge forces us to reevaluate our goals. Do we try to keep up with industry each time it upgrades technologically? Do our programs provide the background for students to compete in both traditional and new media already in existence and those on the horizon? Do changing values in the media, in some cases facilitated by technological change, place an obligation on us to restructure or reevaluate our curricular goals? Do we feel that our mission has changed in any way?

The debate has long ranged about the role of a professionally based curriculum, heavy on skills classes, and largely taught by professional faculty, many of whom do not hold the Ph.D., versus one with fewer hands-on courses and more of a philosophical or theoretical base, largely taught by Ph.D.s, many of whom have spent little or no time working in the communications industry.

No matter how educators line up on both sides of the discussion, there is generally agreement that no matter what the technology dictates or makes possible, or what new media develop on the horizon as potential job markets, or what curricular changes become necessary, journalism and mass communication schools and departments are still going to have to turn out students who can write and edit well, who can think critically, who have a strong foundation in the liberal arts, and who have a sound sense of ethics as it relates to the world around them and to the professions they will enter. The foundations of education for our professions will not change.

These challenges will require a faculty that is well balanced with professional and academic credentials and a commitment to educating well-rounded students who can successfully move into a career in communications. It will also require faculty who are in touch with their counterparts in the professions where their students will work and faculty willing to engage in an ongoing dialogue with those colleagues on the issues facing the media and journalism/mass communication education.

These challenges will not end as the millennium draws to a close, but will direct our programs into the 21st century. There is always change on the horizon in our profession and in the industries for which we train students, and this is exciting. Perhaps one of the most important skills we can teach is how to deal effectively with change because technology will continue to influence existing media outlets and the way communication takes place. The skills necessary for effective communication will remain the same; the tools will evolve. We as a profession must deal with the debates within our ranks and resolve the issues of the priorities in our programs. That will more effectively enable us to work with our counterparts in the media industries to resolve the ongoing debate about what is being taught in our schools and departments of journalism and mass communication.

An open and meaningful dialogue must then continue to deal with the issues that have been longstanding on both sides. Those issues, certainly, are fueled by the new technology and by media organizations being challenged as to the directions in which they, too, are moving, and by the continuing decline in the credibility of media with the public they serve.

With change occurring so rapidly on all fronts, our challenge is to encourage an open and vigorous debate with industry counterparts and our own colleagues across the journalism/mass communication professions to define and redefine our mission and goals, to resolve outstanding issues, and to agree on the priorities that will take us to the close of this millennium and into the new century.

RALPH L. LOWENSTEIN

Ralph L. Lowenstein is dean emeritus of the College of Journalism and Communications at the University of Florida. He has a Ph.D. from the University of Missouri–Columbia. He worked for newspapers in Virginia and Texas and for the United Press. Dean Lowenstein was a journalism educator for 40 years, including 18 years as dean at Florida. He is author or coauthor of five books. He is a recipient of the Society of Professional Journalists' Distinguished Service Award for Research in Journalism and was the Freedom Forum Journalism Administrator of the Year in 1994. He served as president of the Association for Education in Journalism and Mass Communication in 1990– 1991 and has served on the Accrediting Committee of the Accrediting Council on Education in Journalism and Mass Communications.

Journalism education faces the same major problem at the end of the 20th century that it did at its infancy at the beginning of the century: how to achieve academic and professional credibility at the same time.

During the first half of the 20th century, journalism education had more respect from the professions, in relative terms, than it had from academe, since the majority of journalism faculty members had solid professional experience but lacked the educational credentials of colleagues in other fields. Toward the middle of the century, this equation began to change. More and more, communications faculty had the academic degrees equivalent to other professors but less depth in media experience than media professionals thought necessary.

Some journalism schools are doing a good job of maintaining a balance between the so-called "green eyeshades" and "chi squares." Others have become dominated by faculty whose research is so specialized and quantitative that their product bears little relevance to the media with whom their fields are associated. To the extent that this has happened, media practitioners see communications faculty as "blue sky" academicians out of touch with the workaday problems and challenges of the media.

If journalism education is to succeed in its primary task—providing competent and ambitious practitioners to the media—it must bring this professional-theoretical equation back into balance in the 21st century. I am confident that it can be done, but the professions and academe have to recognize the problem and deal with it. There must be more fellowship programs that encourage talented young professionals to seek careers in education. There must be more programs that encourage faculty to return to jobs in the professions for renewal and new insights.

The computer has revolutionized production of print and visual media. For the first time in its history, journalism education can afford the same tools as the media, and can use these state-of-the-art computer tools in the classroom and laboratory. Faculty can also use them in their research. It is not enough simply to have these tools. Communications programs must employ them to design innovative and experimental ways of reaching increasingly specialized audiences.

In short, in the 21st century journalism education will have all the resources to *lead* the media, instead of following 5 to 10 years behind. This is an exciting moment for journalism education, if only administrators and faculty will grasp it.

PAUL K. MCMASTERS

Paul K. McMasters is one of the nation's leading experts on First Amendment and press issues. He is a 31-year veteran of journalism and a former national president of the Society of Professional Journalists. He also served 4 years as the national freedom of information chair for SPJ. He came to The Freedom Forum in 1992 to serve as executive director of The Freedom Forum First Amendment Center at Vanderbilt University. Before that, he was associate editorial director of USA TODAY. Since 1995, he has been First Amendment Ombudsman at The Freedom Forum's headquarters in Arlington, VA. His most recent publications include a chapter titled "A First Amendment Perspective on Public Journalism" in Mixed News: The Public/Civic/Communitarian Journalism Debate, and his essay titled "Free Speech Versus Civil Discourse: Where Do We Go From Here?" was selected for inclusion in the college reader Ten Things Every American Government Student Should Read. His commentary concerning First Amendment issues can be found on his Web site: http://www.freedomforum.org/first/ombudsman.asp

Reporters and editors, correspondents and news directors are held in roughly the same regard as used car salesman, lawyers, and members of Congress these days. So why would anyone aspire to be a journalist? An even more interesting question: Who would encourage such aspirations? That's the job of journalism educators, of course.

Despite the deluge of media criticism and press bashing that permeate public discourse and dinner table conversation, not much is said about the role of these educators. Yet they are the ones who mold the minds and create the credentials of the journalists who determine what we read in our newspapers and view and hear in our newscasts. In other words, journalism educators play a vital role, an increasingly challenging and complex one.

In the classroom, journalism educators are pressured to find new and better ways to teach the fundamentals of news gathering and reporting. They must teach their young charges how to be fact finders, storytellers, gatekeepers, and truth seekers. They also have to teach the internal conflicts among these basics: how the telling of the story can get in the way of the facts and how the gatekeeper must temper the zeal of the truth seeker. Negotiating these conflicts may be the business of the student, but reconciling those conflicts is the task of the educator.

In the journalism schools, deans and administrators struggle to define themselves and their place in the university. Are they more like trade schools, or are they scholarly enterprises embracing a multitude of disciplines and subjects from communications theory to speech therapy to journalism? Should public relations and advertising be part of the journalism program? Does each student need to know the skills of writing, broadcasting, graphics, videography, and Web design in order to be prepared for the 21st century newsroom?

Outside academe, the challenges for educators are equally daunting. Newsroom managers want journalism graduates who combine journalistic skills with knowledge of the economic, technical, and competitive trends afflicting the industry. A young journalist wanting to get ahead must have some idea of "full-time equivalents," "dark time," "churn," and the budget process as well as newsgathering techniques.

Aside from all of this, there is an even larger challenge for today's journalism educators, and that is to make manifest the moral dimension of their calling. Now more than ever, the teacher of journalism must sharply raise the profile of the driving force behind journalists and journalism.

There is a democratic imperative for a free and independent press, and that demands much of those who teach journalists and journalism. They serve as keepers of a flame that would flicker and fade if left to the tender mercies of those on deadline, who are, after all, rewarded for producing copy, not rationales.

Journalism's academic community has a mandate beyond the classroom or the school: To describe and defend the First Amendment rights and values that undergird not just freedom of the press in the abstract but other free-speech activities on and off campus.

Journalism education, no less than its professional counterpart, must have a soul; it must be driven to serve the First Amendment. Too often, too many journalism educators are friends of the First Amendment the same way a biologist is a friend of the bug. The First Amendment has to be more than a specimen or a mere object of study. Too many journalism educators remain silent when free-speech issues arise on their campuses. They allow violations of student and faculty First Amendment rights to go unchallenged. They ignore the protections of tenure and submit to orthodoxy of thought and policy.

Quite simply, when freedom of speech issues arise, too many educators fail to make it clear to their colleagues and their communities that it is quite possible to stand up for the freedom without endorsing the speech. They must show their students, especially, that preaching the First Amendment is not enough. They must practice it, too. When they do that, they put forth a convincing response to the question of why they choose to be journalism educators.

In addition to teaching the skills, they get an opportunity to demonstrate to their students that there is more fulfillment in informing rather than in influencing, that there is more satisfaction in empowering others than in seeking power for oneself. They get an opportunity to teach their students to trust information over secrecy and to trust people over their self-appointed guardians. Most importantly, they get an opportunity to improve and expand a noble and necessary endeavor, to set an example as well as a standard, and to inspire as well as to instruct.

BETTY MEDSGER

Betty Medsger was a professor of journalism at San Francisco State University for 13 years, 10 of them as chair of the department. Before becoming a journalism educator, she worked as a newspaper reporter in Johnstown and Philadelphia, PA, and for the Washington Post. She also has worked as a photojournalists and freelance investigative reporter. She is the writer of or photographer for three books, including Winds of Change: Challenges Confronting Journalism Education. She has served on the Accrediting Council on Education in Journalism and Mass Communications and on the Teaching Standards Committee of the Association for Education in Journalism and Mass Communication. She is a member of the media policy committee of KQED radio and television in San Francisco.

Foremost among the basic issues facing journalism educators at the end of the 20th century is the necessity of having a clear understanding of what journalism is and what it should become. Equally important, journalism education needs to become a mature academic discipline, rooted in the liberal arts and sciences, that helps the profession renew and improve itself continuously in performing its various important missions, especially in performing well its responsibility to inform and educate citizens and promote their involvement in a democratic society.

Some other important issues that educators need to consider as journalism education prepares for the future are:

- Journalism is an essential ingredient of a democratic society, not merely an industry, and as such needs to be improved and protected by journalism educators as they simultaneously critique it and prepare the next generation of journalists.
- Journalism educators need to renew and maintain their own credibility by building faculty who possess expertise that is based on extensive and excellent experience as journalists and/or as excellent scholars of journalism.

- Programs should set standards that will guarantee that journalistic expertise is respected in the academy, that hiring will be based on these standards and promotion, and that tenure will be based on research and writing (or photography or video) that demonstrate intellectual growth as evidenced in each faculty member continuing to produce either depth journalism or scholarly research on matters directly related to journalism.

- Journalism educators need to define carefully and with pride their unique expertise and be prepared to explain its nature to university administrators and other colleagues in the academy who may not understand fully, but can be convinced, of the deeply intellectual nature of fine journalism. The "skills" of journalism (among which are critical thinking, clear expression, artistic expression, service to citizens in a democratic society) should be defined for what they are instead of as nuts and bolts, mere craft, industrial skills—terms that do not do justice to the skills of journalism and that lead to a misunderstanding of the discipline in the academy. Defined accurately, journalism skills are recognized as a vital part of the central mission of any university.

- Research related to journalism should be encouraged, even required, of all journalism educators, whether or not they possess doctoral degrees. By doing so, journalism educators will make vital contributions to their students and the profession and will help the university fulfill its important mission to create new knowledge, as well as its mission to transmit existing knowledge.

- Journalism educators need to face the fact that the declining student interest in journalism has been caused by numerous developments, including some controlled by educators: the declining interest of some communication faculty in journalism, the decline in faculty expertise in journalism, the creation of a curriculum that de-emphasizes journalism and, in some programs, merges all communication disciplines within the same courses, creating an atmosphere that makes it difficult for students to develop deep interest, commitment, or beginning expertise in any discipline.

- In light of the fact that the new journalists who achieve the greatest job satisfaction and who receive the profession's highest awards and fellowships never studied journalism (and instead majored in other subjects, half of them in either literature or history) and bring passion to the profession, it is crucial that journalism educators emphasize the great importance of the liberal arts and sciences in the development of the well prepared journalistic mind.

- Journalism educators should try to undo the disconnect, started in the 1950s by some educators, between journalism educators and the journalism profession. These steps could include:

1. Creating a culture of life-long education for journalists by providing local or regional ongoing professional development/continuing education programs.
2. Engaging professional journalists as mentors and coaches of students.
3. Engaging professional journalists in recruitment, particularly recruitment of students of color, and encouraging news organizations to conduct high school journalism workshops in collaboration with journalism educators. Such joint work recognizes the need for a shared responsibility for growing the next generation of journalists.
4. Encouraging faculty and student research at all academic levels to foster the same creative relationship that exists between medical education and medical practitioners, where collaboration is essential to the development of both good education and good practice.

- Be creative and innovative while also being cautious about trends, particularly ones that divert journalism education programs from their central purposes.
- Emphasize substance over everything else. In recent years, many journalism education programs have moved in directions that took them away from teaching the most important skills of journalism—how to discover stories, how to get to know communities and the needs of people, how to conduct various kinds of research, how to analyze information and ideas, how to organize information and ideas, how to write (photograph, design) clearly and creatively. They have diminished the importance of the essential substance of journalism and emphasized instead the technical aspects of various production and delivery systems.
- Embrace technology for the way it can improve the substance of research, presentation, and delivery of stories. Regard its various forms as new and powerful tools that should be used to improve journalism and that should not be seen as external, uncontrollable forces that drive the content of journalism and that, because of instantaneous delivery now possible, diminish or eradicate the central values of journalism—fairness, honesty, completeness, accuracy.
- Realize that journalism is going through a difficult time and needs wise educators to help it keep its values and responsibilities intact.

In summary, both fields—journalism education and journalism—have been pushed in recent years by forces that caused them to sacrifice important values and goals in the service of ideas and by trends that diminish journalism and journalism education. Journalism education was forced in some institutions to abandon the essence of journalism and adopt the more nebulous umbrella of communications in order, it was told, to acquire greater dignity and respect within the academy. Corporate owners of news organization similarly have caused the essence and values of journalism to be diminished, distorted, neglected, or eliminated in the name of not just profits but excessive profits. However, within each of these fields—journalism and journalism education—there are many people who realize that the essence of journalism is what is essential: its skills, its ideals, its excellent practice and service to the public. Those people need to find each other and, together and separately, renew and transform their institutions in ways that will improve both journalism education and journalism so the public can be served much better by journalism at the beginning of the 21st century than it is being served at the end of the 20th century.

MELVIN MENCHER

Melvin Mencher is professor emeritus at the Graduate School of Journalism at Columbia University. He has also taught at the University of Kansas and at Humboldt State University. He is author of Basic Media Writing (sixth edition) and News Reporting and Writing (eighth edition) and is a frequent contributor to periodicals. Mencher worked for the United Press and newspapers in California and New Mexico. He covered Central America for The Christian Science Monitor and was a Nieman Fellow at Harvard.

If you ask journalism instructors about their problems, they will suggest you sit in a classroom in which students are trying to cope with the elements of reporting and writing. Instruction, it becomes evident, stresses the elements of grammar, punctuation, word usage, and the miscellaneous ingredients of freshman composition. Of course, there are excellent students, well prepared by their high schools. But too many are not ready for journalism.

Indeed, surveys tell us that a significant number of students embarking on media courses say they selected the major because they do not have to write. Journalism programs do little to dissuade these ill-prepared students, or to insist on entrance requirements for the major that will allow instructors to teach at a higher level. Thus, one of the important issues journalism educators must confront is the quality of students in the major. Then journalism educators must agree on a curriculum that prepares students for the practice of journalism. (I am confining this discussion to practitioner training, not to the curriculum that is directed at teaching students how to assess the media or to those who take media courses to supplement another major.)

We are graduating journalism majors who blanche at coping with a percentage and have no idea how to calculate a death rate. We do not usually demand foreign language competence, and we allow our students to skirt the science courses. In short, we must meet the demand society places on us to educate journalists so that they can contribute to the public welfare. We are asked to educate men and women to be discerning, morally responsible journalists. Whether the students find themselves in a small community in Illinois or abroad in the Middle East, they should be given an education equal to the tasks they will face in trying to provide the public with information that will allow citizens to make educated decisions about the issues that they face.

In the great majority of our cities, there is only one journalist covering a beat—education, the city hall, the courts, the environment. Therefore, in all but a handful of our communities, what the people know about major issues is what the education reporter, the city hall reporter, the young man or woman covering an election for mayor tells them through the media. This is an awesome responsibility for them, and for us journalism educators.

The trashing of practitioner training is a consistent refrain in journalism publications, yet we want the highest quality of information in our media. If our practitioner training is not ratcheted up a few notches, we will deserve the criticism.

DOUG NEWSOM

Doug Newsom, Ph.D., APR, Fellow PRSA, teaches at Texas Christian University and is a public relations practitioner and is the senior coauthor of three textbooks: Media Writing (with the late James Wollert); This Is PR (with Judy VanSlyke Turk and Dean Kruckeberg), and Public Relations Writing: Form and Style (with Bob Carrell). She is coeditor of Silent Voices (with Bob Carrell). Professor Newsom has a Ph.D. degree from The University of Texas at Austin. She was a Fulbright lecturer in India in 1988 and was selected as a Fulbright lecturer in Singapore in 1999. Professor Newsom has done public relations workshops in Singapore, South Africa, Bulgaria, Hungary, Romania, Poland, and Vanuatu. She is on the board of directors of a publicly held company and two national nonprofit boards.

The primary issue facing journalism and media-related education at the end of the 1990s is the effect of the new electronic medium on traditional media of all kinds, from mail and other message systems to news and advertising, although to a lesser extent on advertising. Education in all media-related disciplines is affected because most educators will have little or no experience in the new technology, which is changing rapidly. Furthermore, the educational institutions will have difficulty keeping up with the technology, even in a very modest way, so that students can be ready for their first jobs. What this means is teachers preparing students for a communication world that is already history. Every aspect of communication education is affected.

Research is now electronic. Communication between individuals is electronic. Traditional media are getting and sending information electronically. Organizations and institutions have Web pages. Information is sent instantly and available instantly. So the writing and editing process is now one and the same. The editing has to be done before the message is written, the picture taken. Furthermore, distribution is potentially global. Personal messages are more easily intercepted and made public. Thus, the division between what is public and private is blurred. The line between traditional and nontraditional media also is blurred because of the sources the traditional media are using. Furthermore, from an educational perspective, the traditional lines between disciplines are blurring as the arts use electronics to create "reality," and everyone from real estate salespeople to tour guides can give customers a "virtual reality" experience.

Ethical issues and credibility are part of this issue. Global views of ethics are being created as we move from culture-based standards to more universal standards. This is glacial in some areas of ethics and lightening fast in others. It is creating all sorts of difficulties for individuals and for media, not to mention business and nonprofit organizations. Part of this problem is credibility. Ethics are based on values and rooted in belief structures. Conflicting information and an overwhelming amount of information makes it difficult for people at all levels to sort out what approximates reality. Teaching ethics always has been a challenge, but now it is even more so. Credibility of all institutions is problematic because of the sources being used to make judgments.

Although some believe that computers and computer-based information is going to be limited to only a few, that probably is not the case. Many people thought radio wouldn't reach the masses all over the globe because of costs and technology. Now radio probably is the only truly mass medium. However, television and computers are following the same path, only faster. (Radio was delayed until the transistor was developed. Technology is moving faster now.)

A parallel problem will be how to preserve cultures in the face of this computer revolution, although in some ways electronics may be the answer. In some situations where saving languages is an issue, the ability to produce messages electronically is cheaper and easier and may be also a good way to teach new members of those societies their inherited language along with other languages. It's definitely a good way to record and preserve art, from music to dance to drawings and paintings.

As we enter the 21st century, educators are going to have to do what we preach: learn how to learn. We are going to have to ride the crests of these waves of technology or get dashed to bits on the shoals of reality. Our research, our teaching, our preparation has to be visionary in seeing the uses for the new technology to communicate. We also will have to be better at teaching critical evaluation and learning so the students will be better users of information and better communicators. We also can not be as isolated as some educators and also some professionals have been. It may be comfortable, but it's not going to work in a global community.

CHARLES L. OVERBY

Charles L. Overby is chairman and chief executive officer of The Freedom Forum, an independent, nonpartisan foundation dedicated to First Amendment and media issues. Overby was formerly a Pulitzer Prize-winning editor in Jackson, MS. He worked for 16 years as reporter, editor, and corporate executive for the Gannett Company. As a reporter, he covered The White House, presidential campaigns, Congress, and the Supreme Court. He was vice president for news and communications for Gannett and served on the management committees of Gannett and USA TODAY. Overby serves on the Board of Regents of Baylor University and is a member of the foundation board of the University of Mississippi, his alma mater.

The future of journalism education depends on a new and positive relationship with media professionals. In my lifetime, I have never seen less respect by journalism educators and media professionals for one another. Unless the two groups can find common ground for mutual respect and partnership, journalism educators are going to be the 21st century equivalent of Latin teachers. Most Latin teachers can explain why they are needed, but that's the point: They must spend their time justifying their existence.

Journalism education is buffeted from both sides—from elements within academia who see journalism education as a trade school and an unimportant aspect of the higher learning process and from many within the news profession who see journalism educators as irrelevant or unsatisfactory in teaching and preparing future reporters and editors. With diminishing support inside and outside, journalism education is threatened as never before. This disrespect is compounded by the low esteem that many educators have for the media. To make matters worse, many within the news business have developed a self-loathing of their profession. This self-loathing threatens journalism education and journalism itself. It reminds me of the time I was in my dentist's chair, and he decided to confide in me: "I've been thinking maybe I don't want to spend the rest of my life sticking my hands in people's mouths."

Many journalism educators find themselves in the same position today. They find it somewhat distasteful to be educating students for a business that pays students poorly and produces a daily product that they often deride or dislike. If these educators cannot come to grips with the end product of their teaching— namely newspapers and local TV newscasts—then they're no better off than the dentist who doesn't like to stick his hands in people's mouths.

The same can be said for journalists who don't like what they're doing. At the Newseum, we have a collection of movie clips that portray journalists. In one famous scene in "Deadline USA," Humphrey Bogart holds the phone out to the sound of rolling presses and says to a gangster on the other end, "That's the press, baby, the press, and there's nothing you can do about it." We have lost the Humphrey Bogart spirit, and it's up to all of us to put it back, not by pointing fingers but by understanding that we're all in this together.

We must renew our enthusiasm for why we are in this business. We must live up to the nobility of journalism education and the news media. Too often, we all act as if the reporting, editing, and presentation of the news is just another job. It's not unusual for nonjournalists to feel that way, but that mentality is seeping into journalism schools and newsrooms. We must never forget that the free flow of information is the cornerstone of our democracy. If that seems smarmy, then maybe we should check our cynicism levels. Of course, improvements are needed in both journalism education and the news profession, but wringing our hands won't do anything. The role for journalists and journalism educators is to improve journalism, not abhor it.

Enlightened news professionals and journalism educators must find ways to improve journalism together. There are thousands of newsroom professionals and journalism educators. Maybe a few hundred from both sides could lead the way in forging meaningful partnerships for the 21st century. Our future could depend on it.

ELISE K. PARSIGIAN

Elise Parsigian is Associate Director of the Center for Armenian Research, Studies, and Publication, University of Michigan–Dearborn. She holds a Ph.D. degree in Communication Studies–Interdepartmental Program from the University of Michigan, Ann Arbor. She has taught journalism and media-related subjects in the Department of Communication, University of Michigan– Ann Arbor. She is the author of Mass Media Writing and Proposal Savvy: Creating Successful Proposals for Media Projects. Dr. Parsigian won the 1997 Renaissance Award of Excellence from the International Association of Business Communicators. A former print and broadcast journalist, public relations, advertising and film/video writer, she also has her own consulting company.

There's a structural order hidden in the plethora of our problems. Let's not miss it again in the coming century. Anyone who has had real-world experience in all major areas of mass media—print and broadcast journalism, public relations, advertising, film/video—knows very well the features that differentiate one unit from the other. But the similarity that binds them together as a whole emerges for the experienced pro only after exposure to methodologists, particularly those in the social sciences. What emerges is a parallel of habits followed by social scientists and practiced media pros. That shared similarity is a documented, tested, and proven process of problem solving driven by critical thinking throughout a series of procedures in a nonlinear and repeatable system. It's a system that could, should, ought, must be central to our activities in advancing the cause of media education, including an intro course for media students who need basic training in the finer points of research and report *before* entering a specialized media area.

I can already hear the naysayers, but let them look at the consequences of our irresolution. In just the past few decades, we've seen journalism departments and other media units disappear and watched, instead, the rise of "communication studies" programs. That's OK. Such programs are good. They're designed to refine the student's sensibilities for evaluation, objectivity, analysis, synthesis.

The catch? Some students, through association or some mysterious form of osmosis, will be able to transfer those refinements to the science and art of media communication, but most will not. In fact, it's even doubtful the select few will be able to translate those refinements into the kind of performance expected of them in the real world of today's media culture.

Media students and administrators are no longer tolerant of our trial-and-error approach. It's too destructive and too discouraging for both student and instructor. We, along with university administrators and our critics in the professions, have been conducting not only a "dialogue of the deaf," but also explorations of the blind and mute. A dynamic process of problem solving does exist within our midst: one that generates critical thinking, moves through a series of specified procedures toward a substantiated solution, determines the opening and content for the informational or creative message, and provides a reliable discovery structure to fall back on when confronted with a media assignment one may not have experienced in the classroom.

It's time we see the various parts of media communication as an entity and not as a set of independent and exclusive units. Then we might be able to understand the unity of procedure that drives the delivery of messages in each case. What's more, it's even possible we'll be able to explain who we are, what we do, why we do it, and maybe even come to some agreement about our educational agenda and its ethics.

As importantly, we may even be able to argue for the very qualification university administrators insist we must display—the scientific basis of our discipline and how we intend to convey that to communication students. Make no mistake, the art or "craft," as some would have it, of media messages evolves less from a "talent" for composition and much more from a practiced discipline in the specific activities of research and report. In fact, that position should direct our efforts in media education in the next millennium and, at the same time, might even fashion a more balanced view of our discipline as central to the university.

BETSY PLANK

Betsy Plank, APR, Fellow PRSA, is past president of the Public Relations Society of America (PRSA), the first woman to head that professional organization and to chair (in 1980–1981) the U.S. Section of the International Public Relations Association (IPRA). She is the first person to have received both of PRSA's top honors for professionals—the Gold Anvil as the outstanding U.S. professional (1977) and the Lund Award for civic and community service (1989). She was selected by readers of Public Relations News as 1979 Professional of the Year and was named one of the World's 40 Outstanding Public Relations Leaders in 1984. She cochaired the 1987 commission to develop guidelines for the undergraduate PR curriculum. The PRSA Educators Academy presented her its first award honoring a professional for exceptional contributions to public relations education in 1997.

One of the major and unprecedented challenges facing journalism and media-related education in the late 1990s is the fundamental issue being raised by technology. The avalanche of information directly available to the public at large threatens traditional media and their now-and-future gatekeepers with a shift to personal media and control. For the understanding and benefit of its future professionals, it is incumbent on journalism-related education to address that issue from a societal, behavioral, and ethical view, not simply as a risk to vested interests or a need for its students to command state-of-the-art technological skills.

Second, in addition to teaching the new generation, journalism and media-related education also have a renewed responsibility to encourage and enlist professionals to continuing education. If revolution aptly characterizes what's happening in contemporary media, then those now in practice can no longer depend on past academic studies to keep current with professional demands. Editors and other employers have been prompt to recognize that need. Business schools have been prompt to meet it. Schools of journalism, communication, and mass media should also be stepping up to that opportunity and setting standards for relevant and advanced studies.

Third, an unresolved issue in many journalism units is inequitable resources committed to its students majoring in media-related disciplines (e.g., public relations, advertising, compared with those in journalism per se). For starters, consider faculty–student ratios. With fairness, respect, and integrity, responsibility to all students within the unit needs to be recognized, examined and affirmed.

Fourth, in the mix of media-related studies, public relations too often remains the most misunderstood—a victim of outdated perceptions of the 1950s and 1960s and skewed by viewpoints limited to media experience. Yes, writing is its sine qua non, but publicity alone is a diminishing requirement at higher levels. To prepare students for lifetime careers in the field, there must be emphasis on research, analysis of public attitudes and human behavior, identification with the public interest, and actions to achieve public acceptance. The contemporary practice calls for improved understanding of and attention to those objectives by the academy.

In the 21st century, journalism education should see its role and responsibility reaching beyond its student majors to serve all students in its institution, helping them to develop critical thinking skills and judgment and to avoid becoming captive to information overload and undisciplined technology. More than ever before, it is imperative that the educated reader/viewer be equipped to assess information critically and with healthy skepticism, that is, to develop skills traditionally defined as editorial. Who better, more logical, to take that initiative and offer that unique knowledge resource than journalism educators? Should they still serve and train for the responsible professional practice? Of course—and always. But a larger vision can transcend that and position journalism education in a new, even more significant and valued role in the university and in society at large.

LANA F. RAKOW

Lana Rakow is professor in the School of Communication at the University of North Dakota, where she served as director of the school and Associate Dean of the College of Fine Arts and Communication from 1994 to 1996. Prior to that, she served as chair of the Communication Department and then as Associate Vice Chancellor for Undergraduate Studies at the University of Wisconsin–Parkside. She is the author or editor of three books and numerous book chapters and journalism articles. She edits a book series for Sage, with Sonja Foss, on feminist communication. She serves on the editorial board of a number of scholarly journals and has served on national committees for the International Communication Association and the Association for Education in Journalism and Mass Communication.

Market-driven changes in content, format, and delivery of news and information created by the convergence of technologies and industries are being cited by educators as evidence that students need to be prepared differently for a new world of communication careers. These changes in how people receive news and information and how it is "packaged" are not the most important concerns we face as educators, however. What we need to face is the role we should play in creating the communication conditions that must exist if we are to have a truly democratic society. In doing so, we will be living up to our responsibility to the public to serve its interests rather than those of media industries or professions.

Attention being given to new technologies and their consumers detracts from the fundamental issue of voice and access that we have been neglecting in our mass communication programs. The women's and civil rights movements, as well as feminist scholars and race scholars, have shown us that many groups of people are left out of the major systems of communication in the U.S. and elsewhere. Unfortunately, we have persisted in our programs to leave unexamined a model of communication that perpetuates the exclusion of many from the vital democratic processes of voicing one's opinions and experiences. Our predominant model assumes that a few can control the means of communicating while the many listen. It assumes that democratic participation is nothing more than the intake of selected information, representing the opinions and standpoints of elite groups, followed by reactions in the voting booth and the opinion poll. Strangely, we then bemoan the lack of interest we find in many citizens about what we consider important political issues.

Our disinterest in the speech rights of citizens is troubling, especially given our enthusiastic defense of the speech rights of powerful organizations. We appear not to have noticed that the speech rights of business and industry have far surpassed those of individuals, families, and other non-institutionalized groups. Despite the excellent theoretical work done by cultural studies scholars that has problematized the notions of objectivity and representation on which the mass media have been founded, our undergraduate curricula continue to pass along to students the traditional gospel of our field because we see ourselves preparing students to perpetuate the world as it is rather than create the world as it should be.   We are afraid of offending our donors and our students' employers. We are, in fact, afraid to exercise our own speech rights to challenge the industries that we should be critiquing, not advocating.

Once we have faced the need to change our model of communication to one that enables all individuals and groups to have access to the means for *voice*, not simply the means to *listen*, we may be shocked by the obstacles that prevent the free and open speech we profess to cherish. We will need to consider the many ways in which we have institutionalized the speech of powerful organizations at the expense of individuals, whose speech as citizens, as members of communities, as women and members of minority cultural groups, as employees is blocked by lack of access, exclusion by virtue of their "unpopular" opinions, news practices, fear of retaliation, and loss of jobs. We have our work cut out for us as educators of the next generation of citizens who, with our help, can envision a truly democratic system of communication.

STEPHEN D. REESE

Stephen D. Reese is chairman of the Department of Journalism and holds the G.B. Dealey Professorship in journalism at the University of Texas at Austin, where he has been on the faculty since 1982, following graduate study at the University of Wisconsin at Madison. He has headed the Radio–TV Journalism and the Communication Theory & Methodology divisions of the Association for

Education in Journalism and Mass Communication (AEJMC). He is on the editorial board of Journalism & Mass Communication Quarterly (and the new Web Journal of Mass Communication Research). His research has been published in numerous book chapters and in a variety of journals, and he coauthored Mediating the Message: Theories of Influence on Mass Media Content (with Pamela Shoemaker). He is the recipient of the Krieghbaum Under-40 Award for teaching, research, and service from AEJMC.

Journalism education and its companion field, communication, are currently under heavy attack from the professional quarter. Programs are urged, for example, to reject the doctorate as a credential in favor of professional experience and resist encroaching theory with practical skills training. Such criticism is nothing new in this or other professional fields; however, I believe the most recent challenge cannot be easily dismissed.

I would argue that criticism of journalism education is tied to the crisis of legitimacy within journalism itself, leading an ever more concentrated and corporate voice to assert itself, especially in the academy where prestige has historically been sought. This assertion coincides with technology needs and funding cuts that mean today's journalism and other university programs are more dependent than ever before on external support. Journalism on many campuses has left its traditional home in the arts and sciences to join with other communication and media fields to create independent professional schools. In doing so, it has found it easier to enter into symbiotic relationships with the professional community, a relationship that has brought new resources but also corresponding pressures to satisfy those constituencies. Clearly, the academy needs credibility with the professions and relevance to society, but recent attacks often serve to diminish the very features that make the academic tradition so valuable.

The professional pressure on journalism and academia alike cannot be fully understood without grasping changes in the corporate media world. Journalism is today primarily a creature of major concentrated commercial interests. Although law, medicine, and business are typically more remunerative than the average journalistic professional career, the corporate organizations within which journalists are housed are far more concentrated than the more distributed wealth of these other professions. Thus, of them all, journalism has the most corporate face. To preserve legitimacy, the media industry must pay attention to the preservation of what it considers professionalism within journalism education. The current public unease over synergistic media, blurred lines between news and entertainment, and the increasingly conglomerate face of journalism, make the reassertion of authority by the professional community a natural response. Blame can be diverted from a crisis in the profession itself. When the prestige and credibility of the news media decline, academia is one place where influence may be exerted and respect recouped.

The number of firms controlling the news organizations that hire journalism graduates has shrunk with the growing concentration of media ownership, meaning that the potential for a concentrated industry "professional" voice has grown as well. Major philanthropic foundations are associated with these newspaper and other media conglomerates, with the biggest of those involved in journalism education being the Freedom Forum (associated with the Gannett newspaper chain), Knight Foundation (Knight Ridder), and Hearst. Given that journalism is organized with an interdisciplinary liberal arts focus, but must address a professional constituency, it is vulnerable to attack from all sides. Its lesser status and wealth compared to other professional programs make it potentially more dependent on outside help; its relative academic immaturity makes it suspect by the older disciplines. Thus, the academic case for journalism must be clearly thought out to help guide and withstand these cross-cutting pressures.

A more integrated view of journalism and media education is needed that considers a number of links, between academy and society, field and larger university, theory and practice, teaching and research. This goal of integration is a particularly worthy goal of professional teaching. Research makes an inviting target for attack, with professional critics arguing that little academic research in journalism has any value in the "real world." Clearly, much of the research being conducted is not relevant and is of poor quality. As the number of doctoral programs in journalism and communication has grown, with a corresponding imperative to conduct publishable research, too much low quality research is chasing too many journals. Indeed, many professors who are induced to conduct their share of research to advance within the academy would better spend their energies elsewhere. Universities need to broaden the kinds of scholarly activity that are rewarded, not reject such activity altogether.

If this integration is to be carried out within an academic, scholarly, and "intellectual" ethos, we must consider what that means. Although one need not be an academic to be an intellectual, higher education in spite of its flaws is one of the last institutional bastions of free societal critique, where, in the ideal, the taken-for-granted assumptions can be challenged without concern for giving offense or incurring unpleasant sanctions. Partnerships can be productive relationships and necessary in tackling complex problems, and joint ventures are a common fixture of corporate life. It must be clear, however, what one is getting out of the relationship. Academia may properly be a partner but should not become a mere client of the corporate world or the professions.

Educators must think through what they are about, especially in fields with so many constituencies like journalism. For all of its faults, universities provide a valuable source of leadership for society and for journalism that cannot be replicated elsewhere. The value of the academy lies in providing an analytical distance in addressing social issues within an intellectual ethos, and in providing a countervailing influence against short term and parochial social interests.

Academia is a porous institution, absorbing the issues in the larger culture and providing a rigorous, open, and productive way of discussing within and across the various disciplines.

To the extent that professional and academic critics of higher education can find common ground, chances of healthy reform are strong, but encouraging false dichotomies between professional and academic is counter-productive. The never well-defined profession of journalism, with all of its contradictions, is in transition. Before journalism and, therefore, education for journalism can fulfill its proper roles, we must carefully determine what skills and values most deserve preservation. The interests of anyone speaking on behalf of the profession must themselves be evaluated. Professionalism can be misused as an unexamined prop to support corporate information industries in a way that blocks questions of public interest from being raised. At the same time, it can be valuably invoked to protect and guide the laudable goals of journalism to facilitate democratic life.

What guidance are we to be given in developing a new professional model? It must be done collaboratively with the best intellectual leadership informed by a close-hand knowledge of professional practices and problems. We need to challenge the simplistic professionalism that assumes its own validity and prevents turning on itself the kind of questioning that journalism excels in directing at others. Journalism is a microcosm of the issues facing higher education at large. It should be a model of a societally and professionally engaged field, bringing the best thinking of the social sciences and humanities to bear on those issues. Beyond the tired debate between academic and professional lie more interesting discussions about broader reforms, for which journalism education may provide useful guidance.

BILLY I. ROSS

Billy I. Ross is Distinguished Professor at Louisiana State University and Professor Emeritus at Texas Tech University, where he was chairman of the Department of Mass Communications for 17 years. He has Ph.D. in journalism and marketing from Southern Illinois University. He has worked in advertising, publishing, and public relations. Professor Ross received the U.S. Army Legion of Merit award in 1979. He was inducted into the Texas Tech University Mass Communications Hall of Fame in 1991 and was named American Advertising Federation's Distinguished Advertising Educator of the Year in 1989. He has served as president of four national and three regional organizations and is author or coauthor of numerous books and articles. He was cofounder and is coeditor of the national directory Where Shall I Go to Study Advertising and Public Relations, now in its 35th year of publication.

Media-related education first appeared in the catalogs of a few schools 100 years ago. Questions that probably were raised at that time were: What problems face us as we go into the next century? What should we be teaching students? If you asked teachers what they expected of students, the answer might have been, "We want them to think and to write."

Many educators in the field today will tell you that the expectation of the teachers is still the same—students with the ability to think and to write. However, there are many more problems today; journalism and mass communication administrators could provide a long list of other problems that they face. Some of those are:

- Academic and professional acceptability
- Number and quality of students
- Academic and professional qualifications of faculty
- Amount and type of equipment
- Budget support by school and the profession
- Ethics and standards of the profession
- The Internet—is it a mass medium?

Academic and professional acceptability is not a new problem. Journalism education has come a long way in the past 100 years, but it still lacks the kind of acceptability enjoyed by the traditional academic fields on the campus. Since the mid-1960s, when enrollment figures were published in professional publications, the general trend has been upward. In fact, many schools have now placed a cap on the number of students admitted. Also, many schools have set entrance standards that assure them the better students on campus.

The type of faculty is another problem that administrators face when hiring. There is an academic need for faculty with academic credentials, whereas professionals in the field think that new faculty need professional experience. Equipment, the amount and type, becomes a major problem with school administrators. Should the school provide each student with a computer and have labs with the most up-to-date equipment? Or should the school focus its attention on thinking and writing as they did 100 years ago?

The size of the budget has and always will be a problem. Media-related education is no longer a pencil, paper, and typewriter operation. Electronic equipment has become some of the most expensive on a college campus. Equipment is not the only high cost for journalism education. Research, travel, classroom support, and cost of faculty and staff are only a few of other costs.

The ethics of the profession has been marred in recent years to the extent that journalism educators are faced with decisions as to what they can do to improve the education of the students before they enter the field. In fact, academic accrediting agencies encourage schools to offer specific courses in ethics.

Not to be considered as last among the problems, the Internet must be considered both a problem and a blessing to journalism education. In the view of many in the field, the Internet is a mass medium that journalism schools should include as a part of the curriculum. Other educators don't agree. They consider it a personal medium.

Mass communication educators will have to look at the problems that exist at the end of this century to determine the direction for the new century. In some cases the solution of the problems will be he direction for the future. Time and accomplishment of faculty and students will help schools be accepted by both academic and professional critics. The framework has been established; the results will be the grade recorded.

Due to continued growth of journalism school enrollments in the last half of the 1900s, nearly all will have to limit the number of students. Quality will be the criterion. The question will have to include the best way to determine those students who will be able to think and write. The mix of academic and professional qualifications will be the best answer for future educators. The bigger question will be how those hired will meet tenure qualifications.

Budget and equipment form another challenge for the future. In general, the cost of new equipment will be the biggest problem facing schools. The answer is support from the profession. Media have received a black eye during the past decade. The starting place to change the image is within the halls of ivy. Schools can take a sound position in establishing the standards of the professions.

The Internet will have to be considered as the biggest challenge of media-related education. The challenge will be to establish the position that journalism education will take. Not only will the Internet be a source of information, but it will also be a medium for the dissemination of news and advertising. It cannot be ignored by journalism educators, but they cannot stand on the sidelines and see what direction it will take. It is a growth medium in which journalism must take a position.

The challenges of the new century are great for journalism education; however, it offers opportunities that are unparalleled in other parts of academia.

DAVID H. WEAVER

David H. Weaver is the Roy W. Howard Professor in Journalism and Mass Communication Research in the School of Journalism at Indiana University–Bloomington. He received his Ph.D. in mass communication research from the University of North Carolina after working as an editor and reporter on four daily newspapers in Indiana and North Carolina. He is author or coauthor of seven books, including The American Journalist in the 1990s: U.S. News People at the End of an Era, as well numerous book chapters, articles, and reports. Professor Weaver serves on the editorial boards of Political Communication,

Newspaper Research Journal, and International Journal of Public Opinion Research. He was the 1987–1988 president of the Association for Education in Journalism and Mass Communication (AEJMC) and 1986–1987 president of the Midwest Association for Public Opinion Research (MAPOR). He is the recipient of the AEJMC Krieghbaum Award in 1983 and the Sigma Delta Chi Distinguished Service Award for Research About Journalism in 1986 and 1996 (with G. Cleveland Wilhoit).

As for major issues facing journalism and media-related education at the end of the 1990s, I would cite the changing definition of journalism as new media proliferate and the boundaries between information and entertainment dissolve, the lack of growth or shrinking size of many journalism/mass media faculties as compared with the increasing enrollments of students in these programs, an increasing reliance on temporary faculty in nontenure track positions, an increasing interest of many journalism students in business and corporate communication and a decreasing interest in informing citizens, a need for ever more sophisticated and expensive computer-based technology for teaching journalism, the continuing need to balance the teaching of specific skills with more theoretical and critical approaches to journalism and media studies, and the need for faculty members who have a combination of significant journalism experience and high quality advanced degrees.

As for directions that I think that journalism and media-related education should take in the first decade of the next century, I would stress the need to balance the teaching of specific entry level skills with courses that emphasize more abstract, critical thinking about journalism; the need to keep technology in perspective and to not place too much emphasis on the delivery channels at the expense of the content of news; and the need to preserve a view of this field that includes both its academic and professional traditions. This is an extremely difficult balancing act, but a necessary one to ensure that journalism and media studies maintains its academic standards as well as its ties to the real-world problems and issues of those who practice what we preach.

Appendix

Major Reports/Studies
Concerning Mass Media Education

PAUL DRESSEL'S STUDY OF LIBERAL ARTS EDUCATION
AND JOURNALISM (1960)

A study by Dressel (1960) provides a perspective on several issues that remain relevant to journalism education after four decades. He examined four conceptions of journalism education: as technical field, as social science, as behavioral science, and as liberal education. He noted that the first conception, a technical journalism orientation, "seems originally to have connoted concern about techniques and writing in technical fields such as home economics and agriculture" (p. 82). He stated, "Individuals having this technical journalism orientation come to regard knowledge of a field and knowledge of journalism as different facets of education." He added, "Although they may agree that journalism requires a liberal education, it is only because one cannot write very much without knowing something about the subject" (p. 83).

According to Dressel (1960), the second conception, journalism as a social science, views the field as an applied social science concerned with local, national, and international social and political issues and "the journalist who reports and interprets the developments to citizens and influences their point of view must be well grounded in the social sciences" (p. 83). Educators with this conception speak of liberal education but have little interest in students taking courses in literature, art, music, or philosophy because they have no direct application to journalism. Dressel stated that the concept leads to "a superficial contact with introductory courses in the many social sciences, and a lack of sufficient depth to gain any understanding of the real nature of the discipline or of the tentativeness associated with the concepts and generalizations covered in the introductory courses" (p. 84). Another drawback, he stated, was that an emphasis on the social sciences could cause the field to regress to the level of technical journalism because "the requirement of contact with all of the many social science disciplines places a premium on knowledge rather than on real understanding of broad concepts, principles, theory, and methods" (p. 84).

The third conception, that of journalism education as a behavioral science, was, according to Dressel (1960), somewhat broader than conceiving of it as a social science because behavior "broadly construed involves anything that an organism does" (p. 85). He stated:

Ultimately, it is possible that the behavioral science or the communications (study) concept may establish journalism as a discipline in its own right. Necessary and desirable as this development is, there is danger that individuals will become so engrossed in the essential nature of the communication process that their work has little direct relevance for the level at which the journalist operates. (p. 85)

He added that journalism educators had sought "complete respectability among their liberal arts brethren" for a long time and that it would be unfortunate if it achieves that respectability "by assuming their increasingly specialized orientation" (p. 86).

Concerning the fourth conception, journalism education as a liberal education, Dressel (1960) wrote that "the ideal would be for the journalist to be a broadly educated, deeply understanding person who is also versed in the art of discussing intelligently what is going on in the world." In addition, the journalist "should be a person of responsibility and integrity and in addition . . . should know something about the special methods and arts of the various journalistic forms: newspaper, magazines, radio and television" (p. 86). Such traits would require a liberal arts degree, he noted, but the additional requirements for technical abilities made that impossible without the higher salaries that would justify more than a 4-year degree. He added that "journalism courses should be so taught as to have a strong liberal content in the sense that they provoke a spirit of inquiry, relate knowledge from many fields, and encourage further research as needed to attain a depth of insight before attempting to interpret events" (p. 86).

Dressel (1960) wrote that, with such a view, "the first qualification of the journalist is a general and liberal education" (p. 86). In addition, the journalist must have "an understanding of the relationship between press and society and some training in the technical and craft skills of the several mass media of communications" (p. 87). He saw practical courses not so much vocational as art. The difference in trade and art, he wrote, is that "the tradesman unimaginatively performs relatively routine tasks at the behest of another person, whereas the artist sets his own goals and uses equipment to gain them" (p. 87). Such an education would be closer to the ideals of a liberal education than would be found in most liberal arts colleges, he wrote, and would require a journalism faculty that was "truly educated rather than being, on one hand, professionally competent as practicing journalists or, on the other hand, the proud possessors of the doctorate primarily concerned with research" (p. 88). He added, "Such a faculty must hold that the technical aspect of journalism is not unimportant, but a means to an end—a means which at no time must receive such an important role in the curriculum as to obscure the end itself" (p. 88). He called for only a handful of specialties (such as news writing and editing, radio and television, and advertising) and proposed that a minimum of 50% of a student's professional courses be courses taken by all journalism majors because such a small percent of graduates took a job related to their major.

APME JOURNALISM EDUCATION COMMITTEE REPORT (1982)

The Associated Press Managing Editors Journalism Education Committee produced a report titled *1990—Journalism Education in the Next Decade:19 Big Questions & A Host of Answers* (APME, 1982). Robert H. Giles, chair of the committee, wrote that the survey began with a single question: "Can we define the needs of journalism education in 1990?" He answered the question by stating:

> It is, of course, not a single question, but many. And as our project moved ahead, it was clear that we were seeking fresh thoughts from campus and newsroom about dramatic changes or bold new directions for journalism education in the next decade. We also wanted to re-examine some of the basic issues in teaching journalism and in the relationship between educators and journalists. (unpaginated)

The 13-member committee, including three journalism educators, interviewed 20 journalism educators and 29 people with a connection to newspapers. It proposed 19 questions concerning journalism education and included responses by the educators and practitioners. The questions still are relevant for the year 2000. They are:

1. How can journalism schools become more central to the newspaper industry by 1990?
2. How can newspapers help journalism schools recruit better students?
3. Should journalism school admission standards be tougher in 1990?
4. What "futuristic" subjects might be part of the journalism curriculum by 1990?
5. Now, journalism majors take 25% of their courses in journalism and 75% in liberal arts. Should that balance be changed by 1990?
6. Who will carry the load for teaching spelling and grammar in 1990?
7. Teaching management: Is it a journalism school responsibility for the 1990s?
8. Should newspaper marketing—including advertising and circulation—be taught in journalism school?
9. New technology: More or less in 1990?
10. How can journalism schools become more respected members of the academic community?
11. Should research in journalism schools be of genuine value to the

newspaper industry?

12. Does accreditation have a purpose worth continuing in 1990?
13. By 1990, should there be greater differences in the purposes of undergraduate and graduate journalism programs.
14. Is midcareer education the big new role for journalism schools in 1990?
15. What should newspapers be doing by 1990 to help journalism school faculty get professional experience and keep current with trends in the industry?
16. How can newspapers help attract more minorities to college journalism programs?
17. How will the advent of electronic photography change the role of the news photographer?
18. What traditional skills do photojournalists lack that will be in demand in 1990?
19. What "futuristic" skills will photojournalists need to have in 1990?

THE OREGON REPORT (1984)

The major expansion in journalism/mass communication student enrollment in the 1970s and the changing nature of the media led Everette Dennis, dean of the School of Journalism at the University of Oregon, to organize a 2-year, $86,000 study of mass media education funded mainly by a $70,000 Gannett Foundation Grant. The purpose of the study—the Project on the Future of Journalism and Mass Communication Education (Project, 1984; Project, 1987)—was "to assess and evaluate the present status and future needs of the nation's schools and departments of journalism and mass communication through a series of studies and by fostering a national debate wherein interested parties may offer a critique" (Project, 1987, p. v). Dennis suspected that it was the first such report of its kind.

The Oregon Report Project Team surveyed administrators at all 81 accredited schools plus several unaccredited schools and received 82 responses, a 91% response rate. Questions covered five areas of concern: (a) the placement of the journalism/mass communication unit (school or department) within the larger university or college, (b) the internal organizational pattern of the media unit, (c) the primary goals of the media units, (d) the curriculum in place in media units, and (e) changes that media educators would like to implement. The Project Team also sent letters to more than 100 media faculty members and 40 faculty from related fields asking for in-depth comments and received responses from 70%. In addition, the team sent surveys to members of the AEJMC Council of Affiliates asking how successful the media-related programs in the United States had been, how they could be improved, and whether the media industry was living up to its responsibility to act as a partner with journalism educators.

The Oregon Report's Major Conclusions

The report concluded that the academic unit in which media programs are located should be a freestanding professional school unless another organization better met the needs of the institution. It predicted that undergraduate education would be de-emphasized in the future and that continuing education would be given more importance. It predicted that schools of journalism and mass communication would be pushed away from industry-oriented sequence programs and toward more generic mass communication study because of the pace of new knowledge and technology change. It proposed that highly specialized courses be offered in the student's final year and continue in graduate and continuing education and concluded that conceptual and craft courses would merge in many instances. It suggested that some programs might be realigned along competence and knowledge lines with specific instruction in literacy, visual literacy, and computer literacy along with information gathering, and it predicted that conceptual courses (media and society, media economics, etc.) would be organized as linchpins to the liberal arts. It stated that specific professional courses should be organized in modules, with specific outcomes for training stated well in advance and over which students can be tested for competency. Students leaving the university would have personal assessments from faculty to provide them with a suggested continuing education plan to meet their specific needs and deficiencies. All courses would have a 5-year review rule wherein course outlines and plans are submitted voluntarily to outside referees.

The Oregon Report proposed that students get conceptual instruction in the impact and influence of communication technology in society as well as specific hands-on instruction in areas related to entry-level work. It predicted that the media faculty member normally would be a scholar/teacher with limited professional experience but that room should exist for the professional teacher from the media professions. It proposed greater use of professionals in residence and short-term appointments and more opportunity for scholars with little professional experience to get greater exposure to industry experience. It called for the development of more service courses for general university students who are not media majors. It also called for a national strategic plan for media education and a strategic plan on every campus, and it stated that an understanding of the mass media in American society was a critical need for all citizens.

Perhaps the most controversial of the Oregon Report's recommendations was its call for a "generic model" of journalism/mass communication education to replace the "industry model." The Oregon Report stated:

> Essentially, the problem is that journalism schools tend to operate on an industry model. That is, students are taught the entry-level skills they will need to secure their first jobs in a single, specific communication industry such as newspaper or

broadcasting. Reliance on the industry model, however, does not give students the sufficient understanding of the media as a whole that they will need to advance later in their careers. An alternative approach would be to use a generic model of journalism/mass communication education. . . .

In substantive terms, the generic model will enable students to develop a better understanding of the fields in which they wish to work. . . .

Far too much emphasis has been placed on the tactics of accomplishing specific entry-level skills at the cost of preparing students for the changes that are already upon us. (Project, 1987, pp. 9–10)

The report noted that journalism and mass communication education "in its zeal to produce well-trained entry-level people, . . . often fails to give students broader survival skills to prepare them for a communication industry that is rapidly merging into a single field" (Project, 1987, p. 48).

The Oregon Report's Model Curriculum

In addition to its recommendation for a generic curriculum, another controversial proposal in the Oregon Report was its model curriculum. It called for a "creative merger of more generalized mass communication study with the lessons of professional practice" (p. 49). The report concluded that a model curriculum should have the following components:

- *A conceptual map of the field.* Such an approach "explains how communication scholars and professionals do their work, how they think, what methods they use and what the yield of their activity involves. It means introducing knowledge about mass communication as a process as well as an explanation of literature in the field" (p. 49).
- *A linchpin course.* "The journalism/mass communication curriculum through its course structure needs to do more to help students make sense out of the rest of their education" (p. 50).
- *Relating goals to outcomes.* "Specific craft courses must be developed as part of an overall plan that is linked to educational outcomes for the student. . . . A course of study should have a general objective that actually lists both specific knowledge and specific skills that are desired in students completing the program" (p. 50). Outcomes would be determined by a competency test including practical assignments to determine the result of the student's media course work.

The Oregon Report also made two major recommendations concerning assessment. It stated that the curriculum of specific sequences or programs should be submitted to outside experts for review every 5 years and that each media unit should make an inventory of its characteristics and specialties, particular student needs, and particular concerns of the institution. The report also noted that "for a complete communication education in the generic mode, it might be necessary to do a graduate degree and most certainly to be involved in continuing education after completion of the undergraduate degree." It stated that such an education "would not be unlike contemporary legal education" (p. 54).

THE COMMISSION ON UNDERGRADUATE
PUBLIC RELATIONS EDUCATION (1987)

The 26-member Commission on Undergraduate Public Relations Education, cochaired by William Ehling and Betsy Plank, released its report, titled *Design for Undergraduate Public Relations Education*, in 1987 (Commission, 1987) and reissued it in 1993 (Commission, 1993). The commission was established in late 1983 by the Public Relations Division of the Association for Education in Journalism and Mass Communication and the Public Relations Society of America. The committee was charged with a 3-year mission to develop and recommend a public relations program of study for undergraduate public relations in U.S. colleges and universities.

In May 1985, the Commission on Undergraduate Public Relations Education mailed 1,500 questionnaires to professionals. It was thought to be the largest survey ever conducted concerning undergraduate public relations education. The questionnaire also was sent to all educators listed as members of the Public Relations Society of America (PRSA), International Association of Business Communicators (IABC), International Communication Association (ICA), and Speech Communication Association (SCA), as well as a cross-section of practitioners from various areas of public relations practice and associate members of the PRSA. Each respondent was asked to respond to 124 courses using a 1 (*most essential*) to 7 (*not essential*) scale. A total of 544 questionnaires were returned (36.9%). The commission found virtual unanimity of opinion between practitioners and educators about what the content of undergraduate public relations education should be.

English was the general education course rated highest by both practitioners and educators, and an internship/practicum was the highest rated public relations course. Respondents agreed that the arts and sciences should remain the basis for undergraduate public relations study. The report recommended that a minimum of 54% of the student's hours (65 hours in a 120-hour course of study) should be in the liberal arts and sciences and another 21% (25 hours) outside of the professional program. No more than 25% of a student's required credit hours (30 hours of a 120-hour curriculum) should be professional courses. About half of those 30 hours should be in courses clearly identifiable as public relations courses and half of them in communications courses. The guideline was interpreted as following the ACEJMC's 90/65 curriculum rule (Standard 3).

The commission recommended that about half of the student's 15 credit hours in professional education should be production oriented and half management oriented (research, planning, and evaluating). It urged public relations students to consider a minor in business. The report stated that the public relations educator should have practical public relations experience and an advanced degree in public relations/communications, preferably a doctoral degree. It suggested that partnerships between the profession and educators should be strengthened.

The report stated the following goals or responsibilities of the study of public relations that should be conveyed to undergraduate majors: (a) the nature of a public relations activity, (b) the tasks and responsibilities of public relations management, (c) the various intellectual perspectives on which alternative concepts of public relations production and management are based, and (d) the operational and ethical standards that can be and should be used in determining which perspective is the most appropriate in practice (p. 14). The commission stated that the public relations program should seek to reach those goals by determining: (a) the number and types of courses that should make up the undergraduate public relations program, (b) the conceptual content and structure of those courses, (c) the type of emphasis and the standards of course evaluation, and (d) the nature of assessment used to judge student performance (p. 14).

The Model Public Relations Curriculum

The commission proposed that for a complete undergraduate public relations program, the student would take 15 hours in Studies in Communication and 15 hours in Studies in Public Relations. Studies in Communication would have three components: technical/production courses, historical/institutional courses, and communication process/structure courses. Technical production courses would include: Copy Preparation and Editing, Graphic Arts and Typography, Still Photography, Production for Electronic Media, and Public Speaking and Oral Presentation. The historical/institutional course would concern the history of public communications; and the communication process/structure course would cover social and cultural factors affecting communication and the effect of communication on society. Studies in Public Relations would consist of Principles, Practices and Theory of Public Relations; Public Relations Techniques: Writing, Message Dissemination, and Media Networks; Public Relations Research for Planning and Evaluation; Public Relations Strategy and Implementation; Supervised Public Relations Experience; and Specialized Advanced Study.

ROPER ELECTRONIC MEDIA
CAREER PREPARATION STUDY (1987)

The International Radio and Television Society, the Radio–Television News Directors Association, and the National Association of Television Program Executives commissioned the Roper Organization to conduct a study of attitudes of electronic media industry executives concerning the adequacy of the educational background of students seeking to undertake a career in the electronic media. The Gannett Foundation provided additional funding. The study was based on 514 telephone interviews, 403 of them evenly divided among general managers, news directors, program directors, and sales directors and 111 of them with executives at cable systems, syndication companies, and other related media organizations.

Electronic media executives thought that applicants did not measure up to expectations in such areas as writing skills, examples of previous industry work experience, actual experience in work situations, and experience with or even familiarity with broadcast communications technologies. On the other hand, expectations were met in areas considered of secondary importance: experience on a school newspaper, radio station or TV station; a graduate degree; the prestige of the institution attended; and a well-rounded liberal arts background. Thus, the report writers concluded that "executives appear to be making an important distinction between the 'skills' which come from work on school media and an understanding of the 'realities' of the work situation for entry level employees in the electronic media industry" (Roper, 1987, p. 7).

Nearly all executives (88%) favored a closer link between the electronic media industry and higher education tied to a mechanism to expose students and professors to people with current or recent experience in electronic media. Suggestions toward that end included (a) more courses taught by people who work or have worked recently in the industry, (b) lectures or other instructional participation by people currently working in the industry, (c) an opportunity for faculty to take leaves of absences to work in the broadcasting and cable industries, and (d) more internships for credit. They also suggested that higher education put more emphasis on writing skills and hands-on experience with new production technologies. The report writers concluded that executives "credit schools for providing a broad overview, even as they are critical of their failure to prepare students for the realities of what it is like to actually work in the industry" (p. 8).

Rather than rating journalism/mass communication programs, the 403 TV and radio station respondents in the Roper poll were asked to give the higher education system in general a report card. The executives gave higher education a C grade in terms of the overall job it did in preparing students for entry-level positions in broadcasting and cable. Whereas program directors gave the highest rating (2.2 on a 0-to-4 scale, still a low C), general managers and sales directors gave it the lowest rating (1.9). Executives in large markets gave higher education a 1.9, the lowest rating, while those in middle-size markets gave a 2.0 and those in the smallest markets gave it a 2.1.

Nearly all executives (91%) stated that higher education should place more emphasis on courses taught by people with current or recent media experience, 87% noted that input from people in the broadcast and cable industries should be emphasized more, 81% mentioned better writing skills, 79% stated a need for faculty to takes leaves of absence to work in the industry, 77% listed hands-on experience in the new production technologies, and 69% suggested internships for majors. Fewer than half the respondents thought more emphasis was needed on general liberal arts courses (39%) and on communications theory (32%). The report writers noted about the areas of emphasis: "Overall, three of the top four areas that require more emphasis by higher education are of the same nature. These three areas involved providing a stronger link between academic and the electronic media industry by having students exposed to people who have recent experience or are currently employed in the electronic media" (p. 37). The authors of the study concluded that "broadcast executives generally expect students to come to the job knowing the basic elements that are required for work in the industry" (p. 45). Those major areas are writing skills (noted by 39%), the basics of broadcasting (31%), knowing how to operate equipment (25%), and communications skills (19%). The only other area mentioned by more than 10% of respondents was a liberal arts background (10%).

The nonstation executives agreed that a college degree was important but not essential, and they also gave the higher education system a C grade. They agreed with station executives that college gives students a good overview of the industry and a good liberal arts background, and they criticized colleges for not providing students more practical knowledge of the "real world" of work. They basically agreed with station executives about the deficiencies of higher education courses. Nonstation executives, however, were somewhat less likely to state that colleges should give more emphasis to hands-on experience in production. They were more likely to state that colleges should give greater emphasis to the reading of industry publications and to introductory courses stressing the extent of work opportunities in broadcasting and cable. Most nonstation executives wanted a closer relationship between the industry and higher education, but they were not as likely as station executives to say so. They were more likely, however, to favor programs for professionals to lecture or teach and internship programs. Their organizations also were more likely than stations to provide paid internships.

VERNON STONE'S BROADCAST EDUCATION RESEARCH
(1986–1988)

Research by Vernon Stone of the University of Missouri around the time of the
Roper study came to similar conclusions. In a 1986 survey, V. Stone (1987) found
that news directors most often rated journalism and broadcast writing courses as
having been of the most help to them since leaving college. Just over one fifth
(21%) listed journalism writing as most useful to them, 14% listed other
journalism courses, just over 11% mentioned nonjournalism writing courses, and
just over 9% named other radio–TV courses (p. 9).

Stone conducted a study in 1988 partly in response to remarks by ABC's Ted
Koppel to the Radio and Television News Directors Association and the Society of
Professional Journalists in 1987 that broadcast education was "worse than nothing,
requiring unteaching" (V. Stone, 1989, p. 58). Stone polled all 890 TV stations and
a sample of 825 commercial radio stations. He obtained responses from 459 TV
stations (52%) and 373 radio stations (45%). Stone found fairly strong support for
broadcast journalism education. About two thirds of TV news directors (67%) and
radio news directors (63%) responded that broadcast journalism training at
universities generally gives new hires a "head start with solid training in the
basics" with 29% of TV and 32% of radio news directors stating that it was not
much help and about 4% of each group stating that it was "worse than nothing."
Responses did not differ much based on the size of the market or the size of the
staff.

THE TASK FORCE ON THE FUTURE OF JOURNALISM
AND MASS COMMUNICATION EDUCATION (1989)

The Task Force on the Future of Journalism and Mass Communication Education
produced a report titled *Challenges and Opportunities in Journalism & Mass
Communication Education* (Task Force, 1989). The document was divided into
two parts. The first part, "Role of Liberal Arts and Sciences," is known as the
Mullins Report for its author, Ed Mullins of the University of Alabama. The
second part consisted of reports by subcommittees (or task forces) on advertising
curriculum, broadcast curriculum, magazine curriculum, news–editorial
curriculum, public relations curriculum, and visual communication curriculum.
Each subcommittee was asked "to survey memberships of its identified constituent
bodies, academic and professional, to determine the basic programs in the areas
specific to the individual subcommittees" (Task Force, 1989, p. A-2) and "to
identify the integrating principles that should characterize education for mass
communication in the twenty-first century" (p. A3).

Liberal Arts and Sciences Task Force Report

The Liberal Arts and Sciences Task Force wanted its report (a) to assist media units attempting ACEJMC accreditation or reaccreditation; (b) to provide a framework for media units to use in "implementing, monitoring, and demonstrating compliance with the sacred standard of ACEJMC, the much-feared Standard No. 3 of the visiting team report, titled 'Curriculum' "; and (c) to guide the accrediting council itself about the relationship of liberal arts to accreditation (Task Force, 1989, p. A3).

The task force concluded from statements by the founding figures of media education, Willard Bleyer and Joseph Pulitzer, that four desired outcomes exist for a journalism and mass communication major: (a) a set of field-related skills, (b) a broad education grounded in the liberal arts, (c) a value system that emphasizes public service, and (d) the ability to integrate these things "in relation to the life and work of the world." They also concluded that the four outcomes fit well with the "present theory of JMC curricula" and "remain the best superstructure for JMC education." Much like the Oregon Report, the Mullins Report stressed the "commonality among JMC disciplines" (p. A4).

The Liberal Arts Task Force noted that only 8% of jobs taken by media graduates are traditional entry level media positions. In language reminiscent of the Oregon Report, the Mullins Report noted that "such statistics show us the folly of narrow, industrial-based training of our students" (p. A-5). Eschewing the Oregon Report's use of the term *generic* in favor of *holistic* curriculum, the report nevertheless recommended essentially the same thing: a "functionalist (or integrated) rather than a fragmented or segmented approach to curriculum planning and evaluation" (p. A5).

The task force defined the *functionalist* approach as "the specification of how all components of the curriculum interrelate in addressing explicit goals and objectives of the unit." Much like the Oregon Report, the report stated that such goals, both philosophic and operational, should be "the primary determinants of the curriculum." It called for assessment of courses to determine if they were relevant to the unit's overall goals and objectives and evaluation of how well the unit's goals and objectives were being met. The report called for ongoing evaluation of courses inside the unit as well as liberal arts courses outside the unit. The functionalist approach advocated in the Mullins Report meant assessment of courses based on content, not based on whether it was inside or outside the department, as required by ACEJMC Standard 3. Thus courses within the unit deemed to be liberal arts could count toward the 60 hours of required liberal arts courses.

The Liberal Arts Task Force noted that accreditation guidelines and materials "don't fully articulate the real values of liberal arts in the education of all students, not just our own" and that "[l]iberal arts courses and the essential verbal and quantitative skills of analysis our students develop while acquiring a liberal arts and professional education cannot be defined simply in terms of the ACEJMC (curriculum) standard" (p. A8). The report called on media units to develop "programmatic systems to define and defend the liberal arts context of their students' education for purposes of internal planning and external review" and proposed that the ACEJMC units be able to count liberal arts courses both from within and outside the unit to meet the demands of Standard 3 (pp. 8–9). It concluded: "There will be some who view these recommendations as opening a pandora's box leading to anarchy in JMC curricular matters. That's a risk we may have to run in order to improve our curricula and accreditation procedures" (p. 8).

Advertising Curriculum Task Force Report

The Advertising Task Force surveyed the presidents and education chairpersons of 420 local professional advertising associations affiliated with the American Advertising Federation, as well as the entire membership of the Advertising Division of the AEJMC. It received 407 usable responses from AAF members and 116 from AEJMC members and achieved an overall response rate of 80%. The survey found considerable agreement between advertising practitioners and advertising educators.

Educators and practitioners were in substantial agreement about the importance of particular coursework. Both groups rated advertising, marketing, and English composition as the most important areas of study for advertising majors, followed by psychology, journalism writing, and economics. Computer science and literature were in the middle of both lists. However, professors rated sociology slightly higher than did practitioners (7th vs. 10th). Also, practitioners listed management higher (5th vs. 10th).

Practitioners and professors also agreed on most statements concerning the value of advertising education. They agreed about the importance of a broad education for graduates, that graduates of accredited programs were preferable to those from unaccredited programs and were better prepared, and that a master's degree in advertising was not becoming more important in gaining an entry-level position. Professors were somewhat more likely to agree with the statement that "Most programs I am aware of seem alert to the implications of changes in the structure and function of the advertising industry" (Task Force, 1989, p. 12).

Broadcast Curriculum Task Force

The Broadcast Task Force surveyed an unstated number of broadcast educators, receiving only a 15% response rate. Educators listed broadcast production, performance and equipment operation as the strongest skills their students had at graduation, and they rated writing as the weakest skill. Educators listed social sciences, political science, economics, history, and physical sciences as the most important liberal arts disciplines for broadcast graduates. The Broadcast Task Force reported the results of the Electronic Media Career Preparation Study conducted by the Roper Organization (1987).

Magazine Curriculum Task Force Report

The Magazine Task Force conducted a random survey of 100 magazine editors, 100 AEJMC Magazine Division members, and 100 graduates from accredited programs with magazine sequences. A total of 116 people (38%) responded. Respondents ranked writing first and editing second as important skills for graduates to obtain both an entry level job and to move up the career ladder. Eighty-three percent of respondents agreed that basic news writing, reporting, and editing were important, and 75% agreed that graphics was important. Respondents agreed that an internship was important, but they "were not enthusiastic" about courses in media law, media and society, ethics, and history. The task force and respondents recommended the following electives for magazine majors: advanced reporting, media management, public affairs reporting, photography, reviews and criticism, and business magazine journalism. The task force recommended flexibility in sequence requirements and open electives selected through careful academic advisement.

News–Editorial Curriculum Task Force

Each subcommittee member wrote to at least 5 educators and 10 editors. The need for a strong liberal arts background was the major area of agreement by the 21 educators and 29 professionals responding. They saw a need for courses in budgeting, government, modern American history, geography, and the social sciences, and they agreed that courses outside of journalism should be monitored by the media unit to make sure they were appropriate. Respondents suggested "inside" courses in finding information and using databases and in interviewing, as well as for advanced skills in editorial writing and in investigative or in-depth reporting. They agreed on the need for graduates to be clear in their communication, to have a good vocabulary, and to be regular newspaper readers— to be encouraged by regular current events quizzes. Though neither editors nor educators mentioned the topic, the task force recommended a place for discussing minority and ethnic issue reporting.

Public Relations Curriculum Task Force Report

The Public Relations Task Force endorsed "Design for Public Relations Education" (Commission, 1987), produced by the Commission on Undergraduate Public Relations Education.

Visual Communication Task Force Report

The task force surveyed 16 educators and media professionals. First, it recommended that all media majors receive training in the uses of photography, art, infographics, typography, and layout and design. Second, it recommended that visual communication majors take courses in media history, law, and ethics as well as theoretical foundations of visual communication, complete an internship, and take available practical/skills courses. It suggested skills courses in picture selection; use of graphics; aesthetic and emotional qualities of artwork; cropping, sizing and positioning of artwork; design, paste-up and production; budgeting; text and cutline writing; visual communications law, including press access rights; ethics of representing data and facts in photo illustrations; coverage of media events; and picture editing.

INSTITUTION FOR PUBLIC RELATIONS RESEARCH (1990)

In a report for the Institute for Public Relations Research titled "Public Relations Education: The Unpleasant Realities," D. K. Wright and VanSlyke Turk (1990) attempted to identify and examine major issues facing public relations education. They looked specifically at the public relations curriculum, program growth, faculty, research, educators' relationship with practitioners, where public relations programs should be located, administrative support provided, continuing education, recruitment, and graduate education. They identified the main curriculum issue as whether the public relations curriculum should be altered from a technical perspective to a managerial one. Wright and VanSlyke Turk noted the argument that a public relations curriculum should go beyond teaching entry level skills and increase courses in such administrative and managerial topics as strategic planning, problem solving, communication facilitating, and budgeting. They also noted the difficulty of finding a place in the curriculum for such courses without squeezing out skills courses or reducing the number of liberal arts courses a student could take.

As to placement of public relations programs, Wright and VanSlyke Turk rejected the notion that public relations education should be located in business schools. The two authors noted the need that business majors have for public relations courses, but they suggested business students should take such courses in media units. They concluded that few public relations educators or PR programs were doing much to further continuing education or professional development for practitioners. According to the authors, the main reason for the situation was that the educators hadn't been asked to present such programs. Instead, they noted that practitioners turned to other professionals or professional public relations societies. Wright and VanSlyke Turk (1990) wrote: "There's clearly more than just a residue of lingering practitioner doubt about the relevance and value of public relations education and the worth of those who teach public relations" (p. 13). They called on practitioners to provide "clear and consistent hiring standards in the profession" instead of "meddling" with the public relations curriculum. Such standards would include hiring only graduates with both technical and managerial skills. They also called on public relations educators to "weed out the students who study public relations because they 'like people' or want to be party planners" (p. 17).

BROADCAST EDUCATION ASSOCIATION COURSES AND CURRICULA COMMITTEE TASK FORCE (1990)

In fall 1988 and winter 1989, a Broadcast Education Association Courses and Curricula Committee task force undertook a study of institutions belonging to the organization to update a 1985 study. Warner and Liu (1990) reported that the task force sent questionnaires to 258 4-year colleges and universities belonging to the BEA and received 128 responses, almost a 50% return rate. Broadcast program heads were asked to rate their orientation on a 1-to-5 scale from *theoretical* to *professional*. More than 84% of the schools rated their professional orientation as *moderate* to *high* (3 to 5), with the largest schools least likely to have a professional orientation.

Most broadcast units (60%) offered a bachelor of arts degree, almost one quarter (24%) offered a bachelor of arts degree and a bachelor of science degree, and slightly more than 12% offered a bachelor of science degree. The rest offered degrees by a variety of names. The sequences most often offered were broadcast news (39%), television (35%), production (33%), radio (31%), film (24%), management (24%), broadcasting (19%), advertising (13%), telecommunications (12%), sales (11%), video (8%), mass communication (6%), and performance (5%). All other sequences were offered by fewer than 5% of units. Broadcast units tended to have a core curriculum of between two and six courses. The course most likely to be in the core was Introduction to Media, offered by 35% of programs, followed by media law and regulation (28%), and Introduction to Broadcasting (27%).

ASNE COMMITTEE ON EDUCATION FOR JOURNALISM (1990)

The American Society of Newspaper Editors Committee on Education for Journalism was charged to undertake an "examination of changes in journalism education and the attitudes of newspaper editors toward journalism schools and the values they represent" (American Society of Newspaper Editors, 1990, p. 1). Its study was based on a disproportionate stratified sample of 600 editors: 200 each from small (under 25,000 circulation), medium (25,000–100,000) and large (over 100,000) newspapers. A total of 381 editors responded. In its report, titled "Journalism Education: Facing Up to the Challenge of Change," the committee concluded: "Looking at journalism education through the eyes of editors, as the survey attempted to do, one finds signs of dissatisfaction that should be troubling to both ASNE and the educators" (p. 1).

As support for its conclusion, the committee noted that only 4% of editors gave journalism education an A grade based on the quality of training their recent hires had received, that half of the editors didn't care whether their new hires had a degree in journalism or in the liberal arts; and that editors tended to rate journalism graduates lowest in the skills editors thought were most important: reporting, spelling and grammar, and journalism ethics. The report stated that "ASNE must examine these realities as it defines its continuing role as an active supporter of journalism education" (p. 1). The report also concluded that "perhaps for the first time," editors strongly supported "concepts involved in the accrediting system, and particularly its emphasis on liberal arts and sciences" (pp. 1–2).

The two major concerns listed in the report were the decline in the proportion of news–editorial majors in journalism/mass communication programs, and the rising bias against tenuring experienced journalists who do not have doctorates. The ASNE committee proposed that, among other things, journalism educators make the case for a "doctoral equivalency that would make qualified experienced journalists fully competitive for tenure-track positions, including full professorships" and that they build "more effective bridges with journalism administrators and teachers through newspaper internships for teachers and campus visits by editors." The committee also asked educators to assure that "Ph.D.'s in communications who are teaching journalism skills courses have regular opportunities for newsroom experience." In addition, it called on educators to monitor "the career counseling that journalism students get from their teachers to insure that the expectations and preferences of prospective newspaper employers are presented fully and fairly" (p. 2).

Editors' Views of New Hires

The smallest newspapers were significantly more likely to hire recent college graduates; the larger the newspaper, the less likely they were to hire recent graduates. Medium-sized newspapers were more likely to hire an even mix of recent graduates and experienced people. Five of six editors stated that a college degree was a prerequisite for employment. Half of the editors had no preference for a particular type of major, four of 10 had a preference for journalism school graduates, and the rest wanted graduates in a nonjournalism field. The larger the newspaper, the more likely the editor was not to have a preference. Despite the fact that only 40% of editors stated they preferred journalism graduates, just over two thirds of the editors reported that more than half of their newsroom hires in the previous 5 years had been journalism graduates. Three quarters of editors would have liked their recent hires to have more nonjournalism course work rather than more journalism course work. The larger the newspaper, the more likely the editors were to prefer more course work outside of journalism rather than within the field.

The larger the newspaper, the more likely the editor was to rate the liberal arts and sciences background of new entry level hires as "strong" or "somewhat strong." Editors rated journalism graduates strongest for knowledge of a second language, knowledge of geography, understanding computers, knowledge of media law, and capacity for hard work. They rated journalism graduates lowest for being widely read and having a knowledge of ethics, a broad perspective, a capacity for leadership, an ability to gather information, and a knowledge of spelling and grammar. They rated nonjournalism graduates strongest for problem solving ability, capacity for hard work, knowledge of current events, and having a broad perspective. Editors rated them lowest for capacity for leadership, knowledge of media law, spelling and grammar, understanding computers, and writing ability. Editors ranked journalism school graduates stronger than new hires with other majors in 10 of 17 areas.

Two thirds of the editors gave journalism schools an A or B grade (strong and somewhat strong) for teaching news gathering, and just over half gave them an A or B for teaching writing. Editors rated putting more media professionals on the faculty as the highest priority for improving journalism schools, followed by putting more emphasis on "nuts and bolts" of journalism, adding more visiting professionals from the media, and getting better students. Editors at medium-sized papers were most likely to rate having more media professionals on the faculty as the top priority. Editors were about evenly split as to whether advertising and public relations belonged in journalism schools. Those at larger papers were more likely to state that advertising and public relations didn't belong. Just over two thirds of the editors disapproved of eliminating industry-based sequences and instituting courses designed for all media majors. Editors at medium-sized and small newspapers were more likely to oppose the trend than were those at larger newspapers.

Editors overall were fairly well split on whether journalism schools should offer courses that look at all media as interdependent and interrelated. Editors at larger newspapers were more likely to approve of the idea. Editors were overwhelmingly in agreement that "provide a fundamental knowledge of journalism but keep present level of commitment to liberal arts and sciences" was important or very important. The larger the newspaper, the more likely the editor was to rate to "provide a fundamental knowledge of journalism" as important or very important. Also, the smaller the newspaper, the more likely the editor was to rate "educate students in mass communication concepts" as important or very important. Most editors described journalism schools as academic and professional schools, though one eighth of them described journalism schools as vocational schools. Only one sixth of the editors stated that it was important or very important that "training for journalism should be primarily taught in graduate schools, following the model of law and medical schools."

ROSS' STUDY OF ADVERTISING EDUCATION (1991)

Billy I. Ross' 1991 book, *The Status of Advertising Education*, was an update of his 1965 report and was thought to be the largest study of advertising education undertaken at that point. Ross surveyed the 111 institutions offering an advertising major in 1989. In all but 10 of the institutions, advertising was located in a mass media unit. Ninety institutions responded to his survey. The most common requirement was for five required advertising courses or 15 hours (at 32 institutions). The second-most common requirement was for four advertising courses or 12 hours (21 institutions), followed by six advertising courses or 18 hours (15 institutions). The highest number of advertising courses required was nine, and the lowest number was two. Ross found that the most typical 15-hour advertising curriculum was Principles/Introduction to Advertising, Copy and Layout, Advertising Campaigns, Media Planning/Strategy, and Advertising Management/Administration or Advertising Research. Comparing his findings to what earlier researchers had found, Ross noted that more emphasis was put on research, strategy, and management in 1989 than was the case 30 years earlier.

PUBLIC RELATIONS STUDENT SOCIETY
OF AMERICA STUDY (1992)

The Public Relations Student Society of America sponsored a study of 461 public relations professionals and the chief executive officer of the top 50 public relations firms as ranked by the J. R. O'Dwyer Co. (Schwartz, Yarbrough, & Shakra, 1992). The response rate was 77% for the practitioners and 68% for the CEOs. Only one fourth of the practitioners recommended a public relations major as the best preparation for a public relations career. Almost two thirds recommended a minor in public relations. Half of those proposing a major in another field suggested journalism, and the other half suggested a nonmedia major. Eleven percent of practitioners proposed a liberal arts major and a professional minor. Nearly half of practitioners who majored in public relations, communication, or journalism rated a public relations major as the best career preparation. A quarter of them recommended a public relations minor and a nonmedia major, and a quarter suggested a public relations minor with a major in communication or journalism.

Of the practitioners who were media majors, 41% stated that a major in another media field with a public relations minor was the best career preparation. A quarter of them recommended a public relations major and another quarter recommended a public relations minor with a nonmedia major. Fourteen percent of practitioners did not like the idea of public relations as a university program of study, and 10% did not think public relations programs should be offered at the undergraduate or graduate level. Just over half of practitioners stated that they were not sure how good public relations education was, and one fourth of practitioners stated that public relations majors would not likely succeed in public relations. However, 70% of practitioners with experience supervising or working with college public relations interns gave them good marks, and only 11% graded them negatively. Practitioners and CEOs did not differ in many areas; however, CEOs were a little more negative than were practitioners concerning public relations education. They also reported more regular contact with public relations students and graduates.

Public relations practitioners were asked to list the four most important subjects or curriculum areas among 21 suggested and to rate each of them on a 5-point scale. Writing skills were rated quite or very important by 98% of practitioners, internships and work experience by 89%, problem-solving skills by 87%, presentation/speaking skills by 87%, social trends/issue analysis by 83%, people management skills by 83%, media relations techniques by 78%, research skills by 74%, and psychology of persuasion/motivation by 70%.

DICKSON AND SELLMEYER'S
CURRICULAR STUDY (1992)

Dickson and Sellmeyer (1992a, 1992b) surveyed the heads of media programs at colleges and universities listed in the directory of the Association for Education in Journalism and Mass Communication to determine their attitudes toward journalism education. The researchers wanted to compare responses of media administrators to those of editors who participated in the study by the American Society of Newspaper Editors in late 1989 (ASNE, 1990). Dickson and Sellmeyer (1992a) expected that a gap would exist between editors and media administrators over the more-practical aspects of journalism education versus the broader, more-theoretical aspects of mass communication/media studies. Editors and administrators agreed on the following six items (of 21 proposed items) as priorities for journalism curriculum: (a) requiring a course in media economics, (b) requiring a course in media management, (c) tougher grading, (d) de-emphasizing research, (e) recruiting better students, and (f) requiring a course in marketing research. Editors and administrators also agreed on the top two issues for media education: the importance of media ethics and the importance of liberal arts. They had slightly less agreement on the importance of media law and the need for more resources. They also agreed that eliminating media sequences was not a priority.

Dickson and Sellmeyer (1992b) compared responses of administrators with a news–editorial specialization and administrators with some other media specialization. They found statistically significant differences in four areas. Non-news–editorial administrators were significantly more likely than administrators with a news–editorial background to state that research was a priority, that marketing research was a priority, that media should be seen as interrelated, and that advertising belongs in journalism schools. Dickson and Sellmeyer concluded that the largest gap between editors and media administrators appeared to concern what programs should comprise a journalism school. A small majority of editors rejected the concept of a broad-based media unit with public relations and advertising sequences. Both editors and administrators, however, rejected the notion of a holistic mass media program without media sequences.

BLANCHARD AND CHRIST'S
"NEW PROFESSIONALISM" (1993)

Blanchard and Christ (1993) presented their vision of media education in *Media Education and the Liberal Arts: A Blueprint for the New Professionalism*. They proposed the new professionalism as a means of preparing graduates for a profession and not just an occupation. They called for three major outcomes for the undergraduate curriculum, both for higher education in general and media education in particular: more program diversity; a commitment by the units to the institution's general education or core curriculum; and more "interesting, innovative, integrative ways of delivering media education" (p. xi). They stated:

> We argue throughout this book that these and other changes present both challenges and opportunities to communication and media educators. We believe that for the survival of the field, the revitalization of the liberal arts and the benefits of society, these challenges should be met with a restructuring of undergraduate curriculums in media education toward a New Professionalism that replaces the uniformity and expediency of the occupational ethos of today's media programs with the diversity of a liberal ethos more reflective of the university tradition and community values. (pp. 3–4)

Blanchard and Christ (1993) also called for communication and media educators, as well as educators in other professional programs, "to clearly establish in their campus curriculum discussions the culpability of the traditional disciplines in the overall excessive fragmentation and narrowness of undergraduate education in the United States." They charged that the fragmentation and narrowness is considerably more harmful to liberal education than specialties offered by professional programs (p. 8).

Blanchard and Christ (1993) stated that the new professionalism was an outgrowth of the Oregon Report and other calls for a generic (also called generalized, holistic, and integrated) approach to curriculum. They also drew from the ideas of James Carey and proposals for curriculum reform by Ernest Boyer and others not in media disciplines. The two authors envisioned a media curriculum consisting of a conceptual core, a conceptual enrichment component, and an experiential learning capstone that emphasizes familiarity and understanding, rather than practitioner proficiency, with media technology.

The "conceptual core," those courses required for all majors, would serve two purposes: to introduce students to "essential knowledge and literacy skills 'common to all forms of mass communication work, rather than on nuances of particular industries' " and to familiarize them with "connections among the subdisciplines in communication and media studies" (p. 47). The conceptual core could include both interpersonal and mass media content or media content alone. It would consist of: (1) an introduction to a "conceptual map" for the major and communication industry, (2) "technical literacy," and (3) information gathering and media writing and speaking capability (p. 47).

The "conceptual enrichment" component would link the major to "broader ethical, social, economic, and political contexts." It would include "the theoretical underpinnings of the emerging discipline, an overview and history of the United States' and other media systems, and structural relations with other social, especially political and economic, systems." It purpose would be to "expand on the distinction between vocationalism and the New Professionalism introduced in the core" (p. 49).

The "experiential learning" component would consist of " 'hands-on' instruction using new media and information technology." Such learning would be undertaken in the "media workshop," similar to the Oregon Report's "media laboratory," which was proposed to "provide for systematic investigation and experimentation with purposeful challenging of media content and forms." The media workshop, however, would focus on "on-campus apprenticeship experiences that consist largely of informal instruction by peers—on the student newspaper, radio station, television station" (p. 50). The laboratory would be under close faculty supervision along with student management selected by faculty based on previous performance in lower level workshops.

In defining a "liberally educated media professional," Blanchard and Christ (1993) suggested the following attributes: (a) "a self-directed cultural self-consciousness and a high degree of control over one's self," (b) "dedication to public service," and (c) "an ethical commitment" (p. 62). They argued that media education has been a one-way relationship providing entry level hires for the media industries. They differentiated educating media professionals from "occupational" programs, which "duplicate in the classroom the occupational culture of the newsroom and other media 'shops.' " Blanchard and Christ noted about such programs: "Graduates are being prepared to move into the communication industry as refined and standardized cogs, rather than professionals committed to disinterested public service" (p. 63). They concluded that "the discipline's dilemma cannot be resolved and reform cannot take place without an affirmative, purposeful shift from industrial and occupational and individualistic values to liberal university traditions and community priorities" (p. 64).

Blanchard and Christ (1993) stated that the educational experience they endorsed would be beneficial for the industry as well because graduates of professional rather than occupational programs "can help media companies eliminate their internal rigidities," and the authors called for curricular reform that provides for "the anticipation, identification, and monitoring" of employment trends caused by new technologies (p. 64). They found a unifying theme between the media industries and the communication disciplines and within the communication disciplines themselves: "to advance clear, accurate, responsible expression in the public service" (p. 75). They argued that to replace the occupational ethos with a "liberal ethos" at the root of the new professionalism would help to restore "the idea of the public and public life" to media education (p. 78).

TASK FORCE REPORT ON INTEGRATED COMMUNICATIONS (1993)

The Task Force on Integrated Communications was an ad hoc committee consisting of academics and professionals from the fields of advertising, public relations, promotion, direct response, and marketing. The group had a 2-year goal "to assess how rapid changes in the communications industry may impact on the preparation of advertising and public relations majors" (Duncan, Caywood, & Newsom, 1993, p. i). Its report, "Preparing Advertising and Public Relations Students for the Communications Industry in the 21st Century," recommended that ". . . advertising and public relations students must be offered a more conceptually unified and integrated program of communication study," a recommendation it saw as consistent philosophically with such documents as the Oregon Report and Blanchard and Christ's *Media Education and the Liberal Arts*.

The task force looked at the recent phenomenon variously called *integrated marketing communications* and *integrated communications*. It concluded that "traditional methods of teaching advertising and public relations need to be reconsidered and brought more in line with the changes in practice" (p. i). The study reported the results of research presented at the 1992 AEJMC Convention in Montreal by Doug Newsom and Bob Carrell in a paper titled "Tower of Babel: A Descriptive Report on Attitudes Toward the Idea of Increased Communication Programs." Newsom and Carrell surveyed 158 mass media units and found a majority of respondents had little or no knowledge of integrated marketing communications. A total of 34 schools reported they had combined their advertising and public relations sequences, but the authors determined that only 12 were actually integrated.

The report's authors noted studies showing that fewer than 20% of public relations majors and 25% of advertising majors found jobs in their respective fields. They also noted increased scholarly discussion on the topic of integration and listed a number of enrollment and administrative realities in higher education that favored integration. The report concluded that an integrated approach "offers faculty and administrators a logical use of limited resources by finding opportunities to merge and build on the strengths of public relations, advertising, sales promotion and marketing for those programs interested in moving in this direction" (Duncan, Caywood, & Newsom, 1993, p. 15).

The Integrated Communication Curriculum

The Task Force on Integrated Curriculum called for the following components in any integrated communication curriculum: (a) a strong emphasis on liberal arts (including an understanding of multicultural and international groups); (b) training in oral, written, and visual communication; (c) a solid understanding of business and complex organization objectives and practices; (d) an understanding of, and respect for, all of the major communication functions (advertising, direct response, event sponsorship, packaging, public relations, sales promotion, etc.); and (e) a mastery of basic research skills to give insight into problem-solving techniques and strategies (p. 17). The task force also suggested that communication professionals need the following skills: (a) gathering information from a number of sources, (b) translating information from and for many different groups, (c) analyzing research findings and how issues and trends may affect organizational relationships, (d) planning and developing strategies for implementation of those plans, (e) presenting information both visually and orally, (f) counseling others on the most appropriate communication methods and tools (Duncan, Caywood, & Newsom, 1993, p. 18).

The task force noted four stages in creation of an integrated curriculum: (a) awareness and trend education, (b) course merger and coordination, (c) new course development, and (d) new specializations and majors. The report offered two models for an integrated curriculum. The first curriculum model was designed around subject areas rather than specific courses. It would have three components: (a) *personal development* (writing for communications, problem solving, visual literacy, quantitative and qualitative research skills, and presentation skills); (b) *professional development* (audience insight, business understanding, strategy development, "media" understanding, law and ethics, people management, research methodology, issues and trend identification and analysis, targeting, and segmenting); and (3) *integration* (multidisciplinary basic training, measurement and evaluation, and communication mix management) (p. 20). The second model was course-specific. It consisted of an overview course plus modules in research and analysis, communication skills, and application. The specific courses would be: Survey of Integrated Communication, Stakeholder and Customer Behavior, Organizational Analysis, Persuasive Communication, Message Strategy and Design, Message Delivery and Evaluation, Campaigns, and Internship. The task force listed the barriers to implementation of an integrated communication curriculum as cultivation of expertise, philosophical differences, and accreditation.

APME'S AGENDA FOR JOURNALISM EDUCATION (1994)

Jerry Ceppos, the representative of the Associated Press Managing Editors (APME) to the Accrediting Council on Education in Journalism and Mass Communication, and Marcia Bullard, chair of the APME Journalism Education Committee, conducted a survey concerning journalism education among members of the APME in the summer of 1993. More than 75% of the APME members, a total of 310 editors, responded. The respondents were asked what skills would be needed by future journalists in addition to the fundamentals of journalism. The top five comprised the APME's Agenda for Journalism Education: thinking analytically, presenting information well, understanding numbers in the news, listening to readers, and writing concisely. After meeting with two groups of journalism educators in Atlanta in December 1993, Ceppos determined that "any lingering idea of a significant gulf between educators and journalists is inaccurate—which may be as important as the survey results themselves" (Ceppos, 1994, p. 4).

In a parallel survey (Bullard & McLeary, 1994), editors were asked to have their most recent college graduate hired as a reporter or copy editor fill out a similar survey. Responses were received from 216 young journalists, 85% of whom had graduated since 1991. The top five skills as listed by the new hires were the same five selected by the editors, but in a different order: presenting information well, thinking analytically, writing concisely, understanding numbers in the news, and listening to readers. Recent graduates also were asked the topics that journalism schools should emphasize more. They ranked the topics as follows:

1. reporting on governmental affairs;
2. interviewing skills;
3. practical experience;
4. story research and investigative reporting techniques and copy editing, layout and design; and
5. the Freedom of Information Act.

Graduates also were asked in what ways they were least prepared. Their responses were ranked as follows:

1. reporting on governmental affairs;
2. dealing with tragedies;
3. deadline pressure;
4. in-depth research, database research; and
5. copy editing, layout, desktop publishing.

The graduates listed the areas in which they were best prepared as follows (some items made both the "best" and "worst" lists): feature stories, general assignment reporting, spot news, writing on deadline, interviewing, and researching in-depth articles. Most graduates listed an internship as a valuable experience, and a number mentioned the importance of reading newspapers daily. Eleven percent of the new hires gave their journalism school an A, 45% gave it a B, and 30% gave it a C.

AEJMC/ASJMC JOINT TASK FORCE
ON PROFESSIONAL ALLIANCES (1994)

The joint task force surveyed media educators and members of the Newspaper Association of America and made recommendations on increasing professional–academic cooperation. Task Force Chair Charles Self noted that previous studies had found a lack of cooperation and even hostility between educators and media professionals. The task force study of educators, however, found close cooperation on a number of areas, several indirectly related to curriculum. Self (1994) noted surprise at finding that 99% of the schools reported that media professionals speak to classes, that 99% of units provided academic credit for student field experiences such as internships, that 98% encouraged undergraduates to seek field experiences, that 93% reported faculty attended media conferences, and that 89% stated that media professionals serve the unit as adjunct or part-time faculty. In addition, 61% of the media units reported that faculty had worked in the media in the previous 3 years. On the other hand, only 51% of the units reported that they had an advisory board that included media professionals.

Self (1994) noted about the close ties found despite only moderate use of media advisory boards: "Still, what emerges is hardly a picture of disengagement between faculty and professionals. Instead, intense interaction between these academic programs and their professional constituencies is reported" (p. 35). He concluded that the emphasis on internships, job placement, and faculty presentations at media conferences "shows a bias toward reaping the fruits of the educational process . . . rather than supporting the process by which knowledge is produced in both the student and the faculty member" (p. 37).

The Task Force made five major findings from the survey of educators: (a) A great deal of alliance and cooperative activity was already underway among media units; (b) Larger and more diverse programs reported more alliance activity than smaller, more narrowly focused programs; (c) Most alliances appeared to have been pieced together by specific schools with specific media organizations rather than through nationally organized programs of alliance activity; (d) Distribution of alliance activities among schools appeared to be uneven and to vary widely in quality and reach; (e) Many alliances appeared to be driven by a narrow view of self-interest; and (f) Educators and professionals misunderstand the level of involvement of each group in cooperative activity and the motives of each in such activity. Also, educators and professionals disagreed over the most important goals for cooperation, but in surprising ways: Whereas both groups supported student field experiences, educators ranked alliances that provide money and equipment of high importance, and professionals ranked cooperation in curriculum and on-campus training high. Both ranked cooperation in research as of low importance.

AEJMC VISION 2000 TASK FORCE (1994)

The AEJMC Vision 2000 Task Force, established in 1992, was given two missions: to study the identity and structure of Association for Education in Journalism and Mass Communication and to study the viability of journalism and mass communication units within universities. It produced a report on each topic. The Working Group on the Identity and Structure of the AEJMC produced Vision 2000 Task Force Report No. 1 (AEJMC, 1994a). It did not specifically address the organization's role in curriculum matters and, thus, did not clarify the AEJMC's role in promoting education in journalism and mass communication. The Working Group on the Viability of Journalism and Mass Communication Units Within Universities produced Vision 2000 Task Force Report No. 2 (AEJMC, 1994b). It included the reports of six committees.

One of the committees of the Working Group on Viability, the Committee on JMC Curricula, concluded that " 'mass communication' has become a thing of the past; increasingly what we have is a communication system that serves the information needs of individuals and small groups." The committee also concluded that "journalism education has become more general in its content and more central to the educational life of the university," and it proposed that a "mass communications in society" course become part of the core curriculum (AEJMC, 1994b, p. 28). Like the Oregon Report and later reports, the Committee on Curriculum noted that the "notion of 'sequencing'—preparing students for specific jobs in journalism—appears to be increasingly unsound" and that students should "concentrate on core subjects that prepare them generally for journalistic practice in a wide variety of careers." It proposed media core offerings in history, law and ethics, current practice, communication theory, and the social role of communication. It noted that such courses "should enable students to use the media more productively and to participate in the vast communication system that is contemporary journalism" (p. 28).

The Committee on JMC Curriculum also proposed media "skills minors" in such areas as visual communication, computer graphics, data bases, media criticism, persuasive communication and similar areas that would be expected to evolve as the media change. In addition, the committee noted that the "need for accreditation changes as participatory journalism becomes more and more the rule." It suggested that if "communities are themselves responsible for the journalism that they get, then presumably, they can police the system themselves, correcting abuses or learning to tolerate them" (p. 28). Concerning the role of media programs in the university's general education offerings, the report of the Working Group on Viability noted:

> The goal of journalism and mass communication programs is to provide students "and" the larger society with a deeper understanding of mass communication processes and to improve the practices and performance of mass media professionals.
>
> Their goal is to produce socially responsible, informed, skilled citizens who understand how various media technologies and communication processes emerge within particular social, economic, and political contexts, and thereby affect both individual identity and societal processes on a global level. (AEJMC, 1994b, p. 6)

The working group report noted two major changes in the media that have "far-reaching implications for the academy." The first was that journalism in the United States has become much more participatory, the report noted: "Increasingly journalism involves an entire community reporting on itself, in cooperation with professionals. Since professionals have new roles, they need to develop new skills." The skills noted were critical judgment, analytic abilities, and a "highly sophisticated understanding of long-range system planning, as well as an understanding of design, display, and visual meaning" (p. 7). The second change was that because "the whole community participates in journalism, our educational offerings ought to be for the whole university" (p. 7). The working group concluded: "Instead of being on the edge of the university looking in, we should be at or near the center, inviting everyone to participate in our 'core' offerings, which themselves must be broad, inclusive, critical, and interdisciplinary" (p. 7).

Possibly the most controversial of the working group's recommendations concerned the relationship of media education and the media industries. It concluded that attempts for a partnership between both media industries and universities have met with frustration for two major reasons:

> First, both media institutions and industries and universities have criticized journalism educators on the basis of misinformed, or at least now obsolete understandings of the goals and missions of journalism programs. . . .
>
> Ironically, both parties assumed that journalism education and liberal education were inherently at odds. Second, attempts to shore up the relationship with one of the parties has generally [met] with suspicion from the other. Ignoring considerable evidence to the contrary, both press representatives and university leaders have criticized changes in journalism education as representing moves to cater to the interests of the other. (pp. 8–9)

The report noted that media education has seen greater enrollments but less viability within the university. It concluded that "the requirement to provide the professional skills courses in the highly technical manner to which they have been accustomed makes providing service courses to other majors within the university much more difficult . . ." (p. 9).

Based on a case study analysis of 16 programs, the working group also noted that the "partial skills-oriented approach to undergraduate education which many units reported gives these units a trade school reputation" (p. 11). Based upon its case study analysis the working group concluded that self-standing schools of journalism or mass communication or colleges of communication may compete better for university resources than units that are a part of a particular college. It noted that media units were seeking change through hiring faculty "with skills and research interests in desirable areas including visual thinking, international communication and incorporation of new communication technology." It also noted that other "change had been inspired by shifts in the student body to include more female and minority students" (p.11).

The group's case study analysis determined that a number of the units had recently undergone change in their undergraduate curriculum or were soon to undergo such change. Most of the units taught a combination of skills, theory, and application and, to a smaller degree, research methods. Many units required an overview of the mass media but other program requirements vary considerably. It noted that some units were revising their curriculum by offering courses in such things as visual thinking, technology-assisted communication, and courses that are not media-specific. At the graduate level, it found that most units stressed theory and research over skills (p. 11).

It noted that selection of media courses by nonmajors allowed for more varied opinions and perspectives and that service courses for nonmajors should be part of the institution's general education requirements. Like the Oregon Report, it suggested that media units provide midcareer educational and career-development opportunities. It called for instruction taught by media professionals to provide students an understanding of the communications industries, and it proposed that media units include courses for part-time students, members of the community, and nonmajors. It suggested short courses, seminars and workshops for teachers of media courses at feeder institutions, and proposed that media units increase diversity based on race, culture, religion, ethnicity, and lifestyle. It also proposed that media units emphasize "values, skills, attitudes and frameworks essential to mass communication performance and citizenship" (p 16).

The task force concluded that traditions of the craft and skills should be taught at the secondary level and that higher levels of the craft as well as societal aspects of the profession (such as social and cultural perspectives, law, ethics, history, and media effects) should be taught at the bachelor's level. The master's level should lead to greater levels of performance and more understanding of the cultural and social aspects of the media-related field as well as research methods and theoretical foundations. The working group stated that "viability in the twentieth century may be more importantly connected, as a practical matter and based on principle, to the standing of journalism and mass communication departments in their respective universities than their industrial standing." Therefore, it concluded that "the separation of journalism and mass communication units from their industrial moorings becomes increasingly defensible . . ." (p. 21).

The working group also concluded that "die-hard working professionals in mass media may likely never be convinced of the value of a university/journalism education," but in graduating students schooled in the liberal arts and the *New Professionalism*, ". . . eventually the mass media professions themselves will be comprised of people with a somewhat clearer and more 'modern' understanding of the role and function of journalism education" (p. 22). As the group saw the emerging media education, it concluded that "in some sense that more modern understanding looks more like the 'original' definition of journalism education: to provide an ethical foundation for work, to provide the historical and theoretical bases for launching reasonable, useful, intelligent critiques of social and economic institutions" (p. 22).

Despite having found that self-standing media units do best at competing for funding from the institution, the Vision 2000 Task Force working group called into question the viability of the Oregon Report's recommendation that media units be placed in a "free-standing professional school" because such a location might lead to isolation. It also urged media faculty and administrators to demonstrate that their units are essential to the institution's role of providing a liberal education (p. 23). The task force urged units to "distinguish clearly the undergraduate and graduate programs." It called for journalism graduate programs at the master's degree level to use the model of medicine, business, engineering, and architecture (p. 23). It also called for "a national program undertaken at the local level to demonstrate, regardless of how programs are structured or located, how journalism and mass communication fit into the scholarly and educational missions of universities" (p. 24).

DICKSON'S REPORTS ON MULTICULTURAL ISSUES (1993–1995)

Dickson (1993a, 1993b, 1994a, 1995a) investigated media education's response to multicultural issues, including promoting sensitivity and avoiding stereotypes based upon race, ethnicity, gender, disabilities, and sexual orientation. Dickson (1995a) looked specifically at the impact of accreditation on a media unit's curriculum, particularly the importance of Standard 12, which requires that accredited programs should sensitize students not only to "a multi-cultural, multi-ethnic, multi-racial" society but also to an "otherwise diverse society." He found that nearly 90% of media administrators stated that their journalism curriculum increased students' sensitivity to stereotypes and the potential for bias. He concluded that most media units accredited by the ACEJMC have done more than unaccredited units to sensitize students to a multicultural society and to hire minority faculty and recruit minority students.

Administrators at accredited media units were more likely than those at unaccredited programs to state that the unit gave quite a bit of emphasis in its courses to various stereotypes. Accredited programs also were more likely to have more black students and more minority faculty members. He also found, however, that factors other than accreditation—the institution's enrollment, the number of media majors, the proportion of minority faculty, and proportion of black students in the media unit—were more likely to indicate the extent to which the unit emphasized multicultural elements specifically mentioned by Standard 12. Dickson concluded that media units were making progress in improving their curriculum in regard to multiculturalism. He also concluded that lack of success in recruiting minorities was not deterring media units' progress toward a multicultural curriculum and that media units were making curriculum changes to promote diversity no matter what their size and success in recruiting minorities. He also noted that much work lay ahead at many institutions in meeting the goals of Standard 12.

JANE PAULEY TASK FORCE ON
MASS COMMUNICATION EDUCATION (1996)

Jane Pauley provided seed money for a study of broadcast journalism education because of her concern that journalism schools were "investing in degrees that don't have a lot of currency in the newsroom" (SPJ, 1996, p. 4). The task force undertook two surveys, one of television news directors and one of heads of broadcast journalism programs. Research was carried out by Lee B. Becker and Gerald M. Kosicki of Ohio State University. The task force surveyed 1,131 commercial TV stations and received 308 completed surveys and surveys from 86 stations with no news operation, a return rate of 35%. It also surveyed 195 colleges and universities with a broadcast journalism program. It received 108 completed surveys for a response rate of about 56%.

The characteristics news directors stated were most important for their ideal applicant were writing ability (listed by 42%), good attitude and personality (31%), general knowledge (22%), enthusiasm and eagerness (18%), and good work habits and willingness and ability to learn (each 15%). The task force condensed them into four main concerns: writing ability, a good attitude, knowledge, and good work habits. Their main criticism of applicants was writing ability, listed by 44% of news directors. No other area was listed by more than 16% of the respondents. They listed applicants' greatest strengths as enthusiasm and eagerness for work (37%), willingness and ability to learn (20%), good attitude and personality (17%), and their willingness to work hard and for long hours (15%).

When asked for the ideal major for applicants, nearly half of the news directors mentioned a media-related field: 22% mentioned journalism, 20% broadcast journalism, and 4% communication. About 21% mentioned "other," and 33% of news directors stated it didn't matter. Educators listed writing abilities in general as what news directors see as most important (64%), followed by general technical skills (29%), ability to communicate and tell a story (23%), general knowledge (21%), good work habits and audio–visual editing skills (each 19%), and good attitudes and personality (17%). The broadcast educators listed writing ability as the characteristic they thought was most important (listed by 66% of educators), followed by broad general knowledge (37%), general technical skills (29%), ability to communicate (28%), enthusiasm and eagerness (21%), ethics (17%), and good attitude and personality (16%).

Whereas 25% of educators listed writing ability generally as the area of greatest weakness, 29% listed it as the area of graduates' greatest strength. Also, 13% listed general knowledge as the area of greatest weakness, but 19% listed it as the area of greatest strength. In addition, 10% listed general technical skills as students' greatest weakness, and 23% listed it as their greatest strength. Educators were more likely than news directors to state that communication students were better prepared (92% vs. 68%). The task force concluded that "core journalism values" would remain the same in the future but grow in importance despite technological change. That would mean an increased emphasis on good writing as well as "a demand for accuracy, fairness, objectivity, balance, 'gutsy' news judgment and a clear sense of ethics." It added:

> Education and the communications industry are in a period of significant transition and blending. The evolution of technologies with new partnerships of media giants, such as the ventures between major computer and broadcast companies, indicate the need for cross-training to accommodate new applications to package news and information. (SPJ, 1996, p. 21)

VIRGINIA COMMONWEALTH UNIVERSITY/ ASSOCIATED PRESS MANAGING EDITORS STUDY (1997)

Ketchum Public Relations undertook a study for Virginia Commonwealth University and the Associated Press Managing Editors to determine attitudes of print and broadcast media executives toward journalism education (Ketchum, 1997). Questionnaires were mailed to 2,335 news managers, publishers, editors and producers at newspapers, magazines, and radio and TV stations. A total of 554 surveys were returned for a response rate of 24%. Between 92% and 98% of the print and broadcast executives listed writing, reporting, ethics, and interviewing skills as very important aspects of journalism school training. Also, between 86% and 91% of both print and broadcast executives listed government affairs, current events, and communications law as being very important journalism school courses.

References

AASDJ committee recommends accrediting procedure revisions. (1973). *Journalism Educator, 28*(1), 9–12.

Accreditation issues debated at 1983 AEJMC convention. (1984). *Journalism Educator, 38*(4), 5-12.

Accrediting Council on Education in Journalism and Mass Communications. (1997). *Journalism and mass communications accreditation, 1997-98.* Lawrence, KN: Author.

AEJMC plays key role in national commission. (1998, September). *AEJMC News, 37*, p. 21.

Allen, C. L. (1960). *Survey of advertising courses and census of advertising teachers.* Unpublished research study for the American Academy of Advertising.

Allen, C. L. (1962). *Advertising majors in American colleges and universities.* Report prepared for the American Academy of Advertising. Stillwater, OK: American Academy of Advertising.

Allen, E. W. (1924). The journalistic type of mind. *Journalism Bulletin, 1*, 39.

Allen, E. W. (1927). Journalism as applied social science. *Journalism Bulletin, 4*(1), 1–7.

Alridge, R. (1992, October 5). J-schools could put themselves out of business. *Electronic Media*, 30.

Altschull, J. H. (1990). *From Milton to McLuhan: The ideas behind American journalism.* New York: Longman.

American Society of Newspaper Editors Committee on Education for Journalism. (1990). *Journalism education: Facing up to the challenge of change.* Washington, DC: Author.

Anderson, D. A. (1997). *The leaders: Guiding journalism education into the 21st century.* San Francisco, CA: The Freedom Forum Pacific Coast Center.

Anderson, R., Dardenne, R., & Killenberg, G. M. (1996). *The conversation of journalism: Communication, community, and news.* Westport, CT: Praeger.

An Editor (Anonymous). (1872). *Hints to young editors.* New Haven, Charles C. Chatfield & Co.

Armstead, G. B. (1930). The report of the committee on Schools of Journalism to the A.S.N.E. *Journalism Quarterly, 7*, 142–153.

Arnold, E. C., & Kreigbaum, H. (1976) *Handbook of student journalism.* New York: New York University Press.

Associated Press Managing Editors Association. (1982). *1990—Journalism education in the next decade: 19 big questions and a host of answers.* A report of the APME Journalism Education Committee. San Diego, CA: Author.

Association for Education in Journalism and Mass Communication/Association of Schools of Journalism and Mass Communication Task Force on Missions and Purposes of Journalism and Mass Communication Education. (1996, August).

Report from the AEJMC/ASJMC task force on mission and purpose. Report presented at the annual convention of the AEJMC, Anaheim, CA.

Association for Education in Journalism and Mass Communication Curriculum Task Force. (1996). Responding to the challenge of change. *Journalism and Mass Communicator Educator, 50*(4), 101–119.

Association for Education in Journalism and Mass Communication Vision 2000 Task Force. (1994a, August). *Report No. 1: The identity and structure of the AEJMC.* Report presented at the annual convention of the AEJMC, Atlanta, GA.

Association for Education in Journalism and Mass Communication Vision 2000 Task Force. (1994b, August). *Report No. 2: The viability of JMC units within universities.* Report presented at the annual convention of the AEJMC, Atlanta, GA.

Astin, A. (1995, October). Providing students with a solid understanding of democracy. *The Chronicle of Higher Education,* p. B2.

Bagdikian, B. H. (1987). Let's get rid of bad journalism and bad teaching. In Project on the Future of Journalism Education. *Planning for curriculum change in journalism education* (Rev. ed., pp. 82–83). Eugene, OR: University of Oregon School of Journalism.

Bagdikian, B. H. (1990, September). Three problems with j-schools. *Presstime,* 32.

Bales, F. (1992). Newspaper editors' evaluations of professional programs. *Journalism Educator, 47*(3), 37–42.

Bateman, C., & Cutlip, S. (1975). *A design for public relations education.* Report of the Commission on Public Relations Education. New York: Foundation for Public Relations Research and Education.

Beasley, M. (1994, June). Presidential remarks. *AEJMC News, 27,* p. 2.

Becker, L. B., & Kosicki, G. M. (1997). Annual survey of enrollment and degrees awarded. *Journalism and Mass Communication Educator, 52*(3), 63–74.

Berko, R. (1995, October). ACA conference defines the field. *Spectra,* p. 12.

Bernays, E. L. (1978). Education for PR: A call to action. *Public Relations Quarterly, 23*(3), 18.

Bernays, E. L. (1980). Do our educational facilities meet our needs? *Public Relations Quarterly, 25*(4), 18.

Birkhead, D. (1985). Changing the relationship between journalism and time. *Journalism Educator, 40*(3), 34–36.

Bitter, J. (1987). Which came first—journalism or public relations? *Public Relations Quarterly, 32*(3), 21–22.

Blanchard, R. O. (1988, April). Academic values are losing out to the narrow values of industry representatives in the accreditation process. *ACA Bulletin,* 50–53.

Blanchard, R. O. (1991, Summer). Opportunities offered by the triple revolution. *ASJMC Insights,* 12–15.

Blanchard, R. O., & Christ, W. G. (1985). In search of the unit core: Commonalities in curricula. *Journalism Educator, 40*(3), 28–33.

Blanchard, R. O., & Christ, W. G. (1988, July). *Beyond the generic curriculum: The enriched major for journalism and mass communication.* Paper presented at the annual convention of the Association for Education in Journalism and Mass Communication, Portland, OR.

Blanchard, R. O., & Christ, W. G. (1990). Essential outcomes. *Feedback, 31*(3), 8–9.

Blanchard, R. O., & Christ, W. G. (1993*). Media education and the liberal arts: A blueprint for the new professionalism.* Hillsdale, NJ: Lawrence Erlbaum Associates.

Bleyer, W. G., (1919, October). Journalistic writing in high school. *The English Journal, 8,* 193.

Bleyer, W. G. (1931a, February). In behalf of journalism schools. *The Quill, 19,* 17.

Bleyer, W. G. (1931b). What schools of journalism are trying to do. *Journalism Quarterly, 8,* 35–44

Bloom, A. (1987). *The closing of the American mind: How higher education has failed democracy and impoverished the souls of today's students.* New York: Simon & Schuster.

Botan, C. (1998, July). *Perceptions of public relations education: Executive summary of findings.* Report presented at the National Communication Association Public Relations Summer Conference, Washington, DC.

Bovet, S. L. (1992, September). Educators need to communicate better on and off campus. *Public Relations Journal, 48,* 14–17.

Boyer, E. L. (1987). *College: The undergraduate experience in America.* The Carnegie Foundation for the Advancement of Teaching. New York: Harper & Row Publishers.

Boyer, E. L. (1990). *Scholarship reconsidered.* San Francisco: Jossey-Bass.

Brock, S. S. (1993, May). Can professionals be professors? *Presstime,* 51.

Bronstein, C., & Vaughn, S. (1998, June). Willard C. Bleyer and the relevance of journalism education. *Journalism and Mass Communication Monographs* (No. 166).

Budd, R. W. (1985). It's time to set new directions in communication education. *Journalism Educator, 40*(3), 24–27, 44.

Bullard, M., & McLeary, K. (1994, January–February) Young reporters assess skills they gained in j school and the help they need now. *APME News,* 5–6.

Bybee, C. (1999). Can democracy survive in the post-factual age?: A return to the Lippmann-Dewey debate about the politics of news. *Journalism & Communication Monographs, 1*(1). 27-66.

Calkins, E. E. (1905, March). Advertising as it's taught, Part I. *Profitable Advertising, 14,* 1101.

Camp, E. M. (1888). *Journalists: Born or Made?* Philadelphia: Philadelphia Social Science Association.

Carey, J. W. (1978). A plea for the university tradition. *Journalism Quarterly, 55*(4), 846–855.

Carey, J. W. (1989). *Communication as Culture: Essays on media and society.* Boston: Unwin Hyman.

Carter, R. F. (1995). Of the essential contributions of mass communication programs. *Journalism Educator, 49*(4), 4–10.

Casey, R. D. (1932). Journalism, technical training and the social sciences. *Journalism Quarterly, 9*(1), 31–45.

Casiday, H. L. (1935). Journalism in the high schools of California. *California Journal of Secondary Education, 10*, 525.

Ceppos, J. (1990). Media professionals as teachers: Important to editors, but on campus the push is toward Ph.D.'s. In American Society of Newspaper Editors Committee on Education for Journalism. *Journalism education: Facing up to the challenge of change* (pp. 17–22). Washington, DC: Author.

Ceppos, J. (1992, February–March). The industry's role in judging j-schools. *APME News*, 3–4.

Ceppos, J. (1994, January–February). Teach student to think analytically, APME members tell journalism educators. *APME News,* 3–4.

Christ, W. G. (1993, August 12). Speech for plenary session of the annual convention of the Association for Education in Journalism and Mass Communication, Kansas City, MO.

Christ, W. G. (Ed.). (1994). *Assessing communication education.* Hillsdale, NJ: Lawrence Erlbaum Associates.

Christ, W. G. (1995, Winter). J/MC agenda for the 90's . . . the role of journalism and mass communication in the university of the future. *ASJMC Insights,* 1–5.

Christ, W. G. (Ed.). (1997). *Media education assessment handbook.* Mahwah, NJ: Lawrence Erlbaum Associates.

Christ, W. G. (1998). Multimedia: Replacing the broadcast curriculum. *Feedback, 39*(l), 1–6.

Christ, W. G. (1999). Introduction: Administration and Accountability. In W. G. Christ (Ed.), *Leadership in times of change: A handbook for communication and media educators* (pp. 3–21). Mahwah, NJ: Lawrence Erlbaum Associates.

Christ, W. G., & Blanchard, R. 0. (1994). Mission statements, outcomes and the new liberal arts. In W. G. Christ (Ed.), *Assessing communication education* (pp. 31–55). Hillsdale, NJ: Lawrence Erlbaum Associates.

Cohen, H. (1994). *The history of speech communication: The emergency of a discipline, 1914–1945.* Avondale, VA: Speech Communication Association.

Cole, R. R. (1985). Much better than yesterday and still brighter tomorrow. *Journalism Educator, 40*(3), 4–8.

Cole, R. R., & Bowers, T. A. (1975). An exploration of factors related to journalism faculty productivity. *Journalism Quarterly, 52*, 638–644.

College journalism. (1888, March 20). *The Journalist*, p. 8.

Commission on Freedom of the Press. (1947). *A free and responsible press.* Chicago: University of Chicago Press.

Commission on Undergraduate Public Relations Education. (Commission). (1987). *Design for undergraduate public relations education.* Chicago, IL: Author.

Commission on Undergraduate Public Relations Education. (Commission). (1993). *Design for undergraduate public relations education* (Rev. ed.). Chicago, IL: Author.

Cooper, T. (1993). Communication as corpus callosum: A reorganization of knowledge. *Journalism Educator, 48*(1), 84–87.

Copple, N. (1985). Journalism education is in an enviable catbird seat. *Journalism Educator, 40*(3), 16–22, 36.

Corrigan, D. (1993, October 2). Journalism academia out of touch. *Editor & Publisher*, 34–35.

Corrigan, D. (1995, July/August). Does "public journalism" serve the public or the publishers? *St. Louis Journalism Review*, 9.

Council for Aid to Education. (1997). *Breaking the social contract. The fiscal crisis in higher education.* Available: http://www.rand.org/publications/CAE/CAE100/

Council on Education for Journalism (1925). Principles and standards of education for journalism. *Journalism Bulletin, 1*, 30–31.

Council on Radio Journalism. (1948). Radio journalism courses: Their content and titles. *Journalism Quarterly*, 25(4), 398–399.

Council on Radio and Television Journalism (1961). Standards for broadcast journalism education. *Journal of Broadcasting, 5*(2), 161–164.

Council on radio journalism planned. (1944). *Journalism Quarterly, 21*(4), 324–327.

Cowdin, H. P. (1985, July/August). The liberal art of journalism. *The Quill*, 16–19, 23.

Cowles, G. (1928). What one managing editor thinks. *Journalism Quarterly, 4*, 1.

Crawford, J. W., & Sabine, G. A. (1958, November 13). Educators discuss need for better instruction, more broad-gauge instruction. *Advertising Age*, 95–96.

Cunliffe, J. W. (1926). The relation between cultural and technical courses in journalism. *Journalism Bulletin, 3*, 15–20.

Curtis D. MacDougall receives 1983 ASJSA citation of merit. (1983). *Journalism Educator, 38*(3), 24–27, 45.

Cutlip, S. M. (1957). The university's role in public relations education. *Journalism Quarterly, 34*(1), 60–70.

Cutlip, S. M. (1961). History of public relations education in the United States. *Journalism Quarterly, 38*, 363–370.

Dates, J. L. (1990). The study of theory should guide the curriculum. *Feedback, 31*(3), 10–11.

Davis, R. E. (1991, January). Accreditation in mass communication: A negative view. *ACA Bulletin*, 36–43.

De Mott, J. (1982). J-school of 2001: How will it look? What will it do? *Journalism Educator, 37*(1), 20, 54.

De Mott, J. (1984). Journalism courses are essential part of liberal education. *Journalism Educator, 39*(3), 31–33.

Dennis, E. E. (1987a). Journalism education: Failing grades from a dean. In Project on the Future of Journalism Education. *Planning for curriculum change in journalism education* (Rev. ed., pp. 80–81). Eugene, OR: University of Oregon School of Journalism.

Dennis, E. E. (1987b). Journalism education: Storm swirls on campus; changes coming. In Project on the Future of Journalism Education. *Planning for curriculum change in journalism education* (Rev. ed., pp. 84–89). Eugene, OR: University of Oregon School of Journalism..

Dennis, E. E. (1988). Whatever happened to Marse Robert's dream? *Gannett Center Journal, 2*, 1–22.

Dennis, E. E. (1990). Communication education and its critics. *Syracuse Scholar, 10*(1), 7–13.

Dennis, E. E. (1994, June 16). *Troubling trends or anomalous problems? Reflections on the state of the field of communications.* Speech given at the "State of the Field of Communications" conference, University of Texas at Austin, Austin, TX.

Dennis, E. E. (1995, July 29). Raising questions about civic or public journalism. *Editor & Publisher*, 48, 36.

Dennis, E. E., & DeFleur, M. L. (1991). A linchpin concept: Media studies and the rest of the curriculum. *Journalism Educator, 46*(2), 78–81.

Dennis, E. E., Romm, A. N., & Ottaway, J. Jr. (1990). The case for constructive criticism of the press. *Newspaper Research Journal, 11*(2), 2–10.

Dewey, J. (1927). *The public and its problems.* Denver: Alan Swallow.

Dewey, J. (1966). *Democracy and education: An introduction to the philosophy of education* (Rev. ed.). New York: The Free Press.

Dickson, T. (1992, Summer). The liberal arts and J/MC education. *ASJMC Insights*, 11–16.

Dickson, T. (1993a, Winter). Sensitizing journalism students to minority issues. *ASJMC Insights*, 1–5.

Dickson, T. (1993b). Sensitizing students to racism in the news. *Journalism Educator, 47*(4), 28–33.

Dickson, T. (1994a, August 11). *How JMC education rates in its efforts to sensitize students to ableism issues.* Paper presented at the annual convention of the Association for Education in Journalism and Mass Communication, Atlanta, GA.

Dickson, T. (1994b, August 11). *1993–94 report of the AEJMC Curriculum Task Force*. Report presented at the annual convention of the Association for Education in Journalism and Mass Communication, Atlanta, GA.

Dickson, T. (1995a). Assessing education's response to multicultural issues. *Journalism & Mass Communication Educator, 50*(3), 41–51.

Dickson, T. (1995b, August). *Meeting the challenges and opportunities facing media education: A report on the findings of the AEJMC Curriculum Task Force*. Report presented at the annual convention of the Association for Education in Journalism and Mass Communication, Washington, DC.

Dickson, T. (1996, August). *Is journalism education an oxymoron? What editors say about college preparation for journalists*. Paper presented at the annual convention of the Association for Education in Journalism and Mass Communication, Anaheim, CA.

Dickson, T. (1998). Journalism Education, the Media, and the Common Good: Finding the Nexus. *The SMSU Journal of Public Affairs, 2*, 102-116.

Dickson, T., & Brandon, W. (1998). *Differences in journalism educators' and practitioners' attitudes toward media education*. Unpublished raw data.

Dickson, T., & Brandon, W. (1999, April). *The dialogue of the deaf: Does a gap exist between broadcast educators and practitioners concerning what journalism education should be doing?* Paper presented at the annual convention of the Broadcast Education Association, Las Vegas, NV.

Dickson, T., & Sellmeyer, R. (1992a, August). *Green eyeshades vs. chi-squares revisited: Editors' and J/MC administrators' perceptions of major issues in journalism education*. Paper presented at the annual convention of the Association for Education in Journalism and Mass Communication, Montreal, Canada.

Dickson, T., & Sellmeyer, R. (1992b). Responses to proposals for curricular change. *Journalism Educator, 47*(3), 27–36.

Dillon, C. (1918). *Journalism for high schools*. New York: Noble & Co.

Doerner, R. C. (1984). Advertising program revised to prepare for needs of the 1990s. *Journalism Educator, 39*(1), 18–20.

Donnelly, W. J. (1992). Correlating top agency success with educational background. *Journalism Educator, 47*(1), 67–73.

Drechsel, R. E. (1993). Why Wisconsin opted out of the reaccreditation process. *Journalism and Mass Communication Educator, 47*(4), 67–69.

Dressel, P. L. (1960). *Liberal education and journalism*. New York: Columbia University Teachers College.

Duncan, T., Caywood, C., & Newsom, D. (1993, December). *Preparing advertising and public relations students for the communications industry in the 21st century*. A report of the Task Force on Integrated Curriculum.

Durham, F. (1992). Cultural history of a curriculum: The search for salience. *Journalism Educator, 46*(4), 14–21.

Eastman, S. T. (1986, April). *A model for telecommunications education*. Paper presented to the Central States Speech Association, Cincinnati, OH.

Editorial. (1927). *The Journalism Bulletin, 4*, 25.

Emery, E., & McKerns, J. P. (1987). AEJMC: 75 years in the making. *Journalism Monographs* (No. 104).

Falb, R. (1991). Proposal: Join PR and advertising education—away from journalism or business. *Public Relations Quarterly, 36*(4), 42–44.

Falb, R. (1992). The place of public relations education in higher education: Another opinion. *Public Relations Review, 18*(1), 97–101.

Farrar, R. T. (1993). The push for standards and recognition: A history of the American Association of the Schools and Departments of Journalism. In B. I. Ross (Ed.), *Seventy-five years of journalism and mass communication leadership: The history of the Association of Schools of Journalism and Mass Communication* (pp. 54–73). Columbia, SC: Association of Schools of Journalism and Mass Communication.

Fedler, F. (1993). *Growing body of evidence refutes some criticism of j-schools.* Paper presented at the convention of the Association for Education in Journalism and Mass Communication, Kansas City, MO.

Fedler, F., Carey, A., & Counts, T. (1997, August). *Journalism's status in academia: A candidate for elimination?* Paper presented at convention of the Association for Education in Journalism and Mass Communication, Chicago, IL.

Fedler, F., Carey, A., & Counts, T. (1998). Journalism's status in academia: A candidate for elimination? *Journalism and Mass Communication Educator, 53*(2), 31–39.

Fedler, F., & Counts, T. (1982, August). *Professors' satisfaction with jobs related to academic ranks.* Paper presented at the national convention of the Association for Education in Journalism and Mass Communication, Athens, OH.

Fedler, F., Counts, T., Carey, A., & Santana, M. C. (1997). *New study contradicts Medsger's Winds of Change.* Paper presented at the national convention of the Association for Education in Journalism and Mass Communication, Chicago, IL.

Fedler, F., Counts, T., Carey, A. & Santana, M. C. (1998). Faculty degrees, experience and research vary with specialty, *Journalism & Mass Communication Educator, 53*(1), 4–13.

Fedler, F., Santana, M. C., Counts, T., & Carey, A. (1997, August). *JMC faculty divided: Majority finds dozen uses for research.* Paper presented at the national convention of the Association for Education in Journalism and Mass Communication, Chicago, IL.

Fedler, F., & Smith, R. F. (1985). Administrators feel traditional research has highest value. *Journalism Educator, 40*(3), 51–52.

Fellows, H. E. (1957). The expanding sphere of journalism. *Journal of Broadcasting, 1*(3), 211–219.

Financial skills: Missing in action. (1988). *Public Relations Journal, 44*(12), 10–11.

Finney, R. G. (1990). Wanted: Reading and writing skills. *Feedback, 31*(3), 10.

Fitch-Hauser, M.; Barker, D. R.; & Barker, L. (1989, April). A survey of public relations education in the U.S. and Canada. *The ACA Bulletin*, 80–89.

Fitch-Hauser, M., & Neff, B. D. (1997, November). *Where public relations is taught: A 1997 update on a longitudinal study.* Paper presented at the annual meeting of the National Communication Association, Chicago, IL.

Flexner, A. (1930). *Universities: American, English, German.* New York: Oxford University Press.

Flint, L. N. (1924). Comparing notes on courses. *Journalism Bulletin, 1*, 54.

Frasca, R. (1995, August). *Benjamin Franklin's plan for moral reformation of a scurrilous press.* Paper presented at the convention of the Association for Education in Journalism and Mass Communication, Washington, DC.

Freeman, D. S. (1935). *R. E. Lee: A biography* (Vol. 4). New York: Scribner's.

Fryburger, V. (1959). *Better education for advertising.* Proceedings of the 1959 Regional Convention of the American Association of Advertising Agencies, Chicago, IL

Gaddis, W. (1981). Editors, educators agree on many key j-education issues. *Journalism Educator, 36*(2), 26.

Gallop, G. H. (1928). What shall we do about high school journalism? *Journalism Quarterly, 5*(2), 33–36.

Garrison, B. (1983, April). Learning from others: A journalism and mass communication perspective on curriculum accreditation. *ACA Bulletin, 32*–39.

Gibson, D. C. (1987). Public relations education in a time of change: Suggestions for academic relocation and renovation. *Public Relations Quarterly, 32*(3), 25–31.

Good, H. (1984, July/August). Where dinosaurs roam. *The Quill*, 27.

Gray, G. W. (1954). Some teachers and the transition to twentieth-century speech education. In K.R. Wallace (Ed.). *A history of speech education in America* (pp. 422–446). New York: Appleton-Century-Crofts.

Gray. G. W. (1989). The founding of the Speech Association of America. In W. Work & R. C. Jeffrey (Eds.), *The past as prologue: A 75th anniversary publication of the Speech Communication Association* (pp. 9–12). Annandale, VA: Speech Communication Association.

Griffin, W. G., & Pasadeos, Y. (1998). The impact of IMC on advertising and public relations education. *Journalism and Mass Communication Educator, 53*(2), 4–18.

Grunig, J E. (1989). Teaching public relations in the future. *Public Relations Review, 15*(1), 12–24.

Grunig, J. E. (1991). Public relations research: A legacy of Scott Cutlip. *Public Relations Review, 17*(4), 357–376.

Hachten, W. A. (1998). *The troubles of journalism.* Mahwah, NJ: Lawrence Erlbaum Associates.

Harcleroad, F. F. (1981). *Accreditation: History, process, and problems.* Washington, DC: American Association for Higher Education.

Harper, L. (1999, February 9). Can "public journalism" help newspapers win readers? *Wall Street Journal,* p. B4.

Harrington, H. F. (1919). Teaching journalism in a natural setting: An application of the project method. *Educational Administration and Supervision, 4,* 198–199.

Hartman, J. (1990, Fall). Future looks bad for j-school grads. *AEJMC Newspaper Division Leadtime,* p. 5.

Haskins, J. B. (1970). Information needs of publishers: Basis for newspaper research. *Journalism Quarterly, 47,* 31–40.

Haynes, J. (1981). Public relations in the academic institution. *Public Relations Quarterly, 26*(2), 21–24.

Heath, R. L. (1991). Public relations research and education: Agendas for the 1990s. *Public Relations Review, 17*(2), 185–194.

Heckhausen, H. (1972). Discipline and interdisciplinarity. In L. Apostel et al. (Eds.), *Interdisciplinarity* (pp. 83–86). Brussels: Organization for Economic Cooperation and Development.

Henningham, J. P. (1986). An Australian perspective on educators as researchers. *Journalism Educator, 41*(3), 8–12.

Herring study traces growth of journalism instruction. (1956). *Journalism Quarterly, 33,* 362–363.

Hiebert, R. E. (1971). *Trends in public relations education: 1964–1970.* New York: Foundation for Public Relations Research and Education.

Highton, J. (1967, February). Green eyeshades vs. chi-squares. *The Quill,* 10–13.

Hochberger, S. (1958). Fifty years of journalism education. *Journalism Educator, 13*(4), 2–5, 24.

Hochmuth, M., & Murphy, R. (1954). Rhetorical and elocutionary training in nineteenth-century colleges. In K. R. Wallace (Ed.), *A history of speech education in America* (pp. 153–177). New York: Appleton-Century-Crofts.

Hoyt, M. (1995, September/October). Are you now, or will you ever be, a civic journalist? *Columbia Journalism Review,* 27–33.

Hoskins, R. L. (1988, July). *A new accreditation problem: Defining the liberal arts and sciences.* Paper presented at the annual meeting of the Association for Education in Journalism and Mass Communication, Portland, OR.

Hudson, J. C. (1981). Radio-TV news staff employers prefer broadcasting degree, strong liberal arts foundation. *Journalism Educator, 36*(2), 27–28, 46.

Hunt, E. L. (1916). General specialists. *Quarterly Journal of Public Speaking, 2,* 253–263.

Hutchins, R. M. (1936). *The higher learning in America.* New Haven: Yale University Press.

Hutchins, R. M. (1938, March). Is there a legitimate place for journalism instruction? No! *The Quill*, 20.

Hyde, G. M. (1922). *A Course in Journalistic Writing*. New York: D. Appleton & Co.

Hyde, G. M. (1925). Journalism in high school. *Journalism Bulletin, 2*(1), 1–9.

Hyde, G. M. (1928, May). What the high school teacher of journalism can and should do. *The English Journal, 17*, 716.

Hyde, G. M. (1937). The next steps in schools of journalism. *Journalism Quarterly, 14*, 36.

Hynes, T. (1993, August). *Summary report: ACEJMC survey results*. Unpublished committee report.

Iorio, S. H., & Williamson, K. (1995). The role of liberal arts courses within communication curricula. *Journalism Educator, 59*(1), 16–25.

Jandoli, R. J. (1957). Journalism education and the social sciences. *Journalism Quarterly, 34*, 63–67.

Johenning, J. (1982). A national survey of professionals recommends courses for an advertising curriculum. Unpublished manuscript, New York Institute of Technology.

Johenning, J., & Mazey, J. (1984) Professionals rate "ideal" program for ad majors. *Journalism Educator, 39*(3), 38–40.

Johnson, E. M. (1930). What of the future of instruction in journalism? *Journalism Quarterly, 7*(1), 31–39.

Jones, D. M. (1970). Editors, educators are close on what makes a newsman. *Journalism Educator, 33*(2), 17–18.

Kalupa, F. B., & Allen, T. H. (1982). Future directions in public relations education. *Public Relations Review, 8*(2), 31.

Kellogg Commission on the Future of State and Land-Grant Universities. (1997). Returning to our roots: The student experience. Available: http://www.intervisage.com/kellogg/statements/contents.html

Kennedy, J. E. (1910). An institute for advertising research. *Advertising and Selling, 20*, 67–72.

Ketchum Public Relations Research and Measurement Department. (1997, October). *Views of print and broadcast media executives toward journalism education*. New York: Author.

Kittross, J. M. (1989). *Six decades of education for broadcasting . . . and counting*. Unpublished manuscript, Boston: Emerson College.

Kittross, J. M. (1990, May). Getting it right. *The Quill*, 36.

Knowles, J. H. (1974). *A study of courses in methods of teaching secondary school journalism with a proposed ideal methods course*. Unpublished doctoral dissertation, University of Kansas, Lawrence.

Kosicki, G. M., Becker, L. B., Watson, D., & Porter, L. (1998) *1997 annual survey of journalism and mass communication enrollments*. Athens, GA: Henry W. Grady College of Journalism and Mass Communication.

Lambeth, E. B., & Aucoin, J. (1993). Understanding communities: The journalist as leader. *Journalism Educator, 48*(1), 12–19.

Lancaster, K. M., Katz, H. E., & Cho, J. (1990). Advertising faculty describe theory v. practice debate. *Journalism Educator, 45*(1), 9–21.

Leatherman, C. (1991, December 18). Madison shuns journalism accrediting, stirring a curriculum debate. *The Chronicle of Higher Education*, p. A19.

Ledbetter, J. (1997, October 16). Bad news: The slow, sad sellout of journalism school. *Rolling Stone*, 73-81, 99-100.

Lee, A. M. (1947, Spring). Trends in public relations training. *Public Opinion Quarterly, 11*, 83–91.

Lee, M. L. (1918). *Instruction in journalism in institutions of higher education*. (U.S. Bulletin No. 21). Washington, DC: Department of Interior, Bureau of Education.

Lewis, M. (1993, April 19). J-school confidential. *The New Republic*, 20-27.

Lindley, W. (1988, July 30). Message to journalism faculty: Bridge the gap. *Editor & Publisher*, 18–19.

Link, G. Jr., & Dykes, J. E. (1959). Advertising courses offerings of accredited schools. *Journalism Quarterly, 36*(4), 64–65.

Lippmann, W. (1922). *Public Opinion*. New York: The Macmillan Company.

Lovell, R. (1987, October). Triumph of the chi-squares. It's a hollow victory. *The Quill*, 22–23.

Mabrey, D. (1988a, March). The changing curriculum: Integration or fragmentation? *ASJMC Insights*, 10–11.

Mabrey, D. (1988b, April). Journalism, liberal arts and editors. *ACA Bulletin*, 41–45.

MacDougall, C. D. (1947). What newspaper publishers should know about professors of journalism. *Journalism Quarterly, 24(1)*, 2.

MacDougall, C. D. (1973, August). *What journalism education should be all about*. Paper presented at the annual convention of the Association for Education in Journalism. Fort Collins, CO.

Mader, J. H. (1980, August). Should journalism schools teach public relations? *The Quill*, 17–18.

Marlier, J. H. (1980). What is speech communication, anyway? *Communication Education, 29*(4), 324–327.

Mazingo, S. (1991, April 27). In defense of j-schools. *Editor & Publisher*, 40.

McCall, J. M. (1987). Liberal arts focus provides training for media careers. *Journalism Educator, 42*(2), 17–21.

McCall, J. M. (1990). Beyond the Roper Report. *Feedback, 31*(3), 9–10.

McLeod, J., & Blumler, J. (1987). The micosocial level of communication science. In C. Berger & S. Chaffee (Eds.), *Handbook of Communication Science* (pp. 271-291). Newbury Park, CA: Sage.

McMasters, P. (1997). A first amendment perspective on public journalism. In J. Black (Ed.), *Mixed News: The public/civic/communitarian journalism debate* (pp. 188–195). Mahwah, NJ: Lawrence Erlbaum Associates.

Medsger, B. (1996). *Winds of change: Challenges confronting journalism education.* Arlington, VA: The Freedom Forum.

Mehra, A. (1984). Liberal arts help to develop critical judgment. *Journalism Educator, 39*(2), 33-38.

Mencher, M. (1990a). Confronting our critics and ourselves. *Journalism Educator, 44*(4), 64–67, 96.

Mencher, M. (1990b, March). It's time for trade-school partisans to fight back. *The Quill,* 5–6.

Mencher, M. (1994a, May-June). J school Rx: Screen, emphasize reporting. *APME News,* 18–19.

Mencher, M. (1994b). Reconstructing the curriculum for service to the nation. *Journalism Educator, 49*(2), 71–76

Merrill, J. C. (1980). Upside down. *Journalism Educator, 35*(2), 20–22.

Merritt, D. (1998). *Public journalism and public life: Why telling the news is not enough* (Rev. ed.). Mahwah, NJ: Lawrence Erlbaum Associates.

Mills, G., Harvey, K., & Warnick, L. B. (1980). Newspaper editors point to j-grad deficiencies. *Journalism Educator, 35*(2), 12–19.

Mirando, J. A. (1995, August). *The first college journalism students: Answering Robert E. Lee's offer of a higher education.* Paper presented at the convention of the Association for Education in Journalism and Mass Communication, Washington, DC.

Morrill, J. L. (1938). Is there a place for instruction in journalism? *Journalism Quarterly, 15*(1), 32.

Mullins, E. (1987a, October). Task force report on liberal arts and sciences in journalism/mass communication. *ASJMC Insights,* 3–10.

Mullins, E. (1987b, October). Second task forces report on liberal arts and sciences in journalism/mass communication: Feedback. *ASJMC Insights,* 11–13.

Mullins, E. (1991, January). In favor of accreditation. *ACA Bulletin,* 32–35.

Myers, J. S. (1926). The teacher of journalism. *Journalism Bulletin, 2*(4), 12

Nash, V. (1938). *Education for journalism.* New York: Bureau of Publications, Teachers College, Columbia University.

Neff, B.D. (1989, November). *The most desirable preparation for public relations professionals: Fit of existing and model curriculum with theoretical and philosophical developments.* Paper presented at the annual meeting of the Speech Communication Association, San Francisco, CA.

Nelson, H. L. (1967). Some thoughts for the future of AEJ. *Journalism Quarterly, 44,* 745–748.

Newsom, D. A. (1984). Realities, questions and challenges for public relations education. *Public Relations Quarterly, 40*(3), 15–16.

Newsom, D. A. (1985). Journalism/mass comm as an academic discipline. *Journalism Educator, 40*(3), 23, 44.

Niven, H. (1961). The development of broadcasting education in institutions of higher education. *Journal of Broadcasting, 5*(3), 241–250.

O'Dell, D. (1935). *The history of journalism education in the United States.* New York: Teachers College, Columbia University.

O'Neill, J. M. (1989). A message from James M. O'Neill, first president. In W. Work & R. C. Jeffrey (Eds.), *The past as prologue: A 75th anniversary publication of the Speech Communication Association* (pp. 3–4). Annandale, VA: Speech Communication Association.

Paisley, W. (1984). Communication in the communication sciences. In B. Dervin & M. J. Voight, (Eds.). *Progress in the communication sciences* (pp. 1–43). Norwood, NJ: Ablex.

Parisi, P. (1992). Critical studies, the liberal arts, and journalism education. *Journalism Educator, 46*(4), 4–13.

Paulson, S. F. (1980). Speech communication and the survival of academic disciplines. *Communication Education, 29*(4), 319–325.

Pease, E. C. (1992, Summer). Defining communication's role and identity in the 1990s: Promises and opportunities for journalism and communication studies. *ASJMC Insights,* 6–10.

Peterson, T. (1986). In P. F. Parsons (Ed.), Prominent educators assess journalism education's future. *Journalism Educator, 41*(2), 4–5.

Polson, I. I. (1924). *Progress in teaching of journalism in colleges and universities of the United States and an indication of the trends shown.* Unpublished master's thesis, Northwestern University, Evanston, IL.

Project on the Future of Journalism Education. (1984). *Planning for curriculum change in journalism education.* Eugene, OR: University of Oregon School of Journalism.

Project on the Future of Journalism Education. (1987). *Planning for curriculum change in journalism education* (Rev. ed.). Eugene, OR: University of Oregon School of Journalism.

Public Relations Society of America. (1956). *Public relations education in American colleges and universities.* New York: Author.

Public Relations Society of America. (1964). *Public Relations Education in American colleges and universities, 1964.* Mimeographed. New York: Author.

Public Relations Society of America Task Force. (1988). Public relations body of knowledge task force report. *Public Relations Review, 14*(1), 3–40.

Pulitzer, J. (1904). The college of journalism. *North American Review, 178*(50), 641–680.

Rakow, L. F. (1993). The curriculum is the future. *Journal of Communication, 43*(4), 154–162.

Rayfield, B. (1992, Winter). Letter to the editor. *Leadtime,* p. 5.

Reardon, K. K., & Rogers, E. M. (1988). Interpersonal versus mass communication: A false dichotomy? *Human Communication Research, 15*(2), 284–303.

Report sees antagonism growing between schools, newspaper. (1931, April 25). *Editor and Publisher, 63,* 72.

Research Committee of the National Association of Academic Teachers of Public Speaking. (1915). Research in public speaking. *Quarterly Journal of Public Speaking, 1,* 24–32.

Richard, W. C. (1979, January 1). Advertising education pays off in job—or does it? *Advertising Age,* 51.

Rivers, W. L., & Schramm, W. (1969). *Responsibility in mass communication* (Rev. ed.). New York: Harper & Row Publishers.

Robb, A. T. (1941). Education for journalism—one of its problems. *Journalism Quarterly, 18*(1), 33–39.

Roberts, C. L. (1988, October). ACEJMC accreditation. *ACA Bulletin,* 17–19.

Rogers, E. M. (1994). *A history of communication study: A biographical approach.* New York: The Free Press.

Rogers, E. M., & Chaffee, S. H. (1983). Communication as an academic discipline: A dialogue. *Journalism of Communication, 33*(3), 18–30.

Rogers, E. M., & Chaffee, S. H. (1993). The past and the future of communication study: Convergence or divergence? *Journal of Communication, 43*(4), 125–131.

Rogers, E. M., & Chaffee, S. H. (1994). Communication and journalism from "Daddy" Bleyer to Wilbur Schramm: A Palimpsest. *Journalism Monographs* (No. 148).

Romell, R. (1999, February 27). Thomson to train journalists in Oshkosh; center a bid to counter staff flight from papers. *The Milwaukee Journal Sentinel* [On-line]. Available: http://www.jsonline.com

Roosenraad, J., & Wares, D. (1983). Academics vs. experience. *Journalism Educator, 38*(2), 17–18, 30.

Roper Organization. (1987, December). *Electronic media career preparation study.* New York: Author.

Rose, P. B., & Miller, D. A. (1993). Integrated communications and practitioners' perceived needs. *Journalism Educator, 48*(1), 20–27.

Rosen, J. (1995, November–December). What should we be doing? *IRE Journal,* p. 7.

Rosen, J. (1996). *Getting the connections right: Public journalism and the troubles in the press.* New York: The Twentieth Century Fund Press.

Rosenberg, M. (1998, November 9). Maryland J school expels public relations sequence. *The New York Times* [On-line]. Available: http://www.nytimes.com

Ross, D. K. (1957). Willard G. Bleyer and journalism education. *Journalism Quarterly, 34*, 466–474.

Ross, B. I. (1965). *Advertising education.* A report of the American Academy of Advertising and the American Association of Advertising Agencies. Lubbock, TX: Texas Tech Press.

Ross, B. I. (1990). *Where shall I go to college to study advertising?* Lubbock, TX: Advertising Education Publications.

Ross, B. I. (1991). *The status of advertising education.* Lubbock, TX: PrinTech.

Ross, B.I. (Ed.). (1993). *Seventy-five years of journalism and mass communication leadership: The history of the Association of Schools of Journalism and Mass Communication.* Columbia, SC: Association of Schools of Journalism and Mass Communication.

Rotzoll, K. (1985). Future advertising education: Ideas on a tentative discipline. *Journalism Educator, 40*(3), 37–41.

Rotzoll, K., & Barban, A. M. (1984). Advertising education. In *Current issues in advertising education 1984* (pp. 1-18). Ann Arbor, MI: University of Michigan.

Rudolph, F. (1962). *The American college and university: A history.* New York: Vintage Books.

Ryan, M. (1978). How educators, editors view aspects of j school's role in press criticism. *Journalism Quarterly, 55*, 295–300.

Sandage, C. H. (1955). A philosophy of advertising education. *Journalism Quarterly, 32*, 209–211.

Sanders, K. P. (1972). Q study of editors' attitudes toward journalism research. *Journalism Quarterly, 49*, 519–530.

Schramm, W. (Ed.) (1949). *Mass communications.* Urbana: University of Illinois Press.

Schramm, W. (Ed.). (1954). *The process and effects of mass communication.* Urbana: University of Illinois Press.

Schramm, W. (1963). The challenge to communication research. In R. O. Nafziger and D. M. White (Eds.). *Introduction to mass communications research.* Baton Rouge: Louisiana State University Press.

Schramm. W. (1981, April 14). *There were giants in the earth in these days.* Les Moeller lecture, Iowa City, University of Iowa, School of Journalism and Mass Communication.

Schramm, W. (1997). *The beginnings of communication study in America: A personal memoir.* Thousand Oaks CA: Sage.

Schudson, M. (1978). *Discovering the news.* New York: Basic Books.

Schultze, Q. J. (1980, August). *The quest for professional advertising education before 1917.* Paper presented at the annual convention of the Association for Education in Journalism, Boston, MA.

Schultze, Q. J. (1982). "An honorable place": The quest for professional advertising education, 1900-1917. *The Business History Review, 56*(1), 16-21.

Schwartz, D. F., Yarbrough, J. P., & Shakra, M. T. (1992, September). Does public relations education make the grade? *Public Relations Journal, 48*, 18–25.

Schweitzer, J. C. (1985). Practical research can bring respect to j-schools. *Journalism Educator, 40*(2), 38–41.

Schweitzer, J. C. (1988). Who are all these advertising majors and what do they want? *Journalism Quarterly, 65*, 837–739.

Scott, F. N. (1912, October). The Round Table. *The English Journal, 1*, 173–176.

Self, C. (1994). University–industry task force finds complex alliance activity. *Journalism Educator, 49*(1), 32–38.

Serafini, A. (1984, July/August). A little bit of heresy: Let's put the education back in journalism and the journalism back in the newsroom. *The Quill*, 23–26, 28.

Shepard, A. C. (1996, April). The Pew connection. *American Journalism Review*, 25–29.

Shoemaker, P. J. (1993). Communication in crisis: Theory, curricula, and power. *Journal of Communication, 43*(4), 146–153.

Simon, R. (1957). PRSA's 1956 study of public relations education. *Journalism Quarterly, 34*(1), 71–73.

Sloan, W. D. (1990). In search of itself: A history of journalism education. In W.D. Sloan (Ed.), *Makers of the media mind: Journalism educators and their ideas* (pp. 1–22). Hillsdale, NJ: Lawrence Erlbaum Associates.

Smith, D. K. (1954). Origin and development of departments of speech. In K.R. Wallace (Ed.), *A history of speech education in America* (pp. 447–470). New York: Appleton-Century-Crofts.

Smith, K. O. (1982). Report of the 1981 Commission on Public Relations Education. *Public Relations Review, 8*(2), 61–70.

Smith, L. (1964). Education for broadcasting: 1929–1963. *Journal of Broadcasting, 8*(4), 383–398.

Smith, L. (1977, Winter). Whither journalism-school reform? *The Masthead*, 26–28.

Society of Professional Journalists. (1996). *Tomorrow's broadcast journalists: A report and recommendations from the Jane Pauley Task Force on Mass Communication Education*. Greencastle, IN: Author.

Soloski, J. (1994,). On defining the nature of graduate education. *Journalism Educator, 49*(2), 4–11.

Spevak, J. E. (1959). *An analysis of undergraduate public relations courses*. Boston: Boston University School of Public Relations and Communications.

Stacks, D. W. (1998, July). *Perceptions of public relations education: A survey of public relations curriculum, outcomes, assessment, and pedagogy*. A report presented at the National Communication Association Public Relations Summer Conference, Washington, DC.

State of the field: Academic leaders in journalism, mass communication and speech communication look to the future at the University of Texas. (1994). Austin, Texas: The University of Texas at Austin College of Communication.

Steel, R. (1980). *Walter Lippmann and the American century.* London: Bodley & Head.

Steiner, L. (1994). Career guidance books assess the value of journalism education. *Journalism Educator, 49*(1), 49–58.

Stephenson, W., & Merrill, J. (1975). Missouri profs want to turn j-education upside down. *Journalism Educator, 30*(1), 12–14.

Stone, G. (1982). Professional experience gap between PhDs, non-PhDs narrows, "Roundtable" discloses. *Journalism Educator, 37*(1), 3–5.

Stone, G. (1984). Survey reflects disagreement on 25 percent accrediting rule. *Journalism Educator, 39*(4), 13–16.

Stone, G., & Norton, W. Jr. (1980). How administrators define the term "faculty research". *Journalism Educator, 35*(2), 40–42.

Stone, V. (1987, November). News directors say writing helped them most. *RTNDA Communicator*, 9–10, 14.

Stone, V. (1989, September). J-grad quality and entry-level hiring surveyed. *RTNDA Communicator*, 58–59.

Stratton, J. C. (1940–1941). The modern journalism course. *Phi Delta Kappan, 23*, 284.

Sutton, A. A. (1945). *Education for journalism in the United States from its beginning to 1940.* Evanston, IL: Northwestern University.

Swanson, D. L. (1993). Fragmentation, the field, and the future. *Journal of Communication, 43*(4), 163–171.

Talbott, T. (1990, May). Academic mush. *The Quill*, 36.

Tankard, J. W. Jr. (1990). Wilbur Schramm, definer of a field. In W. D. Sloan (Ed.), *Makers of the media mind: Journalism educators and their ideas* (pp. 239–248). Hillsdale, NJ: Lawrence Erlbaum Associates.

Task Force on the Future of Journalism and Mass Communication Education. (1989). Challenges and opportunities in journalism and mass communication education. *Journalism Educator, 44*(1), A1–A24.

Teeter, D. (1985) Liberal education is the key to defending our liberties. *Journalism Educator, 4*(3), 12–16, 44

Trayes, E. J. (1973). Recommendations to ACEJ prompted by many deviations from guidelines. *Journalism Educator, 28*(2), 42–43.

VanderMeer, A. W., & Lyons, M. D. (1978). Opinions of professors of journalism regarding the liberal arts in journalism education. Unpublished manuscript. (ERIC Document Reproduction Service No. ED 226 674).

Van Ommeren, R. (1991, Fall). Stone throwing solves no problems. *ASJMC Insights*, 7.

Wakefield, G., & Cottone, L. P. (1986). Education for the '80s and beyond. *Public Relations Review, 12*(2), 37–46.

Wakefield, G., & Cottone, L. P. (1992). Public relations executives' perceptions of disciplinary emphases important to public relations practice for the 1990s. *Public Relations Review, 18*(1), 67–78.

Walker, A. (1988). *The public relations body of knowledge.* New York: Foundation for Public Relations Research and Education.

Walker, A. (1989). Where to anchor public relations education? The problem persists. *Public Relations Quarterly, 34*(3), 22–25.

Warner, C., & Liu, Y. (1990). Broadcast curriculum profile: A freeze-frame look at what BEA members offer students. *Feedback, 31*(3), 6–7.

Wartella, E. (1994). Foreword. In *State of the field: Academic leaders in journalism, mass communication and speech communication look to the future at the University of Texas* (p. 1). Austin, Texas: The University of Texas at Austin College of Communication.

Wartella, E. (1996, May). Strategies for the communications unit: How can we become central to the university and its mission? *Journal of the Association for Communication Administration, 2,* 150–152.

Weaver, A. T. (1989). Seventeen who made history—the founders of the association. In W. Work & R. C. Jeffrey (Eds.), *The past as prologue: A 75th anniversary publication of the Speech Communication Association* (pp. 13-17). Annandale, VA: Speech Communication Association.

Weaver, D., & Wilhoit, C. (1988). A profile of JMC educators: Traits, attitudes and values. *Journalism Educator, 43*(2), 4–41.

Weinberg, S. (1990, October). Bridging the chasm: dark thoughts and sparks of hope about journalism education. *The Quill,* 26–28.

Weinberg, S. (1991, May 29). Requiring all journalism professors to have doctorates is wrong headed. *The Chronicle of Higher Education,* pp. B1–B2.

Welke, J. W. (1985, Winter). The generic curriculum menace. *Feedback,* 21–27.

Westland, A. (1974). We must remove "stepchild" label from PR student. *Journalism Educator, 29*(2), 49–50.

What makes a great journalism school. (1995, May). *American Journalism Review. A Special Report on Journalism Education.*

White, A. D. (1884). *What profession shall I choose, and how shall I fit myself for it?* Ithaca, N.Y.: Cornell University.

Whitelaw, K. (1996, March 18). Is j-school worth it? *U.S. News & World Report,* 98-100.

Wilcox, W. (1959). Historical trends in journalism education. *Journalism Educator, 14*(3), 2–7, 32.

Will, A. S. (1928). Concerning the status of teachers. *Journalism Quarterly, 5*(1), 18–19.

Williams, S. L. (1929). *Twenty years of journalism education: A history of the School of Journalism of the University of Missouri.* Columbia, MO: E. W. Stephens Publishing Co.

Williams, W. (1908, December). The college of journalism. *The World Today, 15,* 1233.

Williamson, L. K., & Iorio, S. H. (1994). *Communication curriculum reform and the liberal arts: A research report.* Unpublished manuscript, Wichita, KS: Wichita State University.

Wingate, C. F. (1875). *Views and interviews on journalism.* New York: F.B. Patterson.

Woolbert, C. H. (1916). The organization of departments of speech science in universities. *Quarterly Journal of Public Speaking, 2,* 64–67.

Wright, J. S. (1980, November 15). Our working adpeople and educators must agree on basic ad curriculum. *Advertising Age, 78,* 88.

Wright, D. K. (1982). Public relations education and the business schools. *Public Relations Review, 8*(2), 11–16.

Wright, D. K. (1991). A tribute to Scott M. Cutlip, father of public relations education. *Public Relations Review, 17*(4), 335–342.

Wright, D. K., & VanSlyke Turk, J. (1990). *Public relations education: The unpleasant realities.* New York: The Institute for Public Relations Research and Education.

Wright, J. S. (1980, November 13). Our working adpeople and educators must agree on a basic ad curriculum. *Advertising Age, 78,* 87–88.

Wyatt, J. (1991, April 27). Future of journalism education: Editors, journalism educators lay it on the line at Colorado session. *Editor & Publisher,* 12–13, 40.

Wylie, F. W. (1990). The challenge of public relations education. *Syracuse Scholar, 10*(1), 57–66.

Zarefsky, D. (1990, October). Rethinking the shape of our discipline. *Spectra, 2,* 4.

Author Index

A

Accrediting Council on Education in Journalism and Mass Communications (ACEJMC), 18.
Allen, C. L., 39
Allen, E. W., 23, 24, 27, 126
Allen, T. H., 162
Alridge, R., 101
Altschull, J. H., 118
American Society of Newspaper Editors, 100, 105, 109, 113, 114, 142, 157, 164, 234, 237
Anderson, D. A., 188
Anderson, R., 119
An Editor (Anonymous), 5
Armstead, G. B., 26
Arnold, E. C., 28
Associated Press Managing Editors Association, 240
Association for Education in Journalism and Mass Communication, 87, 88, 102, 113, 126, 139, 144, 149, 154, 155, 244, 245
Association of Schools of Journalism and Mass Communication, 88, 126, 144
Astin, A., 120
Aucoin, J., 120, 121

B

Bagdikian, B. H., 79, 98
Bales, F., 107
Barban, A. M., 35, 37–39, 41
Barker, D. R., 54
Barker, L., 54
Bateman, C., 52
Beasley, M., 84, 182
Becker, L. B., 148–150
Berko, R., 74
Bernays, E. L., 162
Birkhead, D., 84
Bitter, J., 87

Blanchard, R. O., 81, 84, 86, 128, 136–138, 146, 152–154, 188, 238–240
Bleyer, W. G., 20, 22, 27, 30
Bloom, A., 128
Blumler, J., 60
Botan, C., 108, 117
Bovet , S. L., 166
Boyer, E. L., 3, 9, 86, 111, 128, 137
Bowers, T. A., 93
Brandon, W., 125
Brock, S. S., 91, 94
Bronstein, C., 19, 171
Budd, R. W., 76, 77, 79, 128
Bullard, M., 107, 262
Bybee, C., 118, 119, 121

C

Calkins, E. E., 35
Camp, E. M., 7, 126
Carey, A., 89, 95, 114, 116, 119
Carey, J. W., 9, 10, 13, 14, 18, 81, 84
Carter, R. F., 87, 88, 143
Casey, R. D., 26–27
Casiday, H. L., 30
Cottone, L. P., 56, 163, 165, 166
Caywood, C., 160, 165, 186, 240, 241
Ceppos, J., 113, 134, 138, 184, 242
Chaffee, S. H., 60, 67, 69, 70, 71, 151, 171
Cho, J., 83, 94, 105, 115
Christ, W. G., 81, 84, 86, 128, 137, 152–154, 185–188, 238–240
Cohen, H., 60, 62–66
Cole, R. R., 99, 132
Commission on Freedom of the Press, 31
Commission on Undergraduate Public Relations Education, 53, 165, 224, 232
Cooper, T., 86
Copple, N., 99, 112
Corrigan, D., 92, 101, 122
Council for Aid to Education, 186, 187,

271

Subject Index

ABOUT THE AUTHOR

Tom Dickson is professor of journalism and mass media at Southwest Missouri State University in Springfield, where he has taught since 1987. He also has taught at the University of Evansville (IN) and Arkansas State University. He holds a bachelor of arts degree in political science and journalism from Arkansas State, a master's of arts degree in political science from Tulane University, and a doctor of education degree with an emphasis in mass communication from Oklahoma State University. His media experience includes acting radio wire editor of the Associated Press in Little Rock, AR; reporter for the *Jonesboro* (AR) *Evening Sun*; editor of the 18th Military Police Brigade *Roundup*, Long Binh, Vietnam; sports editor of the *Blue Springs Examiner*, a daily newspaper in suburban Blue Springs, MO; managing editor of the *Blue Springs Examiner;* and acting editor of the *Arkansas Sun*, a weekly newspaper. He is co-author of *Journalism Kids Do Better: What Research Tells Us About High School Journalism* (ERIC/Edinfo Press, 1994). He also has contributed chapters to *School Publications: The Business Side* (MOLATX Press, 1989), *Media Education Assessment Handbook* (Lawrence Erlbaum Associates, 1997), and *Censorship: Opposing Viewpoints* (Greenhaven Press, 1997).